THE FSA/OWI PHOTOGRAPHERS AND THE AMERICAN RAILROAD

RAILROADS PAST AND PRESENT

Thomas Hoback and Carlos Arnaldo Schwantes, editors

H. Roger Grant, *founding editor*

THE FSA/OWI PHOTOGRAPHERS AND THE AMERICAN RAILROAD

TONY REEVY

Foreword by Jeff Brouws

INDIANA UNIVERSITY PRESS

This book is a publication of

Indiana University Press
Herman B Wells Library
1320 East 10th Street
Bloomington, Indiana 47405 USA

https://iupress.org

For customers in the European Union with safety or GPSR concerns, please contact Mare Nostrum Group B.V., Mauritskade 21D, 1091 GC Amsterdam, The Netherlands. Email: gpsr@mare-nostrum.co.uk

Manufactured in China

First printing 2026

Cataloging information is available from the Library of Congress.

ISBN 978-0-253-07472-0 (hdbk.)
ISBN 978-0-253-07474-4 (ebook)

TO IAN

who studies

the steel wheel

on the steel rail

CONTENTS

They've Got What it Takes
CAMELS
ACE TEST PILOT
EXPRESS AGENCY

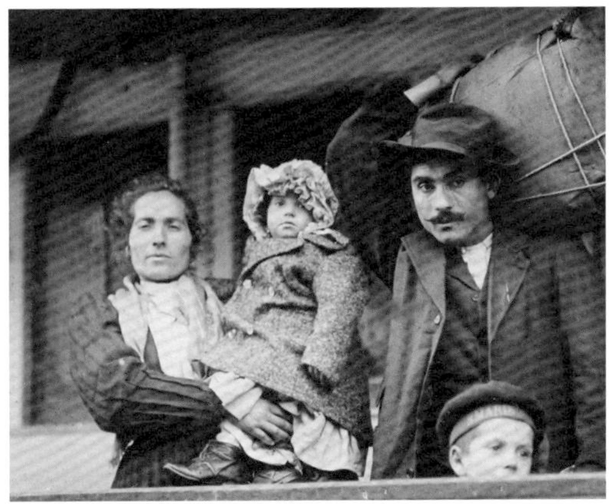

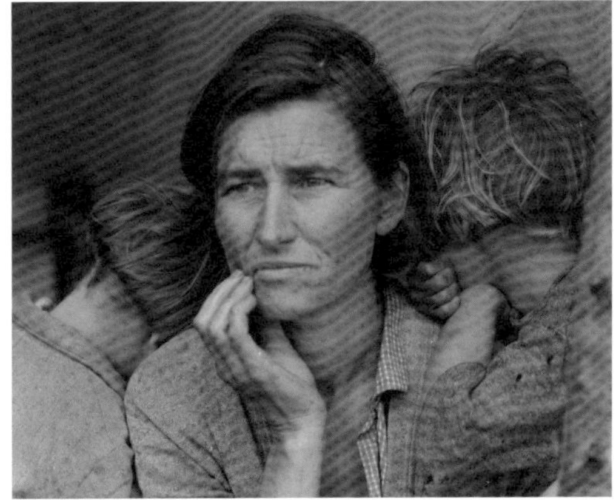

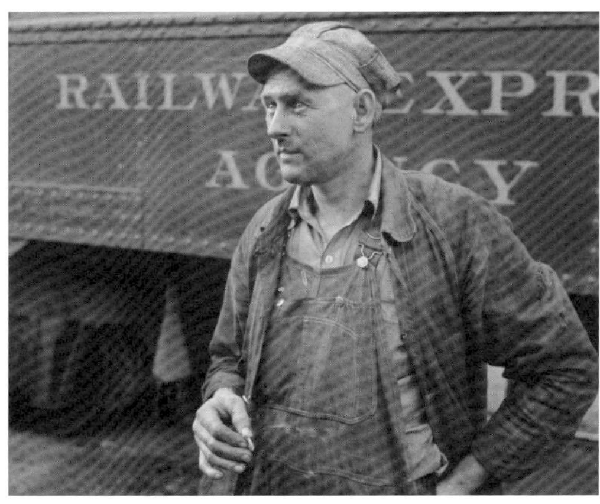

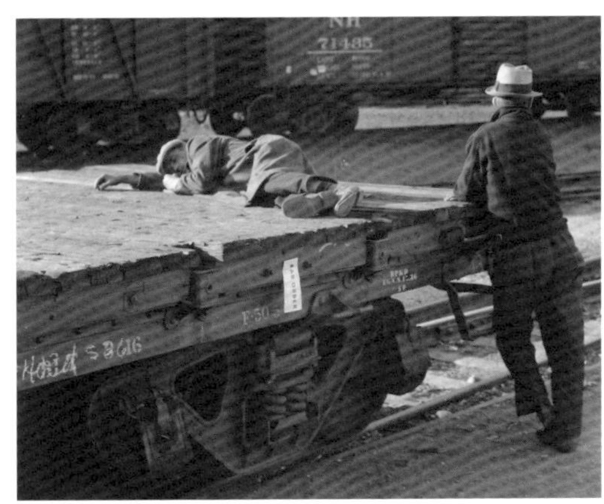

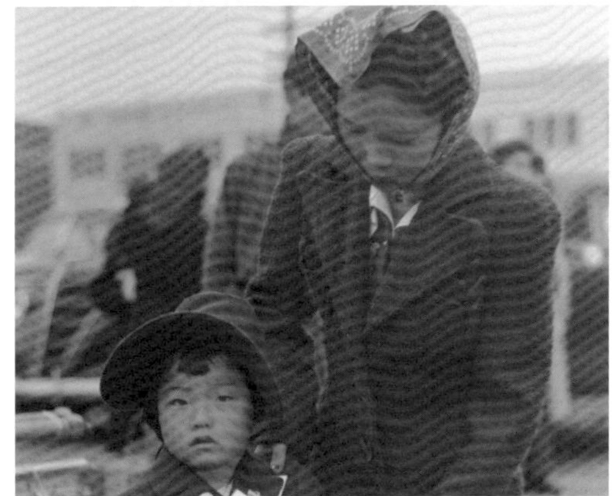

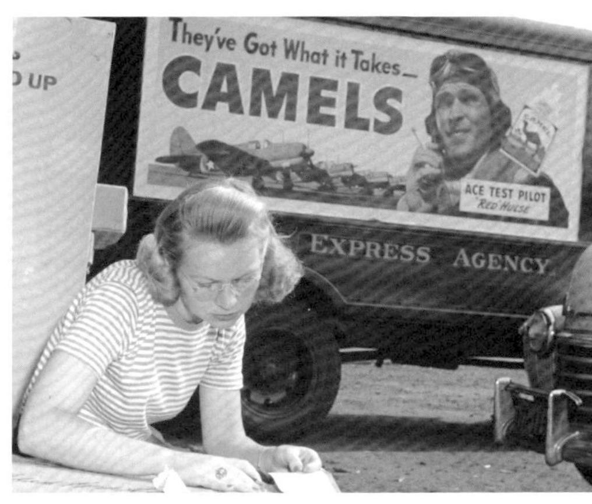

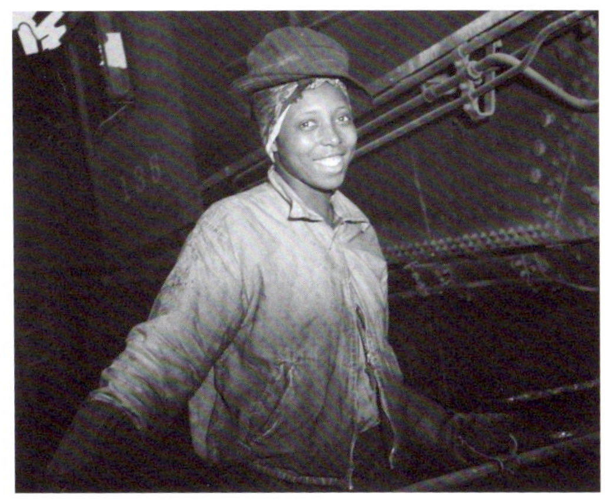

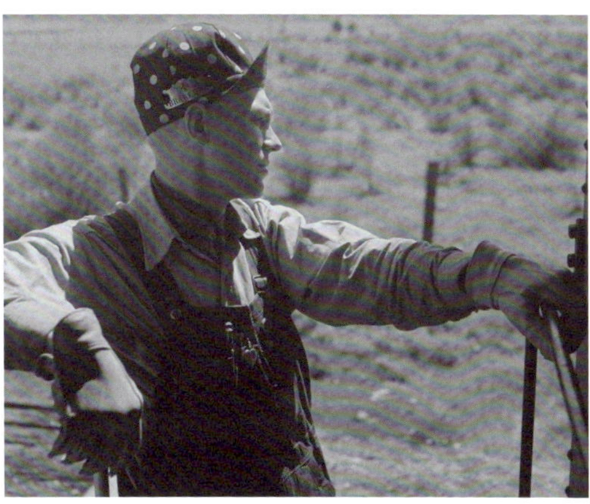

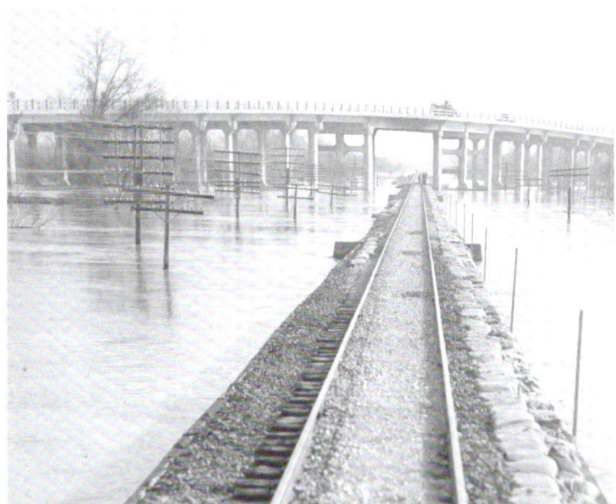

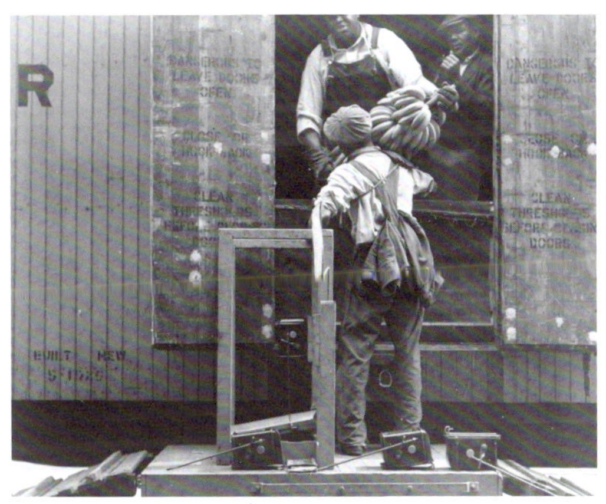

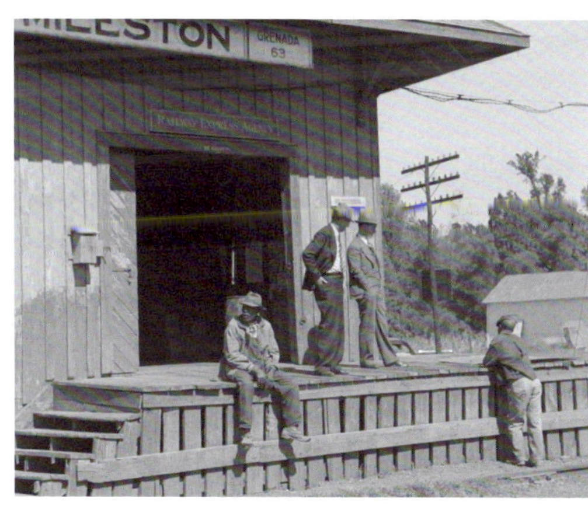

FOREWORD

As one of the preeminent photo researchers of the twenty-first century surveying the historical antecedents of railroad photography in America, Tony Reevy has assembled this splendid volume of photos and text that casts a fresh perspective on the important work done by Roy Stryker and the first-class bevy of talented photographers he hired between 1935 and 1943. First working for the Resettlement Section and then later for the Farm Security Administration, these image makers, with elaborate shooting scripts in hand suggested by Stryker himself, initially documented a country and its people struggling through economic hard times. They would later employ their sturdy 4 × 5 Speed Graphics and Rolleiflexes to record the important intersection of railroad culture woven with the social and economic fabric of American life as it pictorially manifested itself in the early years of World War II. In small towns and major industrial centers, or out on the prairies or coursing through the Intermountain West, these photographers intrepidly aimed their lenses at all aspects of the railroad scene and captured the workers, the architecture, the landscapes, and the rolling stock and locomotives as they traversed the nation and went about their work in plainclothes fashion. Brimming with humanistic appeal, these clearly seen, straight-ahead examples of documentary photography are of the first magnitude. Made by image makers on a mission, they reward us with their earnest and thoughtful vision.

While some photographs are icons of the era deserving to be seen anew—like Walker Evans's *View of Railroad Station, Edwards, Mississippi* (plate 43) and Dorothea Lange's *Toward Los Angeles, California* (plate 52)—Reevy has also done extensive research in the Library of Congress's archives to unearth new gems previously unseen. Many of these are by lesser-known and underrepresented photographers operating at that time like Marjory Collins and Marion Post Wolcott—women who were often overshadowed by their male counterparts like Evans and Jack Delano. The women nonetheless were making significant work that admirably adds to the canonical visual record of American railroading during that crucial time.

Reevy also gives us concise and well-researched biographical information on each photographer, many accounts suffused with unusual and interesting anecdotal material that further fleshes out the interesting story of how this important collection of railroad imagery came into being. He also outlines how, in some cases, individual photographers found fame and received overdue recognition later on in their lives. Interesting, too, are the artistic ties that Reevy uncovers: Who knew that important twentieth-century artists like Maynard Dixon and Paul Strand would be mentors to John Collier or that while some of the photographers came from privileged/patrician backgrounds (like Evans and Post Wolcott), others like John Collier and Dorothea

Lange suffered youthful traumas that undoubtedly led them to empathically infuse their photographs with a deep sense of humanity, giving their individual styles of photography a social justice or anthropological underpinning? These important stylistic decisions would later open a pathway for others, informing and inspiring the camera work of the next generation of photojournalists that followed.

Reevy further analyzes and comments on the backstory for each individual photo; the photos are arrayed in portfolio fashion, giving the reader added insights to enhance the captions first written by the photographers themselves when the images were made. These tangential tributaries of photographic knowledge and the book's fine-art structure set *The FSA/OWI Photographers and the American Railroad* uniquely apart from previous volumes of FSA imagery, making it a must-have publication for every student or train enthusiast interested in the history of American railroad photography.

Jeff Brouws

PREFACE

WHAT WE HAVE LOST

This book provides a brief review of the Farm Security Administration (FSA) and Office of War Information (OWI) railroad-subject photographs of the United States, 1935–1943. This period saw one of the greatest series of challenges to our country: the Great Depression; the rise of fascism, egged on by economic desperation; and the advent of World War II. Looking back, this period rivals only the early years of the United States, the pre–Civil War / Civil War / Reconstruction period, and our present political division as a time of serious threat to the continuation of an America "of the people, by the people, for the people."

The United States did not speak with one voice during the Great Depression, but a majority of Americans abandoned the laissez-faire policies followed during twelve years of Republican control for President Franklin Delano Roosevelt (FDR), a Democrat, and his promised "new deal for the American people." And when the country entered World War II as a result of Japan's attack on Pearl Harbor, the United States was arguably the most united as a nation as it has ever been.

Roosevelt's inauguration in 1933 led to a time of intellectual ferment in government and beyond. Roosevelt was a pragmatic experimenter and a patrician from one of America's oldest families of wealth. But Roosevelt showed deep empathy for the struggles of all Americans—he clearly learned a bit about weakness and compassion when he was stricken by polio at age thirty-nine in 1921, leaving him paralyzed from the waist down. His efforts to help Americans overcome the effects of the Great Depression included bringing Rexford Tugwell into his administration, and Tugwell in turn brought in Roy Stryker, who hired photographers to document the struggles of rural and small-town Americans during the Great Depression.

In doing so, Stryker and his team documented American railroading as it was at the time. This was a natural development, as rural America then still depended on the railroad for passenger and freight mobility in a way that is almost unimaginable today.

A present-day observer can learn many lessons from the FSA/OWI photos. One apt lesson is an understanding of what we have lost, as a nation, in terms of the transportation options we once had, especially outside of certain large urban areas. In the rural United States of today, abandoned first by railroads and more recently by bus lines, and usually never served by air, the automobile is generally the only transportation choice available. This reality has many ramifications—for example, those who are too poor to own a car or unable to drive because of age or disability enjoy little or no mobility in their lives. It also means that as we grapple with the challenge of climate change and greenhouse-gas emissions, the most efficient land transportation mode and the one easiest to electrify, rail, is often simply not available. This lack leaves us with the possible stark future of a nation crawling with battery-powered autonomous vehicles, bringing with them a drastic increase in power-grid infrastructure and the serious environmental impacts of lithium mines.

As we review these photos, let us consider the transportation infrastructure we have lost and how this is one more life disadvantage for the Americans who have been left behind by deindustrialization, by the concentration of farming, by the loss of transportation infrastructure, and more. Would it be good policy—and would it be politically and financially possible—to re-create at least some infrastructure offering the people of North America transportation options? Only time will tell.

ACKNOWLEDGMENTS

The FSA/OWI photographers are well known, as is the story of their work. Some of them—Jack Delano, Walker Evans, Dorothea Lange, Russell Lee, Gordon Parks, John Vachon, and Marion Post Wolcott—are well documented. Others, such as John Collier Jr., Marjory Collins, and Arthur Rothstein, have not been covered as well. This book benefited greatly from the work of many previous authors who have written about the FSA/OWI Historical Section.

The FSA/OWI photographs are available through the Library of Congress and benefit from that staff's expert curation. My photo orders for this book were handled by Tomcka Myers and Rebecca Rose, and Leigh Gleason provided curatorial assistance. Thank you also to Kristi L. Finefield from the Library of Congress for reference information.

Finding a usable photo of John Collier Jr. proved to be a challenge. Diane Tyink, museum archivist at the Maxwell Museum of Anthropology, University of New Mexico, located the portrait used in this book. John Collier Jr.'s collection is held by the Maxwell Museum of Anthropology.

Many thanks go to author and photographer Jeff Brouws for his outstanding foreword. Best wishes, Jeff, and thank you! Thank you also to the indexer for this book, Susan Certo.

This is my fourth book with Indiana University Press, and each of these projects has been a joy to work on with the press's outstanding staff. Many thanks to Dan Crissman, my original editor for the project, and to Gary Dunham, who replaced him when Dan left the press. And thank you to Anna Francis, Stephen Williams, and Dave Miller from Indiana University Press.

This book was preceded and informed by my articles "Walker Evans, American Communities, and the Railroad," published in *Railroad Heritage*; "Jack Delano: Artist of the Rails," published in *Railroad History*; and "Off to War: Gordon Parks' Photographs of Washington Union Station During World War II," published in *Railroad History*, and by my book *The Railroad Photography of Jack Delano*, published by Indiana University Press. Thank you again to those who assisted with these articles and the book.

And, as always, my family—Caroline, Lindley, and Ian—are supportive of my work and have near-infinite patience. Thank you!

Finally, let me recognize and acknowledge that this book was written in Durham, North Carolina, on lands once occupied by what is today the Occaneechi Band of the Saponi Nation.

If I have missed thanking anyone for a work that began, in many ways, with my 2009 articles focusing on Walker Evans and Jack Delano, I apologize. And, of course, errors and omissions are the fault of this author alone.

THE FSA/OWI PHOTOGRAPHERS AND THE AMERICAN RAILROAD

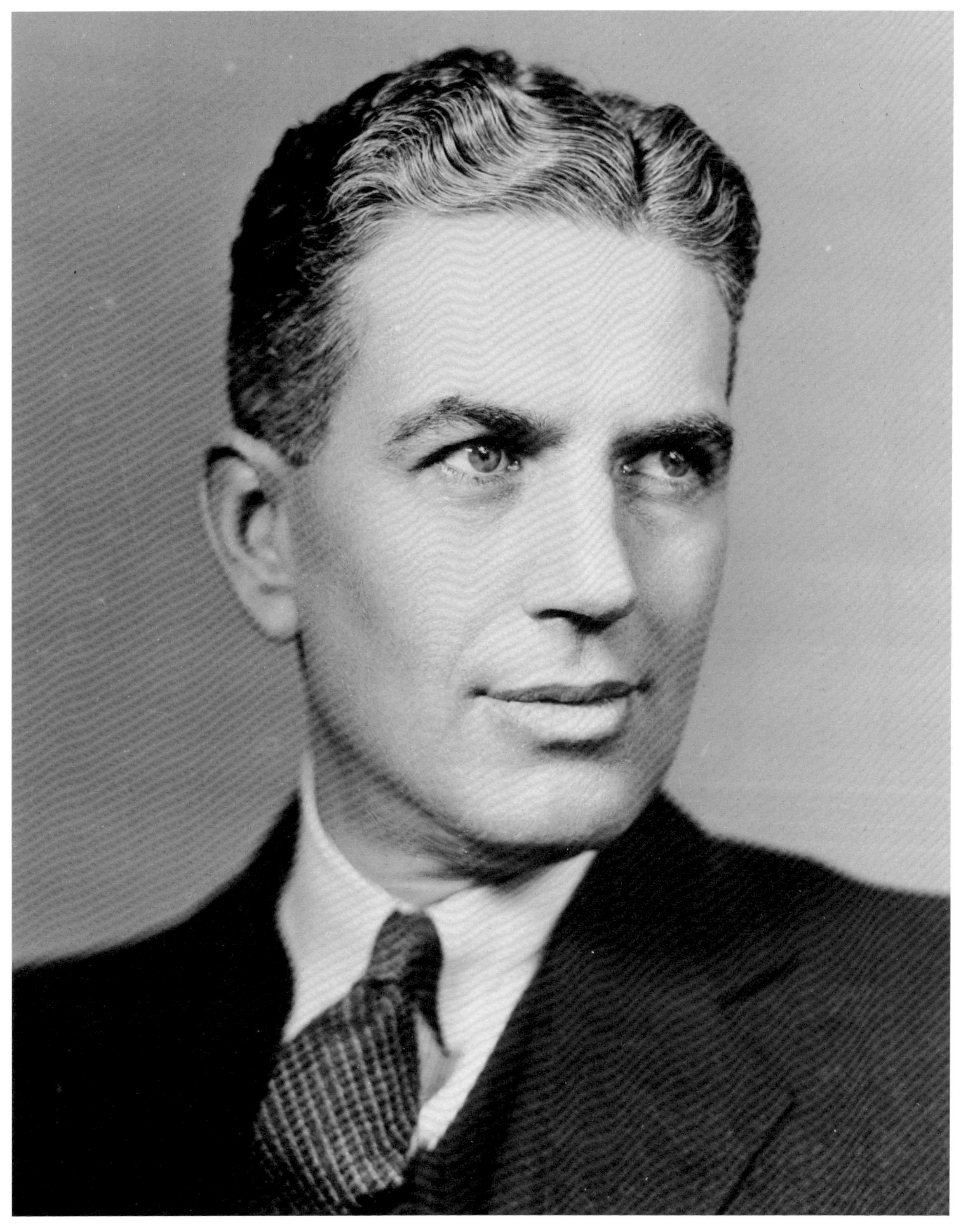

INTRODUCTION

The story of the formation of the Historical Section of the Farm Security Administration (FSA) by Roy Stryker is an oft-told tale.[1] The photographers employed by the section included some of the greatest of the twentieth century, such as Walker Evans and Dorothea Lange.

Despite the fame of FSA/OWI photographer Jack Delano's railroad-subject work, the substantive and wide-ranging coverage of the US railroad by the FSA photographers and by the Office of War Information (OWI) photographers who followed them is less known. This book brings together significant work by ten FSA/OWI photographers who documented American railroading as it was from 1935 to 1943 for the first time. One of the purposes in doing so is to make this easily accessible trove of exceptional railroad-subject images of 1930s and 1940s American railroading better known.

***Facing,* Figure 0.1.** Rexford G. Tugwell, administrator, Resettlement Administration.

Photographer and date unknown. Library of Congress, Prints & Photographs Division, FSA-OWI Collection, LC-USF344-003487-ZB.

THE FSA/OWI PHOTOGRAPHERS, ROY STRYKER, AND THE HISTORICAL SECTION

The Historical Section's connection to President Franklin Delano Roosevelt was deep in the organizational chart of the federal government, but the intellectual connection was close. The founder of the Resettlement Administration, the first home of the Historical Section, was Rexford G. "Rex" Tugwell, one of the members of President Roosevelt's "brain trust" and one of his closest advisers.[2] Tugwell and Roosevelt founded the Resettlement Administration in 1935, a new agency with the mission of "resettling" destitute farmers and others to locations where they had a chance to build new lives. The political unpopularity of this agency's mission led to Rexford's nickname, Rex the Red.[3]

Tugwell brought his graduate student Roy Stryker from Columbia University into the administration to form its Historical Section. Tugwell and Stryker agreed on the importance of photography as a means to document history and influence policy and were coauthors, with Thomas Munro, of the classic book *American Economic Life*.[4] Stryker was influenced by the work of Jacob Riis and Lewis Hine as well as by the work of Dorothea Lange and Paul Taylor. As Gabriel Bauret has pointed out,

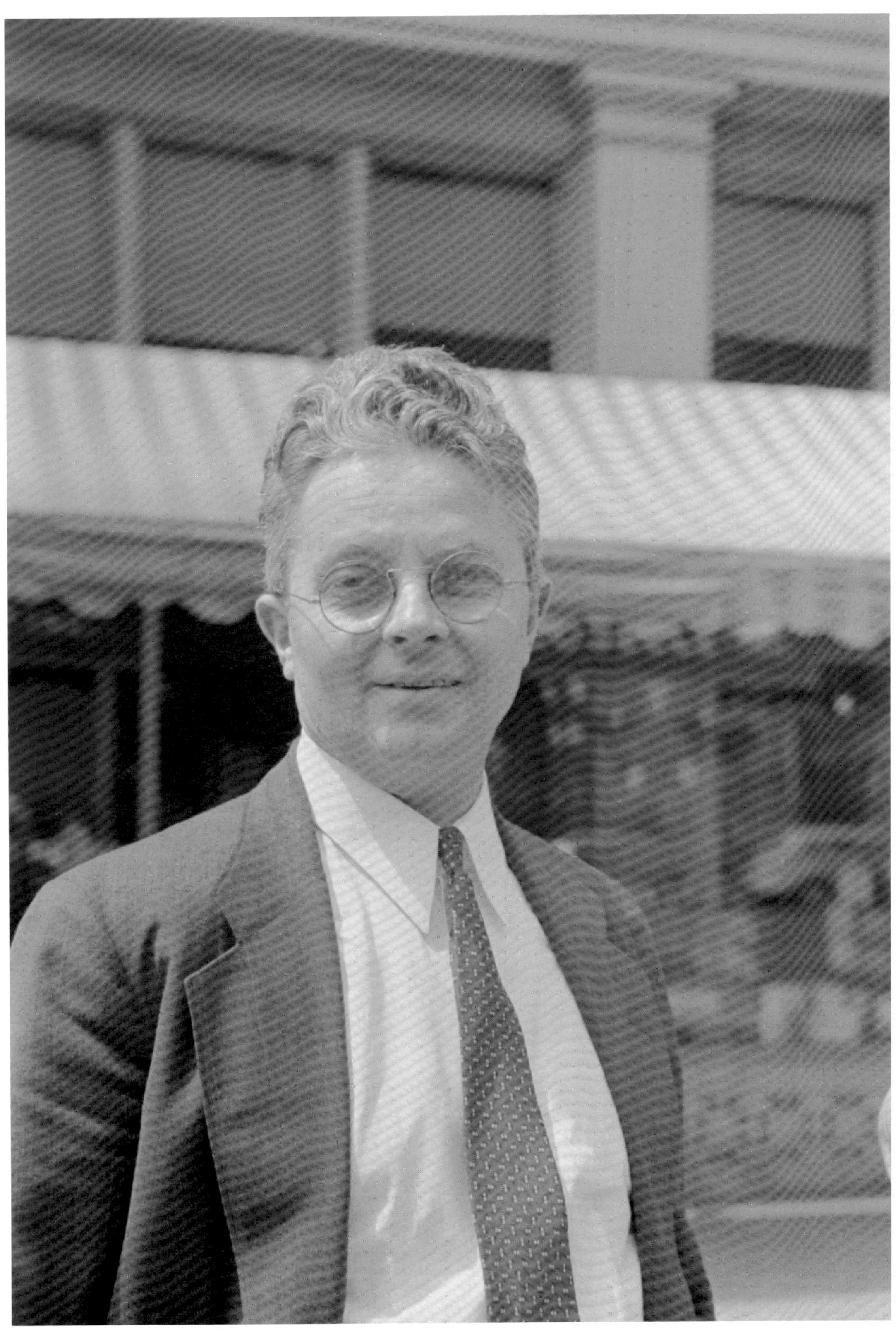

Figure 0.2. Roy E. Stryker, photograph chief of the US Farm Security Administration, standing in street, probably in Washington, DC.

Russell Lee. August 1938. Library of Congress, Prints & Photographs Division, FSA-OWI Collection, LC-USF33-011585-M5.

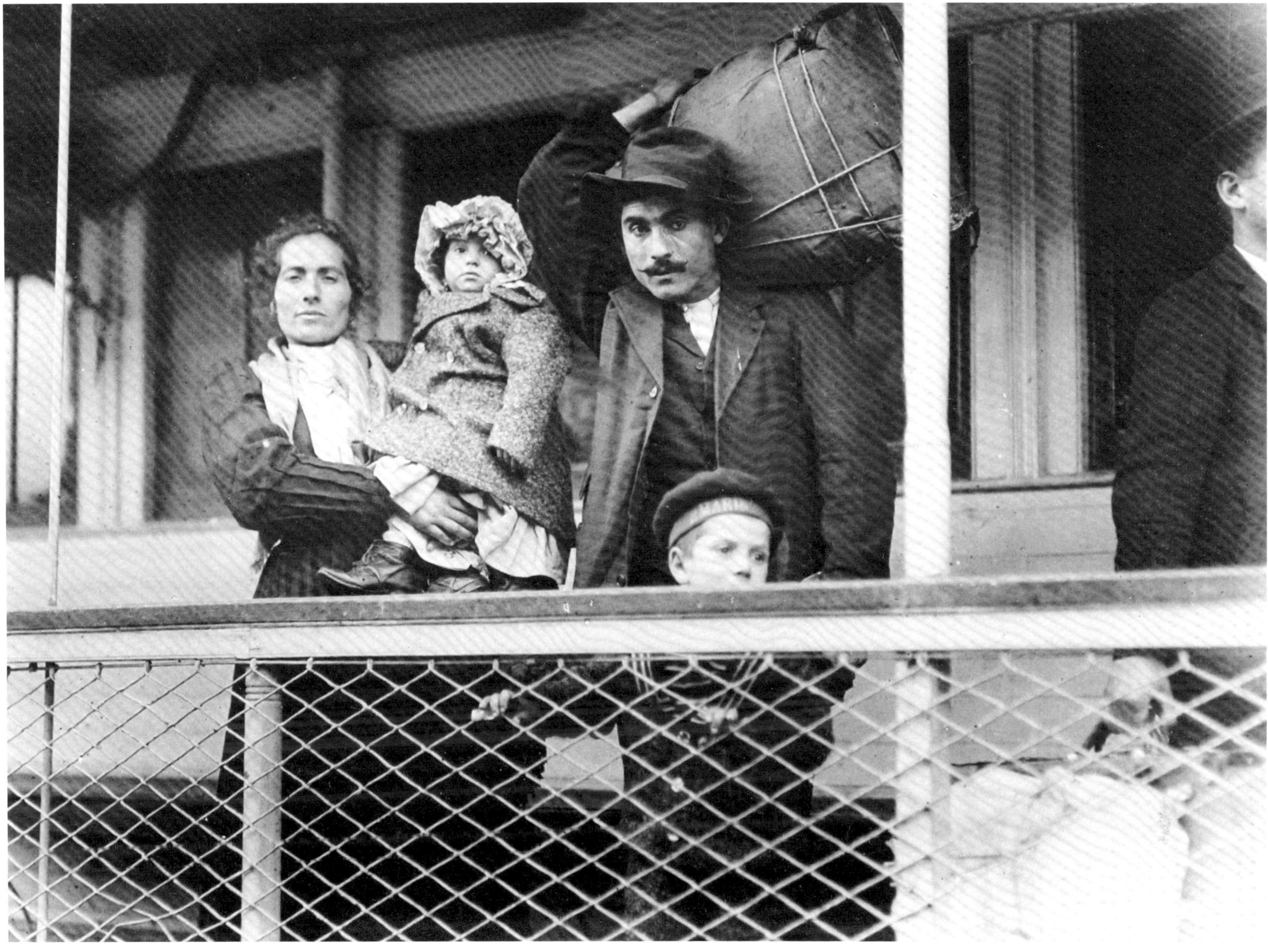

Figure 0.3. Italian immigrant family on ferry, leaving Ellis Island.

Lewis Hine. 1905. Library of Congress, Prints & Photographs Division, FSA-OWI Collection, LC-USW34-000897-ZB.

the group of photographers Stryker created "was more important than the individuals within it"—but, somewhat paradoxically, with "each of them being very much driven by their own agenda."[5]

Stryker made a few initial missteps but eventually showed exceptional judgment in choosing the photographers who would document the US for the Historical Section. Two of his early hires, Theodor Jung and Paul Carter, did not work out. Another early hire, Carl Mydans, was an excellent photographer but stayed only a year.

The other three early hires were outstanding. Ben Shahn, an established artist, and Walker Evans, a New York–based photographer, advised Stryker as he set up the Historical Section, and he soon hired them. He was familiar with Dorothea Lange's work, and he soon hired her as well. Evans and Lange, whose status as photographers was already established when Stryker hired them, are now considered two of the greatest photographers of the twentieth century. Stryker's Columbia University undergraduate intern, Arthur Rothstein, was also an early hire. He developed into a noted photographer and one of the most influential members of the photojournalism movement in photography.[6]

In 1937, following Tugwell's resignation from the Roosevelt administration, the Resettlement Administration was renamed the Farm Security Administration and transferred to the Department of Agriculture. As a result, the first period of FSA/OWI photographic work came to a close.

The second period, 1937–1942, with the FSA as part of the Department of Agriculture, found Roy Stryker an outspoken but politically and programmatically experienced leader. The strong artistic personalities—Evans, Lange, and Shahn—left during this period and were replaced by less-experienced photographers who, while they may have had other mentors in the past, were then advised and led by Stryker. These included two who would prove to have long careers in photojournalism: John Vachon and Russell Lee. Also joining the Historical Section during this time were Jack Delano, a multitalented artist who later became a public media leader, and Marion Post Wolcott, who essentially gave up photography soon after she married in 1941. Delano and Post Wolcott are now recognized as significant photographers of the twentieth century.[7] Stryker also worked with a married team, Edwin and Louise Rosskam, during these years.

As the world moved into the shadow of the Axis powers, Fascism, and world war, the Historical Section's work had to refocus from an emphasis on the disadvantaged people of the United States to images demonstrating the strength and unity of the country and its people. Images from this period of the FSA's work also tended to emphasize the diversity of the US population. Finally, as World War II took hold of the nation's attention and resources, the Historical Section transferred from the FSA to the OWI in 1942.

Stryker's skill in hiring new photographers and others continued to shine during this period. He hired John Collier Jr., son of a prominent New Dealer, in 1941; Collier would go on to be one of the founders of visual anthropology. In 1942, he hired a photographer interested in women's issues, Marjory Collins. At about the same time, he hired another woman photographer, Esther Bubley, who would enjoy a long photographic career.

In 1942, Stryker made perhaps his most momentous personnel decision by hiring a Black photographer, Gordon Parks, the only person of color to work for the Historical Section.[8] Showing brilliant artistic leadership, Stryker assigned Parks to photographic assignments in Washington, DC, then a highly segregated city. Parks would go on to become an acclaimed photographer and, like Jack Delano, was a polymath—directing films, writing fiction, and entering the elite world of fashion photography.[9]

By 1943, the work of the Historical Section had run its course. Stryker's photographers had left the OWI, and he remained, filling requests for photos from what had become known simply as the "file." Stryker arranged with an old friend, Archibald MacLeish, head of the Library of Congress, for the transfer of the file to the library.

With the safety of the file assured—though many critics would have preferred it be destroyed—Stryker resigned, taking a similar position with Standard Oil of New Jersey. He would employ many former FSA/OWI colleagues there, as would Rexford Tugwell in Puerto Rico during his stint as its last appointed governor. Stryker later directed the Pittsburgh Photographic Library and a photographic documentation project for Jones and Laughlin Steel Corporation.[10]

THE FSA/OWI HISTORICAL SECTION AND THE US RAILROAD

Initially, the FSA photographers focused on the people the Resettlement Administration was founded to serve—economically disadvantaged Americans, especially the rural poor. As the project proceeded, the scope expanded to include extensive coverage of small towns. Finally, in the OWI period, the Historical Section's coverage changed to include war-related industries, military subjects, and surveys of ethnic minorities joining together with others to advance the war effort.

The railroad was a prominent part of all of these subjects. It linked rural areas with markets and served most small towns in the US. It was indispensable to industries critical to the war effort, such as coal mining, steel making, and food production, and so was a war industry itself. Railroading's place as a war industry led to the greatest portfolios of railroad-subject photographs in the file: Jack Delano's work on railroading in the Chicago, Illinois, area and on the Atchison, Topeka and Santa Fe Railway in late 1942 and early 1943.

Stryker, using his "shooting scripts"—written outlines of shots to take of certain photographic subjects—consciously directed his photographers to include views of the railroad in their work.[11] He recognized the importance of the railroad to rural and town life but also saw its decline as an active influence on the people of the United States. In the preamble to one of these scripts, Stryker said,

> The railroad has been a part of the everyday affairs of a large proportion of the villages and towns in the United States for the past several decades. It was the tie to the outside world. Watching the train arrive and depart was one of the eventful occasions of each day enjoyed by a surprising number of the local citizens. The railroad is now fast losing its place as a direct influence on the social habits of these people. The bus, the pleasure car and the truck are in so many towns and villages, relegating the "little red" railroad station to a memory. No longer does it function as one of the meeting places of the town.[12]

As the United States faced another world war, Stryker also saw the critical role that railroading had—and continues to have in our time—in moving freight through a country that spans a continent. In the OWI shooting script for Delano's work on the railroads of Chicago, Stryker said,

> The Railroads of Chicago are today doing a more difficult and more important job than at any other time in their history. The gigantic scope of the operations involved, connecting the great Northwest with the industrial East, with lines tying it directly to the South and Southwest, make [*sic*] Chicago the center through which flows the food, merchandise and war materials needed to win the war. Hundreds of war plants throughout the country, millions of consumers both east and west, as well as many of our allies abroad, depend upon the efficiency with which the Railroads of Chicago do their work.[13]

Jack Delano, the most prolific railroad-subject photographer in Stryker's group, wrote Stryker about taking railroad-subject images:

> Other than taking a few shots of the engineer and fireman, there is not much point in riding in the engine cab. It is very difficult to see out of the cab and quarters are very crowded, so I spent most of my time in the caboose. When there is switching to do, however, the engine is the place to be and I was always having to work out a compromise on the basis of what I could expect at the next stop.
>
> I could take along with me only a limited amount of equipment—just what I could carry in my arms and *on my back*. Railroad yards are usually far from train or bus stops and walking is the only means of transportation. Although I took the Graphic along I was seldom able to use it, and had to rely a great deal on the Rollie [*sic*]. Trying to stand in a caboose and take pictures is worse than in any rocking boat and I had to shoot all the pictures at very fast shutter speeds. Anyhow, there is not much room inside the caboose and the wider angle of the Rollie [*sic*] was a great help. As usual, the weather remains bad and shooting with the Graphic was very often impossible.[14]

Being from Montrose, a small town in Colorado, Stryker himself also had a special feeling for the American railroad.[15] In reaction to a Walker Evans photo, *View of Railroad Station, Edwards, Mississippi*, plate 43, Stryker said,[16]

> I remember Walker Evans' picture of the train tracks in a small town, like Montrose. The empty station platform, the station thermometer, the idle baggage carts, the quiet stores, the people talking together, and beyond them, the weatherbeaten houses where they lived, all this reminded me of the town where I had grown up. I would look at pictures like that and long for a time when the world was safer and more peaceful. I'd think back to the days before radio and television when all there was to do was go down to the tracks and watch the flyer go through. That was the nostalgic way in which those town pictures hit me.[17]

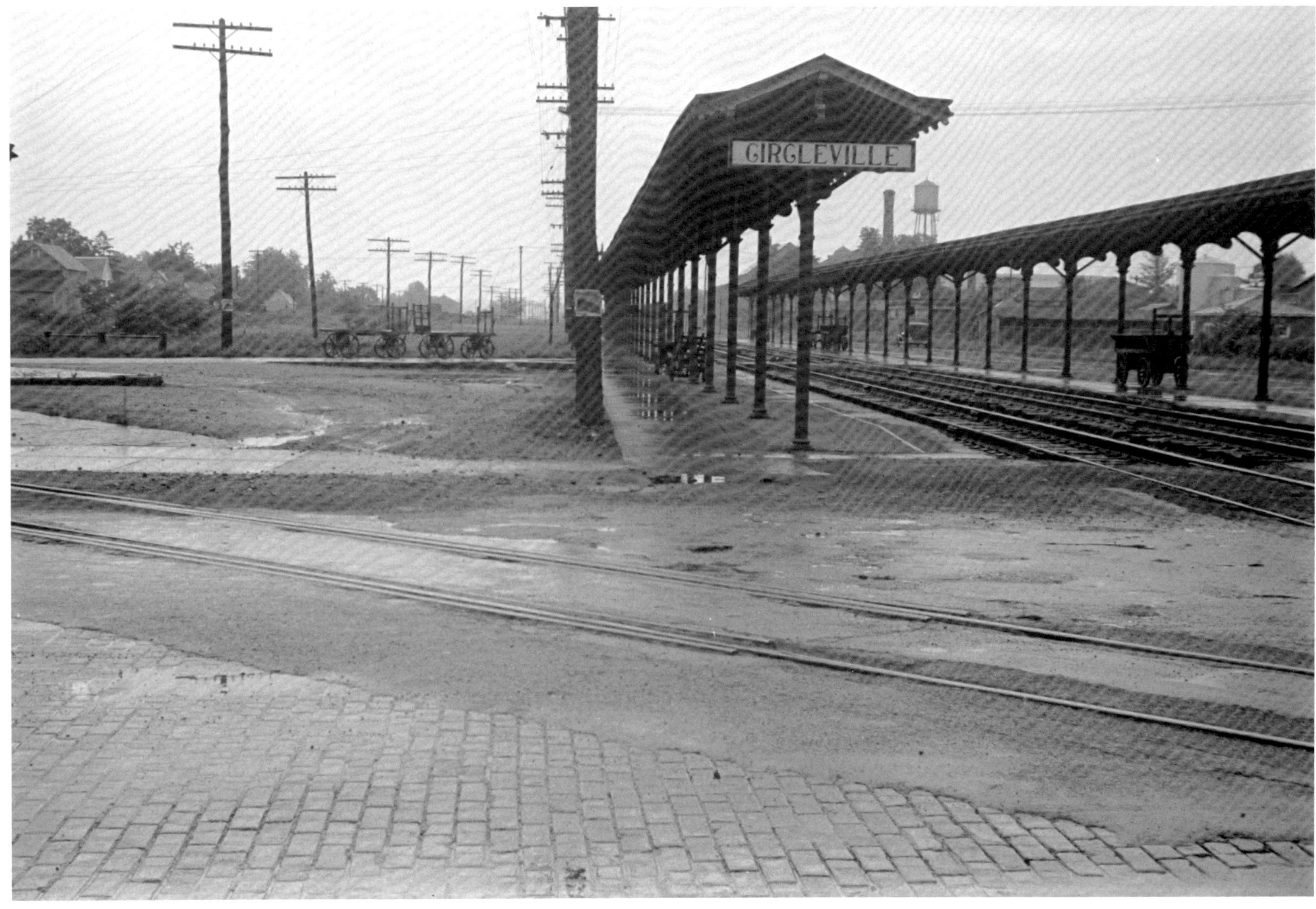

Figure 0.4. Railroad station of Circleville, Ohio.

Ben Shahn. Summer 1938. Library of Congress, Prints & Photographs Division, FSA-OWI Collection, LC-USF3301-006577-M4.

THE FSA/OWI PHOTOGRAPHERS RESPOND TO THE US RAILROAD

In response to Stryker's guidance and the ubiquity of the railroad in American society in the 1930s and early 1940s, almost all of the FSA/OWI photographers took images of American railroading. Ten of the photographers—John Collier Jr., Marjory Collins, Jack Delano, Walker Evans, Dorothea Lange, Russell Lee, Gordon Parks, Arthur Rothstein, John Vachon, and Marion Post Wolcott—took a considerable number of railroad-subject images. Each of these photographers is profiled in the note preceding the portfolio of their railroad-subject work later in this book.

In terms of output of railroad-subject photographs, Jack Delano is head and shoulders above the others, with about 2,700 black-and-white images.[18] His work on railroads is extensive because of his noted Chicago-area and Atchison, Topeka and Santa Fe Railway assignments. John Vachon and Russell Lee are also prolific chroniclers of the subject, each having hundreds of such images to their credit.[19]

At least four FSA/OWI photographers would continue to produce significant railroad-subject images after leaving Stryker's team. As staff photographer for *Fortune* magazine, Evans would produce four enormously skilled and influential railroad-subject photo-essays for the magazine. He would mentor both Robert Frank, who produced a similar essay for *Fortune*, and David Plowden. Finally, he helped move the historic preservation movement in the United States forward with a plaintive photo-essay in *Life* focusing on the demolition of New York City's Pennsylvania Station.

Delano, who led a fascinating life after leaving the OWI, relocated permanently to Puerto Rico following World War II. As part of documenting that US territory, he produced an extensive photo-essay focusing on the American Railroad Company, which circled part of the island to connect San Juan with Ponce and Guayama.[20] This work was presented to the public much later with the 1990 publication of *From San Juan to Ponce on the Train*.

Esther Bubley and Russell Lee both followed Roy Stryker to Standard Oil of New Jersey.[21] Since railroads both used and moved petroleum products, Stryker's Standard Oil project continued to document the US railroad to some extent.[22] This collection, which includes about seventy thousand photographs, is held by the University of Louisville, which also holds the Roy Stryker Papers, a Lewis Hine study collection, and the Jones and Laughlin Steel Corporation collection.[23] The 1949 book *Granger Country*, edited by Lloyd Lewis and Stanley Pargellis, showcases photos of the Chicago, Burlington and Quincy Railroad taken as part of this project by Bubley and Lee.[24]

THE LEGACY OF THE FSA/OWI RAILROAD-SUBJECT PHOTOGRAPHS

The FSA/OWI Historical Section file has had an immense influence on US popular culture, on other photographers and those who study their work, and on railroad-subject photographers.

The overall impact of the Historical Section's work on US society stems from a number of factors. The first is the size and breadth of the file and the fact that it documents two of the most difficult challenges the United States has faced—the Great Depression and World War II. Several of the images in the file, such as the photo usually titled *Migrant Mother* by Dorothea Lange and *Farmer and Sons Walking in the Face of a Dust Storm* by Arthur Rothstein, are popular icons conveying the impact of the Great Depression and the coincident Dust Bowl. The output of books and articles focusing on the FSA/OWI photographs remains strong, and the images are all easily accessed from the Library of Congress website.[25] As government documents, they are not copyrighted and so are easy and inexpensive to use as illustrations. Within this large body of work, Jack Delano's railroad-subject work is widely known, and Walker Evans's *View of Railroad Station, Edwards, Mississippi* (plate 43) and Dorothea Lange's *Toward Los Angeles, California* (plate 52) have earned positions as iconic images of our culture.

The influence of the FSA/OWI photographers, both while they were with the agencies and afterward, on photographers who have followed is immense. Two of the FSA/OWI photographers, Walker Evans and Dorothea Lange, have earned recognition as being among the greatest photographers of the twentieth century. With the exception of Marion Post Wolcott, all of the photographers profiled in this book remained active after leaving the FSA or OWI. Gordon Parks, Arthur Rothstein, and John Vachon had long photographic careers with *Life*, *Look*, and *Look*, respectively, and Rothstein authored a key book in the field of photojournalism.[26] John Collier Jr. joined academia, as did Russell Lee, and Collier authored a seminal book in the field of visual anthropology.[27] Marjory Collins spent many years as a magazine publisher. Jack Delano, like the Rosskams and Rex Tugwell, moved to Puerto Rico. Unlike them, he and his wife settled there, raised a family, and spent the rest of their lives in this US territory. Delano and Parks were polymaths, generating creative output in a number of different fields. Many of the FSA/OWI photographers, including Esther Bubley, Collier, Lee, Parks, Edwin and Louise Rosskam, and Vachon, would continue

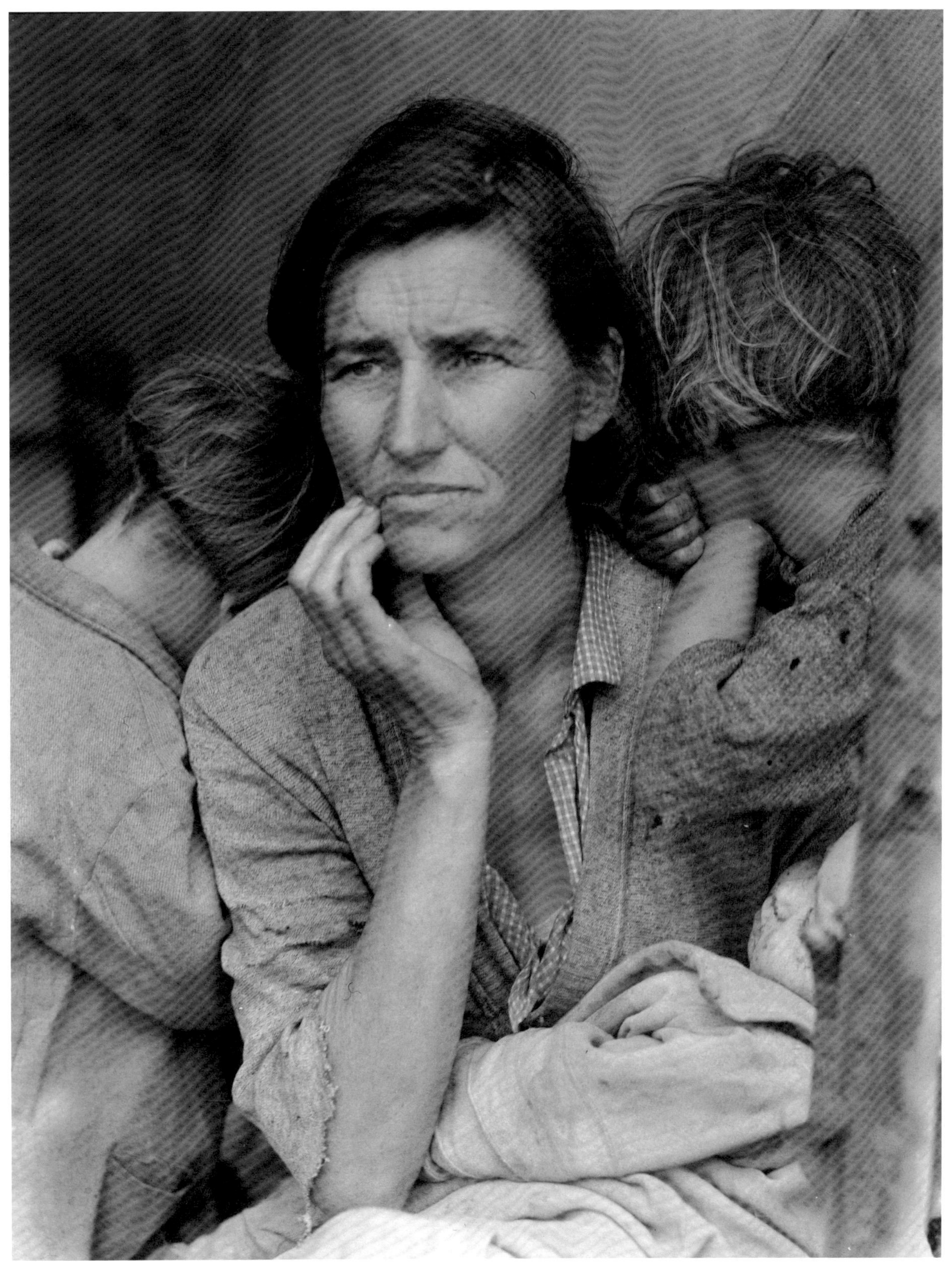

Figure 0.5. Destitute pea pickers in California. Mother of seven children. Age thirty-two. Nipomo, California. (Commonly titled *Migrant Mother.*)

Dorothea Lange. March 1936. Library of Congress, Prints & Photographs Division, FSA-OWI Collection, LC-USF34-T01-009058-C.

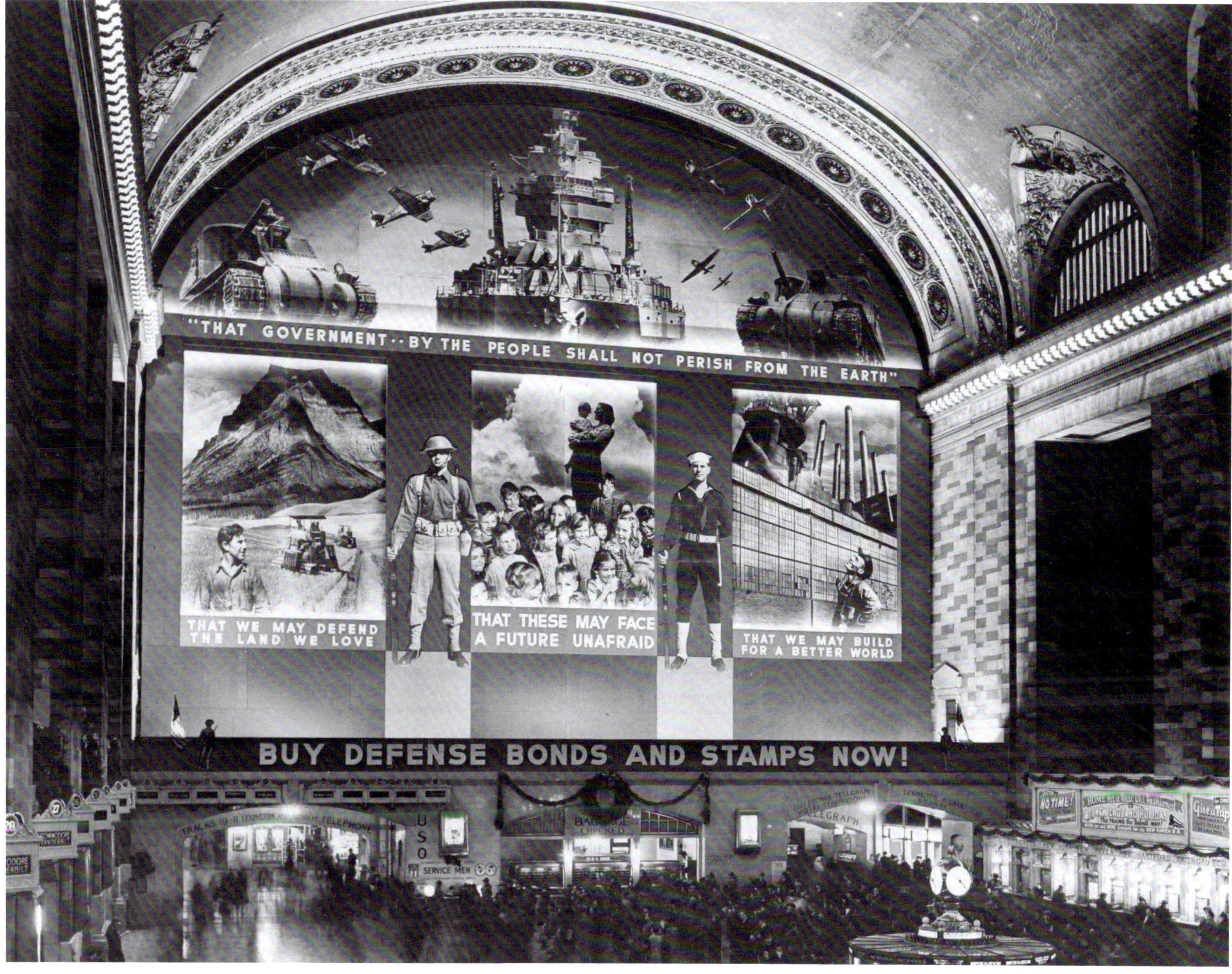

Figure 0.6. New York, New York. Photo mural to promote the sale of defense bonds, designed by the Farm Security Administration, in the concourse of Grand Central Terminal.

Arthur Rothstein. 1941. Library of Congress, Prints & Photographs Division, FSA-OWI Collection, LC-USF34-024495-D.

to do at least some work with Roy Stryker at Standard Oil of New Jersey, the Pittsburgh Photographic Library, and Jones and Laughlin Steel Corporation.

With their photographic work, writing, and teaching, the fifteen significant FSA/OWI photographers had a tremendous impact on photography, in the United States and beyond, with a collective sweep of work that spans from about 1920 to about 1990.[28] Consider the personal history of the best-known of these photographers, Walker Evans. He was a close friend of the American writers Hart Crane and James Agee and mentored—mentorship was and is important in the photography genre—Robert Frank and David Plowden, among others. He was a partner with James Agee in a classic book, *Let Us Now Praise Famous Men*, and led photography for an influential magazine, *Fortune*, for two decades. He had an enormously influential exhibition at the Museum of Modern Art in 1938, its first solo photography exhibition, and taught photography at Yale from 1961 to 1971.[29] Similar, if not usually as expansive, stories may be told about the rest of these talented individuals.

What about the FSA/OWI photographers and their influence on railroad-subject photographers who followed them? Because of the awareness his railroad-subject work has earned, Jack Delano stands above the others as an influence on railroad-subject photography. His influence started late—his work first became well known with the release of two books in 1977, James E. Valle's *The Iron Horse at War* and Don Ball and Rogers E. M. Whitaker's *Decade of the Trains: The 1940s*.[30] After a period of relative inactivity, two more books focusing on Delano's railroad-subject photographs were issued in the mid-2010s: John Gruber's *Railroaders: Jack Delano's Homefront Photography* and this author's *The Railroad Photography of Jack Delano*.

Railroaders is an unforgettably creative work, combining Delano's 1942/1943 portraits of railroad workers with the stories of these men and women's lives. The book is illustrated by contemporary photos of the railroad workers' family members by Delano's son, Pablo Delano, and its release was accompanied by a successful exhibition, also entitled *Railroaders: Jack Delano's Homefront Photography*. Meanwhile, one of the portfolios in *The Railroad Photography of Jack Delano* featured Delano's groundbreaking color images of US railroading during the 1940s. Because of this attention, Delano's railroad-subject images are now well known, particularly his portraits of railroad workers during World War II.

Beyond its artistic and historic value, another reason that Jack Delano's work has resulted in so many books to date is the breadth of his coverage of the US railroad, with thousands of such images in his FSA/OWI oeuvre. The next most prolific bodies of work, by Russell Lee and John Vachon, number in the hundreds—probably not enough to justify single-artist books featuring their railroad-subject work.[31]

The extensive railroad-subject work of Walker Evans is perhaps less known today than Delano's, but it was influential in the 1950s and 1960s due to his occasional portfolios in *Fortune* magazine and a notable article in *Life*. The cost of reproducing Evans's work for *Fortune*, because of the usage fees charged by the copyright holder, has limited its visibility in recent years, and so his excellent railroad-subject portfolios are essentially stranded in back issues of that magazine.

Although the FSA/OWI photographers beyond Jack Delano produced at most a few hundred railroad-subject images, they did produce interesting portfolios of work that certainly at least justify photo-essay articles. The most notable examples include Marjory Collins's images of female railroaders during World War II, Russell Lee's coverage of the narrow-gauge railroads of Colorado, Arthur Rothstein's photographs of the Virginia & Truckee Railroad, and John Vachon's images of the Frisco (St. Louis–San Francisco Railway) operations in Tulsa, Oklahoma.[32]

ABOUT THE PORTFOLIOS

Railroad-subject images by ten of the most notable FSA/OWI photographers are presented in the portfolios, which are in alphabetical order based on the name of the photographer in question. Each portfolio begins with a biographic sketch of the photographer, including information about the strongest aspects of their work and notes on key life events that influenced their work.

The images are presented as high-resolution, full-page photographs. The captions for the photos are those assigned to them by the photographers.[33] Some of the photos were originally uncaptioned, and in these cases, the practice was to caption them as "possibly related" to a similar captioned photo. In deference to the artistic and administrative practices of the photographers, the FSA/OWI, and the Library of Congress, the captions shown are the captions the photos have in the file.

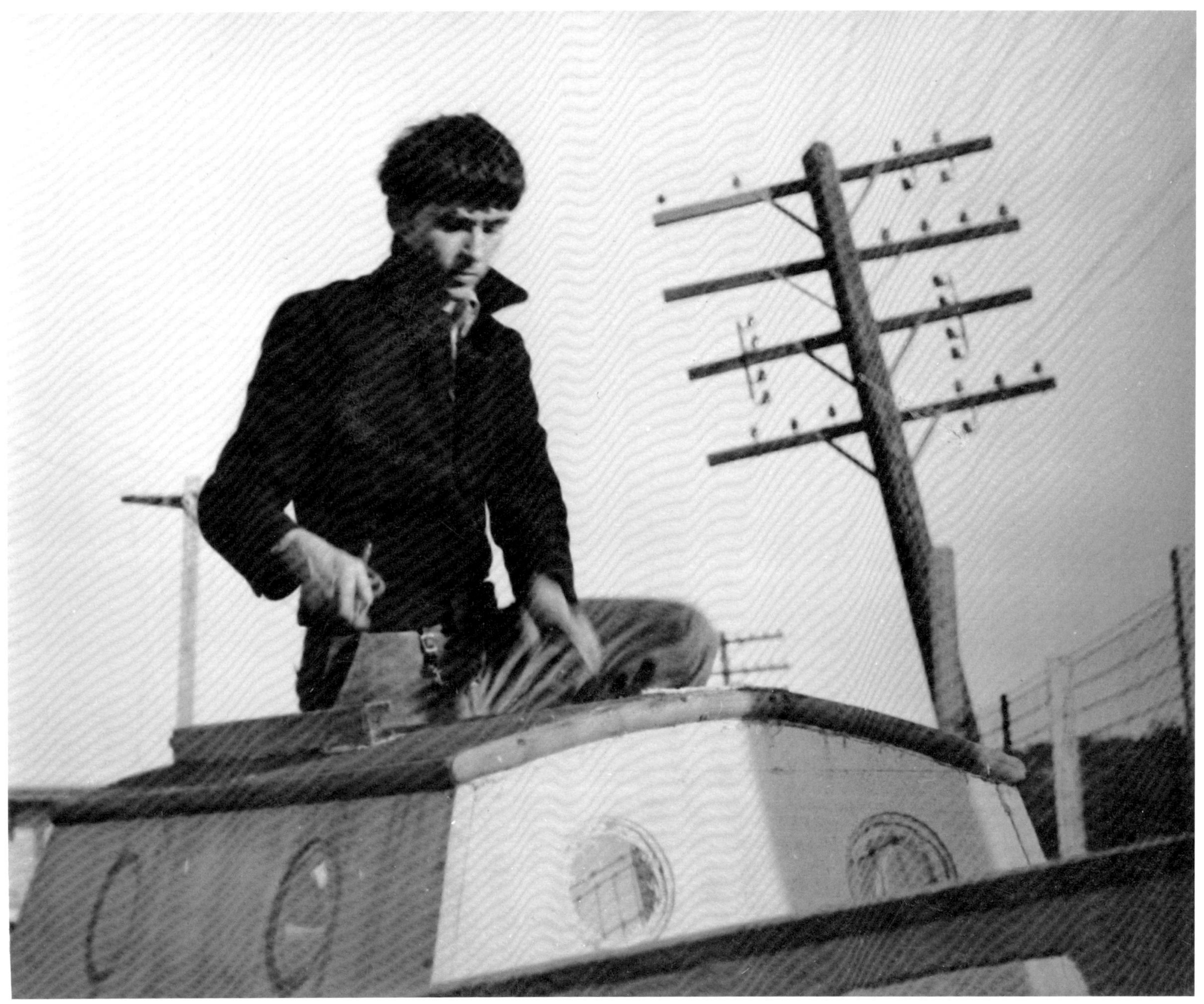

Figure 1.1. John Collier Jr. aboard the *Spring Fever*, Sausalito, California, 1930s.

Catalogue No. 2006_117_3426. Courtesy of the Maxwell Museum of Anthropology, University of New Mexico.

PORTFOLIO ONE

JOHN COLLIER JR.

When John Collier Jr. was seven, he was hit by an automobile and suffered a skull fracture. The brain damage that resulted was unusual and debilitating, affecting Collier's sense of hearing and spelling and mathematics skills.[1] This may have predisposed Collier to view the world in a concretely visual way. Despite his disability, Collier forged a career as an artist, photographer, and anthropologist. His book *Visual Anthropology: Photography as a Research Method* is a classic of the field. Collier is best known for his documentary projects focusing on Native Americans in New Mexico, including extensive work on the Navajo Reservation. Despite this record of achievements, and like Marjory Collins, Collier has not found a biographer, nor is his work featured in the Fields of Vision series of short books featuring FSA/OWI photographers.

Collier's father, John Collier, a writer and reformer, was the commissioner for the Bureau of Indian Affairs during the entire New Deal and World War II periods, 1933–1945. The elder Collier became interested in Native Americans through visiting Taos, New Mexico, in 1920. He was from Atlanta, but he and his family moved to California, and Collier taught at San Francisco State College. The Collier family also maintained ties with Taos, New Mexico, beginning in 1920, and the elder Collier eventually moved there and died in Taos in 1968.[2]

A few years after the younger Collier's accident, at age twelve, he was apprenticed to painter Maynard Dixon, who was Dorothea Lange's first husband. This apprenticeship was intended to replace formal schooling for Collier, which was difficult due to his disability. Collier also served on a ship as a teenager. He then met Paul Strand and set up his first studio in Strand's old Taos darkroom. Like his family, Collier established a home in the Taos area in the 1930s. He married Mary Elizabeth Trumbull, also a photographer, in 1943.[3]

Collier joined the FSA, soon to become a part of the OWI, in 1941 and worked there until 1943. He was also associated with Stryker's photographic project for Standard Oil, including projects in South America and Canada. Collier also worked with Cornell University, conducting fieldwork in New Mexico, Canada, and Peru.

In later life, Collier taught at the California School of Fine Arts and at San Francisco State University and lived in Muir Beach, California, and Talpa, New Mexico. Collier died in 1992 in San José, Costa Rica, from internal bleeding following surgery while on vacation.[4] His collection is held by the Maxwell Museum of Anthropology at the University of New Mexico in Albuquerque, New Mexico.

Our review of Collier's work for the FSA/OWI begins with plates 1–5. These were all taken in Richwood, West Virginia, in September 1942 on the Baltimore & Ohio Railroad (B&O). Plate 1 depicts a probable reason for Collier's visit there, documenting a special train taking area people to do migrant farm work in New York state. By this time, Stryker and his team, including Collier, were focused on documenting the war effort, and food production was a critical aspect of the World War II home front.

While in Richwood, Collier composed an excellent photo series showing railroad operations on the B&O there—a group of photos that deserves a dedicated article. The next four plates give an overview of this series. Plates 2 and 3 depict B&O engineers in a compelling portrait and in a traditional cab window view. B&O 5123, shown in plate 3, was a Class P-3 Pacific (4-6-2 in the Whyte notation). Plate 4 depicts a B&O baggage man in his car, an image replete with period details such as the spare brake hoses and the shelves for paperwork. Collier's caption to plate 5 states it is a view of a "baggage car," but what we are seeing in this view is the side door of a railway post office car (RPO car), or at least the RPO section of a car. The employee shown here is probably a federal railway postal clerk. At stations that received mail where the train did not stop, he kicked the arriving mail bag out of the door shown here and used the hook apparatus shown to pick up a received mail bag on the fly.

One of Collier's best-known series of photos for the FSA/OWI depicts coal mining in Pennsylvania.[5] Since coal mining was and is an extractive industry producing a heavy, low-value-per-weight product, it was dependent on the availability of rail service. For this reason, Collier's coal-mining images include a number that also may be viewed as railroad-subject images. Plate 6, part of this work, shows coal being loaded into coal cars at the Pittsburgh Coal Company's Montour No. 4 mine, which was located in Lawrence, Pennsylvania, and served by the Montour Railroad.

Plate 7 shows another scene exemplifying the railroad industry's importance in the home-front food industry. In the image, taken in Cambridge, Maryland, on Maryland's largely rural and agricultural Eastern Shore, canned foods are loaded into a Pennsylvania Railroad boxcar (Cambridge was served by the Pennsylvania Railroad) at the Phillips Packing Company plant. This company canned seafood, fruits, and vegetables and still exists today.[6]

Our review of Collier's railroad-subject photographs closes with an image taken in a very different place: the border between Florida and Alabama. Plate 8 depicts an abandoned railroad line crossing the mill pond in Falco, a ghost town in Alabama just north of the Alabama-Florida border. Established by the Florida-Alabama Land Company in 1903, Falco was largely abandoned in the 1920s when its timber was exhausted.[7]

***Facing*, Figure 1.2.** Grand Central Terminal, New York City.

John Collier Jr. October 1941. Library of Congress, Prints & Photographs Division, FSA-OWI Collection, LC-USF34-080907-E. Collier took a handful of images of Grand Central Terminal, the only such images in the FSA/OWI file other than ones covering construction and installation of a photomural promoting war bond sales in the iconic station.

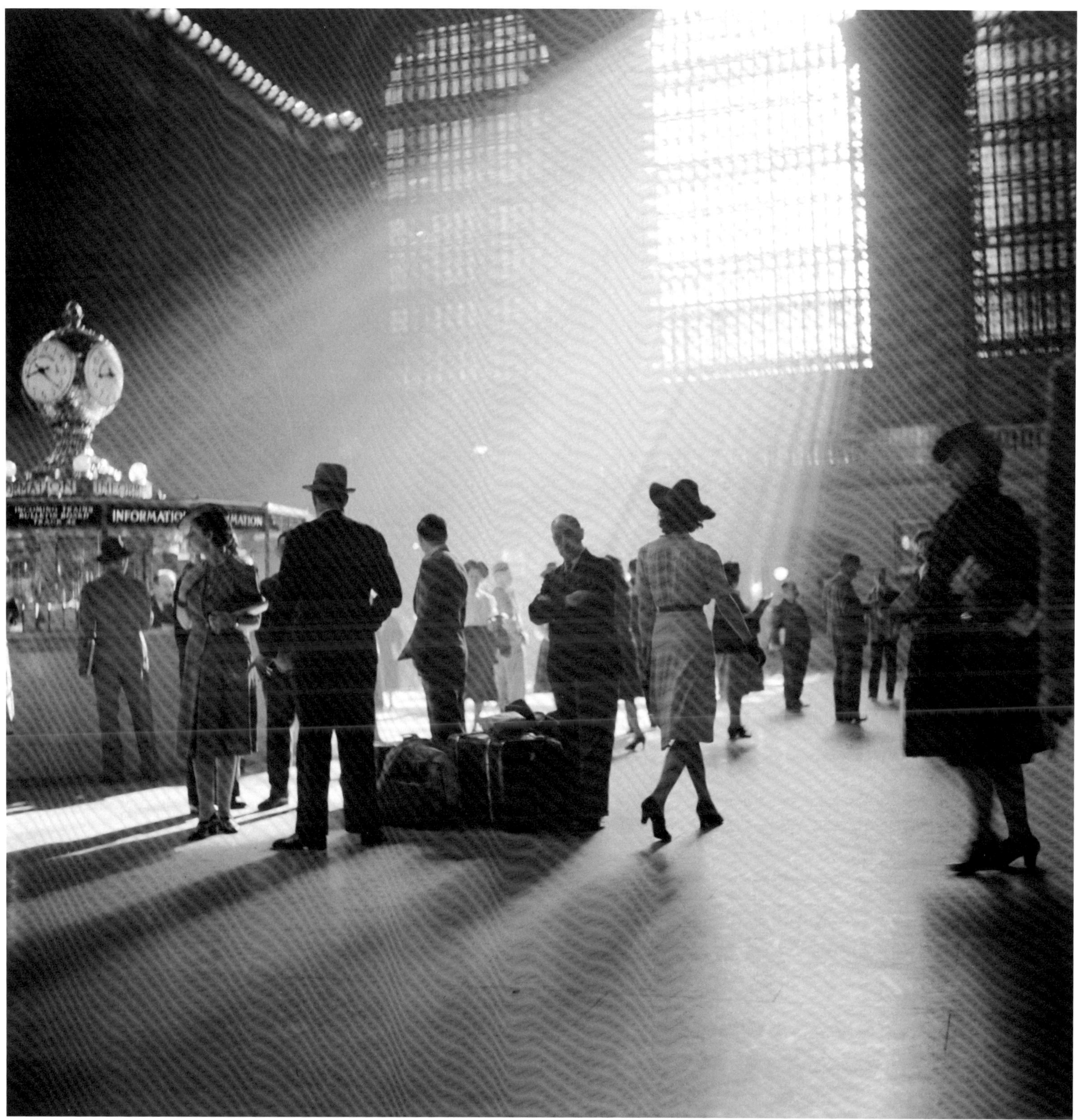
INFORMATION

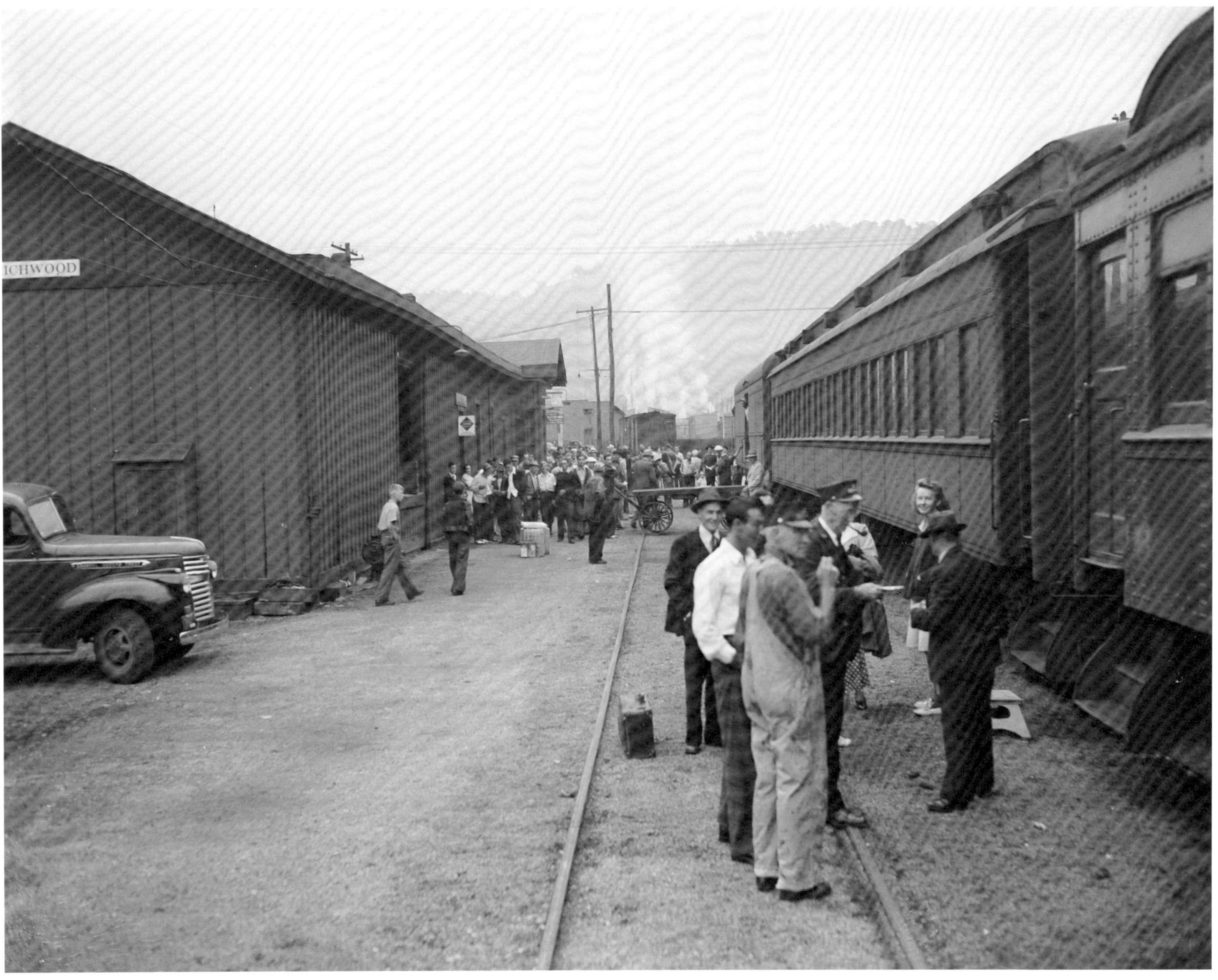

***Above,* Plate 1.** Richwood, West Virginia. The Baltimore & Ohio Railroad furnished a special train to carry the three hundred men, women, and children to upper New York state, where they would work in the harvest.

John Collier Jr. September 1942. Library of Congress, Prints & Photographs Division, FSA-OWI Collection, LC-USF34-083922-C.

***Facing,* Plate 2.** Richwood, West Virginia. An engineer on the Baltimore & Ohio Railroad.

John Collier Jr. September 1942. Library of Congress, Prints & Photographs Division, FSA-OWI Collection, LC-USF34-084047-E.

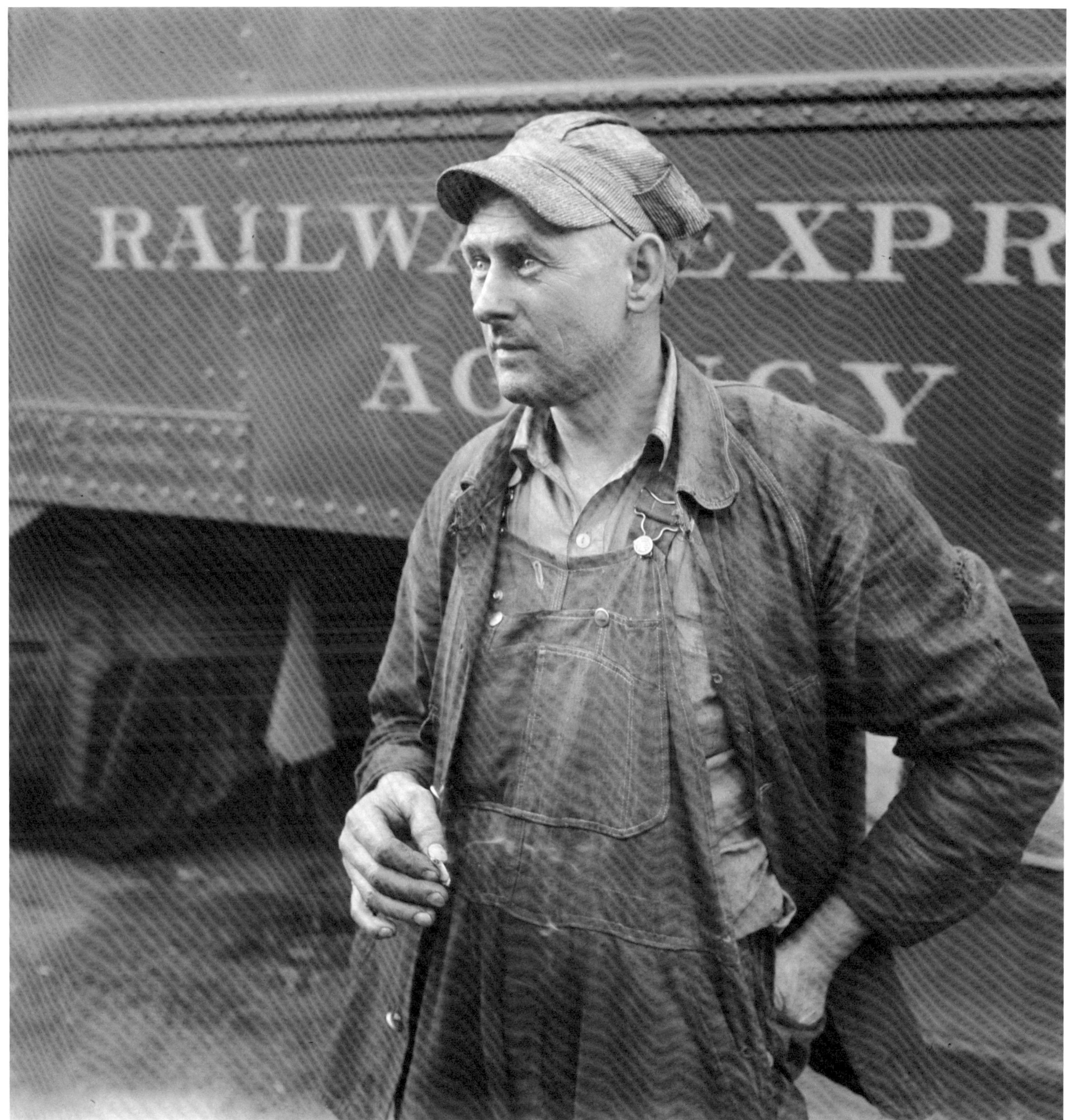

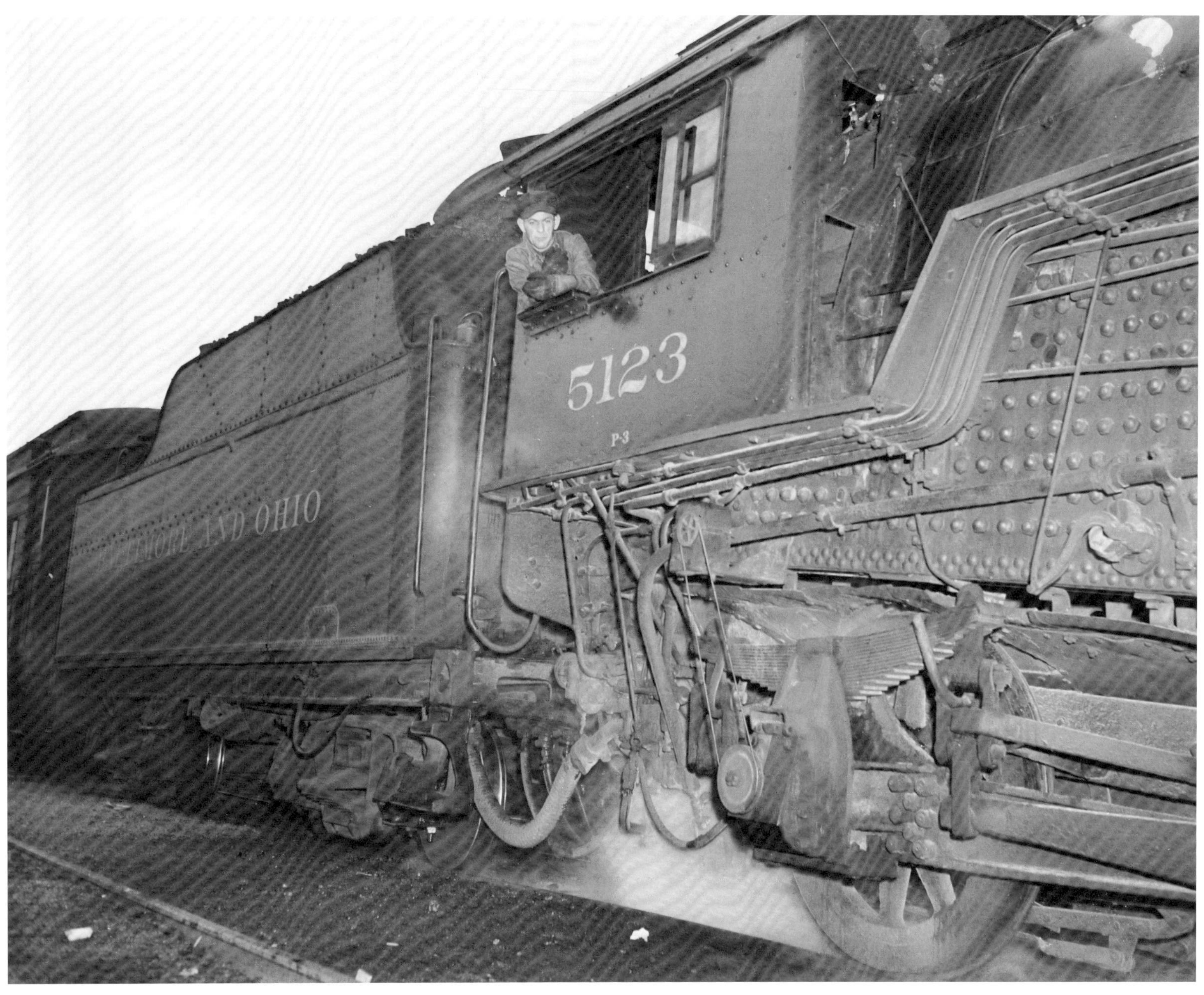

Plate 3. Richwood, West Virginia. An engineer on the Baltimore & Ohio Railroad.

John Collier Jr. September 1942. Library of Congress, Prints & Photographs Division, FSA-OWI Collection, USF34-083989-C.

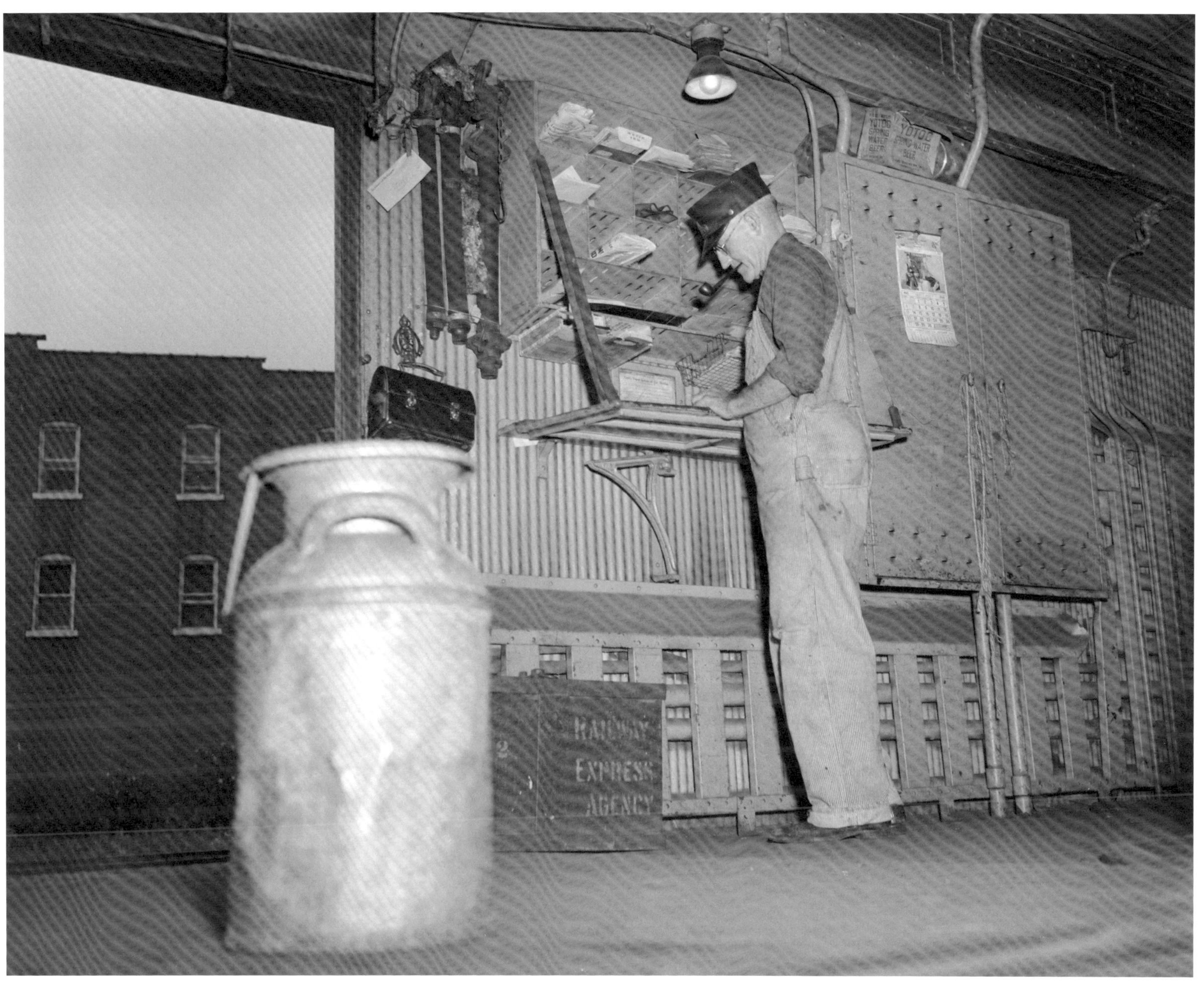

Plate 4. Richwood, West Virginia. A baggage man on the Baltimore & Ohio Railroad.

John Collier Jr. September 1942. Library of Congress, Prints & Photographs Division, FSA-OWI Collection, LC-USF34-083986-C.

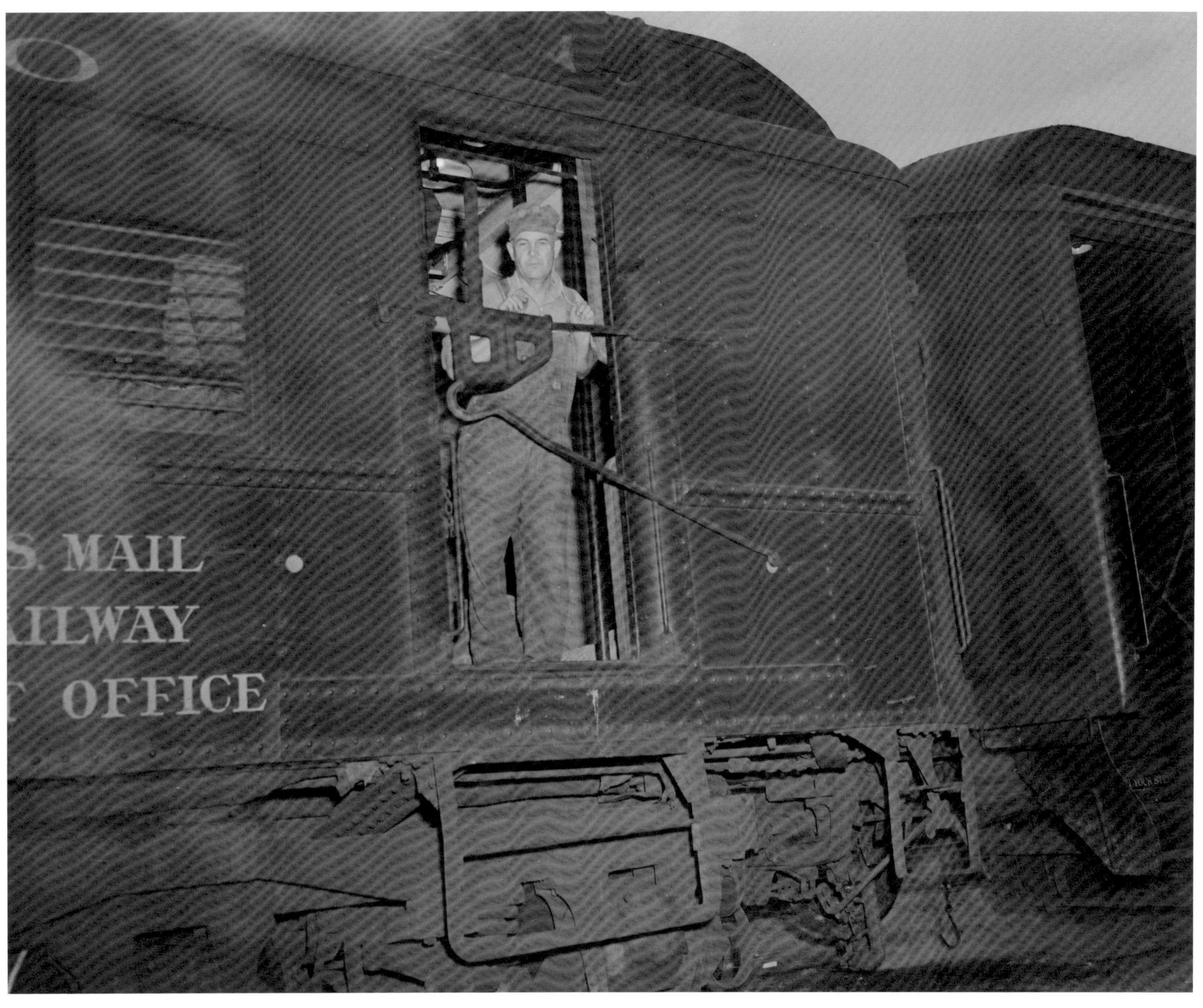

Plate 5. Richwood, West Virginia. Baggage car on the Baltimore & Ohio Railroad.

John Collier Jr. September 1942. Library of Congress, Prints & Photographs Division, FSA-OWI Collection, LC-USF34-083990-C.

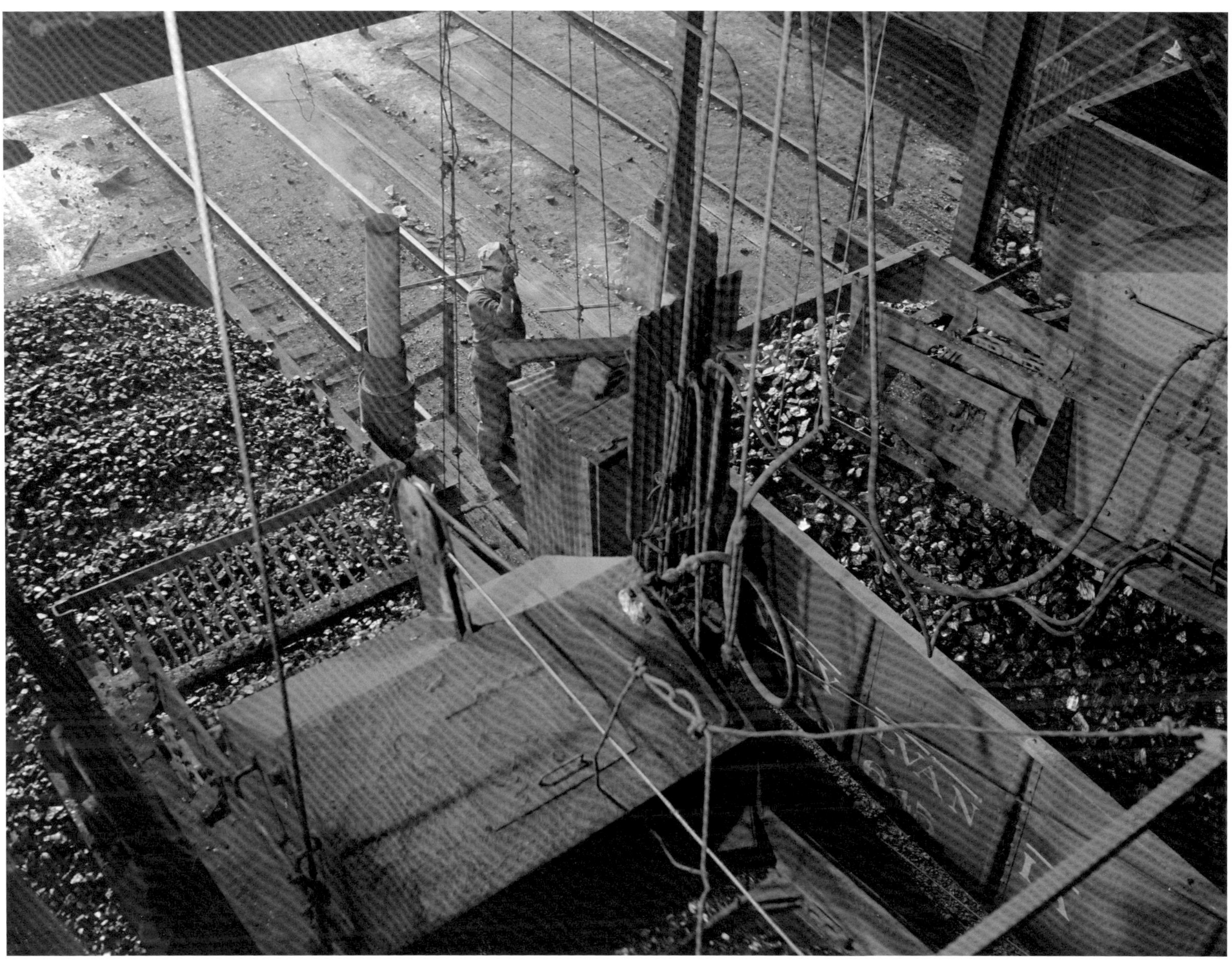

Plate 6. Pittsburgh, Pennsylvania (vicinity). Montour no. 4 of the Pittsburgh Coal Company. Loading cleaned coal into railroad cars.

John Collier Jr. November 1942. Library of Congress, Prints & Photographs Division, FSA-OWI Collection, LC-USW3-012141-C.

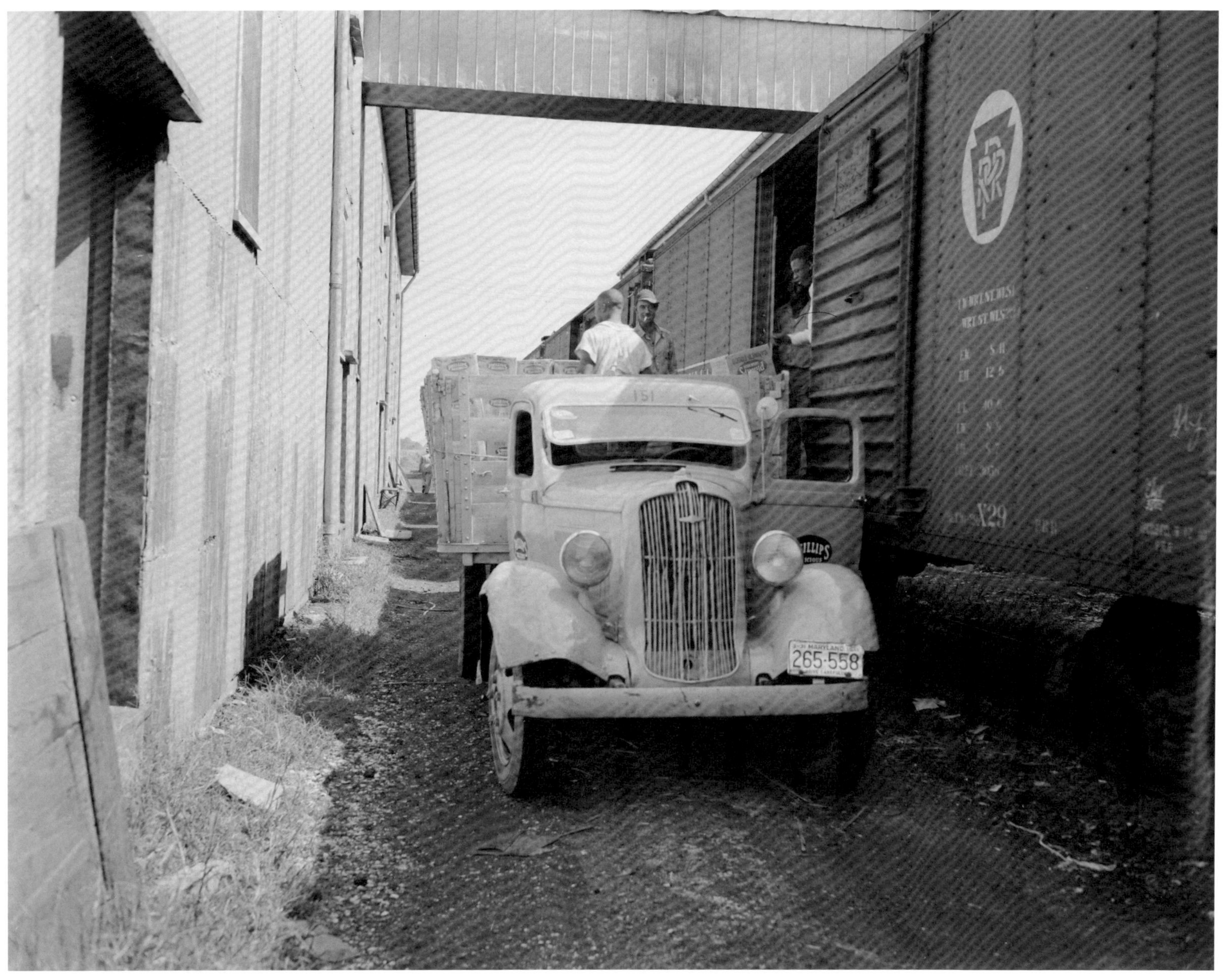

Plate 7. A railroad spur enters the Phillips Packing Company plant to load canned goods for distant points not reached by truck line. Cambridge, Maryland.

John Collier Jr. August 1941. Library of Congress, Prints & Photographs Division, FSA-OWI Collection, LC-USF34-080651-C.

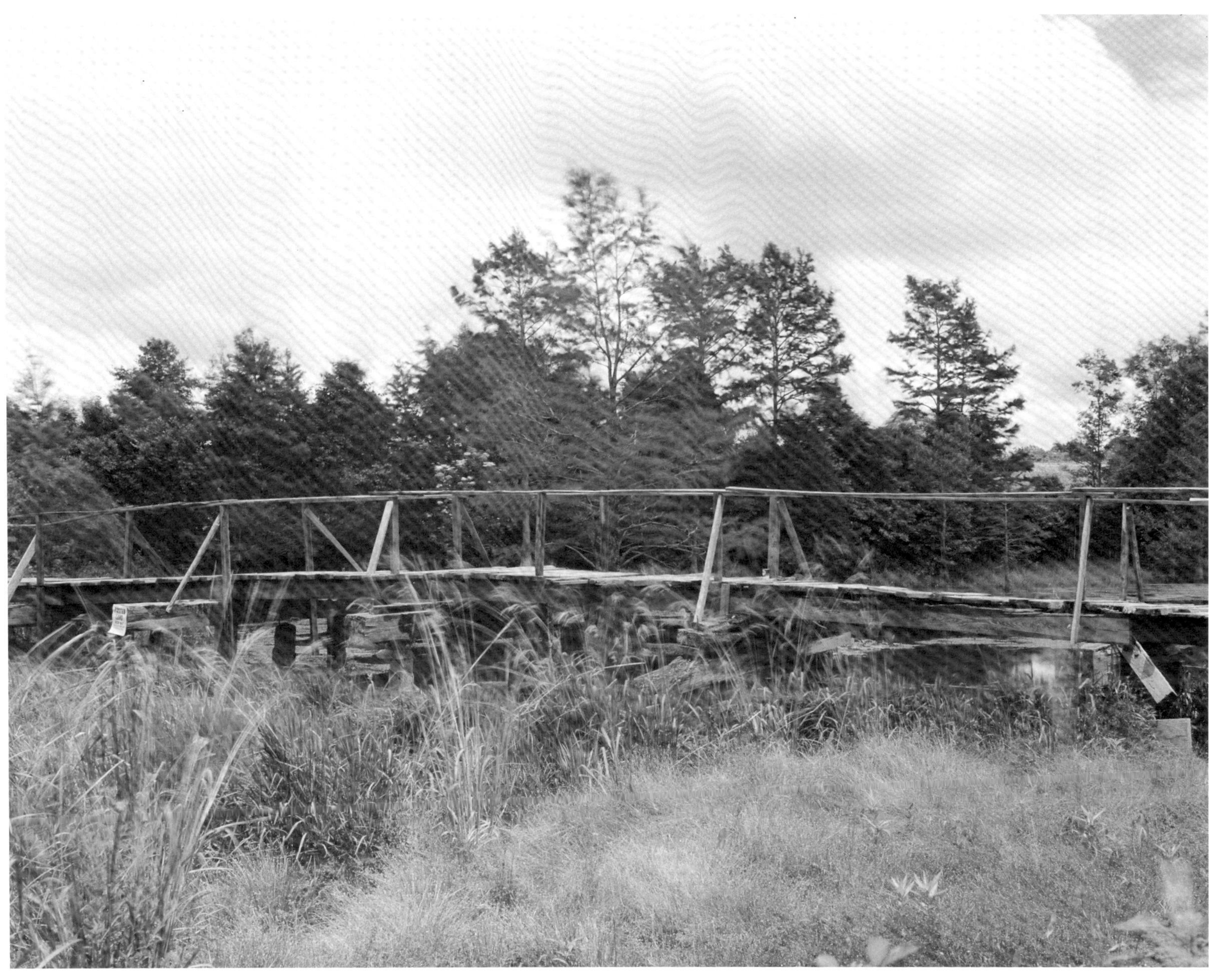

Plate 8. Falco, Florida [i.e., Alabama]. All that is left of the railroad line running to the Falco lumber mill as it crosses the old log pond (mill closed in 1923).

John Collier Jr. June 1942. Library of Congress, Prints & Photographs Division, FSA-OWI Collection, LC-USF34-082705-C.

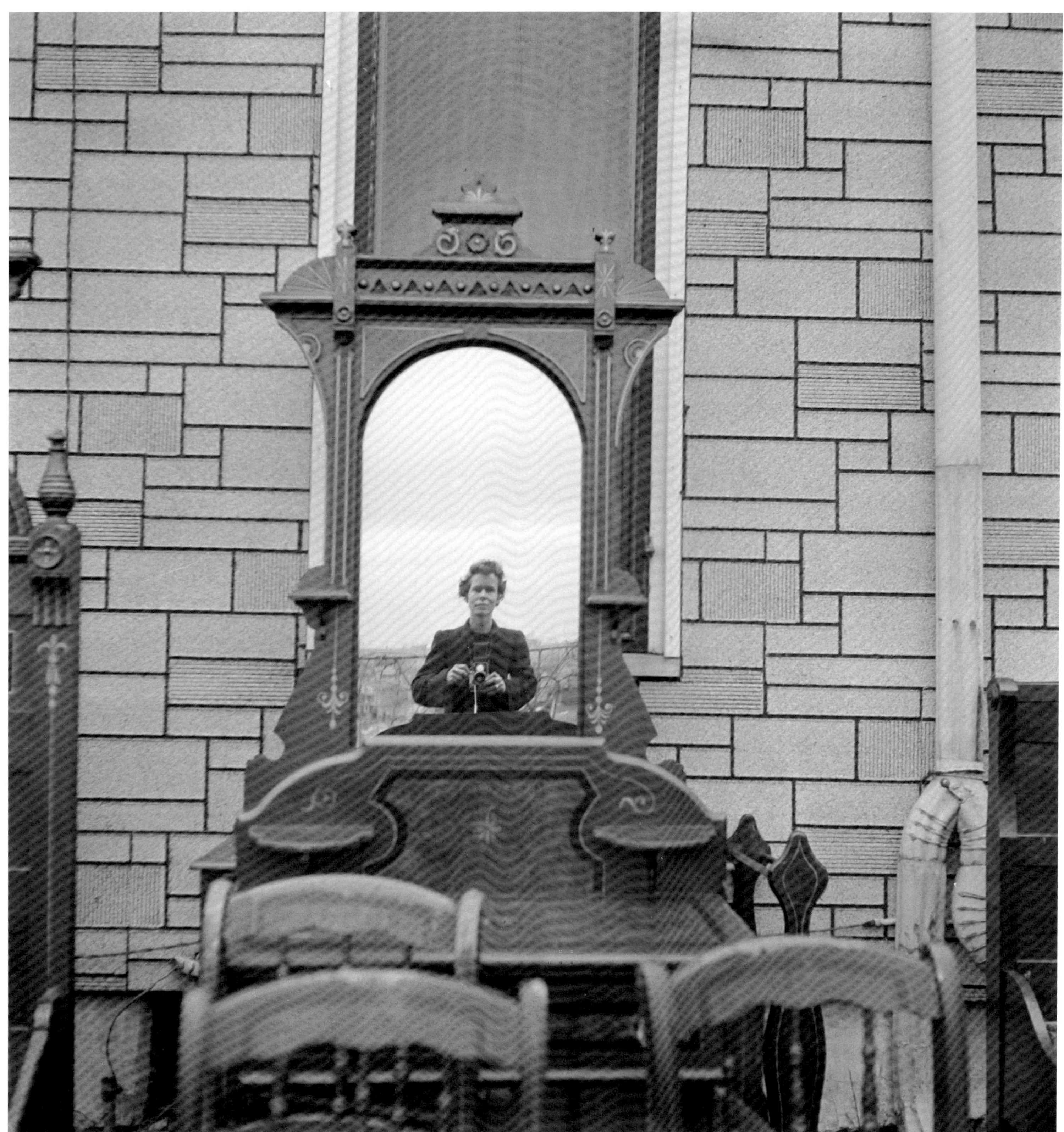

PORTFOLIO TWO

MARJORY COLLINS

Marjory Collins is arguably the least-known photographer featured in this book. She has not even been accorded an appearance in the Library of Congress's Fields of Vision series of brief books focusing on the FSA/OWI photographers.

An available source about her life, a biographical essay by Beverly Brannan, provides a tantalizingly brief view of Collins and her work.[1] She began her life as a socialite and married a Yale student in 1933; the marriage ended in divorce in 1935.[2] Collins then studied with and became a protégé of noted art photographer and avant-garde filmmaker Ralph Steiner, in turn a protégé of Clarence White and a member of a circle that also included Walker Evans and Paul Strand. Collins worked for *PM*, where Steiner was the photo editor, and *US Camera*.

Collins's work at *US Camera* helped her find a position at the OWI in New York, but she soon transferred to Roy Stryker's team in Washington, DC, beginning work there in early 1942. According to Brannan, her closest colleagues at the OWI were Gordon Parks and John Vachon. During 1942 and 1943, she would take more than three thousand OWI photographs.

Collins was criticized by fellow OWI photographer Alfred Palmer for sometimes showing "the seamy side of life."[3] Although Collins did not have a close relationship with her boss, Roy Stryker, her work reflected his influence.[4] Palmer's comment shows how much the orientation of governmental photography in the US had changed as a result of World War II and suggests why Stryker would leave the OWI before the end of the war.

After her brief but productive stint at the OWI, Collins worked on freelance assignments in Alaska, Africa, and Europe. She later broadened her freelance career to work as a writer and editor covering issues that were clearly of great concern to her: civil rights, the Vietnam War, and the women's movement. She lived in Vermont much of this time but later moved to San Francisco.

Collins was an activist in the women's movement and founded the feminist journal *Prime Time*. She died of cancer in San Francisco, California, in 1985. Her personal papers, unlike many of her photographs, survive and are held by Harvard University.

In her essay, Brannan focuses on Collins's OWI work and its focus on "hyphenated Americans," including subjects of Chinese, Czech, German, Italian, and Turkish heritage. These

***Facing,* Figure 2.1.** Lititz, Pennsylvania. Self-portrait at a public sale.

Marjory Collins. November 1942. Library of Congress, Prints & Photographs Division, FSA-OWI Collection, LC-USW3-011699-E.

images served the US government's aim of showing a country united against the Axis powers. Brannan also mentions Collins's work on women's wartime entrance into industry in the US. Collins also gave wartime views of Pennsylvania Station extensive coverage, as Gordon Parks did for Union Station in Washington, DC, and Jack Delano did for Chicago Union Station.[5]

To this observer, Collins's OWI views are most notable for their coverage of women in the World War II–era workforce, including the railroad workforce. While serving the OWI's purpose of showing a country united to fight the Axis, they also presage Collins's later work as a feminist activist, editor, and scholar. In viewing them, one is reminded of contemporary work focusing on women and US railroading by Linda Niemann, Shirley Burman, and others. Collins, her work, and her life certainly deserve more study.

Our look at Marjory Collins's railroad-subject work for the OWI begins with plate 9, a portrait of an express agent in Lititz, Pennsylvania, O. K. Bushong. Lititz was served by the Reading Company.

Plates 10–13 show New York's Pennsylvania Station almost overwhelmed by wartime train traffic while it is also being used to house a military induction center. Plate 12 is especially telling, showing a middle-aged white man stealing a glance as an attractive woman bends over her baby, while a Black railroader, perhaps a Red Cap, studiously looks away. This is an image that has much to say about US society then and now.

Plates 14 through 20 are the fruit of Collins's work on women in US industry, including railroading in Pennsylvania, during World War II. All these images were taken at Pitcairn, Pennsylvania, which was served by the Pennsylvania Railroad. Her captions give journalistic but telling details, noting, for example, that a female freight stower is a "mother of four children" and is married to a coal miner, or that a twenty-eight-year-old locomotive preparer is a "mother of six children." Plate 18 is a rare image, a period portrait of a Black female railroader, while plate 19 shows twin young women using air hammers, then an uncharacteristic pose. The Pennsylvania Railroad locomotive seen in plate 18 is 135, an L1s 2-8-2. Two of these images, plates 16 and 20, show women working with male railroaders.

This portfolio closes with plate 21, a portrait of a male worker at a railroad supply company, the New York Car Wheel Company, teaching a female colleague to use an axle lathe. While many—perhaps most—of the World War II female railroaders left those positions soon after the end of the war, the 1970s saw a new and more lasting entrance of women into the railroad workforce.[6]

***Facing,* Plate 9.** Lititz, Pennsylvania. Mr. O. K. Bushong, express agent. Two trains a day pass through Lititz on the Lancaster-Reading Railroad. He says that passenger trade has increased 100 percent since war.

Marjory Collins. November 1942. Library of Congress, Prints & Photographs Division, FSA-OWI Collection, LC-USW3-011254-E.

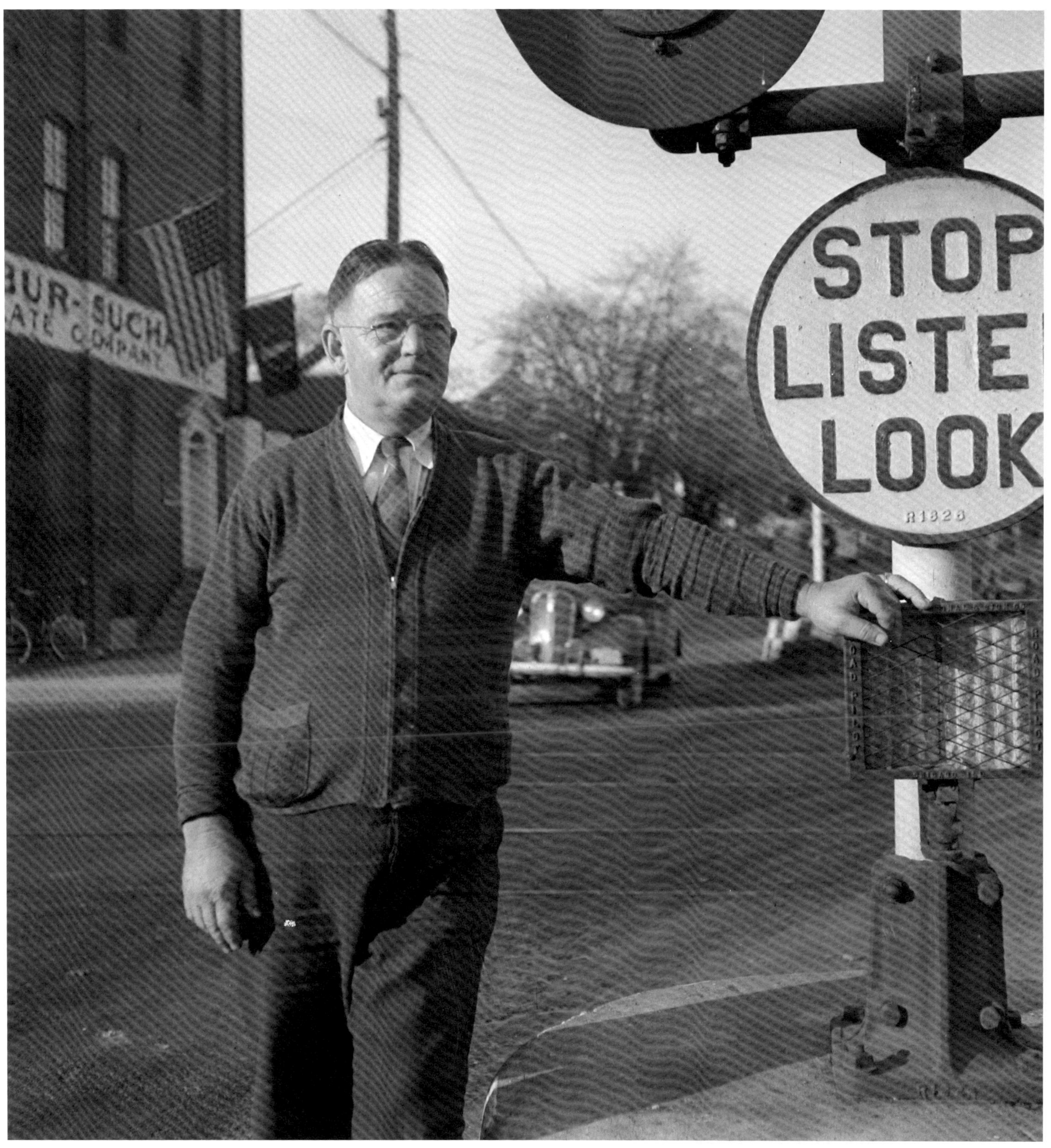
STOP
LISTE
LOOK
R1828
BUR-SUCH
ATE COMPANY

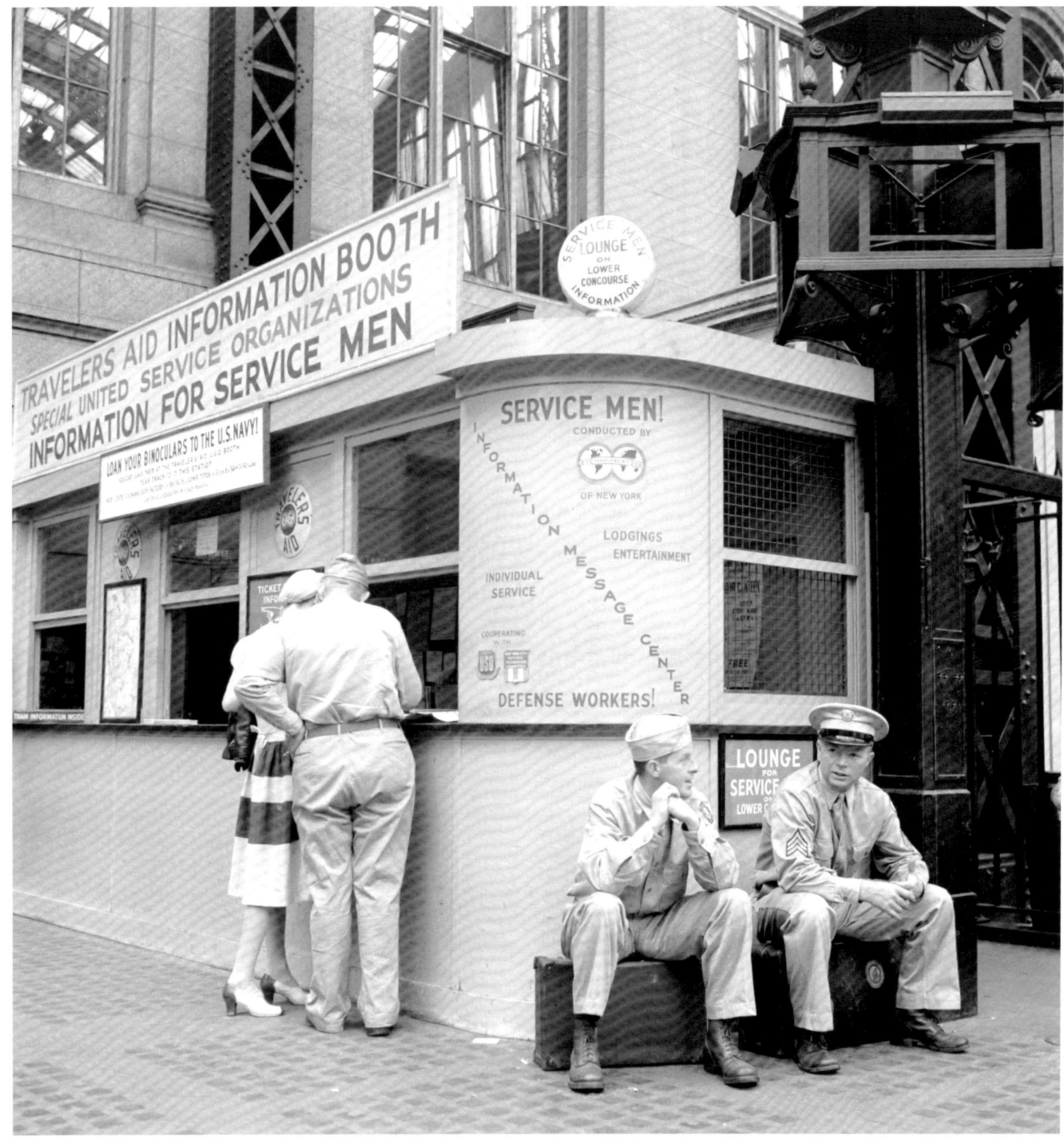

***Above*, Plate 10.** New York, New York. Pennsylvania Railroad Station.

Marjory Collins. Circa August 1942. Library of Congress, Prints & Photographs Division, FSA-OWI Collection, LC-USW3-006960-E.

***Facing*, Plate 11.** New York, New York. Waiting for trains at the Pennsylvania Railroad Station.

Marjory Collins. Circa August 1942. Library of Congress, Prints & Photographs Division, FSA-OWI Collection, LC-USW3-006976-E.

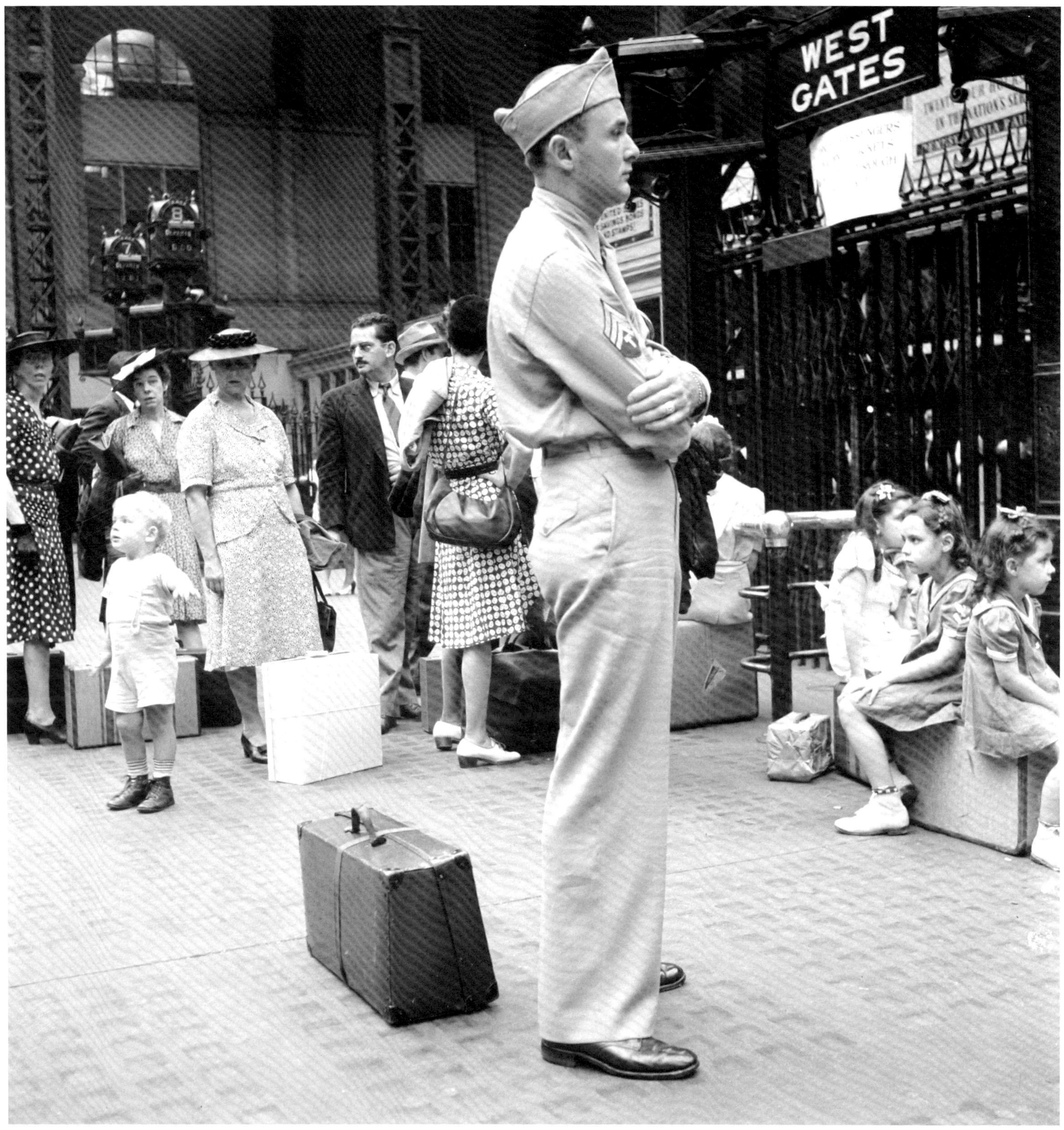
WEST
GATES

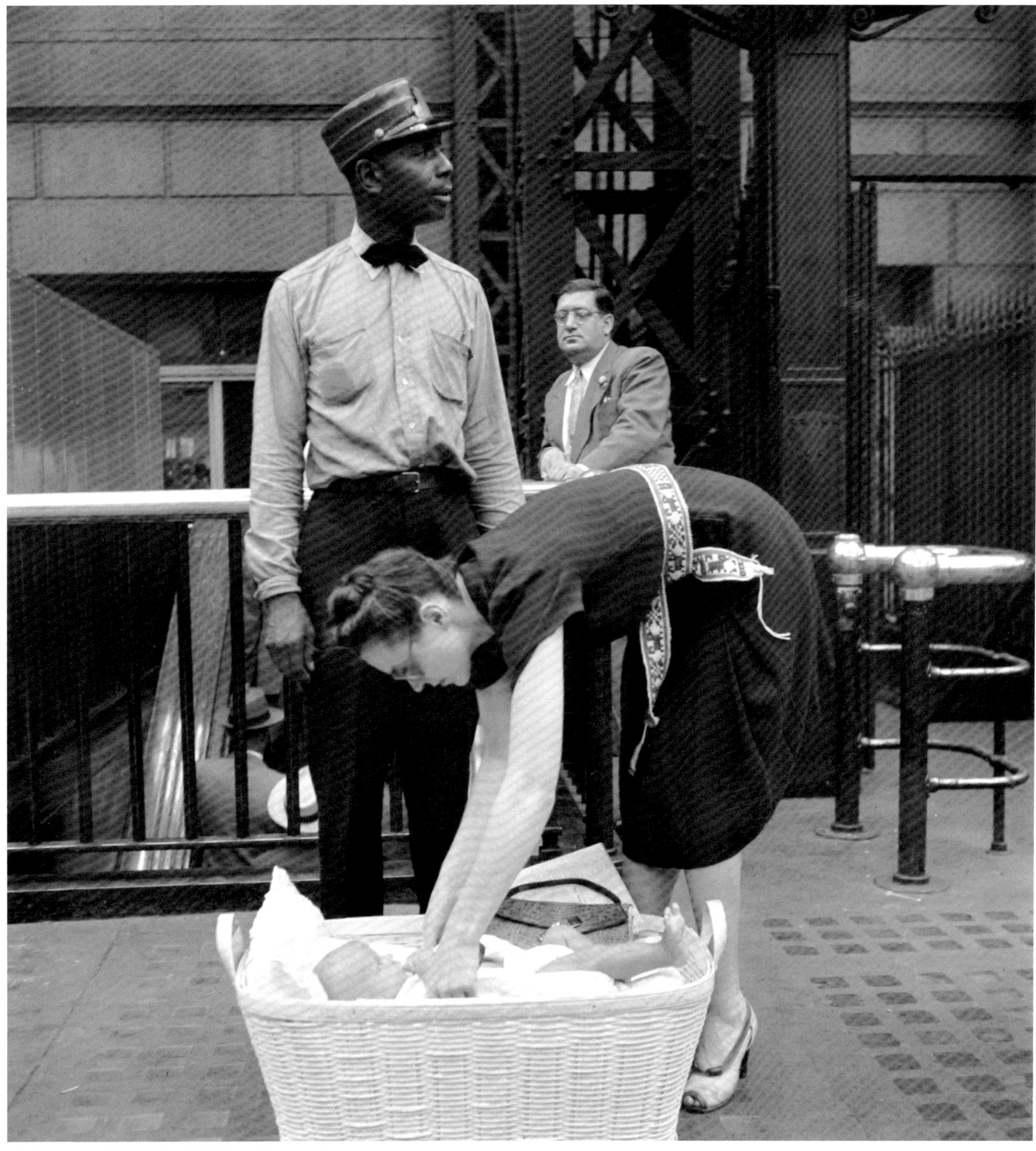

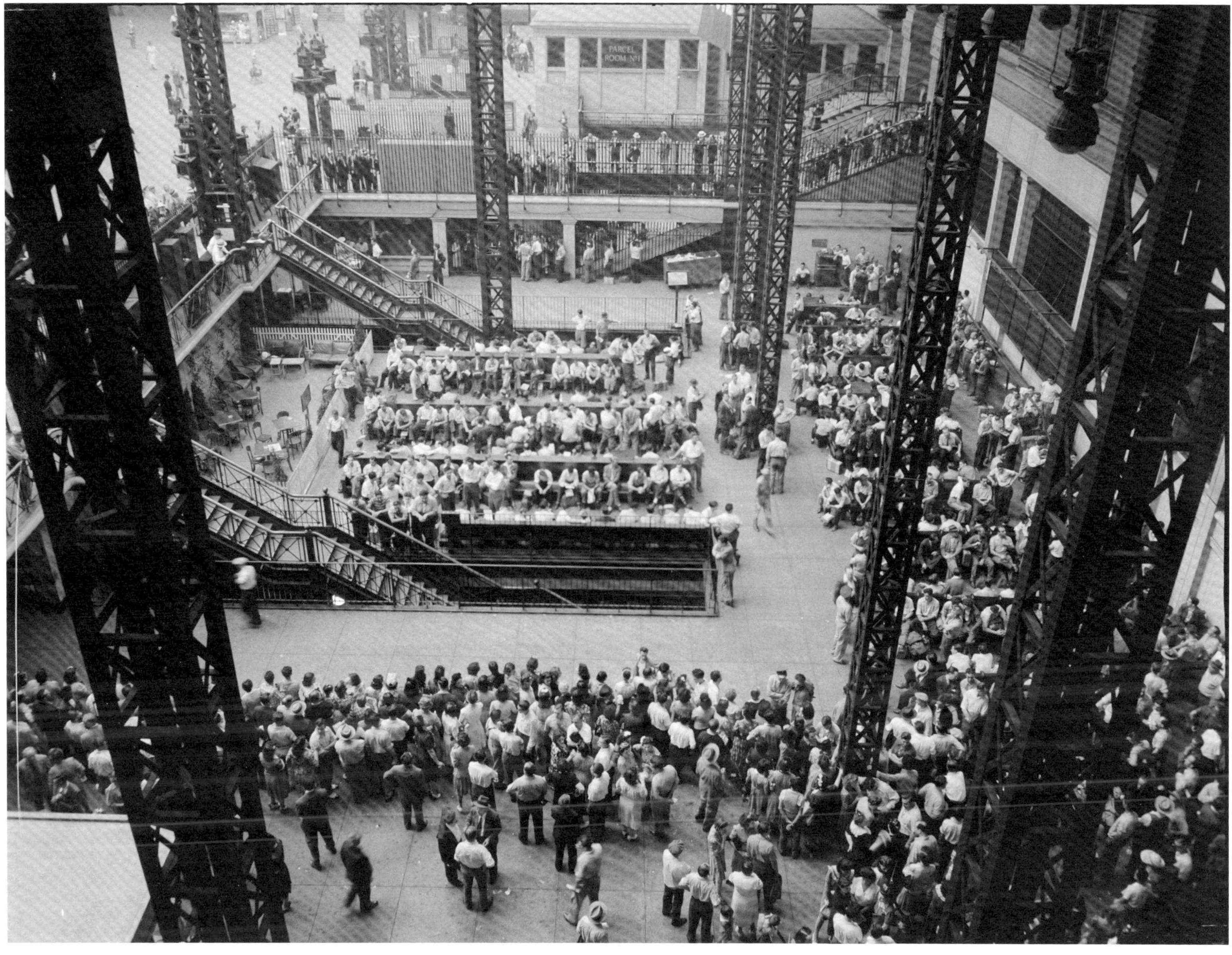

***Facing*, Plate 12.** New York, New York. Waiting for trains at the Pennsylvania Railroad Station.

Marjory Collins. Circa August 1942. Library of Congress, Prints & Photographs Division, FSA-OWI Collection, LC-USW3-006965-E.

***Above*, Plate 13.** New York, New York. Draftees on their way to the induction center at the Pennsylvania Railroad Station.

Marjory Collins. Circa August 1942. Library of Congress, Prints & Photographs Division, FSA-OWI Collection, LC-USW3-007023-D.

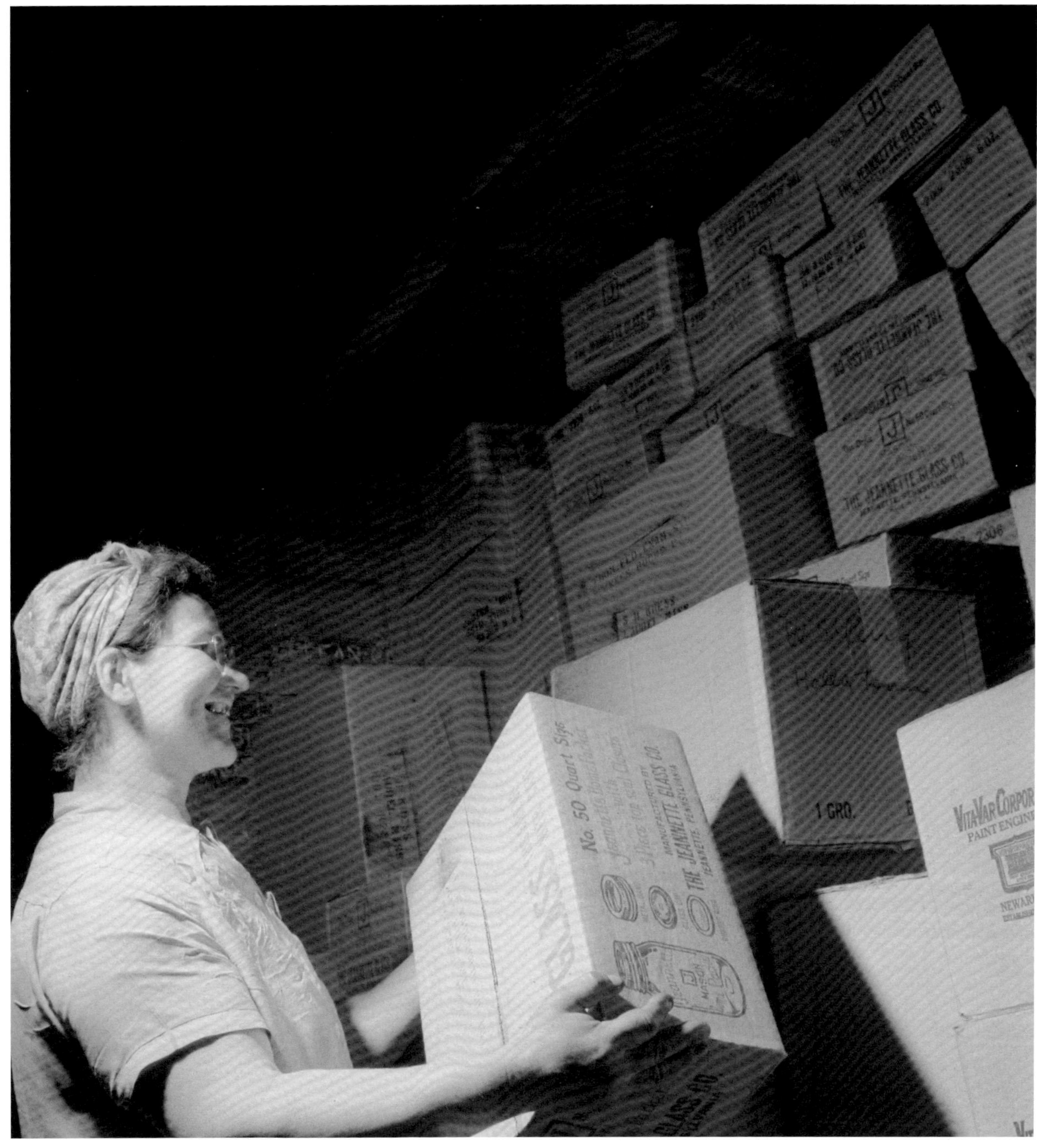

***Above,* Plate 14.** Untitled photo, possibly related to: Pitcairn, Pennsylvania. Mrs. Anna Matecko, a Lithuanian, mother of four children, employed as a stower of freight at the transfer service of the Pennsylvania Railroad, earns seventy cents per hour. Her husband, of Russian descent, is a coal miner.

Marjory Collins. June 1943. Library of Congress, Prints & Photographs Division, FSA-OWI Collection, LC-USW3-030578-E.

***Facing,* Plate 15.** Pitcairn, Pennsylvania. Mrs. May Watson, thirty-eight, mother of three children, employed as a freight trucker for the Pitcairn transfer service of the Pennsylvania Railroad, earns sixty-eight cents per hour. Mrs. Watson's husband works for the Carnegie-Illinois Steel Company.

Marjory Collins. June 1943. Library of Congress, Prints & Photographs Division, FSA-OWI Collection, LC-USW3-030572-E.

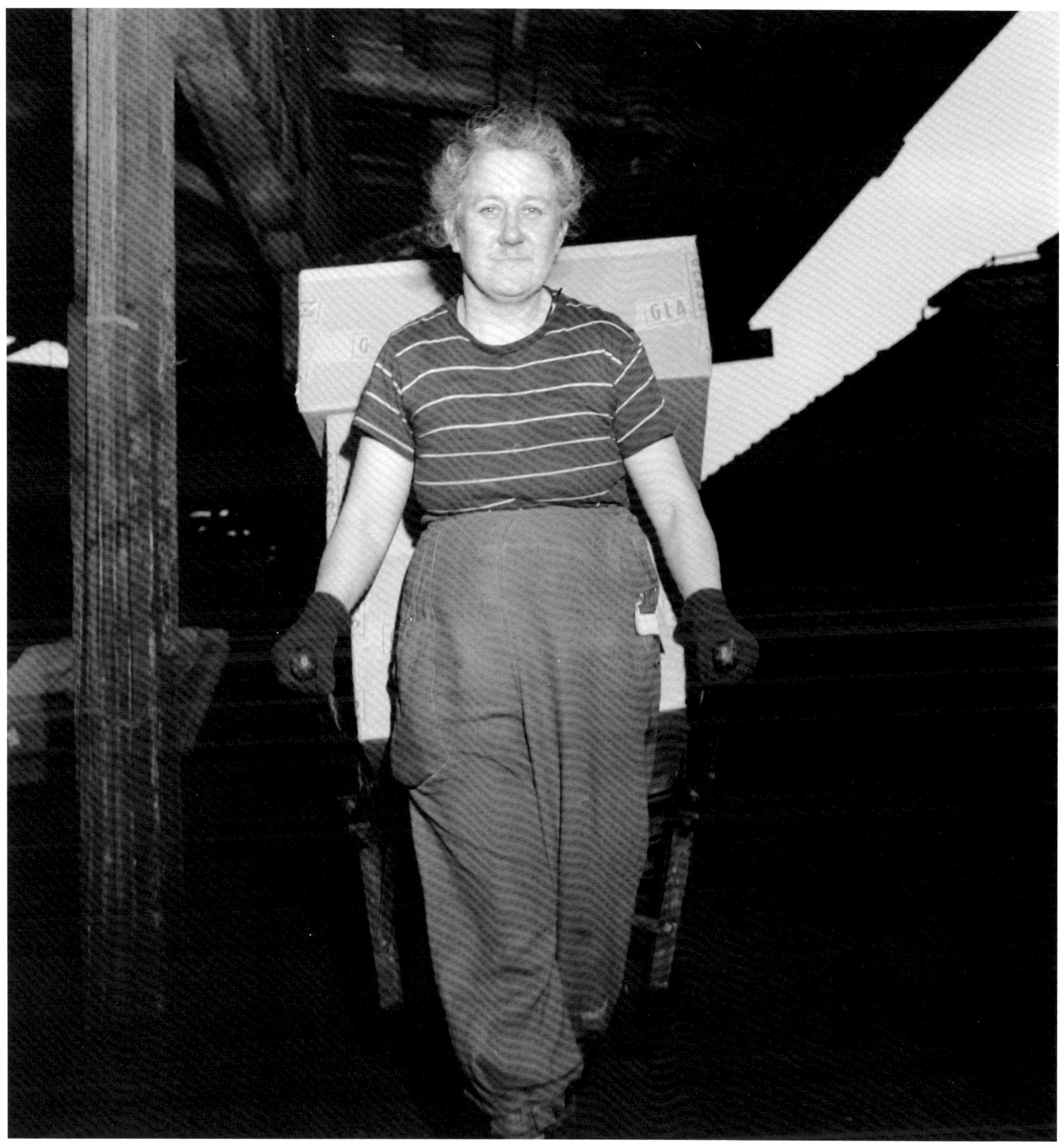

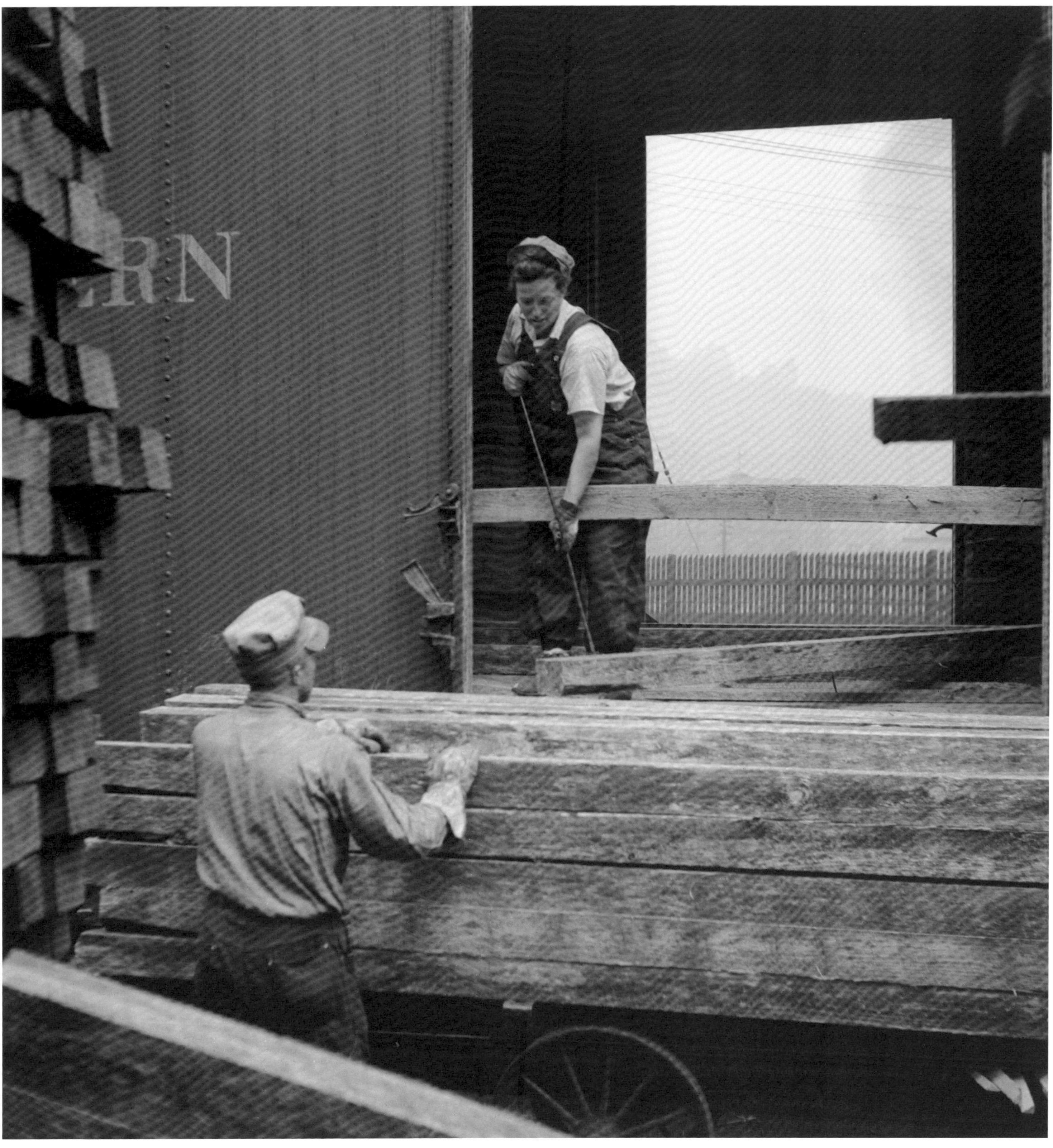
RN

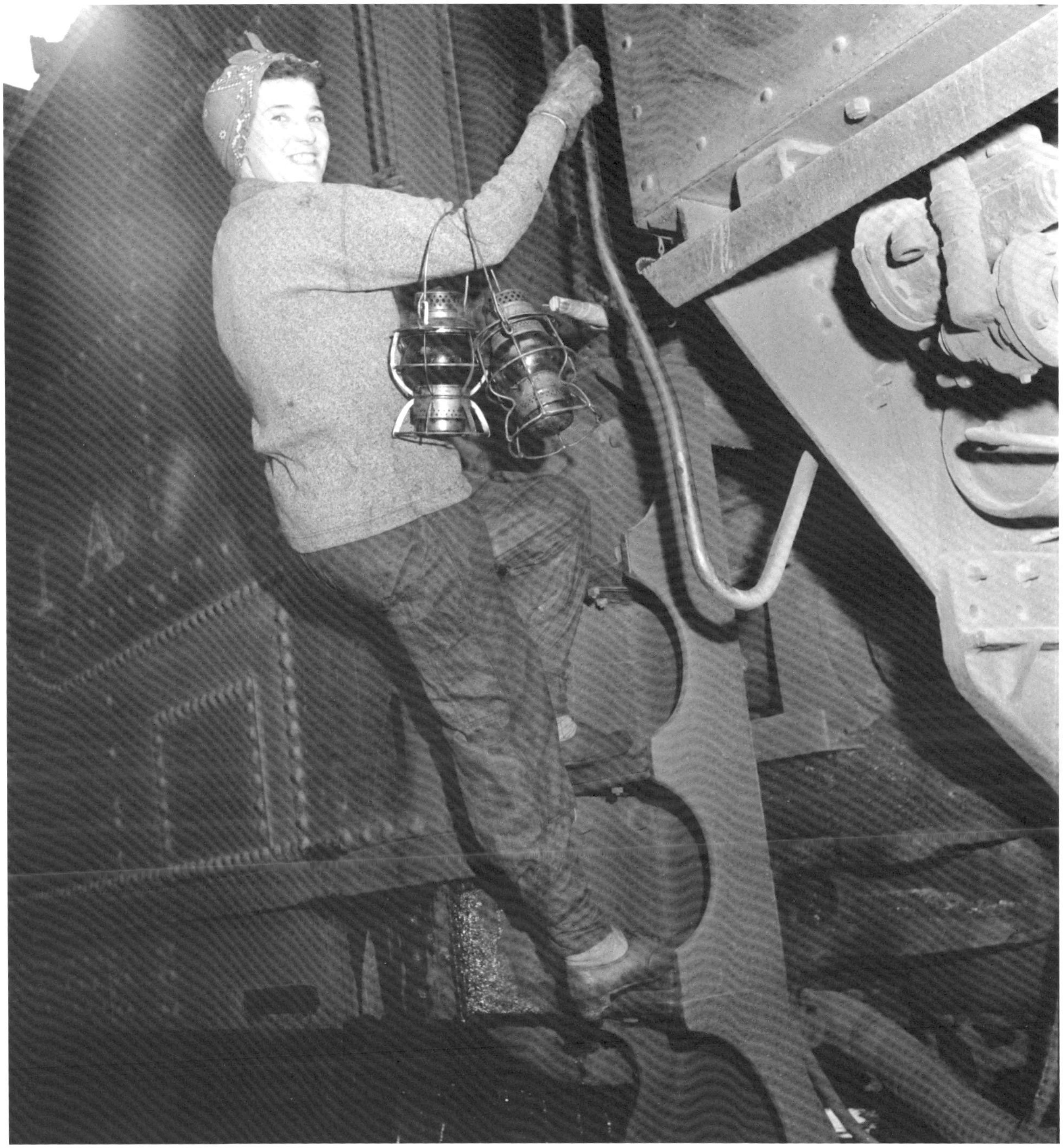

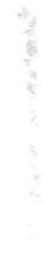

***Facing,* Plate 16.** Pitcairn, Pennsylvania. Mrs. Lois Micheltree, thirty-six, employed as a laborer at the Pennsylvania Railroad lumberyard, earning fifty-five cents per hour. She helps to load and unload lumber from cars. Mrs. Micheltree has a son in the US Navy.

Marjory Collins. May 1943. Library of Congress, Prints & Photographs Division, FSA-OWI Collection, LC-USW3-030041-E.

***Above,* Plate 17.** Pitcairn, Pennsylvania. Mrs. Mary Ankrom, twenty-eight, mother of six children, employed at the Pennsylvania Railroad engine house as a locomotive preparer, earning fifty-eight cents per hour. Her father takes care of her children while she is working.

Marjory Collins. May 1943. Library of Congress, Prints & Photographs Division, FSA-OWI Collection, LC-USW3-030020-E.

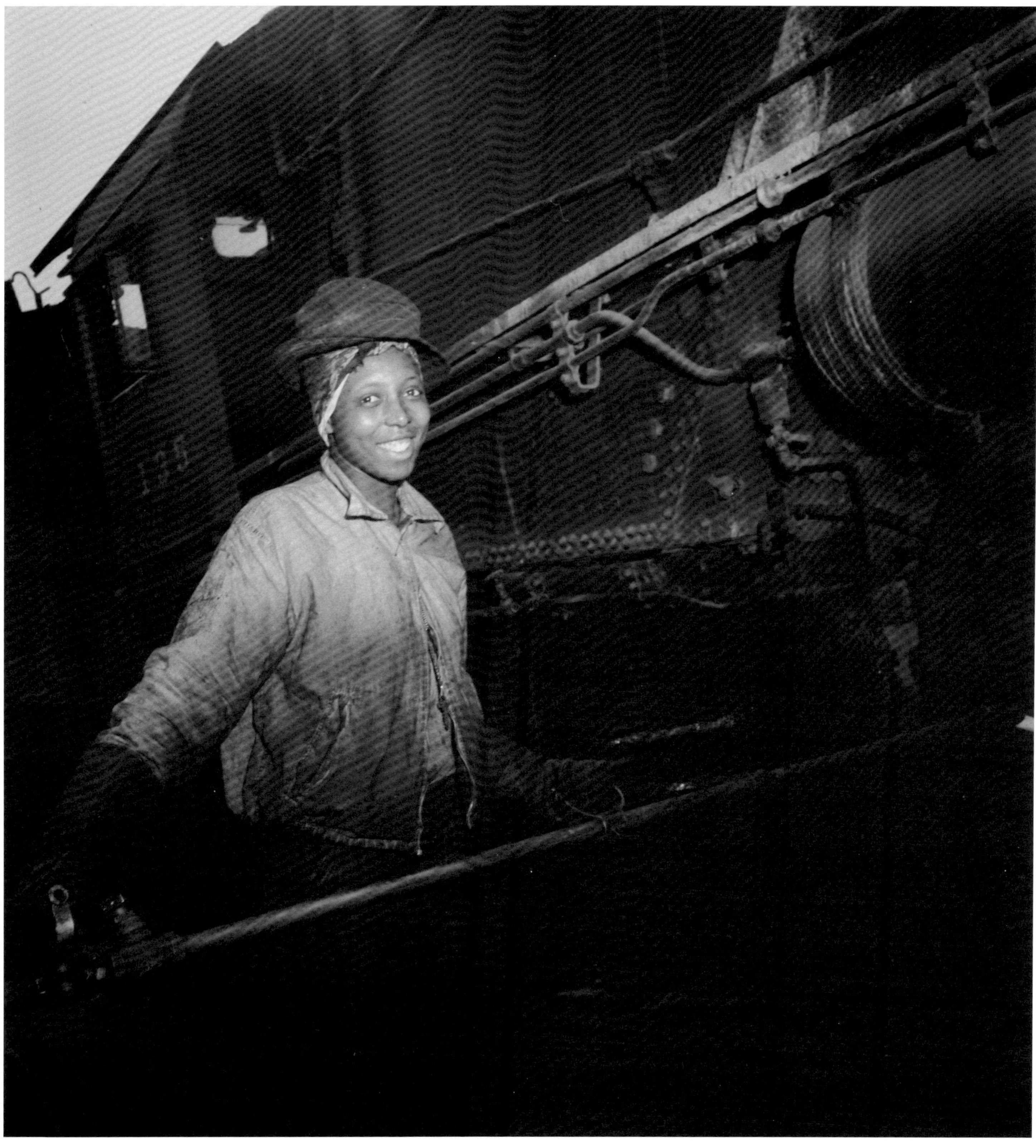

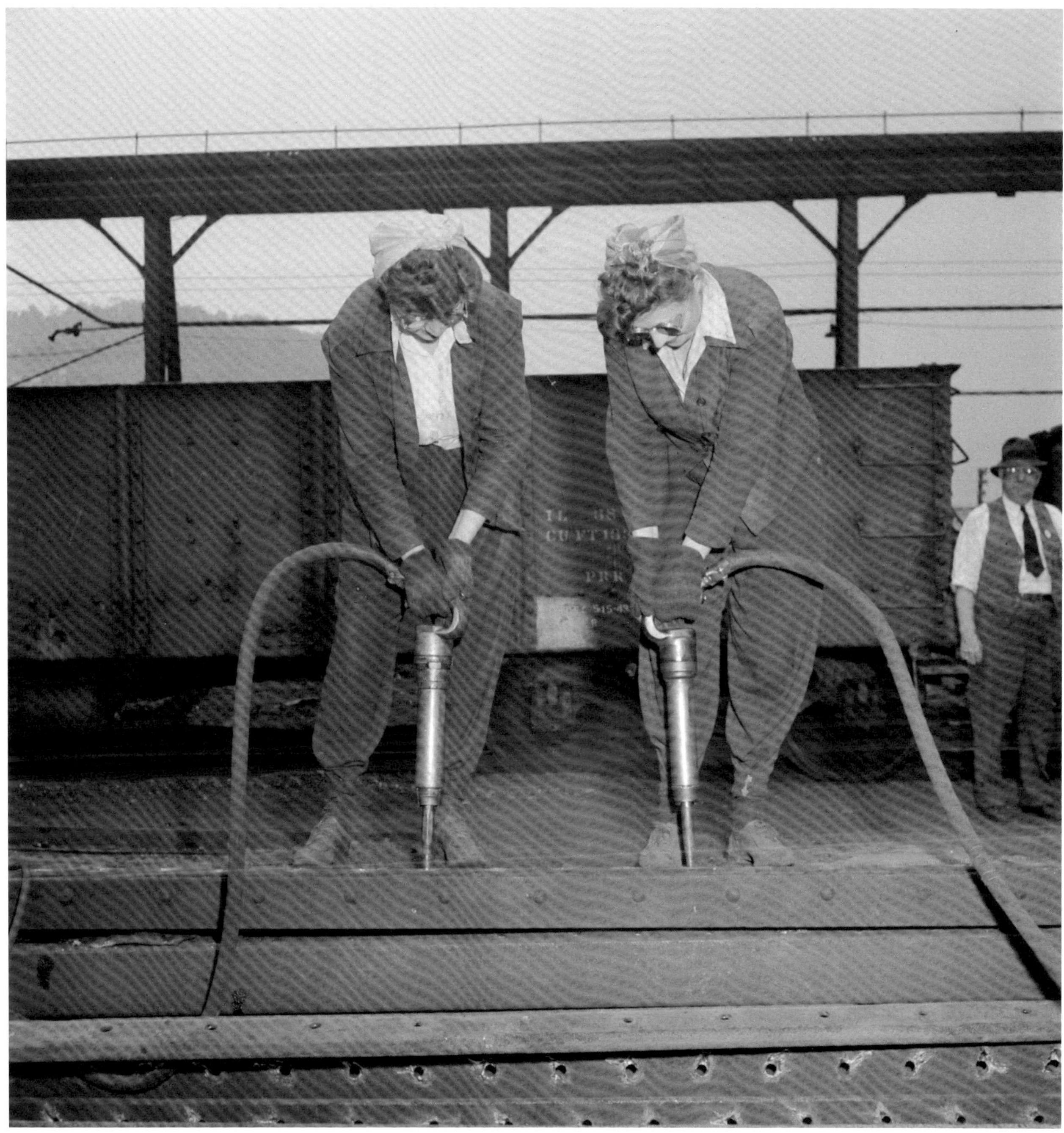

***Facing*, Plate 18.** Pitcairn, Pennsylvania. Mrs. Bernice Stevens of Braddock, Pennsylvania, mother of one child, employed in the engine house of the Pennsylvania Railroad, earns fifty-eight cents per hour. She is cleaning a locomotive with a high-pressure nozzle. Mrs. Stevens's husband is in the US Army.

Marjory Collins. June 1943. Library of Congress, Prints & Photographs Division, FSA-OWI Collection, LC-USW3-030577-E.

***Above*, Plate 19.** Pitcairn, Pennsylvania. Twins Amy and Mary Rose Lindich, twenty-one, employed at the Pennsylvania Railroad as car repairmen helpers, earning seventy-two cents per hour. They reside in Jeanette, Pennsylvania, and carpool with fellow workers. Dismantling sides of the old hopper cars.

Marjory Collins. May 1943. Library of Congress, Prints & Photographs Division, FSA-OWI Collection, LC-USW3-030031-E.

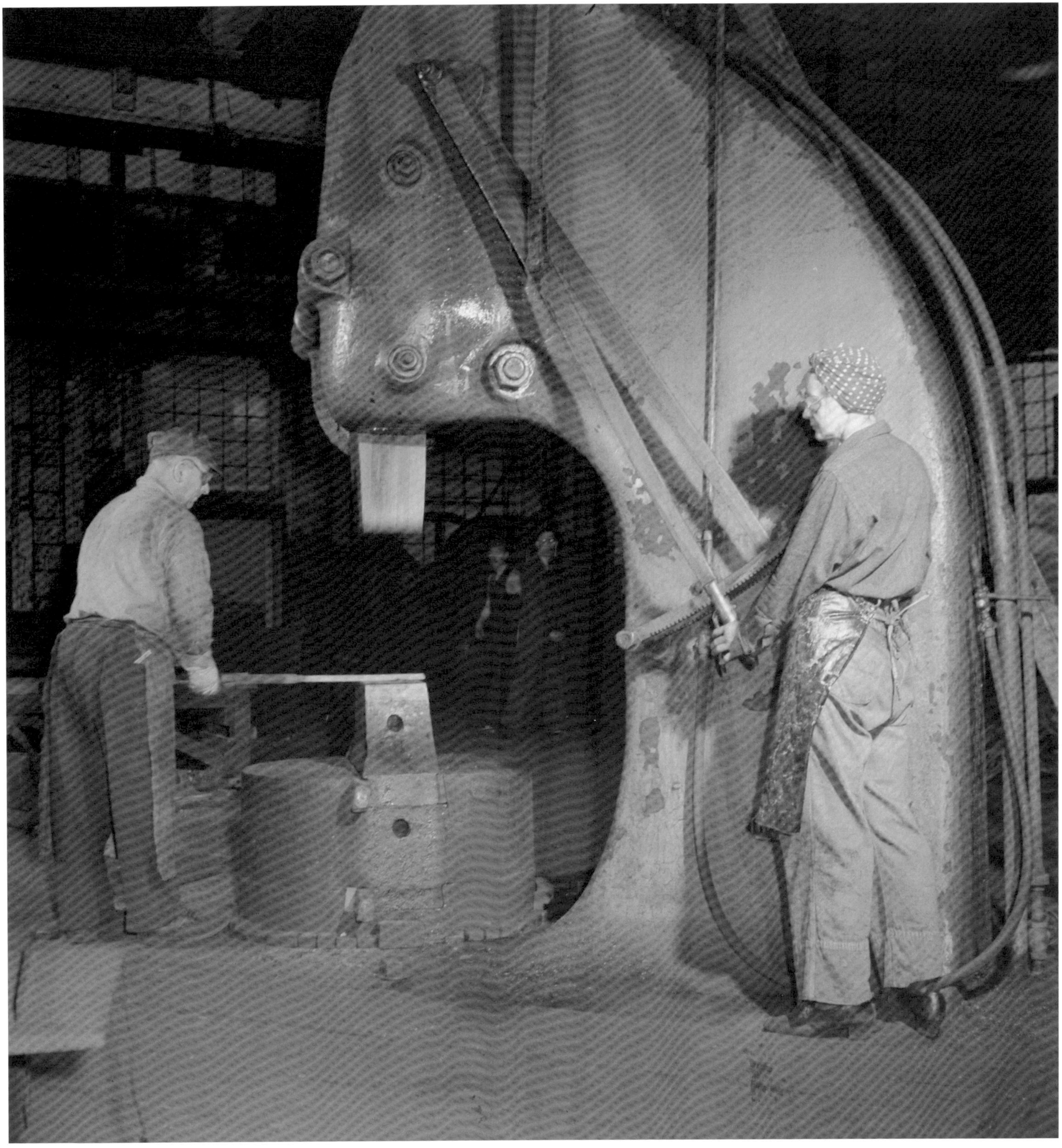

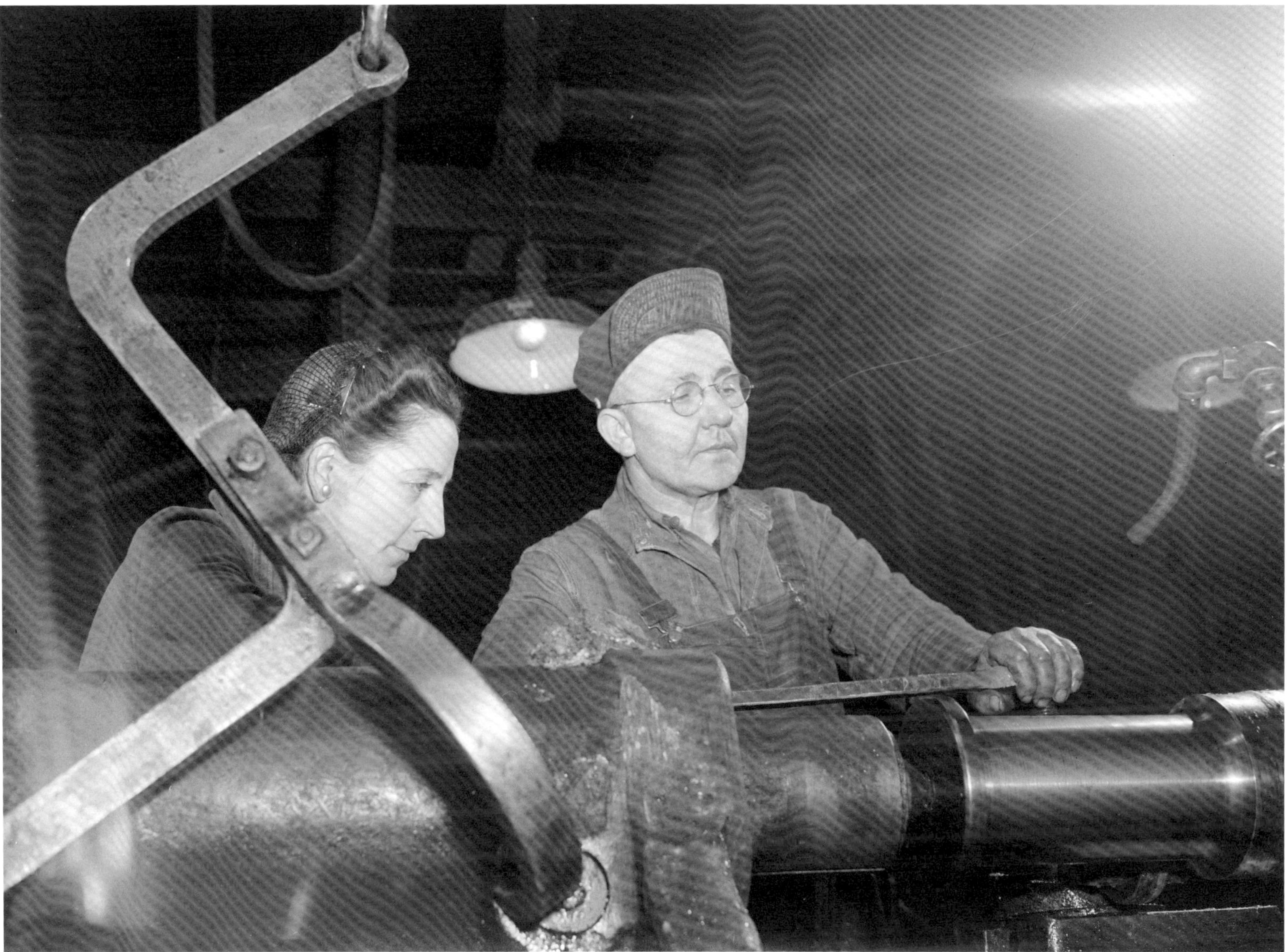

***Facing,* Plate 20.** Pitcairn, Pennsylvania. Mrs. Katie Sablejack, forty-five, a Hungarian, employed as a blacksmith's helper in the Pennsylvania Railroad yards, earning seventy-two cents per hour. She is operating a half-ton steam hammer. Mrs. Sablejack is a widow and mother of two children.

Marjory Collins. May 1943. Library of Congress, Prints & Photographs Division, FSA-OWI Collection, LC-USW3-030033-E.

***Above,* Plate 21.** Buffalo, New York. Woman learning to operate an axle lathe at the New York Car Wheel Company, makers of locomotive wheels for the railroads.

Marjory Collins. April 1943. Library of Congress, Prints & Photographs Division, FSA-OWI Collection, LC-USW3-023784-D.

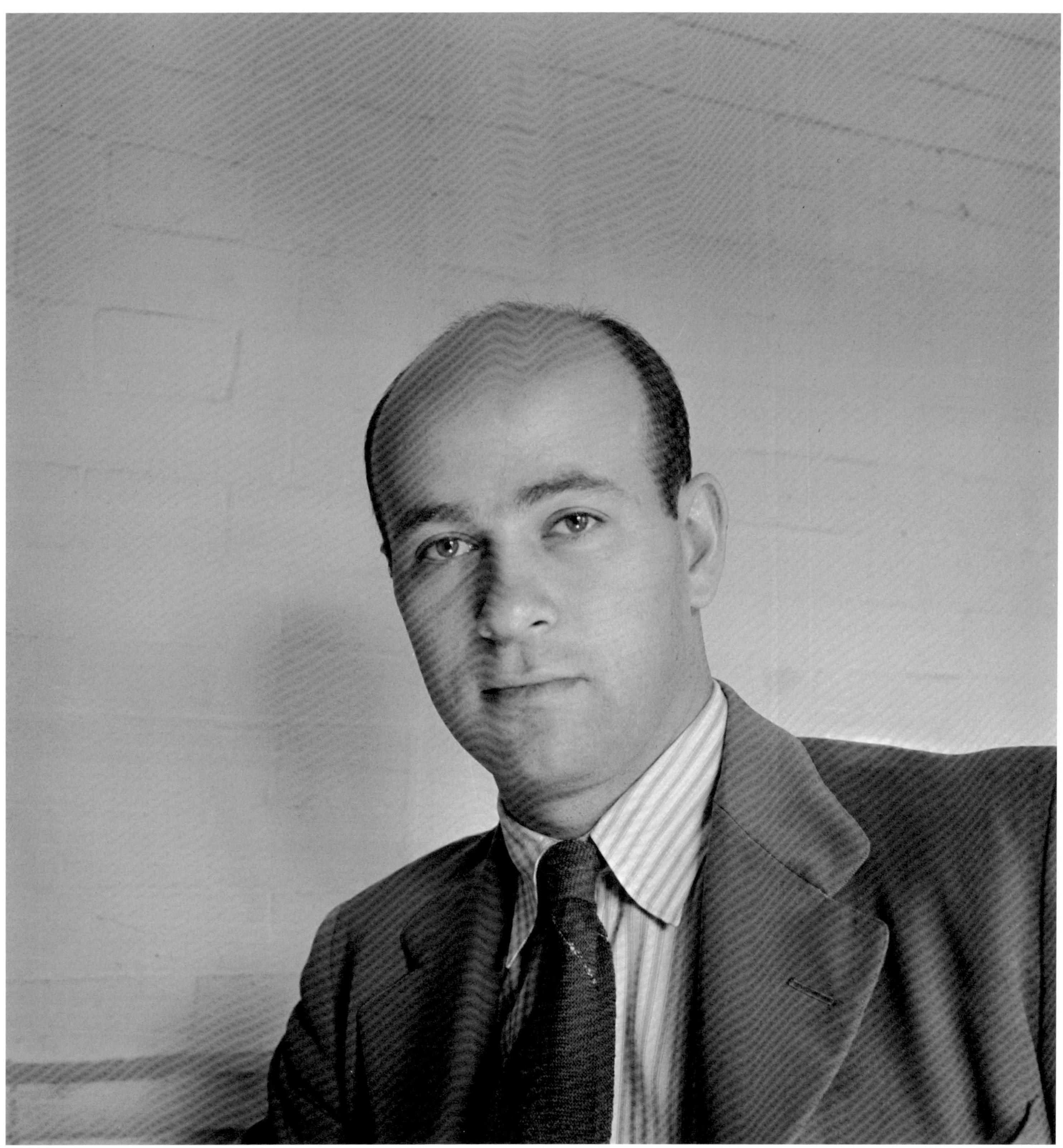

PORTFOLIO THREE

JACK DELANO

Jack Delano is notable for the way he transcended both societies and art forms. Born in 1914 in what is now Voroshilovka, Ukraine, as Jacob Ovcharov, he immigrated with his family to the United States in 1923. After a brief stay in New York, he spent the remainder of his childhood in Pennsylvania. He attended the Pennsylvania Academy of Fine Arts. After graduating in 1936, during the Great Depression, his job search led him to work with the Works Progress Administration (WPA) as a photographer.

He began using the anglicized name Jack Delano in the 1930s and later legally changed his name to this new, more pronounceable one. Delano sought a job at the FSA Historical Section for about a year before Roy Stryker hired him in 1940 to replace Arthur Rothstein. Soon after joining the FSA, Delano married his long-term girlfriend, Irene Esser. She was a distant cousin of painter and FSA photographer Ben Shahn.

***Facing*, Figure 3.1.** Washington, DC. Portrait of Jack Delano, Office of War Information photographer.

John Collier Jr. September 1942. Library of Congress, Prints & Photographs Division, FSA-OWI Collection, LC-USF34-014739-E.

Delano first encountered Puerto Rico when documenting it and the US Virgin Islands in 1941 and 1942. World War II broke out during this assignment for the FSA, and Delano endured long delays and a perilous journey before he could return to the US mainland. He stayed with Stryker when Stryker's team transferred to the OWI. Soon after that, in 1943, Jack Delano entered the US Army as a photographer and filmmaker; he served in the armed forces until 1946.

He received a grant from the John Simon Guggenheim Memorial Foundation to conduct a photography project in Puerto Rico in 1945 and moved there with Irene in 1946.[1] The Delanos' children, Pablo and Laura, would be born there, and Delano and his wife lived the rest of their lives in Puerto Rico. In addition to living in three different cultures during his lifetime, Delano was successful in a number of very different art forms, including music, film, illustration, and photography.[2]

Irene Delano died in 1982. Delano's noted photo book about Puerto Rico, *Puerto Rico Mio: Four Decades of Change*, was published in 1990. Death claimed Jack Delano in 1997, the same year his autobiography, *Photographic Memories*, was published.

During his photographic career, Delano took a number of important railroad-subject images. These photos were largely taken during three distinct periods: photographing migrant workers and other subjects for the FSA in 1940 and 1941; photographing US railroads during World War II for the Office of War Information; and photographing the transportation system of Puerto Rico for the government of Puerto Rico in 1946.[3] Delano's railroad-subject work was little known until 1977, when two books showcasing his OWI images of US railroading appeared. After a hiatus of attention, additional books appeared in the late 1980s and early 1990s. With the publication of *Railroaders: Jack Delano's Homefront Photography* in 2014, the success of its accompanying exhibit, and the publication of *The Railroad Photography of Jack Delano* in 2015, Delano's place in the pantheon of great railroad-subject photographers was solidified. Given the publication of *Photographic Memories*, *Railroaders*, and *The Railroad Photography of Jack Delano*, Delano's life is fairly well documented, but he has never been the subject of a biography.

Delano's railroad-subject images are notable for his outstanding portraits of US railroad workers. In addition, his FSA and OWI images included a number of color transparencies of American railroading, rare for the time period in which they were taken. Finally, despite the technical challenges inherent in the form at the time, Delano was an early experimenter with color and black-and-white night images of US railroads.

This portfolio of Delano's work avoids the now well-known images and focuses only on his black-and-white images. It includes a sequence focusing on his night/darkness images.

Delano joined the FSA in 1940. His early work on US railroads for the FSA focused on the northeastern and southern areas of the nation. Plates 22 and 23 represent this aspect of Delano's work and introduce his portraiture. Both views show railroaders living and working in Pennsylvania. DuBois, Pennsylvania (plate 22), was served by the Baltimore & Ohio Railroad and the Pennsylvania Railroad; the railroad Delano mentions in his caption for plate 23 is the Central Railroad of New Jersey, also known as the Jersey Central.

World War II caused a dramatic shift for Delano and his work. By the fall of 1942, the FSA Historical Section had been transferred to the Office of War Information. Delano stayed with Roy Stryker and the former FSA team as they made this transition. Soon after this, Stryker sent Delano to Chicago—then and now the center of the US railroad industry—to document the area railroads' contribution to the war effort.[4] Delano traveled to Chicago in late 1942 and worked extensively there through early 1943. It was winter in Chicago, the Windy City: always challenging but exceptionally tough in 1942–1943 as area railroaders struggled with war traffic. Plates 24, 25, and 26 represent this segment of Delano's OWI work, with plate 26 showing the diesel-electric locomotive, the interloper that would soon change railroading in dramatic ways. Santa Fe 2202, shown in plate 26, was a Baldwin Vo-1000.

In March 1943, Delano received a new assignment from Stryker, and he rode the rails of the Atchison, Topeka and Santa Fe Railway (usually known as the Santa Fe) from Chicago to Southern California—the line known today as the Southern Transcon, one of the busiest railroad corridors in the world. Plates 27–31 represent Delano's Santa Fe journey. Santa Fe 3770, shown in plate 31, was a 4-8-4 Northern type.

In plates 32 through 36, we see Delano's innovative black-and-white photographs of railroading at night, both in Chicago and on the Santa Fe. Delano's night/darkness photography precedes that of Phil Hastings and O. Winston Link by about a decade and is still too little known. The locomotive shown in plate 35 is Santa Fe 3167, a 2-8-2 Mikado, often called a MacArthur during World War II.

We leave Jack Delano's railroad-subject work with plate 37, a modernistic view of railroad wheelsets on the Illinois Central Railroad in Chicago. This photo in many ways foreshadows the innovative photographic views taken in today's consolidated railroad environment in the US.

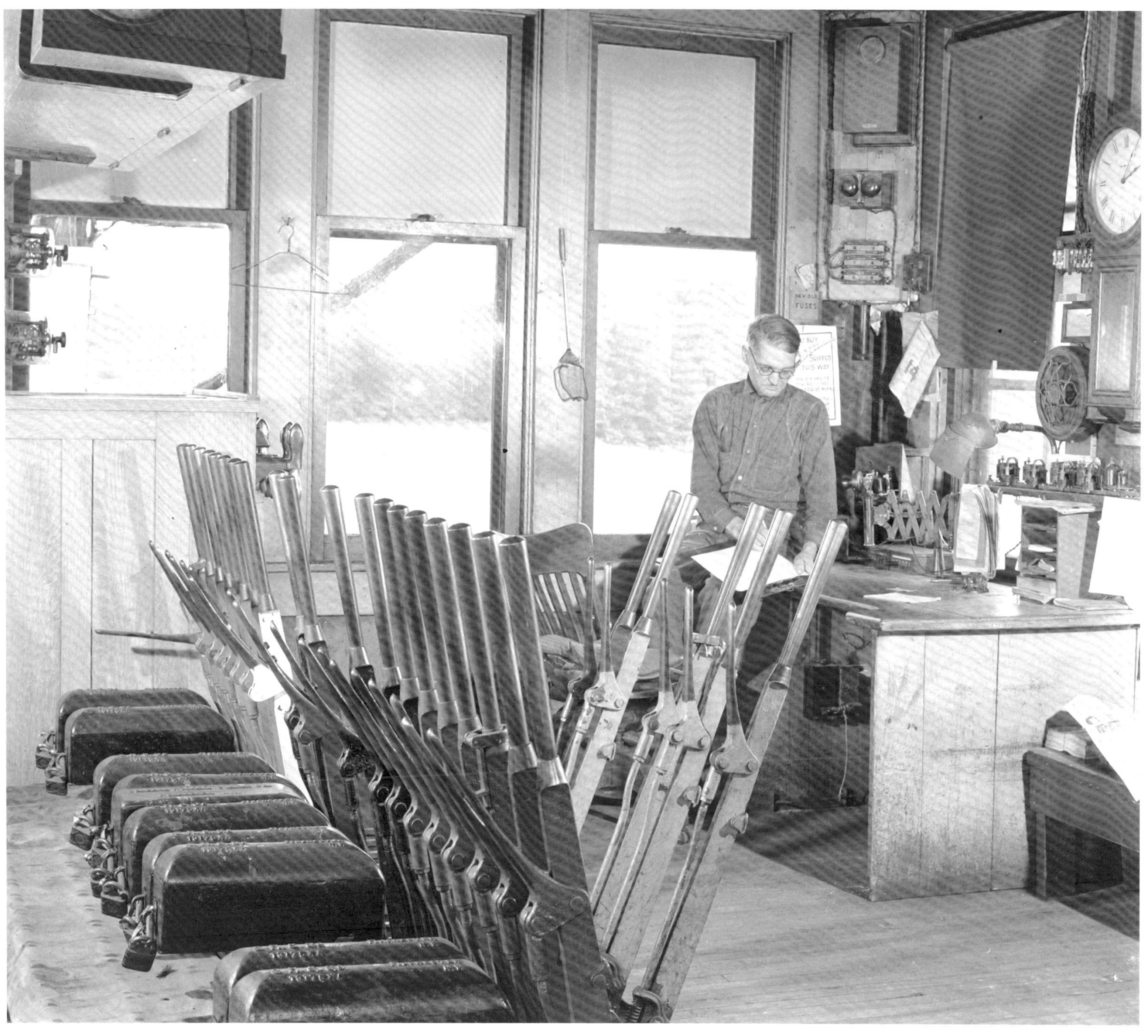

Plate 22. Mr. T. J. Long, president of the Tri-County Farmers Co-op Market in Du Bois, Pennsylvania, at his work in a railroad tower near Du Bois, Pennsylvania.

Jack Delano. September 1940. Library of Congress, Prints & Photographs Division, FSA-OWI Collection, LC-USF34-041329-D.

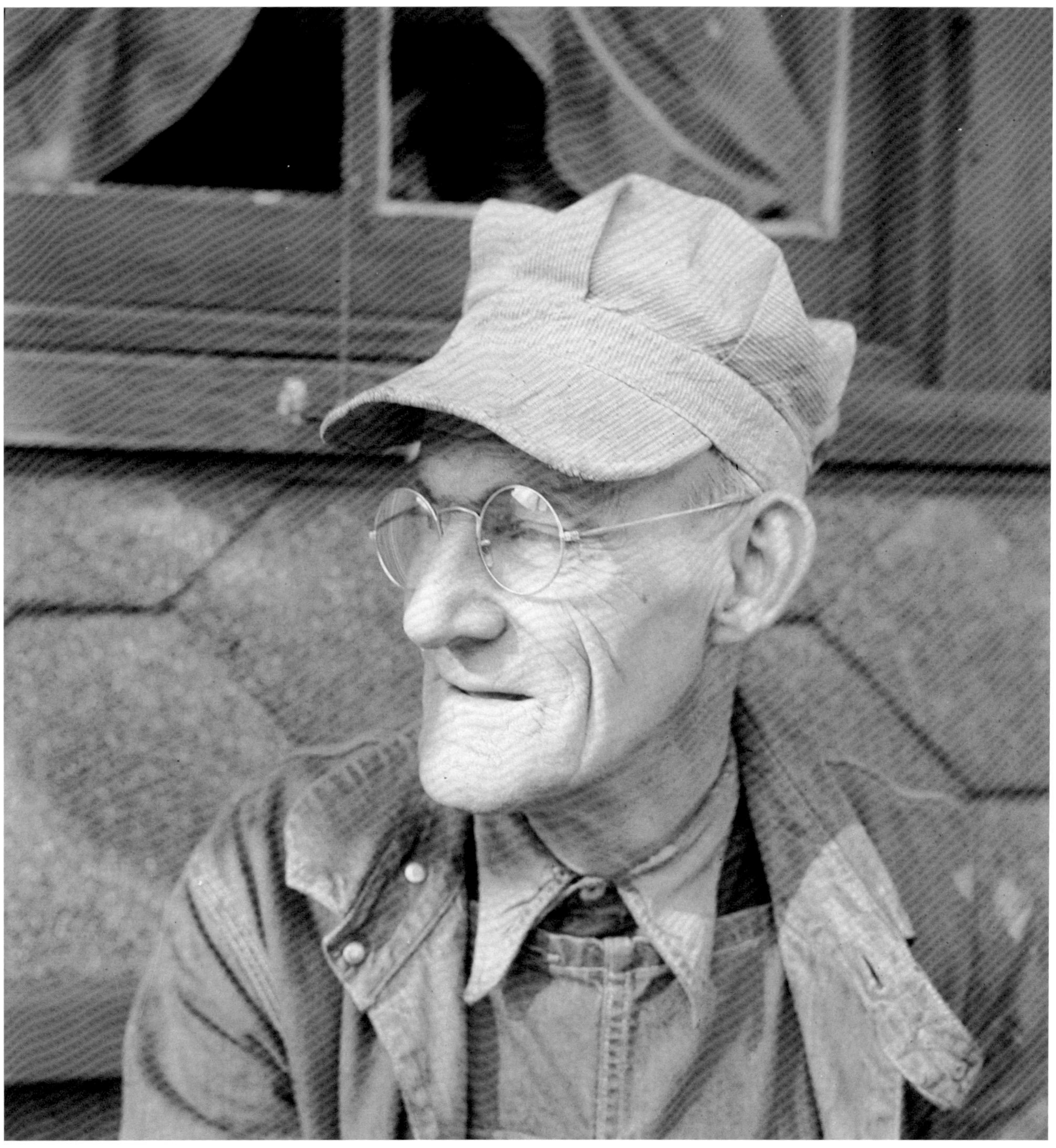

***Above,* Plate 23.** Robert Perry, railroad engineer working on the Central Railroad in New Jersey and living on Center Street. Upper Mauch Chunk, Pennsylvania.

Jack Delano. August 1940. Library of Congress, Prints & Photographs Division, FSA-OWI Collection, LC-USF34-041133-E.

***Facing,* Plate 24.** Untitled photo, possibly related to: Chicago, Illinois. The turntable at the roundhouse at an Illinois Central Railroad yard.

Jack Delano. November 1942. Library of Congress, Prints & Photographs Division, FSA-OWI Collection, LC-USW3-010584-E.

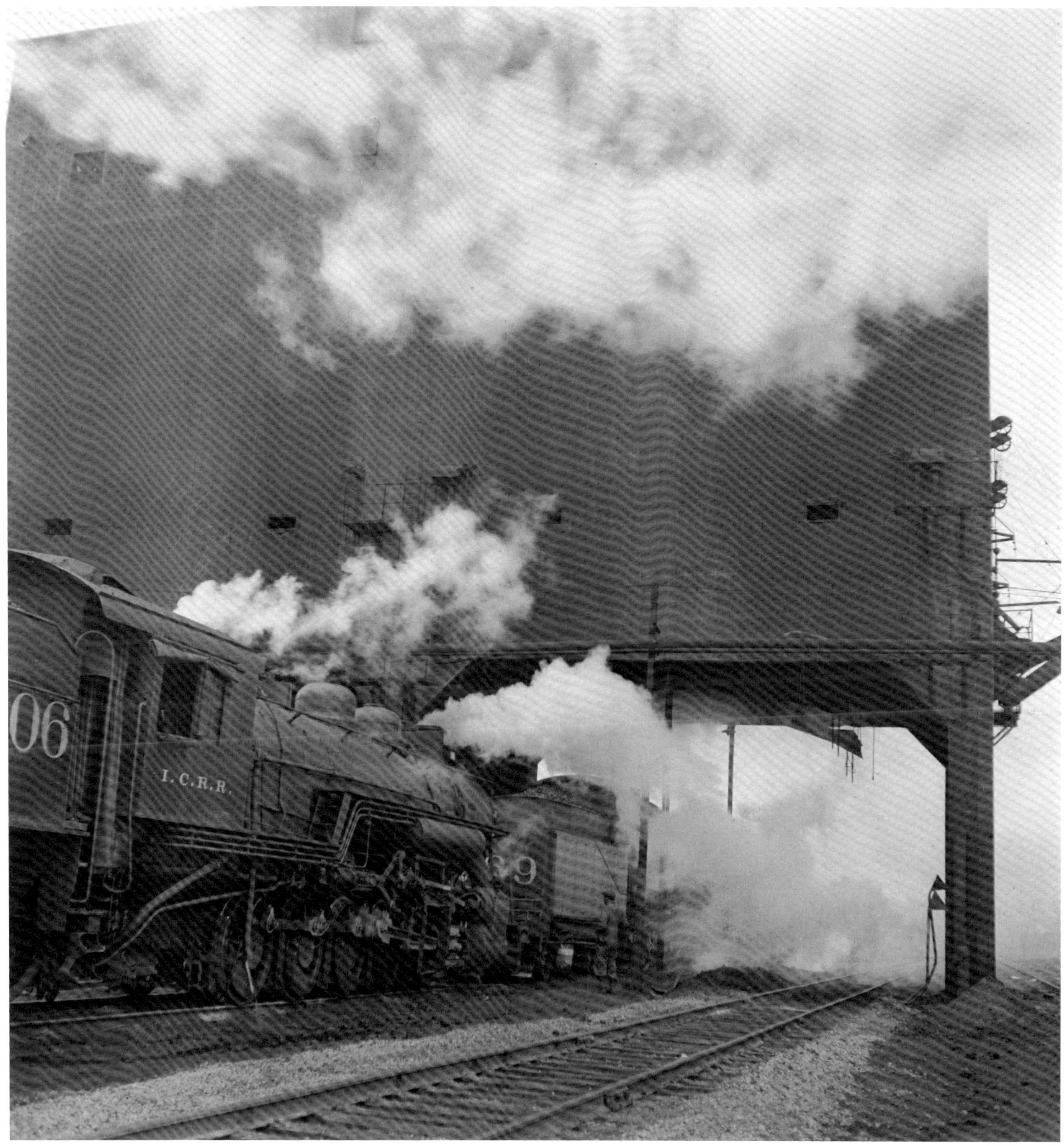
I.C.R.R.

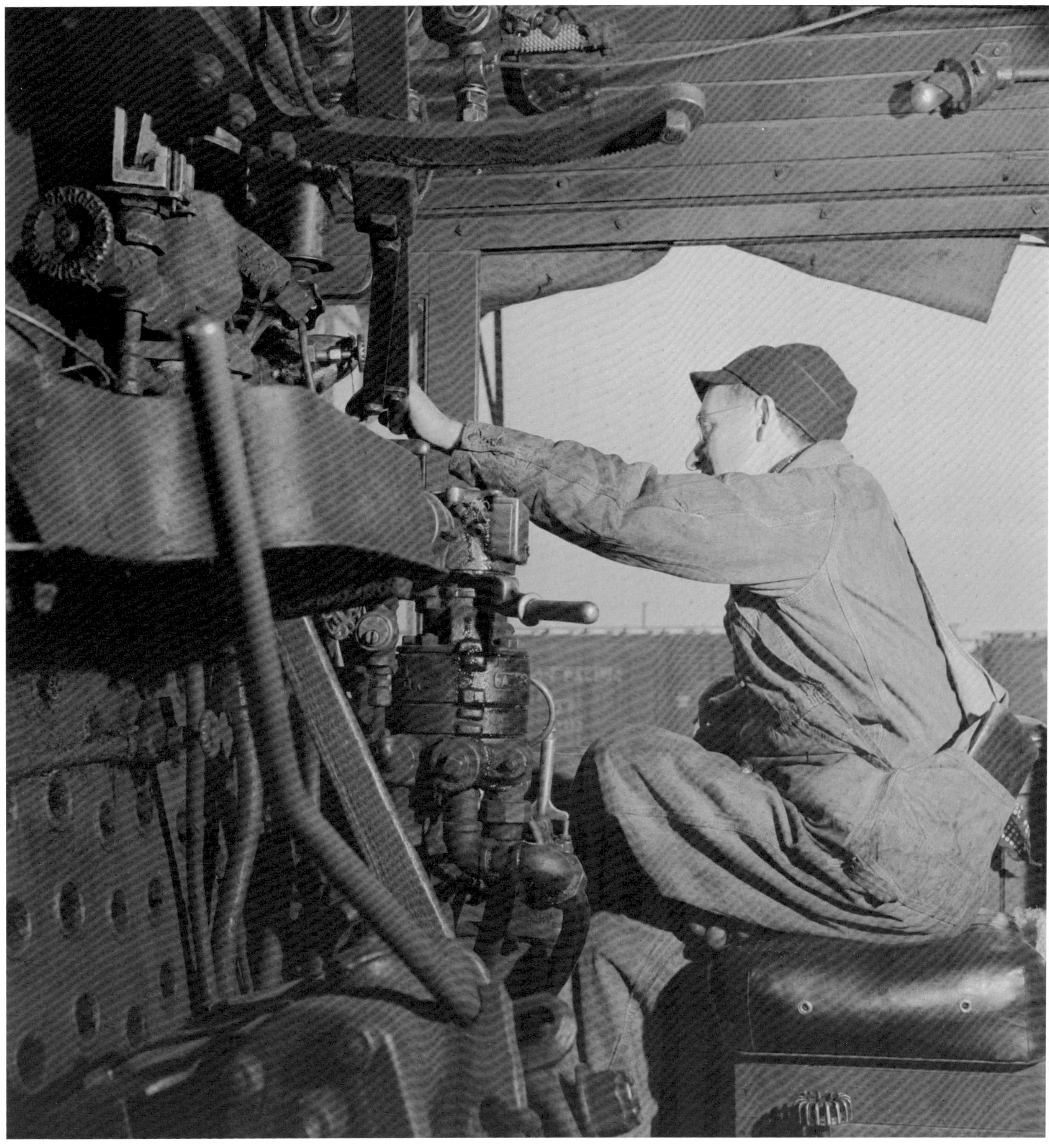

***Facing,* Plate 25.** Chicago, Illinois. Engineer of an incoming locomotive in his cab at a Chicago and North Western Railway yard.

Jack Delano. December 1942. Library of Congress, Prints & Photographs Division, FSA-OWI Collection, LC-USW3-012392-E.

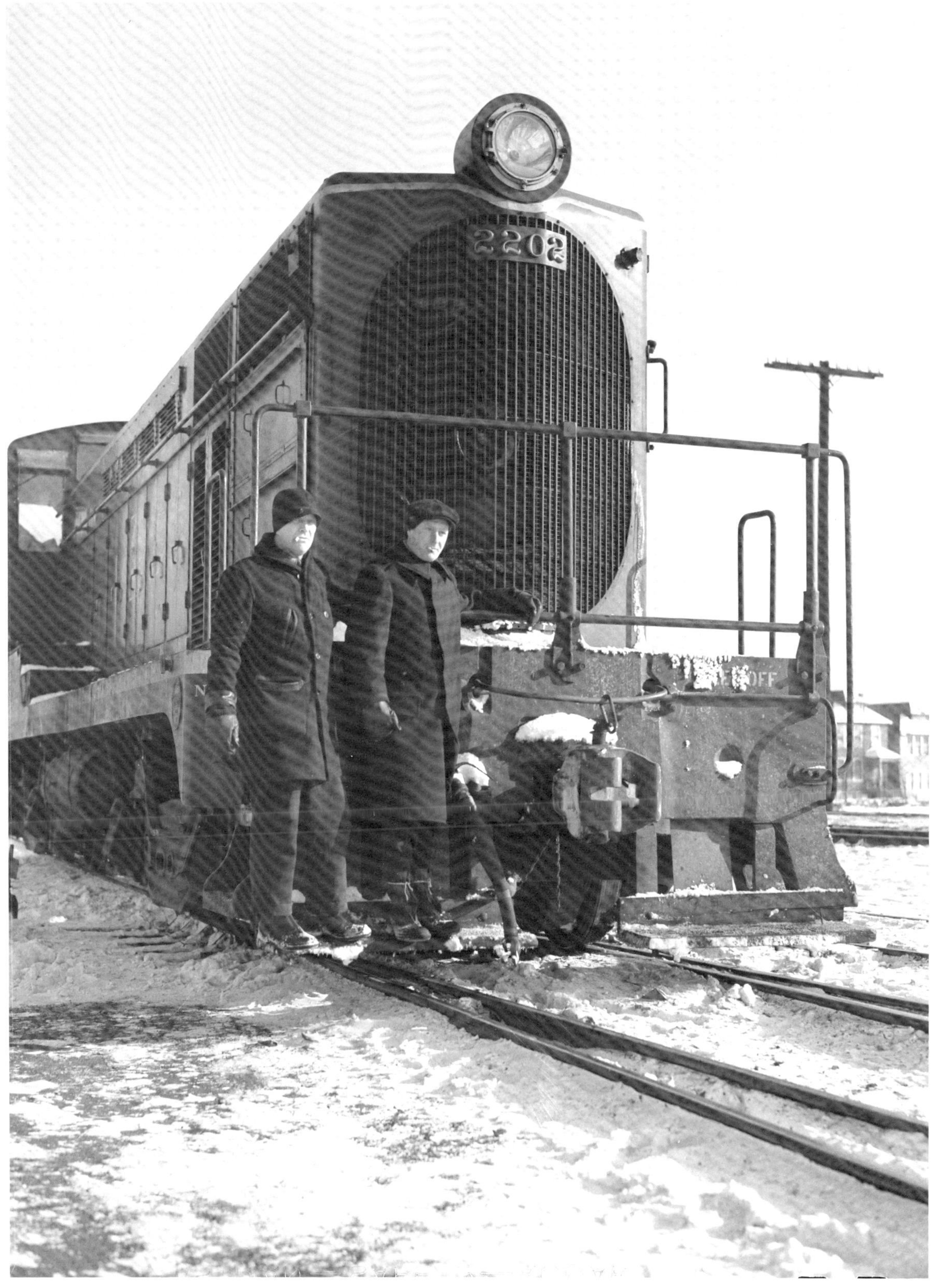

***Right,* Plate 26.** Chicago, Illinois. Switchmen riding one of the Atchison, Topeka and Santa Fe Railway diesel switch engines.

Jack Delano. March 1943. Library of Congress, Prints & Photographs Division, FSA-OWI Collection, LC-USW3-019374-D.

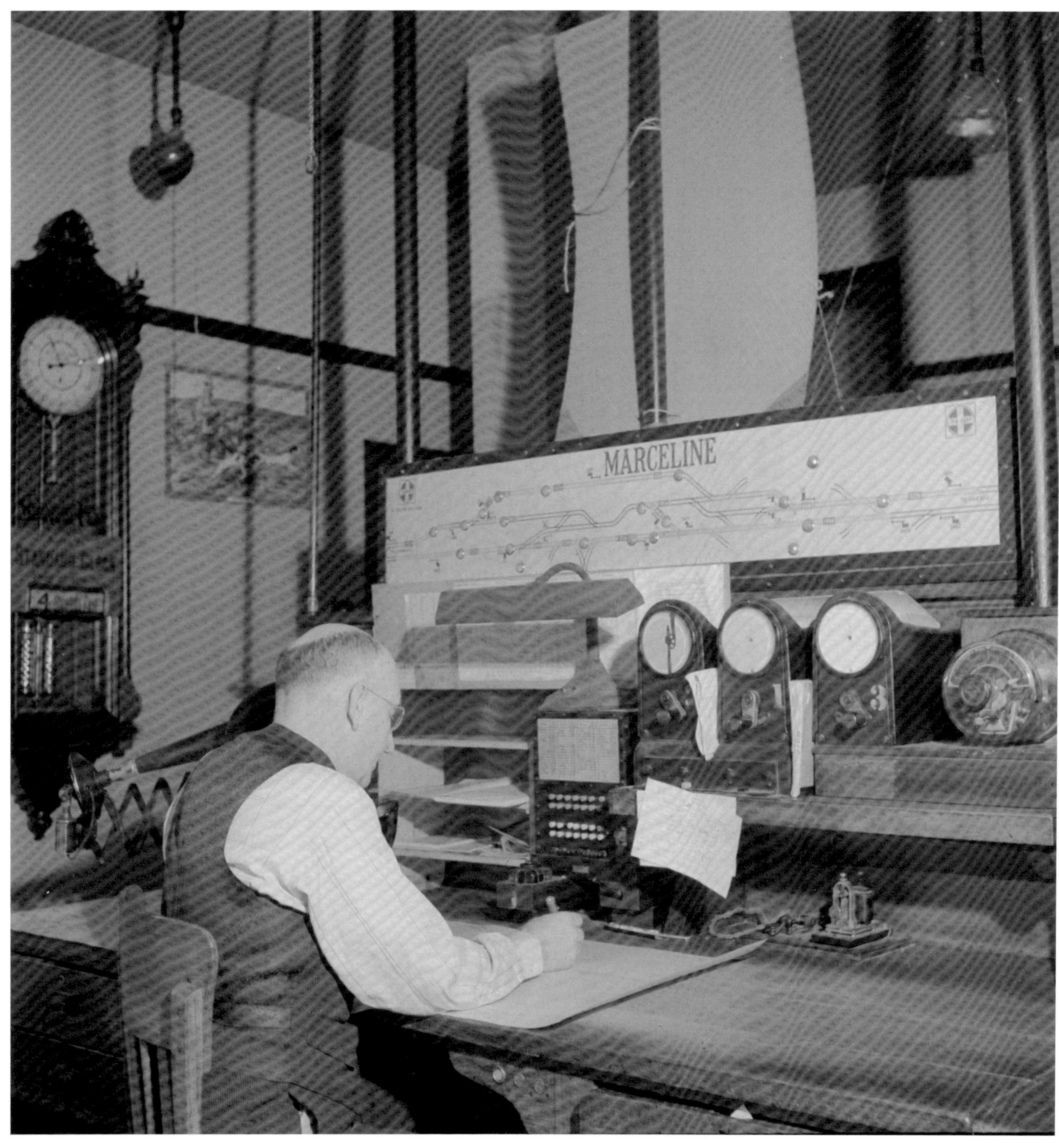

Plate 27. Marceline, Missouri. A dispatcher at work in the Atchison, Topeka and Santa Fe Railway offices.

Jack Delano. March 1943. Library of Congress, Prints & Photographs Division, FSA-OWI Collection, LC-USW3-019644-E.

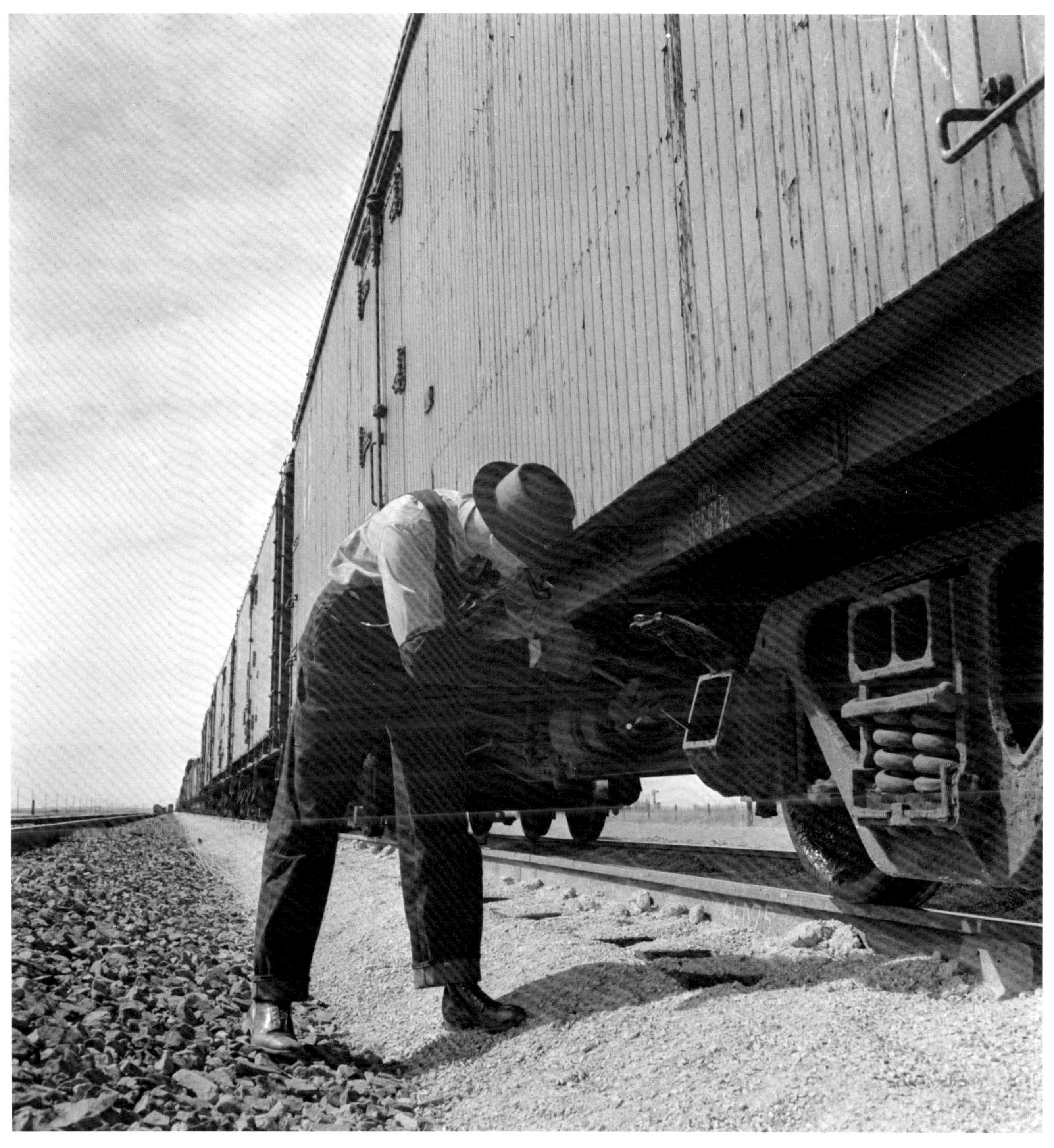

Plate 28. Texico, New Mexico. Conductor E. K. Hill inspecting the Atchison, Topeka and Santa Fe Railway train in a siding.

Jack Delano. March 1943. Library of Congress, Prints & Photographs Division, FSA-OWI Collection, LC-USW3-035238-E.

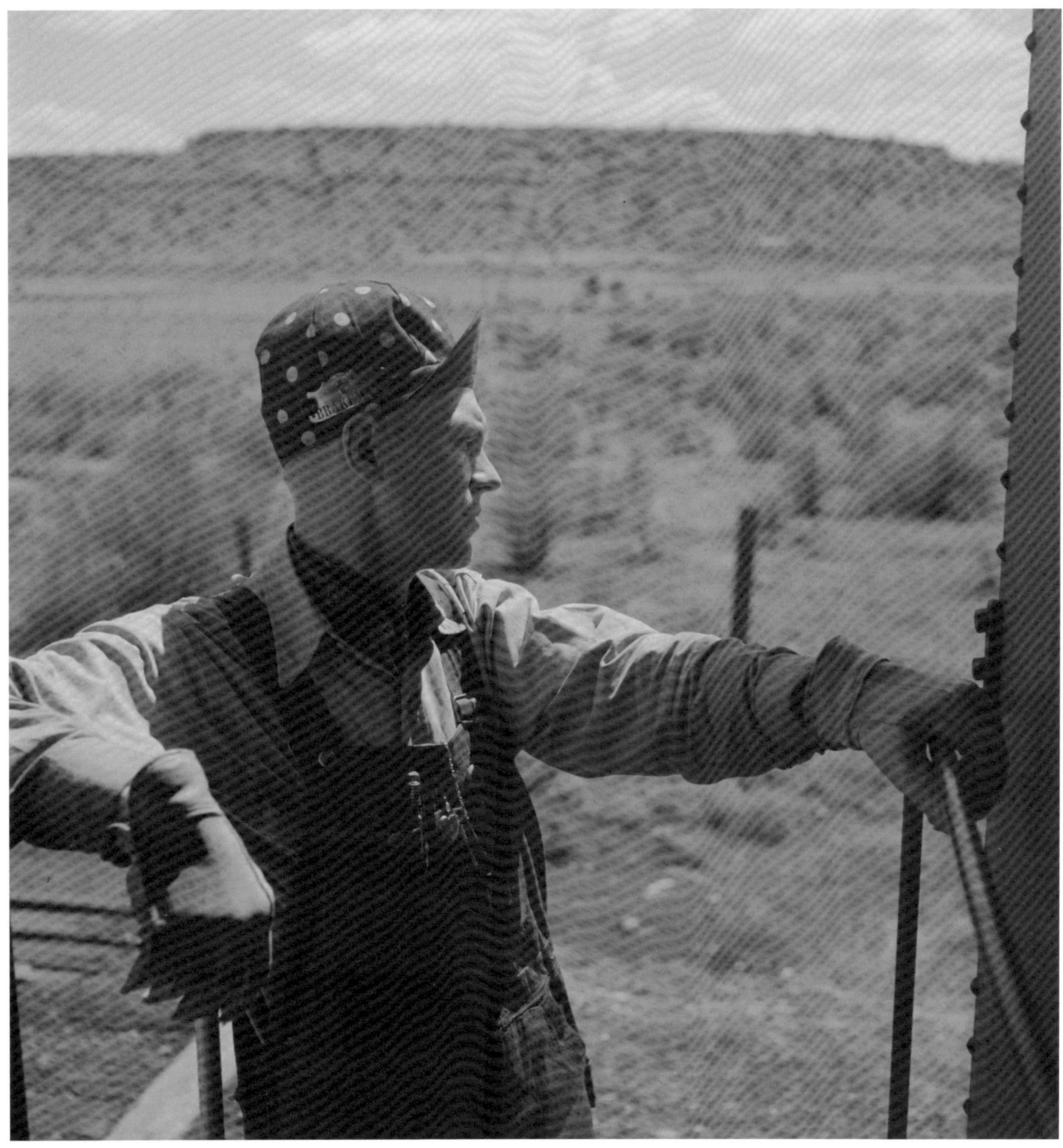

***Above,* Plate 29.** Acomita, New Mexico. Brakeman R. E. Capsey standing on the platform of the caboose waiting to hop off as the train on the Atchison, Topeka and Santa Fe Railway between Belen and Gallup, New Mexico, pulls out to a siding.

Jack Delano. March 1943. Library of Congress, Prints & Photographs Division, FSA-OWI Collection, LC-USW3-021154-E.

***Facing,* Plate 30.** Untitled photo, possibly related to: Yucca, Arizona. A section crew returning from work on the Atchison, Topeka and Santa Fe Railway between Seligman, Arizona and Needles, California.

Jack Delano. March 1943. Library of Congress, Prints & Photographs Division, FSA-OWI Collection, LC-USW3-021369-E.

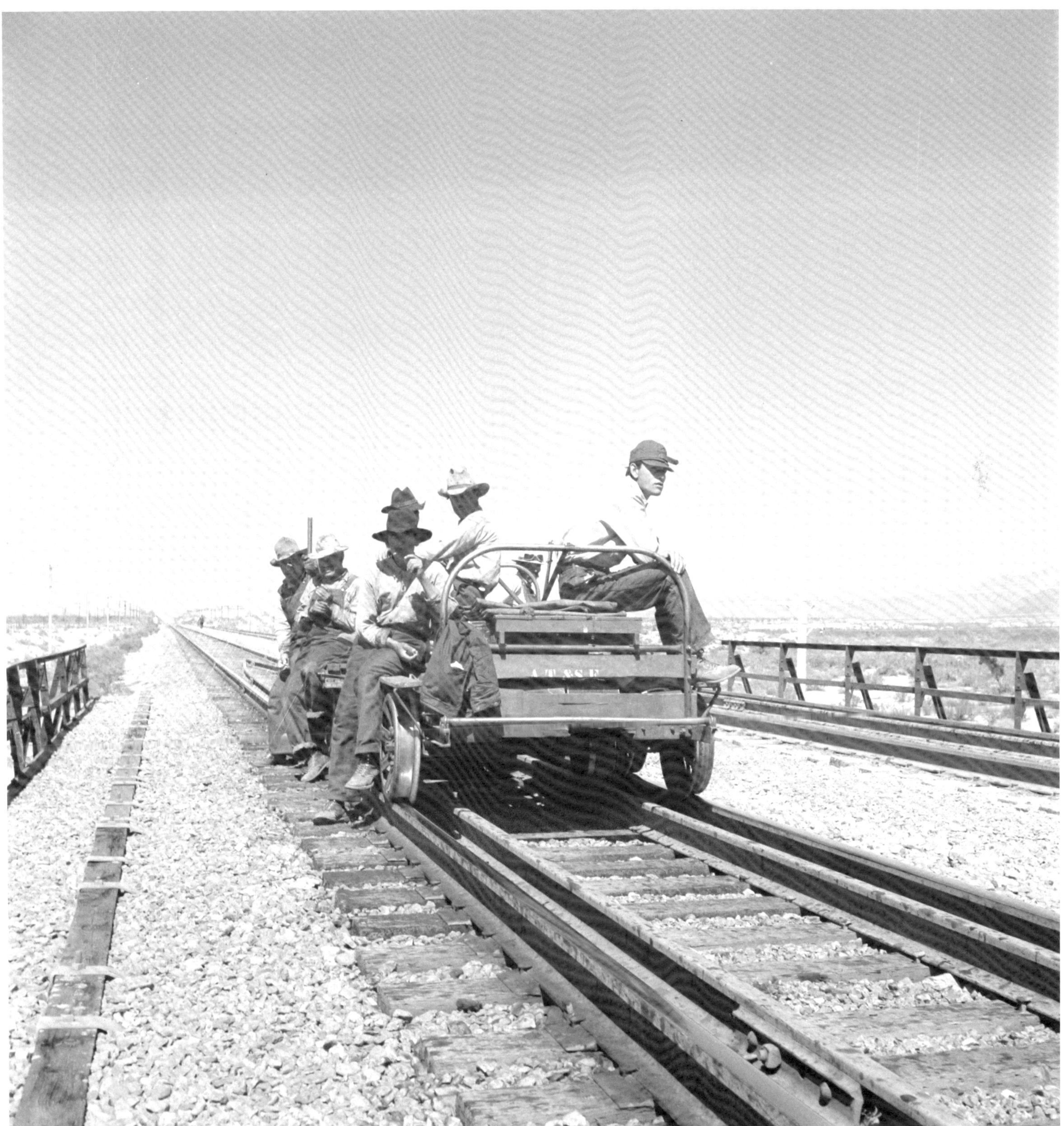
A T &S F

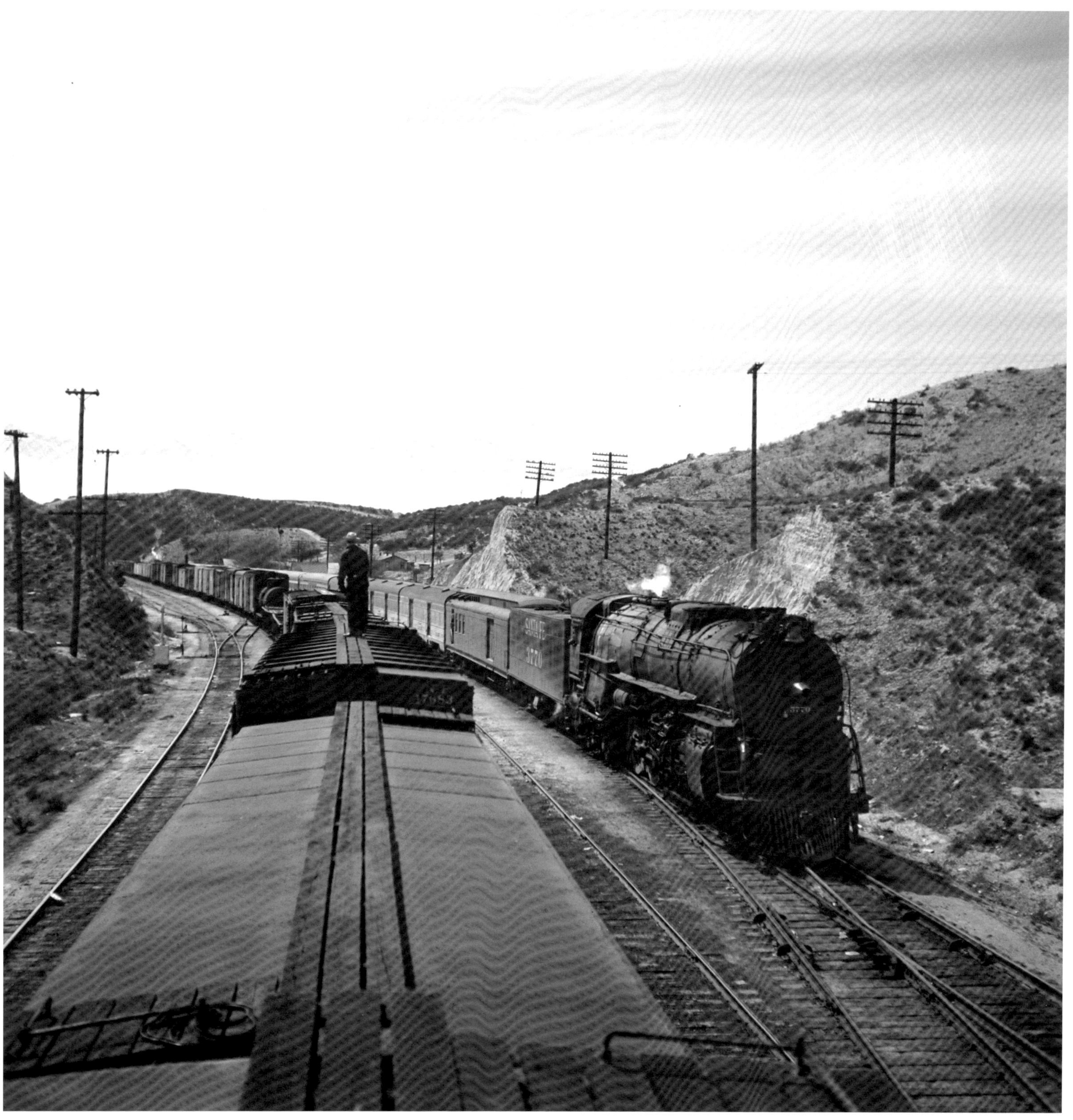
SANTA FE
3720

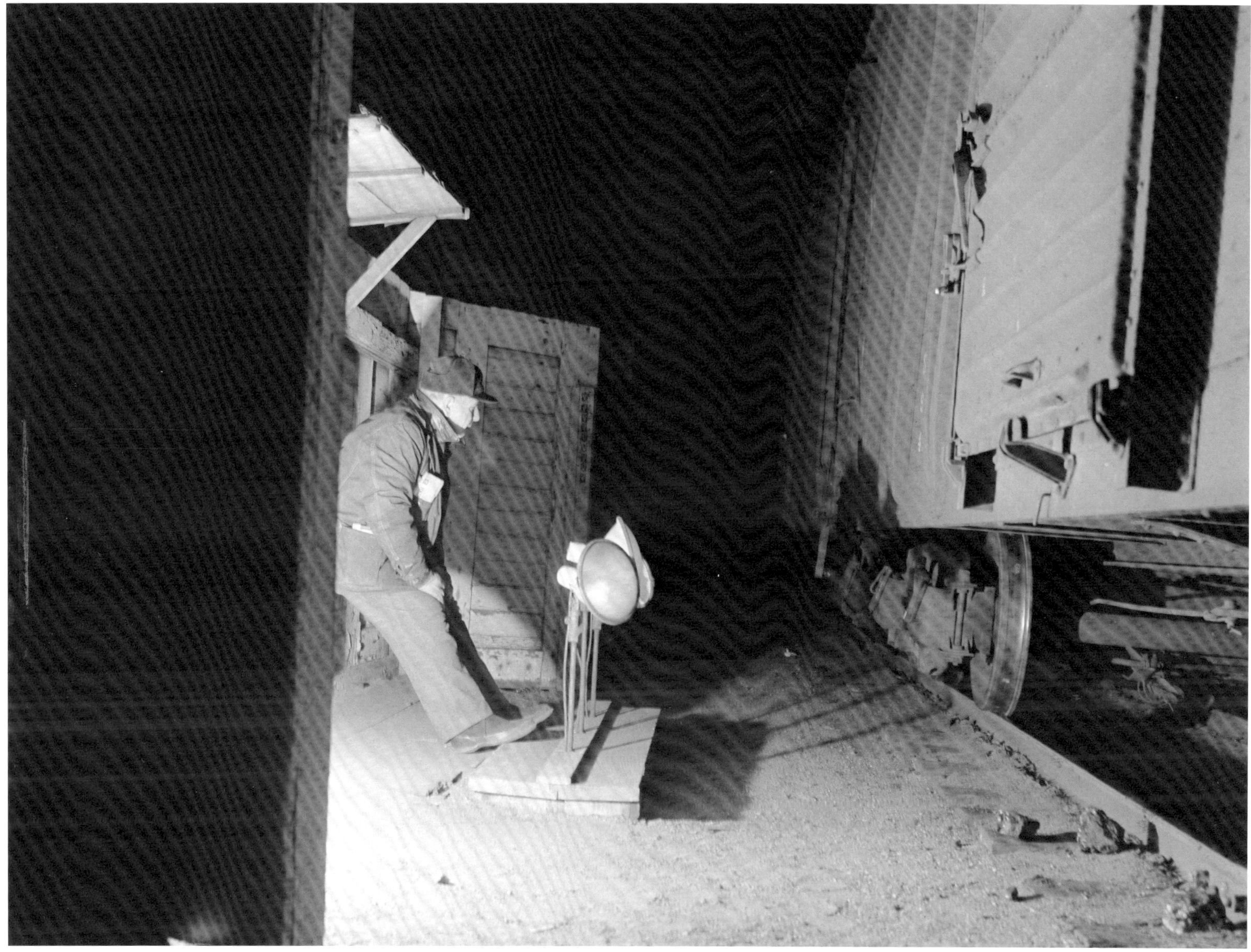

***Facing,* Plate 31.** Summit (vicinity), California. Passing an eastbound passenger train, the *Chief,* while coming down the mountain on the Atchison, Topeka and Santa Fe Railway between Barstow and San Bernardino, California.

Jack Delano. March 1943. Library of Congress, Prints & Photographs Division, FSA-OWI Collection, LC-USW3-021514-E.

***Above,* Plate 32.** Chicago, Illinois. Car inspector working at night at the hump at a Chicago and North Western Railway yard.

Jack Delano. December 1942. Library of Congress, Prints & Photographs Division, FSA-OWI Collection, LC-USW3-012365-D.

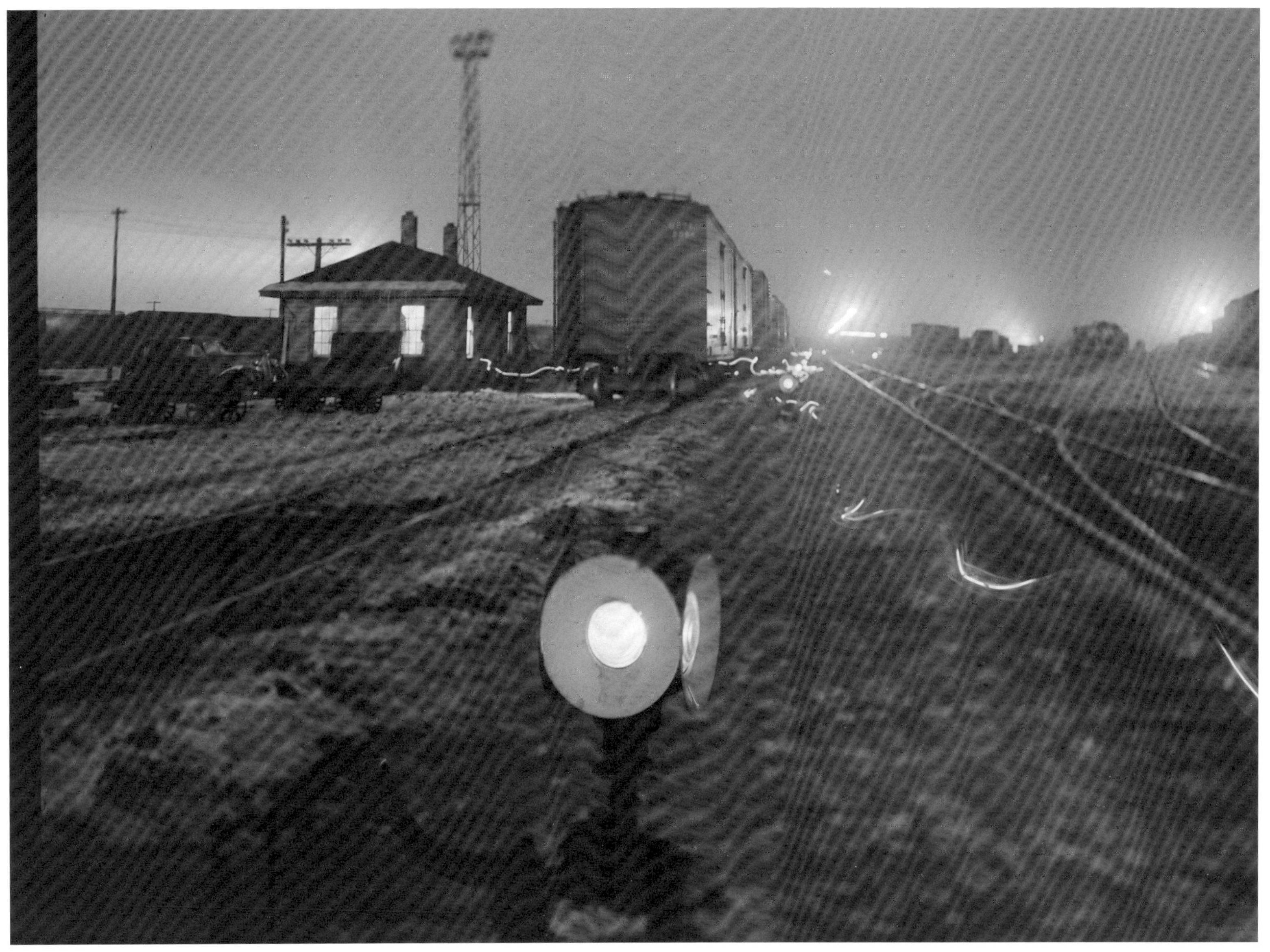

Plate 33. Chicago, Illinois. One of the yards of the Chicago and North Western Railway at night. The light streaks are caused by lanterns of men going in and out of the yard office.

Jack Delano. December 1942. Library of Congress, Prints & Photographs Division, FSA-OWI Collection, LC-USW3-012681-D.

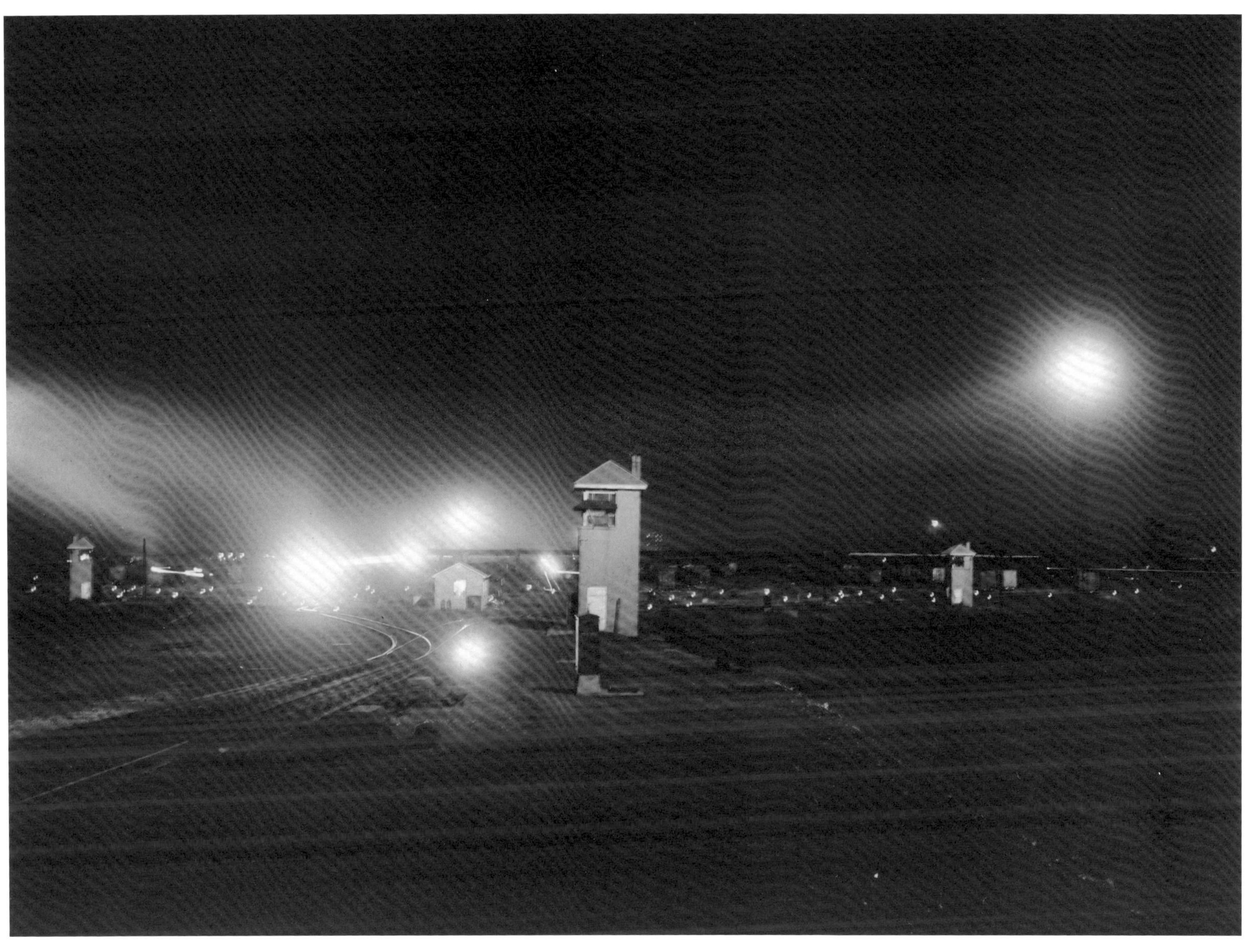

Plate 34. Chicago, Illinois. Work goes on twenty-four hours a day at this Chicago and North Western Railway yard.

Jack Delano. December 1942. Library of Congress, Prints & Photographs Division, FSA-OWI Collection, LC-USW33-014783-D.

***Above,* Plate 35.** Untitled photo, possibly related to: Argentine, Kansas. Freight train about to leave the Atchison, Topeka and Santa Fe Railway yard for the West Coast.

Jack Delano. March 1943. Library of Congress, Prints & Photographs Division, FSA-OWI Collection, LC-USW3-019719-E.

***Facing,* Plate 36.** Belva, Oklahoma. Helper engine coming to help push the train on the Atchison, Topeka and Santa Fe Railway as far as Curtis, Oklahoma.

Jack Delano. March 1943. Library of Congress, Prints & Photographs Division, FSA-OWI Collection, LC-USW3-019882-E.

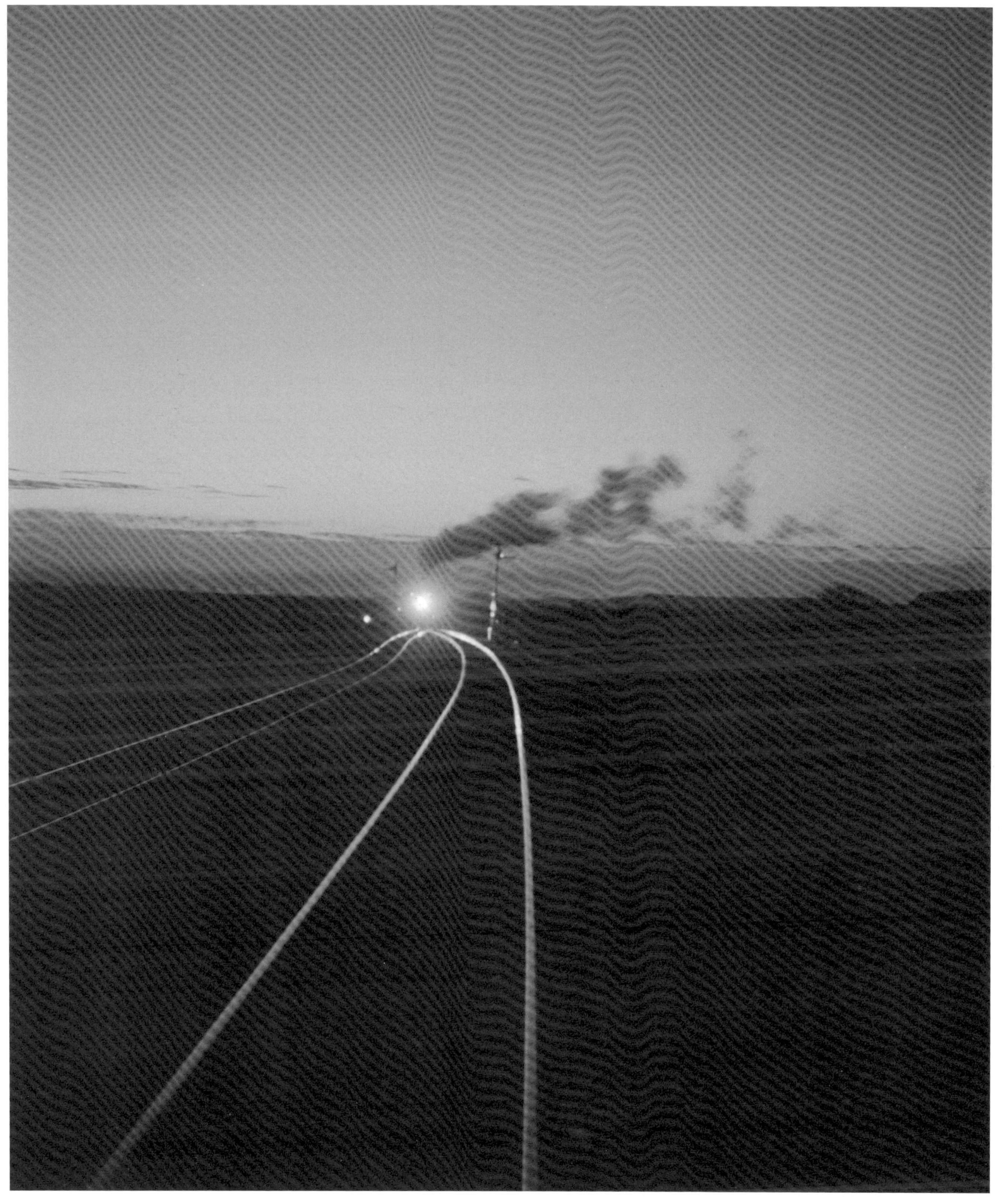

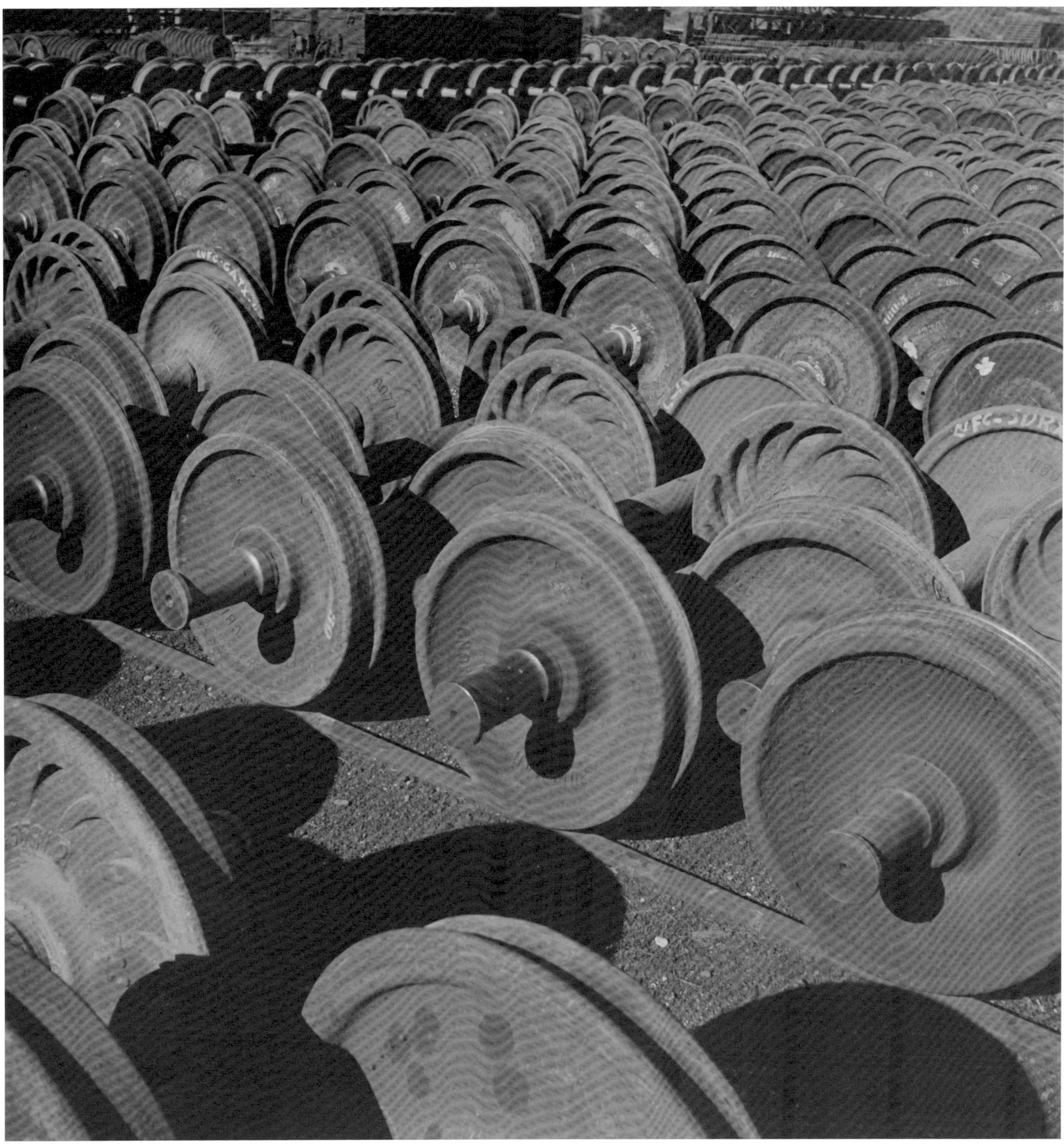

***Facing*, Plate 37.** Chicago, Illinois. Wheels and axles outside the locomotive shops at an Illinois Central Railroad yard.

Jack Delano. November 1942. Library of Congress, Prints & Photographs Division, FSA-OWI Collection, LC-USW3-010673-E.

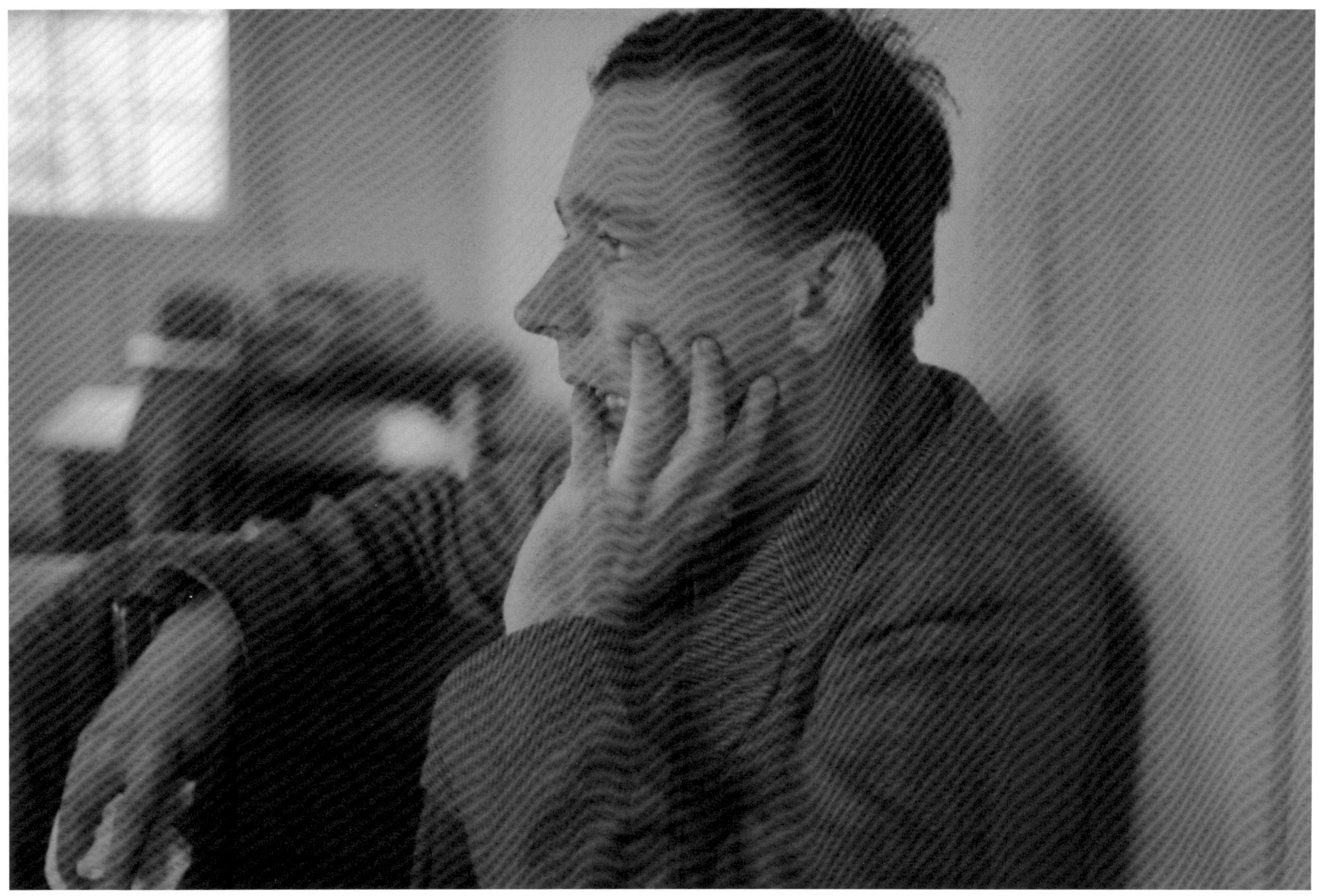

Figure 4.1. Walker Evans, profile, hand up to face.

Edwin Locke. February 1937. Library of Congress, Prints & Photographs Division, FSA-OWI Collection, LC-USF33-004225-M4.

PORTFOLIO FOUR

WALKER EVANS

When Walker Evans joined the Resettlement Administration, later the Farm Security Administration (FSA), in 1935, he was already well known, especially for photographs featured in the 1930 first edition of *The Bridge*, an epic poem by his friend Hart Crane. Evans, along with Dorothea Lange and Ben Shahn, connected the FSA with the art world, providing a cachet that Historical Section head Roy Stryker valued.[1]

At the time he joined Stryker's team, Evans, like Lange, was a fairly established artist who wanted—and probably needed—to go his own way. Throughout his career, he focused on producing specific images of great content and quality rather than a broad set of images defining a subject. Given his orientation, Evans was bound to clash with Stryker, and clash with him he did. Their disagreement was not only due to the relatively small number of images Evans photographed but also the result of Stryker's search for documentarian images focusing on rural and small-town US life vis-à-vis Evans's focus on art photography. Evans produced about 870 images for the Resettlement Administration/FSA during 1935, 1936, and 1937. This is a small number compared to his colleagues, but these images include some of the most artistically important photographs of the twentieth century. Evans left Stryker's team in 1937 to become a freelance photographic artist.[2] However, he would soon join *Fortune* magazine, a part of Henry Luce's Time Life empire, as a staff photographer. Evans worked for *Fortune* from 1945 to 1965 and then closed his career teaching at Yale. He died of a stroke in 1975. New York's Museum of Modern Art (MOMA), a great showcase for and promoter of his photography, owns an outstanding collection of his work, as does the J. Paul Getty Museum in Los Angeles.

Despite the discord between Stryker and Evans, Evans's work for the FSA produced great fruits, including two enormously influential books. The first, *American Photographs*, published by MOMA in 1938, was the catalog to Evans's renowned one-person exhibition at MOMA that year. Many of the images in *American Photographs* were taken for the FSA, and Evans included several railroad-subject FSA images in *American Photographs* (see plates 38, 39, and 41). The second, a joint project with noted author James Agee, *Let Us Now Praise Famous Men*, included FSA images. Although a commercial failure when first published, *Let Us Now Praise Famous Men* was, and is, enormously influential.[3]

Evans's work on American railroading continued in the 1950s in four portfolios he shot for his long-term employer, *Fortune* magazine. He would oversee a 1955 railroad-subject portfolio in *Fortune* focusing on the Pennsylvania Railroad's *Congressional*

by his famed mentee, Robert Frank.[4] Evans's railroad-subject work also includes his 1966 book of clandestine portraits taken while riding the New York City subways, *Many Are Called*, which features an essay by James Agee.[5] Evans helped launch the historic preservation movement in the US with his article in the July 1963 issue of *Life*, "America's Heritage of Great Architecture Is Doomed . . . It Must Be Saved." This article is how many Americans learned about the demolition of New York City's majestic Pennsylvania Station.[6]

Evans enjoyed a long and productive career, and his work has been described with many labels, including formalist, minimalist, and modernist. Perhaps the most lasting legacy of his work is its clean—even detached—view of American architecture and of American signs and advertising logos and materials.

This Walker Evans FSA railroad-subject portfolio reflects the quality and paucity of his work. Plates 38 and 39, photos taken for the Resettlement Administration/FSA and featured in *American Photographs*, are clean and iconic representations of the railroad in the US landscape: a presence understated here perhaps to emphasize its ubiquity. Phillipsburg, New Jersey, was served by the Delaware, Lackawanna and Western Railroad, the Jersey Central, the Lehigh Valley Railroad, and the Pennsylvania; Easton, Pennsylvania, was served by these railroads and the Lehigh and Hudson River Railway. Plate 40, which is not a well-known Evans image, is a railroad station in Bethlehem, Pennsylvania, with the dirt embankment in the foreground seeming to foretell the building's decline to collapse or demolition. Bethlehem was served by five railroads; the station shown in plate 40, which still exists, was the Jersey Central station.

Plate 41, a well-known image also featured in *American Photographs*, shows company houses along the railroad tracks in a coal-mining "camp" in Scott's Run, West Virginia (see also plate 126). Scott's Run is not shown in period railroad station lists, but nearby Pursglove was a station on the Monongahela Railway. Plate 42 is part of Evans's coverage of the disastrous floods of January 1937, showing a train track flanked on both sides by floodwater.

Finally, plate 43, *View of Railroad Station, Edwards, Mississippi*, is probably Evans's best-known railroad-subject image, depicting a station on the Illinois Central. The noted photograph is featured in later editions of *Let Us Now Praise Famous Men*.

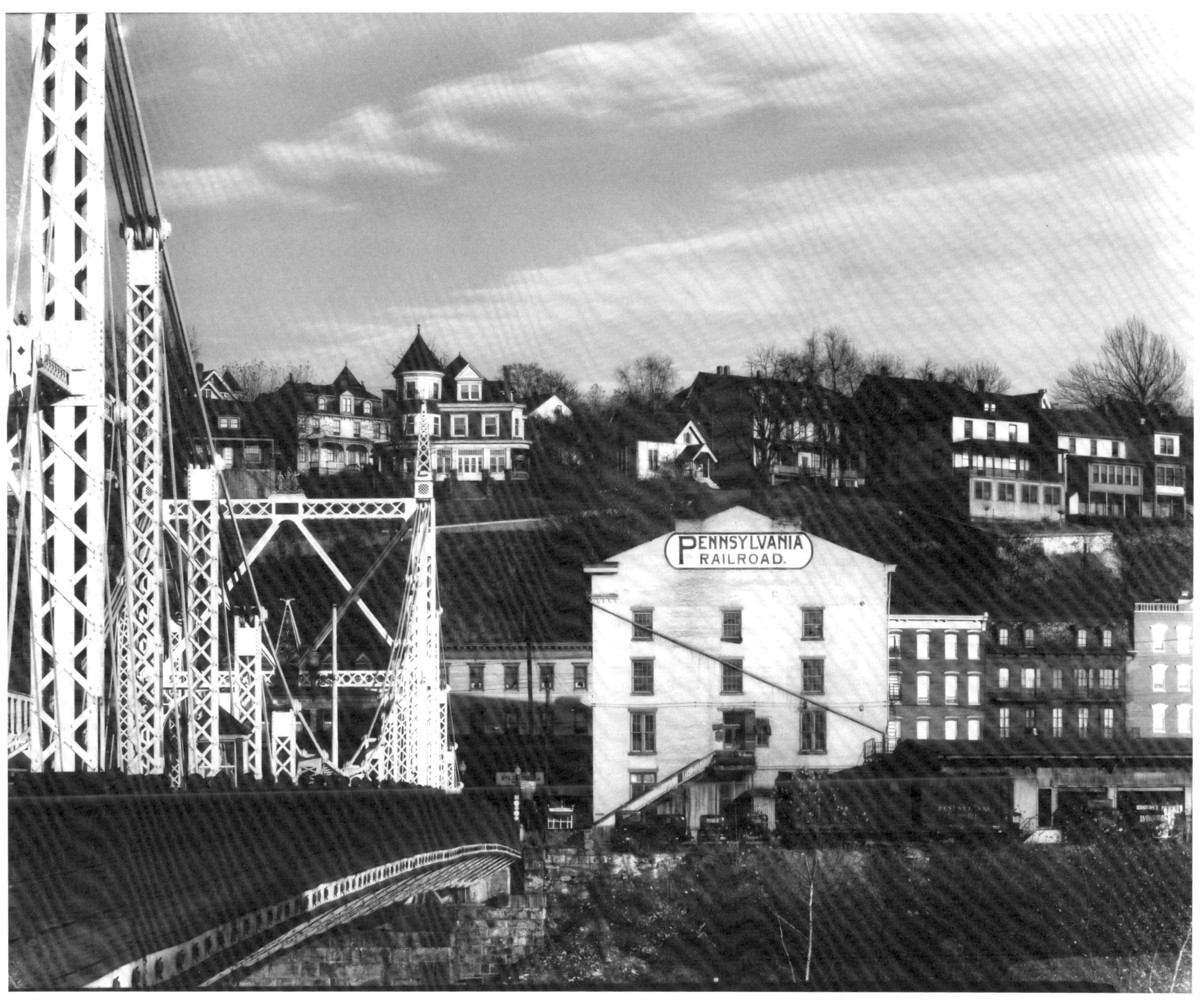

Plate 38. Bridge and houses in Phillipsburg, New Jersey; seen from Easton, Pennsylvania.

Walker Evans. November 1935. Library of Congress, Prints & Photographs Division, FSA-OWI Collection, LC-USF342-001171-A.

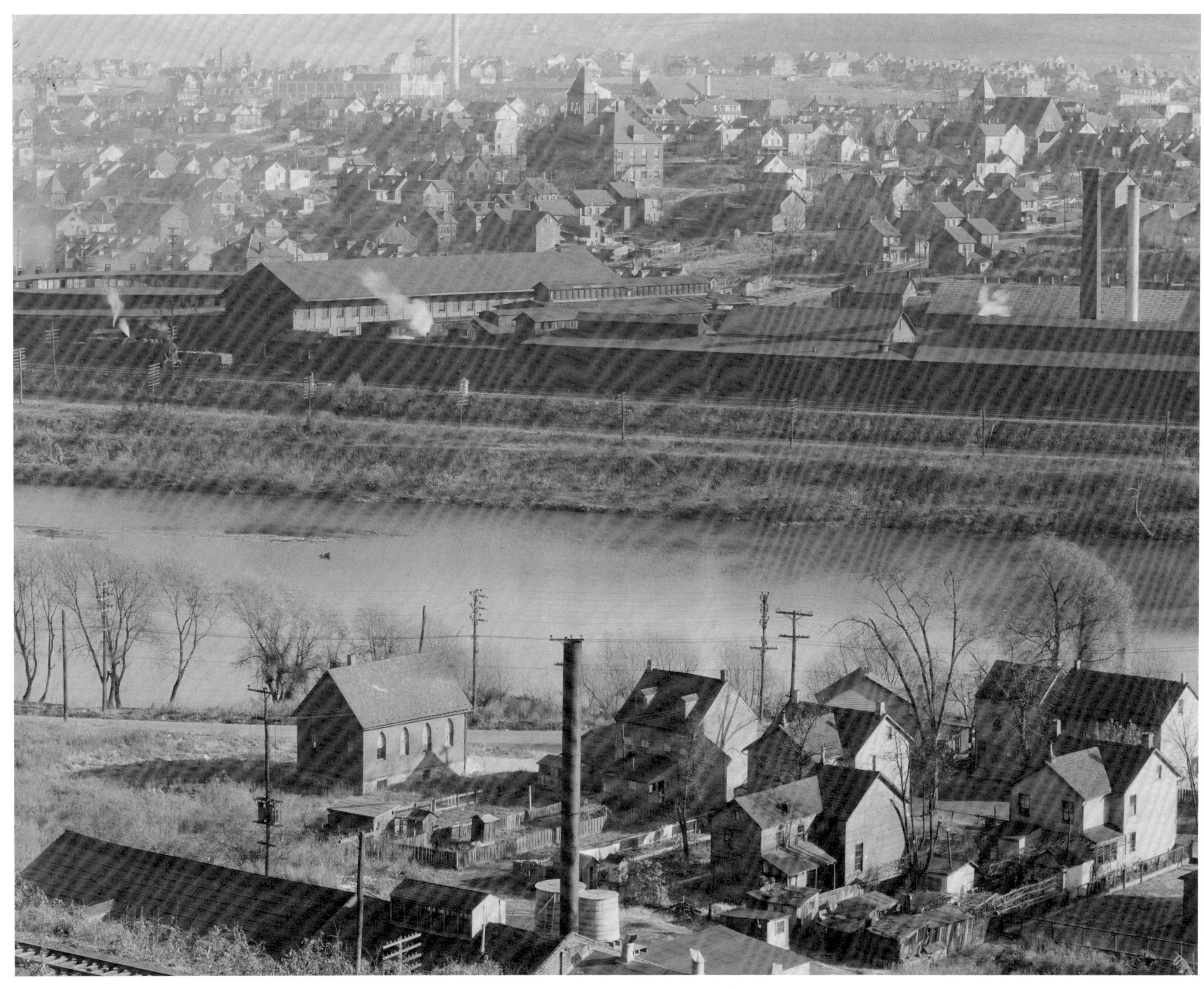

Plate 39. View of Easton, Pennsylvania, on the Lehigh River.

Walker Evans. November 1935. Library of Congress, Prints & Photographs Division, FSA-OWI Collection, LC-USF342-001163-A.

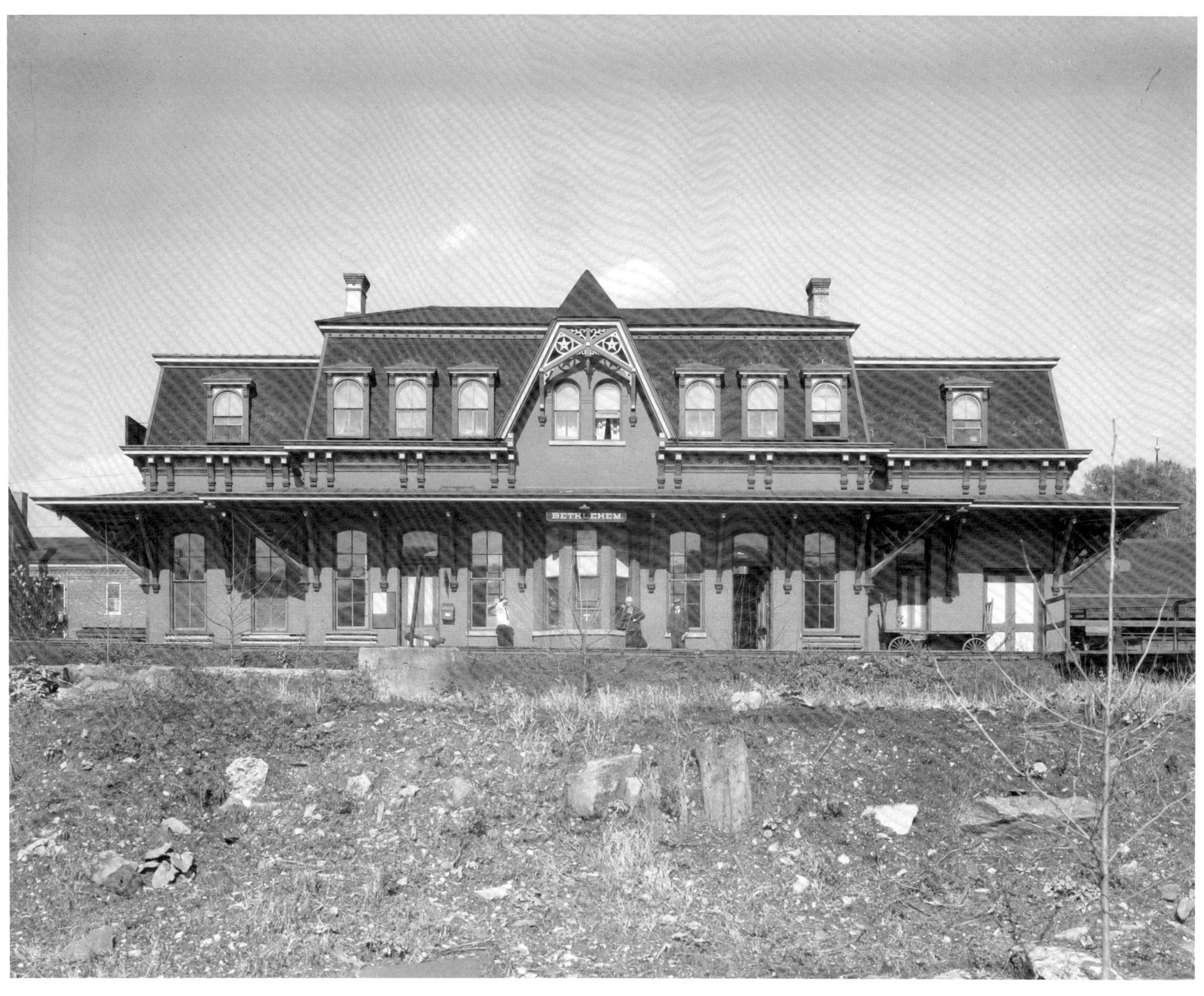

Plate 40. Depot in Bethlehem, Pennsylvania.

Walker Evans. November 1935. Library of Congress, Prints & Photographs Division, FSA-OWI Collection, LC-USF342-001169-A.

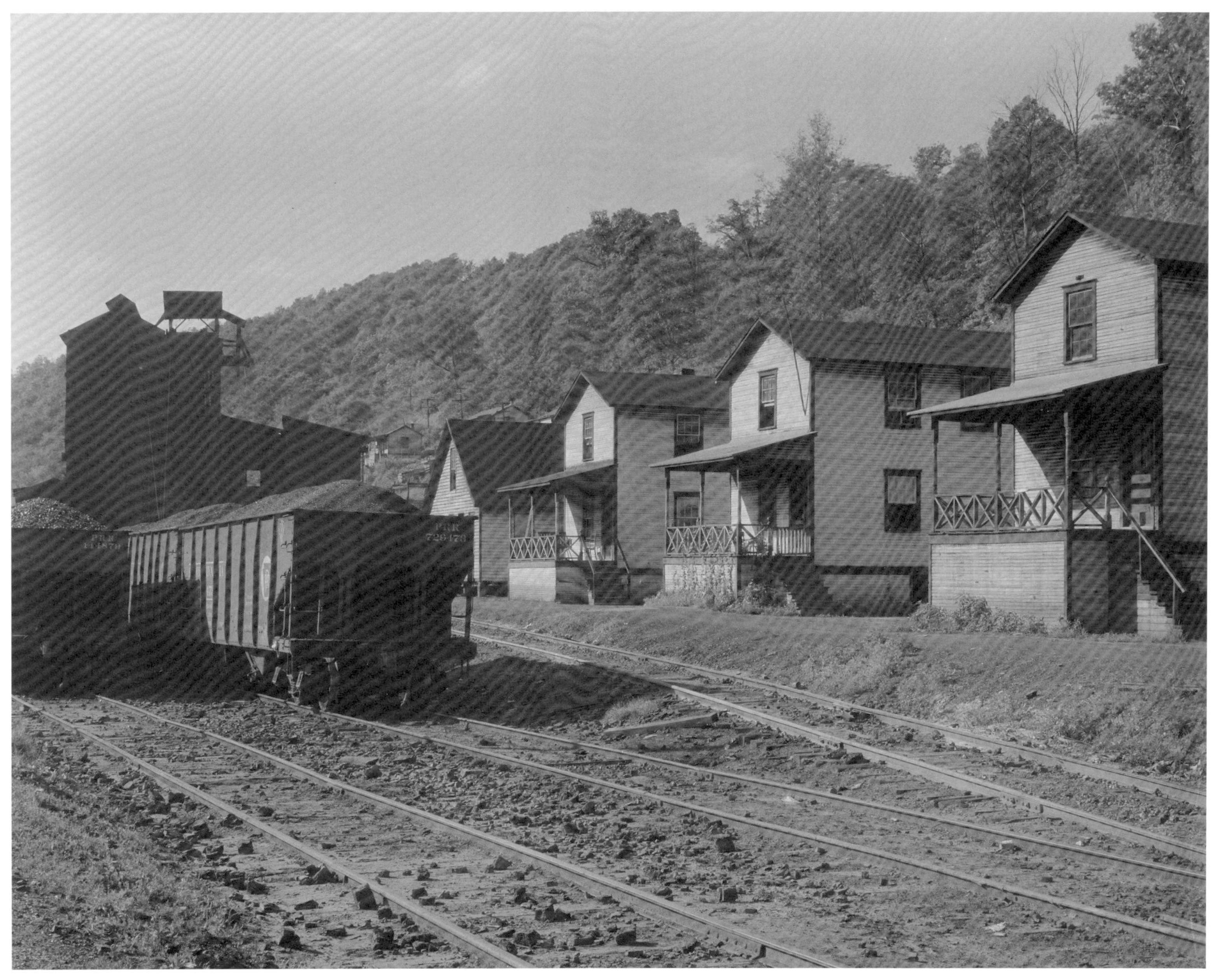

Plate 41. Company houses along railroad tracks. Scott's Run near Morgantown, West Virginia. Osage, West Virginia.

Walker Evans. July 1935. Library of Congress, Prints & Photographs Division, FSA-OWI Collection, LC-USF342-000892-A.

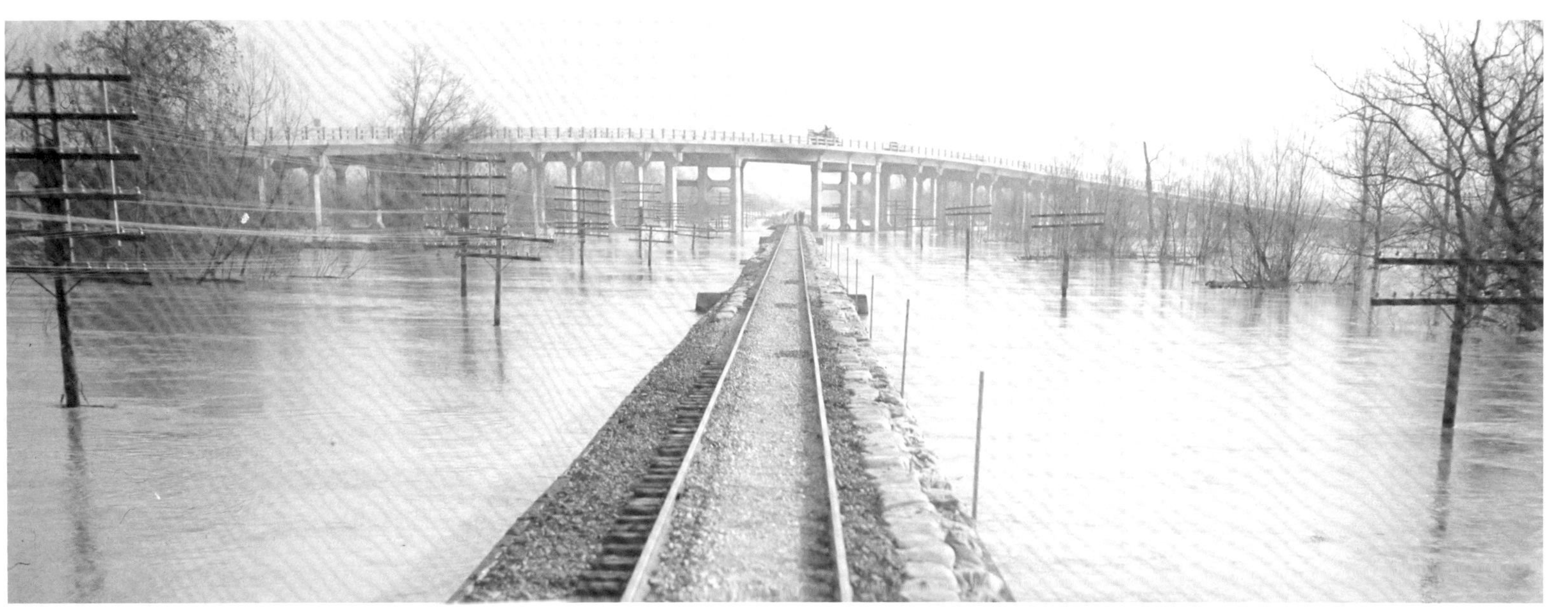

Plate 42. View taken from train between Memphis, Tennessee, and Forrest City, Arkansas.

Walker Evans. February 1937. Library of Congress, Prints & Photographs Division, FSA-OWI Collection, LC-USF34-008189-E.

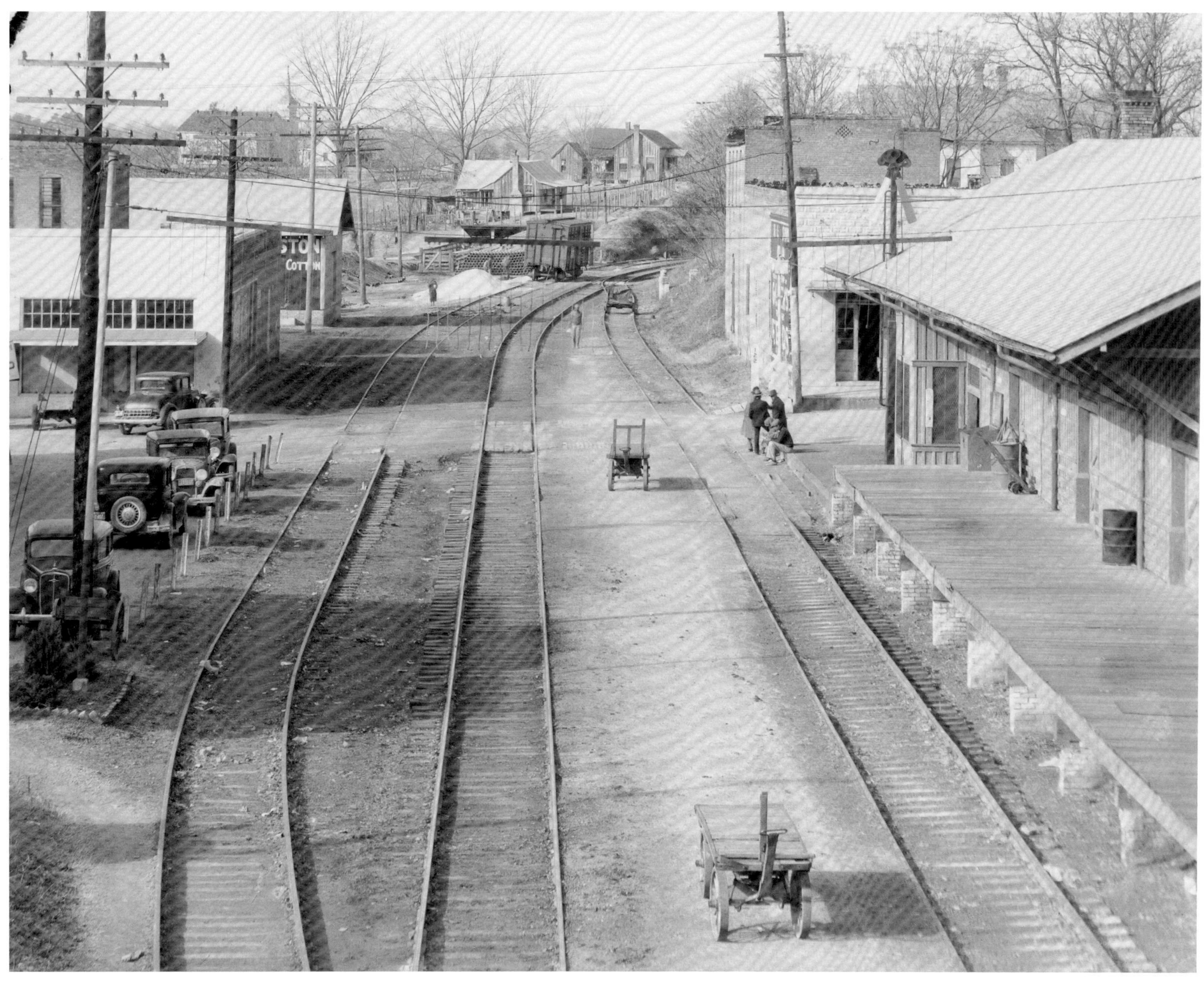

Plate 43. View of railroad station, Edwards, Mississippi.

Walker Evans. February 1936. Library of Congress, Prints & Photographs Division, FSA-OWI Collection, LC-USF342-001295-A.

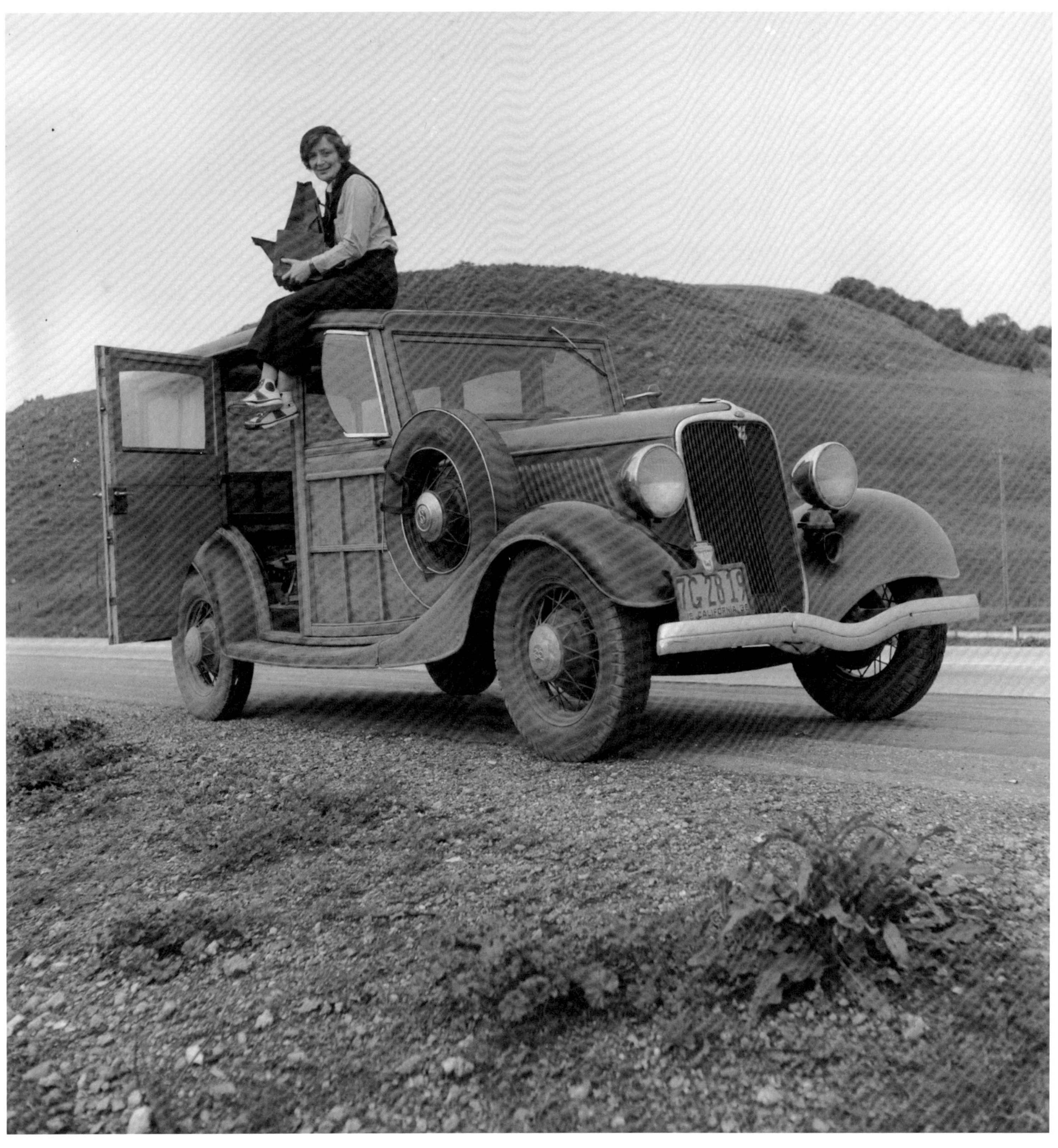
CALIFORNIA

PORTFOLIO FIVE

DOROTHEA LANGE

Like President Franklin Delano Roosevelt, whose administration founded the Resettlement Administration/Farm Security Administration (FSA), Dorothea Lange led a life that was changed by polio. Born in Hoboken, New Jersey, in 1895 as Dorothea Margaretta Nutzhorn, Lange was raised by her mother in New York City after her father abandoned the family.[1] She contracted polio as a child and was left with a deformed foot and a limp.

Soon after graduating from high school, Lange decided to become a photographer—even though she had no camera and had never taken a photograph.[2] Lange found a position with Arnold Genthe, and noted Photo-Secessionist photographer Clarence White became her mentor.

In 1918, she decided to travel around the world with a friend, but a robbery led to the end of their trip in San Francisco, California, where Lange was to spend much of her life. She befriended noted photographer Imogen Cunningham, and benefactors helped her establish a photography studio in San Francisco that was very successful. Lange specialized in family portraits.

In 1920, Lange married painter Maynard Dixon, and they had two sons.[3] The coming of the Great Depression dramatically affected commissions for both Lange and Dixon and also led Lange to walk the streets of San Francisco with a camera, documenting the Depression's toll on the people of the area. During this period, she took one of the iconic images of the Great Depression in the United States, *White Angel Breadline*. It would soon be followed by others. Her works began to show the influence of Jacob Riis and Lewis Hine.

Like Walker Evans, Dorothea Lange had attained status as a noted photographic artist before joining the FSA. In 1934, Paul Taylor, an associate professor of economics at the University of California, Berkeley, saw Lange's photos on display in an Oakland gallery.[4] Taylor hired her to take photographs for the California Division of Rural Rehabilitation when he became its director in 1935.[5] Lange and Dixon divorced, and Lange married Taylor. She then devoted herself to photography focused on social justice.

***Facing*, Figure 5.1.** Dorothea Lange, Resettlement Administration photographer, in California.

February 1936. Library of Congress, Prints & Photographs Division, FSA-OWI Collection, LC-USF34-002392-E.

In 1935, Lange was hired by Roy Stryker, and she worked for the FSA, albeit off and on, until 1939. Her photography for the FSA is characterized by portraiture demonstrating the lives and needs of disadvantaged Americans. Like Walker Evans, Lange had a complex relationship with Stryker, who valued her experience and artistic excellence but found her independence challenging. Her insistence on remaining resident in California was also a challenge for her work with the Washington, DC–based FSA.

At about the time she left the FSA, Lange collaborated with her husband, Taylor, on the book *An American Exodus*, published in 1939. Like *Let Us Now Praise Famous Men*, *An American Exodus* is today considered a landmark book, but it was not a commercial success when published. The attention of the American people at the time was turning away from economic challenges to the advent of war in Europe.

Like Russell Lee, Lange documented the internment of Japanese Americans in the early 1940s, but her images, taken for the US government, were not released for three decades. Lange's health deteriorated after World War II, and she had to give up photography for almost a decade.

In the late 1950s, Paul Taylor began a period of extensive world travel, consulting with officials in the developing world. Lange's health had improved, and she traveled with her husband, photographing people in places such as Indonesia and Korea. After this period of travel was over, Lange returned to her home in Berkeley, California, and devoted herself to documenting the details of her life there.

By 1965, Lange was dying of cancer.[6] She spent the remainder of her life working on a retrospective exhibit of her work being organized by the Museum of Modern Art (MOMA). She died in October 1965, and the MOMA exhibit appeared in 1966.

Walker Evans and Dorothea Lange are two of the greatest photographers of the twentieth century, and they both documented the Great Depression extensively. A comparison of their work is instructive. If Evans's photographs showed detachment and often depicted architectural details, Lange's are steeped in social justice. Her portraits depict disadvantaged people facing daunting odds with dignity. This approach is reflected in the railroad-subject photographs included in this portfolio, which focus on what then would have been called migrants, itinerants, tramps, or even bums and today would be termed the homeless or the unhoused.

Plate 44 shows the ferry dock at the Central Railroad of New Jersey terminal in Jersey City, taken from one of the ferries that linked this railroad station with New York City.[7] Plate 45 is one of several iconic period views of grain elevators included in this book. Lange's photo shows a grain elevator in North Platte, Nebraska, foregrounded by a Union Pacific switch engine, 4432, a 0-6-0. These grain elevator images presage later work by photographers such as David Plowden.

Plate 46 is an evocative detail photo of a small Union Pacific railroad station in Irrigon, Oregon. The ties in the track, the planks in the station ramp, and the boards forming the deck of the baggage cart all align with each other, providing visual interest. Plate 47, while still a detail view, shows more about this typical small-town station.

Plates 48–51 form a short portfolio of Lange's views of homeless people using the railroad for free transportation and the challenges they faced in doing so. Plate 48 shows that some things have not changed much since the 1930s: it depicts a uniformed man inspecting a train for "smuggled immigrants" in El Paso, Texas. This official is accompanied by what appears to be a railroad "car knocker" (car inspector). Migrants attempting to enter the United States today still sometimes try to use freight trains, which they often term "the beast."[8]

Plate 49 depicts a family who traveled by freight train to Toppenish, Washington, a town on the Northern Pacific Railway. They sit, with their meager belongings, in the shade formed by a railroad freight car that towers over the family. The woman of the family looks directly at the photographer, a detail helping to make this a classic image.

Plate 50 depicts two weary men leaning or lying on a disabled flat car in a railroad yard in Sacramento, California. The railroad tag indicating a piece of rolling stock needs repair, "bad order," shows prominently, and ironically, just below one of the sleeping hobo's shoes. Plate 51 shows two "itinerants" sitting on the railroad track near Calipatria, California, on the Southern

Pacific. Both men have their rolled belongings, their "bindles." One sits at the base of a railroad signal, and the other, in a very dangerous pose, sits on one of the rails in the track. The period railroad signal, a semaphore, under which they are posed, towers over the men, and the railroad track reaches a vanishing point in the arid surroundings.

This view of Lange's railroad-subject work closes with one of her most famous images, *Toward Los Angeles, California*, plate 52, which owes its notoriety to its inherent irony as well as to its visual excellence. Two men, one with a suitcase and one with a bindle, walk the dirt and gravel to one side of what appears to be a state or federal highway.[9] A utility line borders the highway to the left of the image, but otherwise the surroundings are desolate, with the majority of the view composed of bare dirt. Both men wear visually interesting hats. Just to the right of one of them is a billboard stating "Next time try the train. Relax. Southern Pacific." As viewers, we certainly believe the men would take the train—if they could afford it.

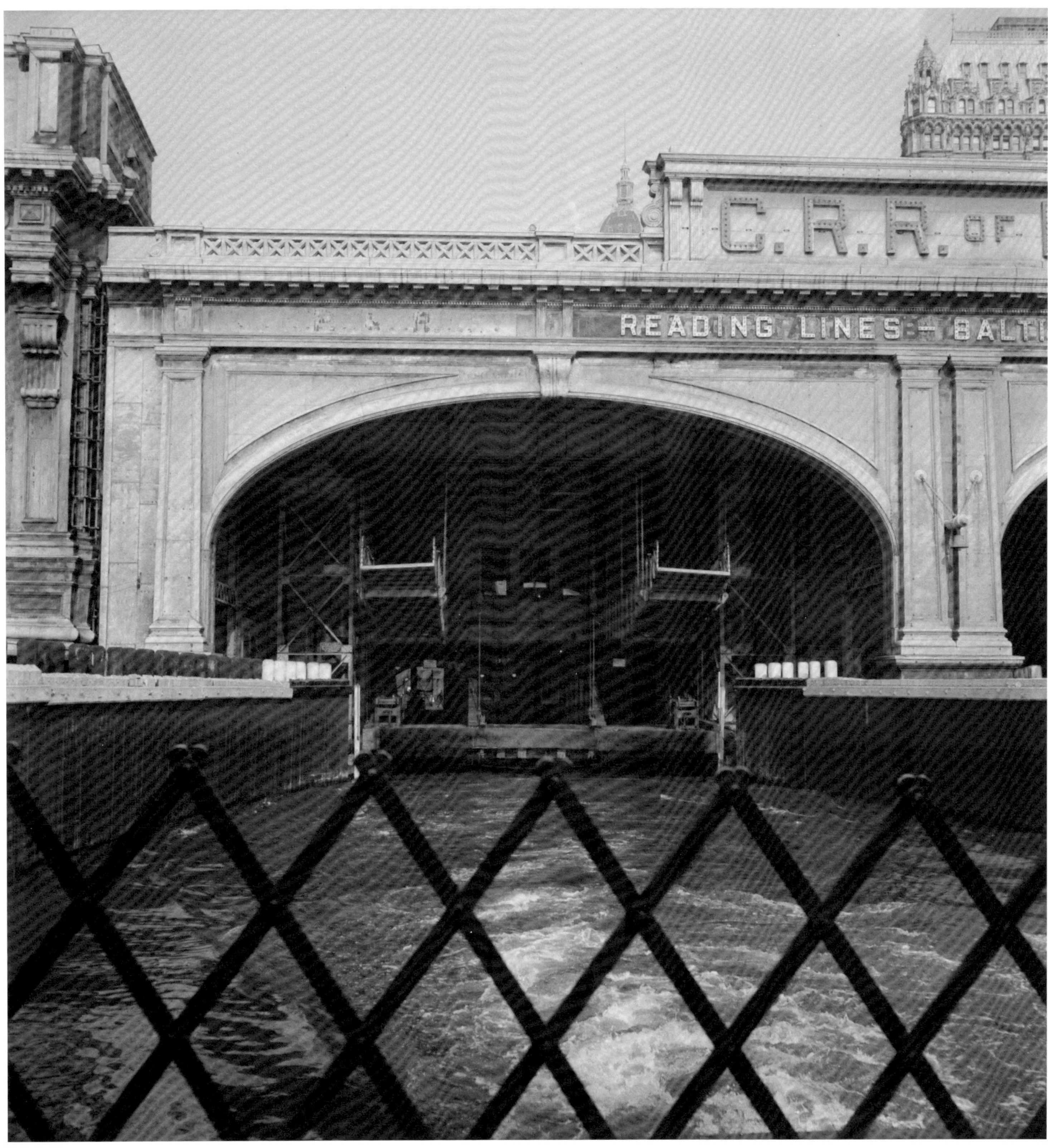
C.R.R. OF
READING LINES BALTI

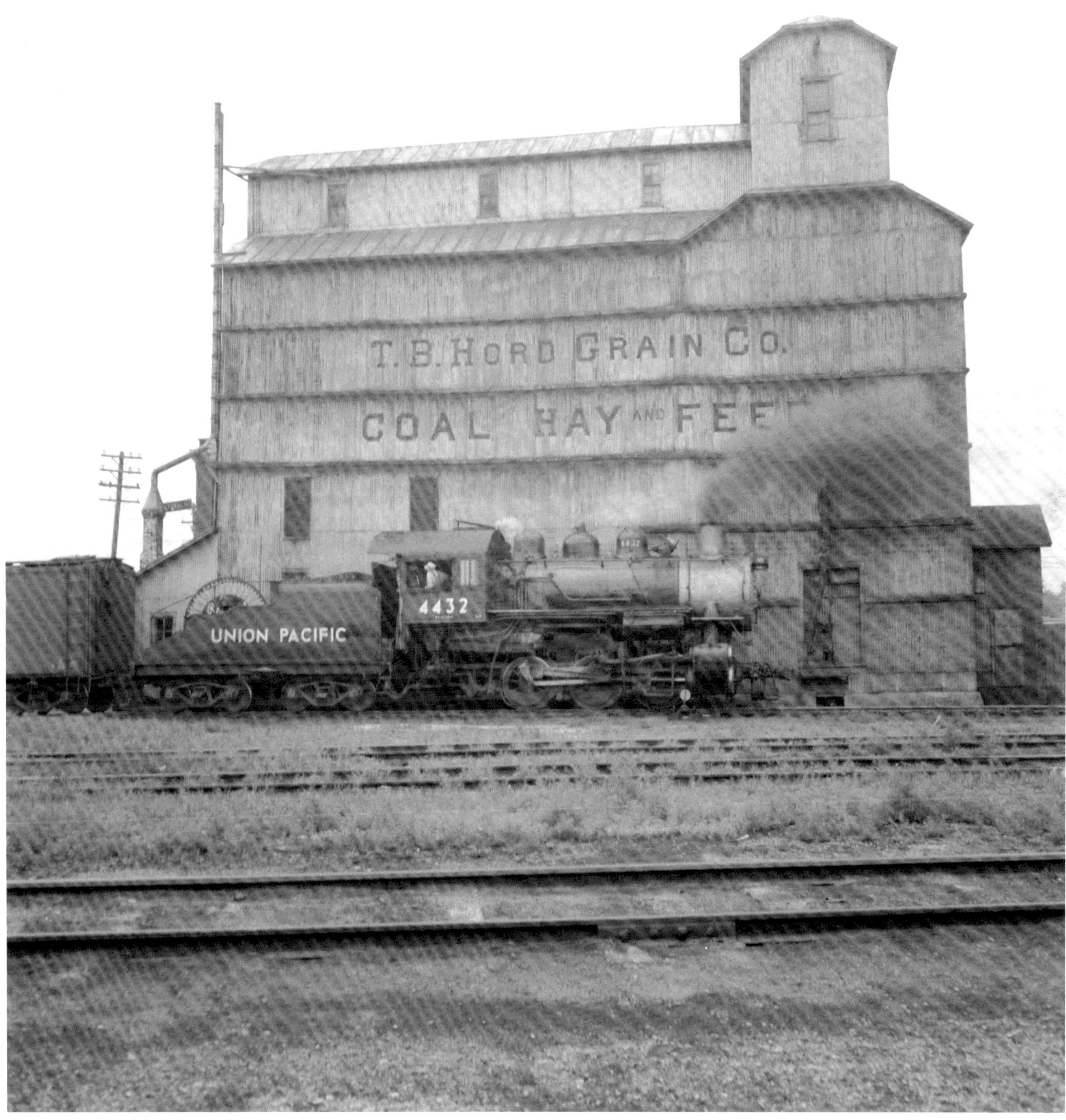

***Facing,* Plate 44.** Ferry slip seen from ferry that transports passengers across the Hudson River by bus to trains on the Jersey side. New York City.

Dorothea Lange. July 1939. Library of Congress, Prints & Photographs Division, FSA-OWI Collection, LC-USF34-019820-E.

***Above,* Plate 45.** Grain elevator along railroad yard. North Platte, Nebraska.

Dorothea Lange. June 1939. Library of Congress, Prints & Photographs Division, FSA-OWI Collection, LC-USF34-019691-E.

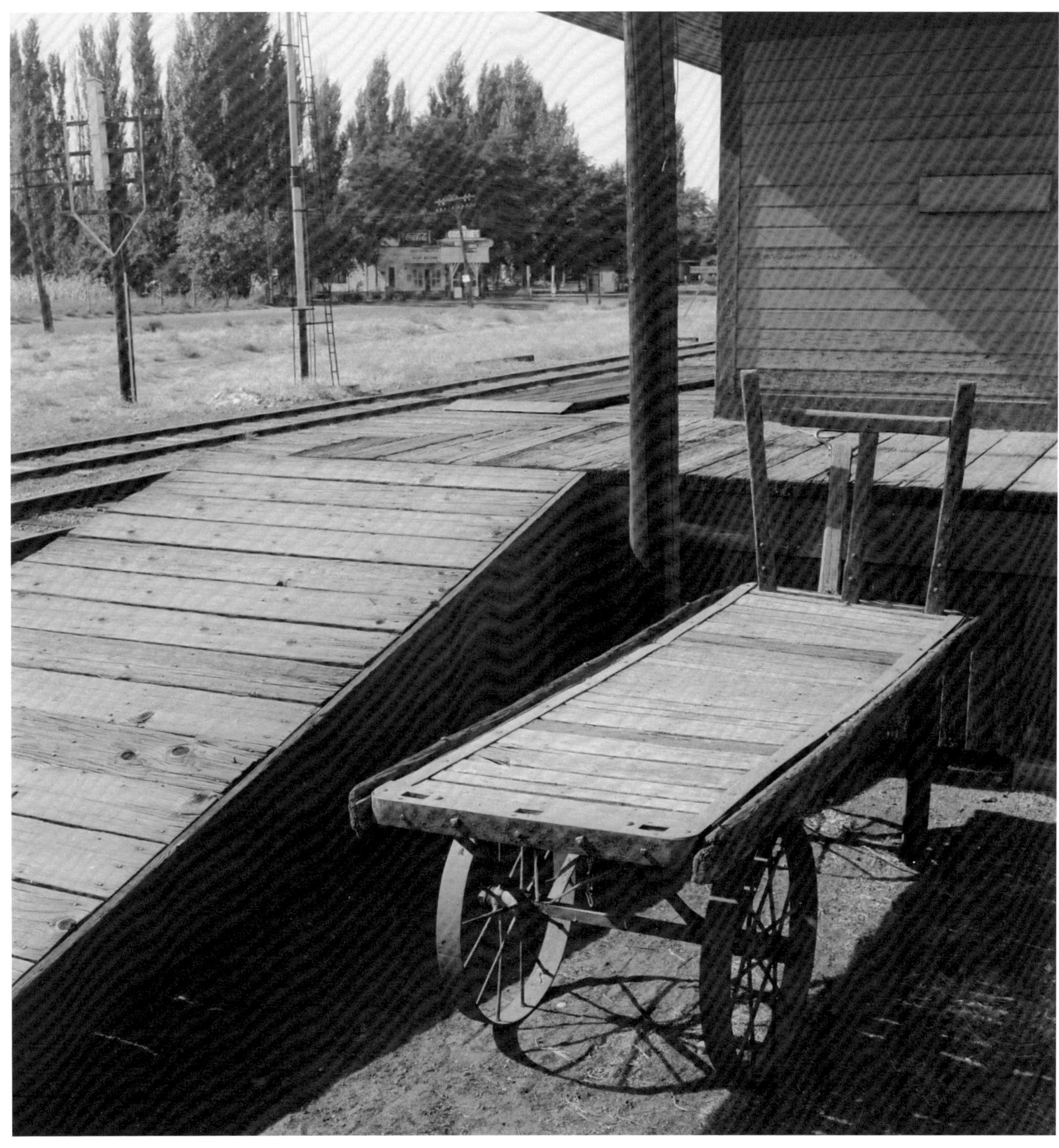

***Above*, Plate 46.** Detail of old railroad station. Small farming town, population 108. Irrigon, Oregon.

Dorothea Lange. October 1939. Library of Congress, Prints & Photographs Division, FSA-OWI Collection, LC-USF34-021130-E.

***Facing*, Plate 47.** Detail of railroad station painted "railroad yellow." Irrigon, Morrow County, Oregon.

Dorothea Lange. October 1939. Library of Congress, Prints & Photographs Division, FSA-OWI Collection, LC-USF34-021123-E.

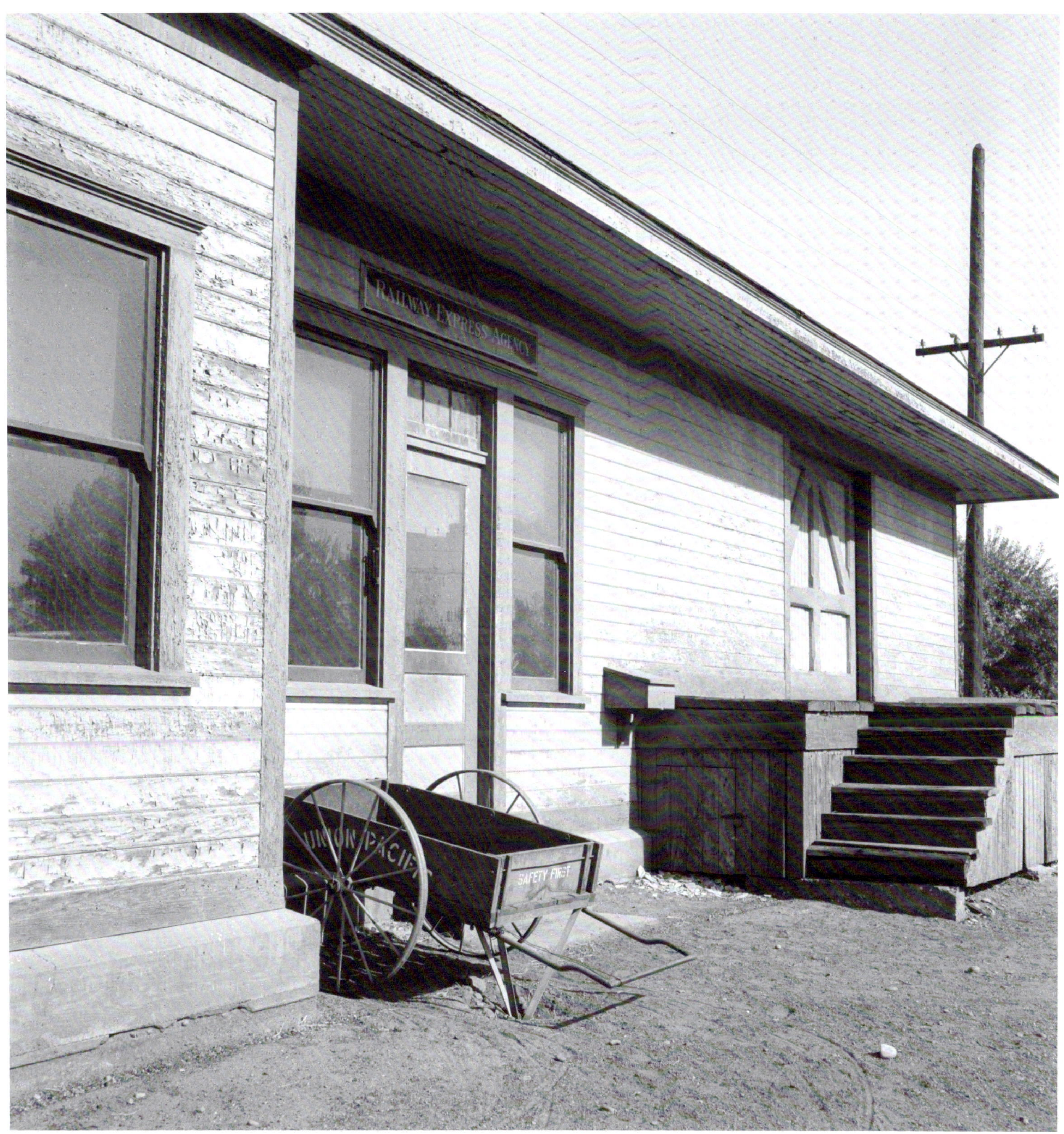
RAILWAY EXPRESS AGENCY
UNION PACIFIC
SAFETY FIRST

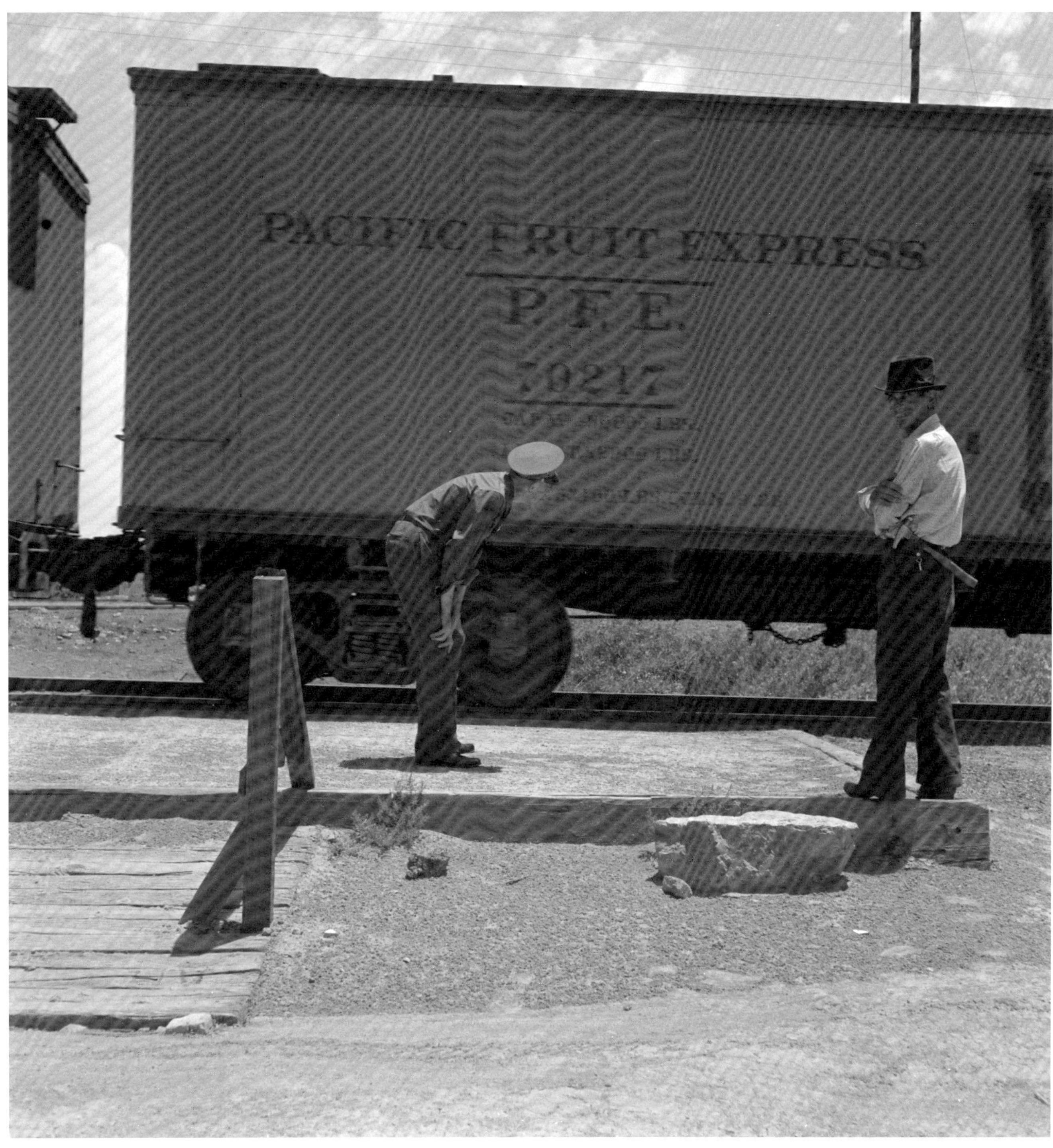

***Above,* Plate 48.** Inspecting a freight train from Mexico for smuggled immigrants. El Paso, Texas.

Dorothea Lange. June 1938. Library of Congress, Prints & Photographs Division, FSA-OWI Collection, LC-USF34-018222-E.

***Facing,* Plate 49.** Family who traveled by freight train. Washington, Toppenish, Yakima Valley.

Dorothea Lange. August 1939. Library of Congress, Prints & Photographs Division, FSA-OWI Collection, LC-USF34-020312-E.

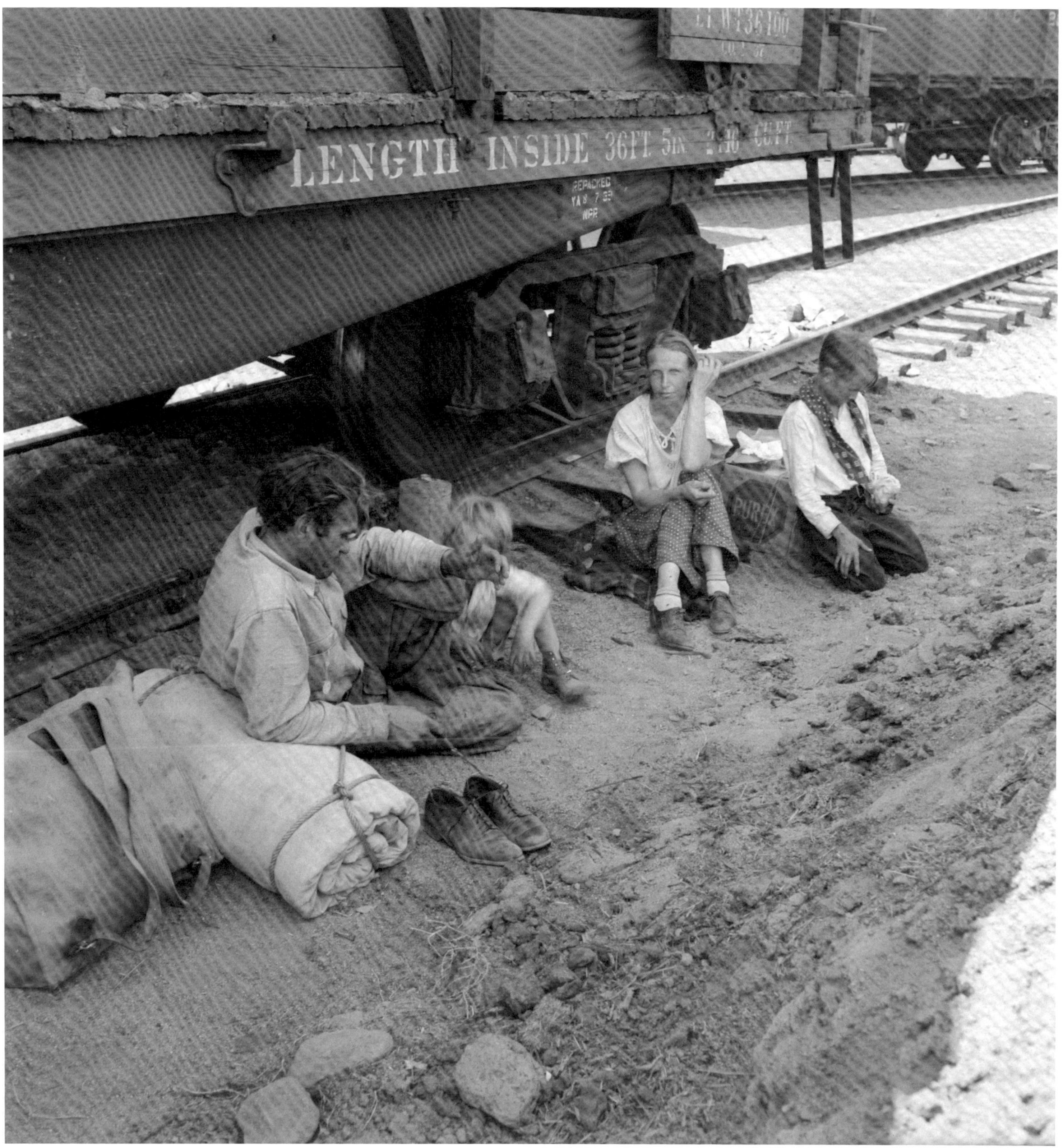
LENGTH INSIDE 36FT. 5IN

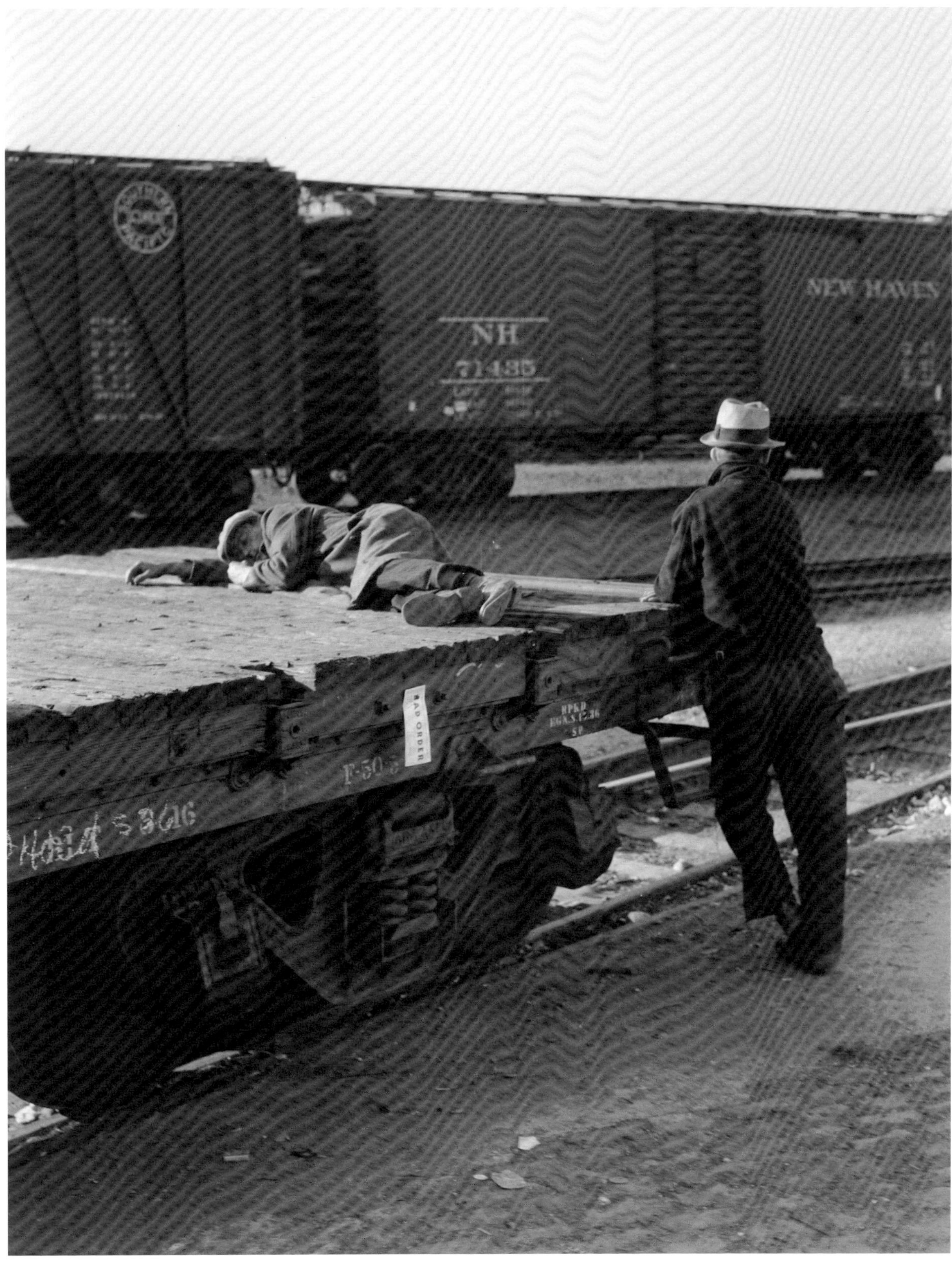

Plate 50. Scene in railroad yard. Sacramento, California.

Dorothea Lange. November 1936. Library of Congress, Prints & Photographs Division, FSA-OWI Collection, LC-USF34-016101-C.

Plate 51. Looking east down the railroad track, near Calipatria, California. Single men, itinerants with bindles waiting for the freight.

Dorothea Lange. February 1939. Library of Congress, Prints & Photographs Division, FSA-OWI Collection, LC-USF34-019355-C.

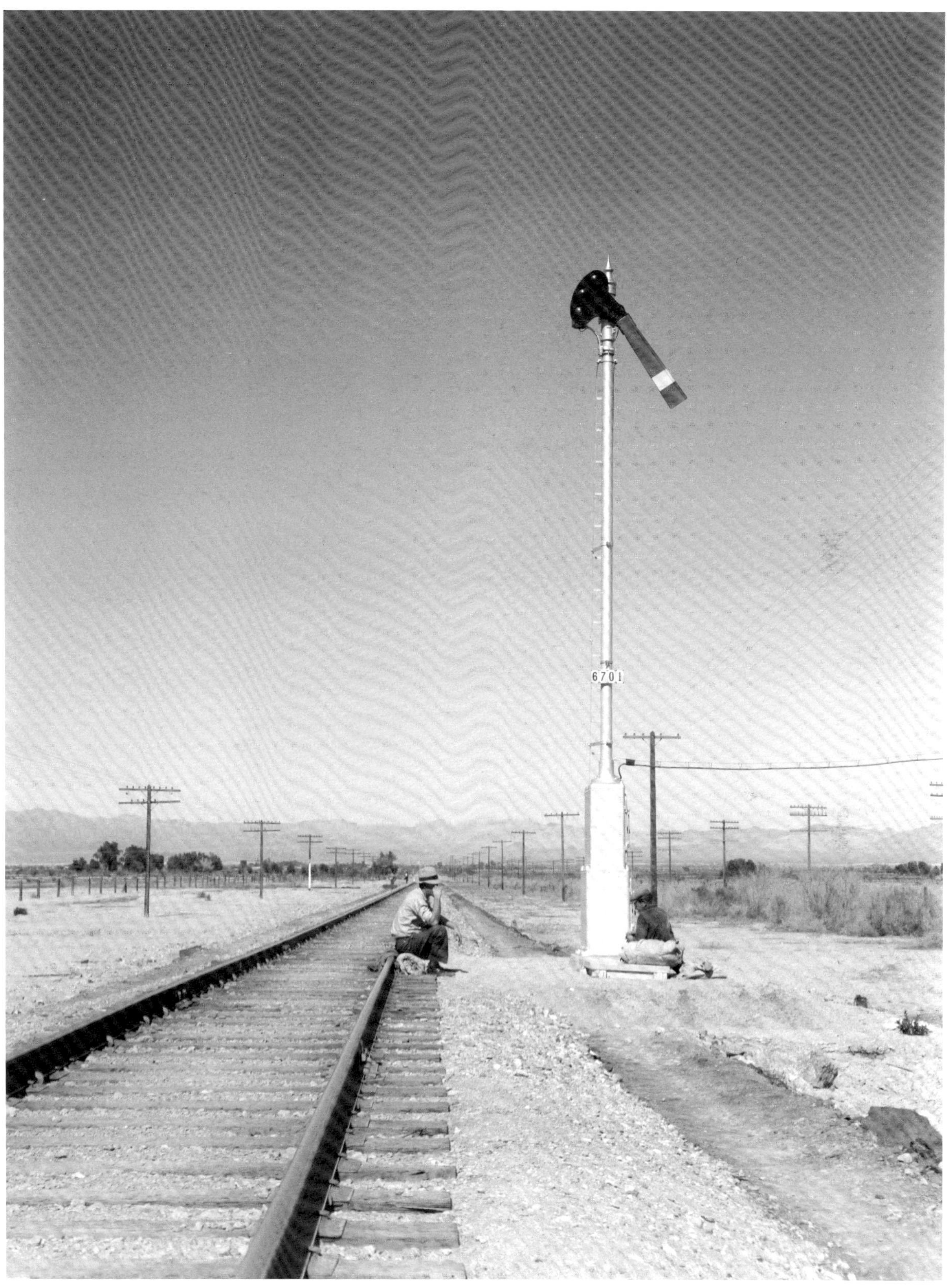

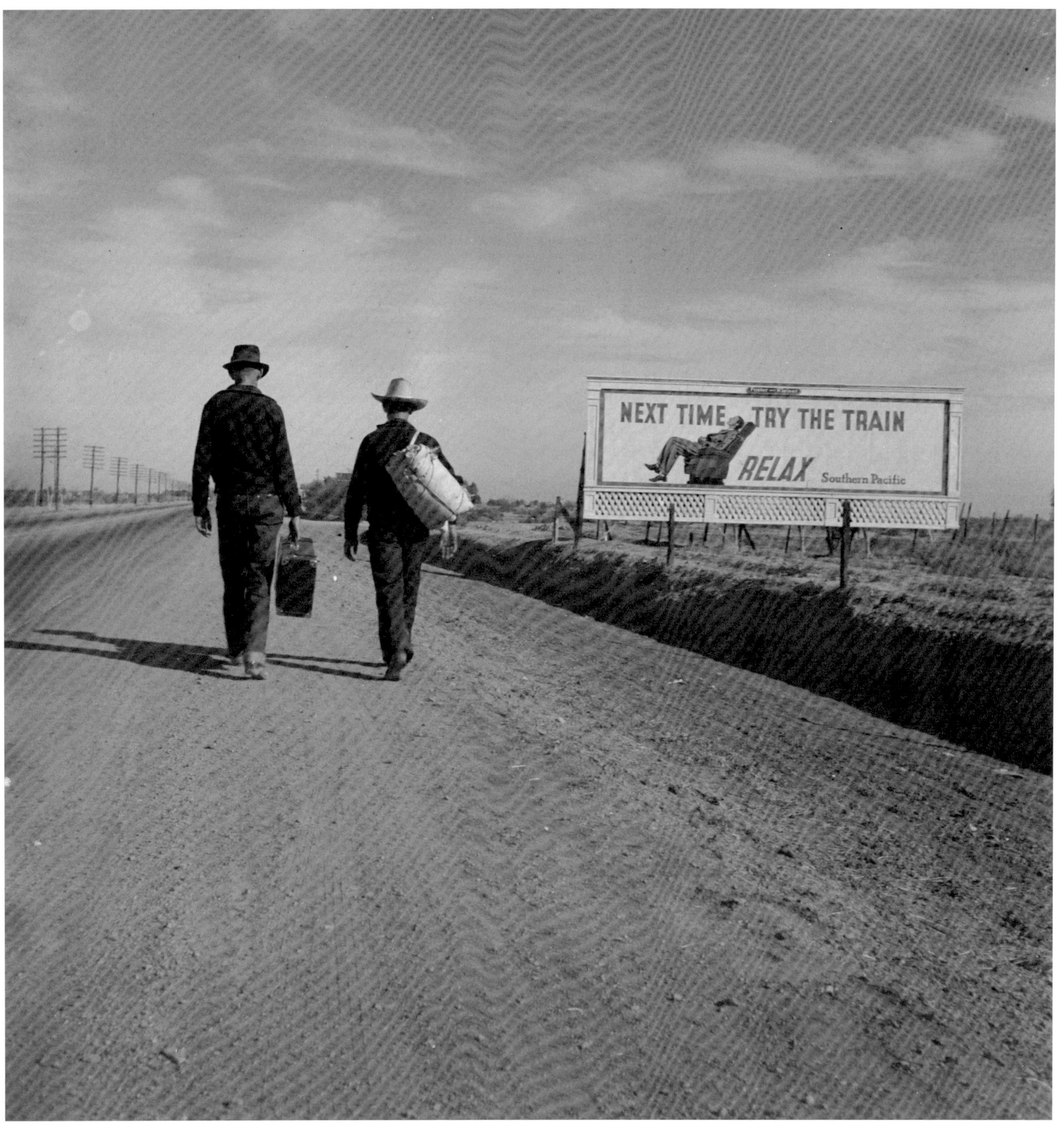
NEXT TIME TRY THE TRAIN
RELAX
Southern Pacific

***Facing*, Plate 52.** Toward Los Angeles, California.

Dorothea Lange. March 1937. Library of Congress, Prints & Photographs Division, FSA-OWI Collection, LC-USF34-016317-E.

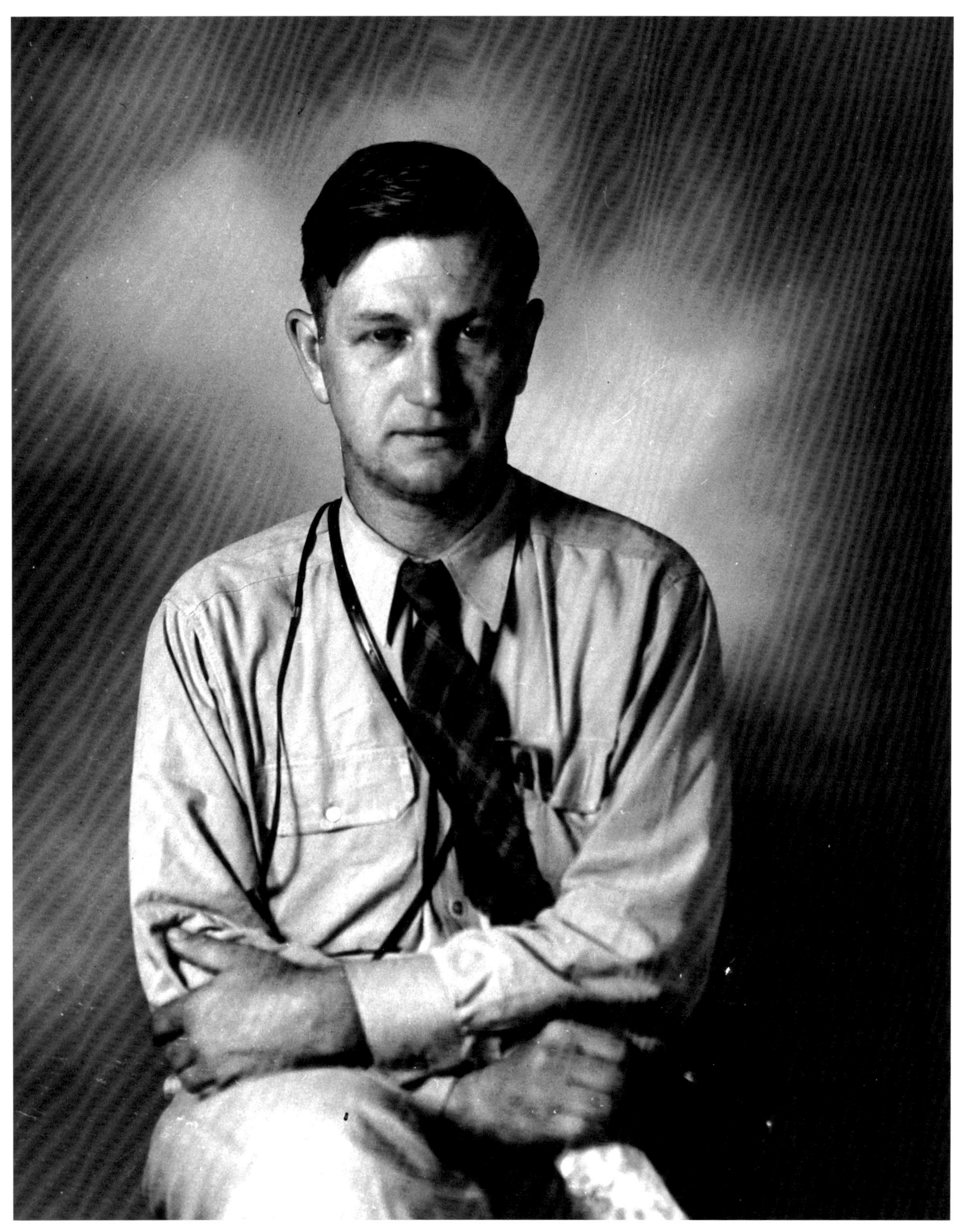

PORTFOLIO SIX

RUSSELL LEE

Russell "Russ" Lee's work as an FSA/OWI photographer is, in some ways, a paradox. Hired in 1936, Lee stayed with Roy Stryker until he joined the Army Air Forces as a photographer in late 1942.[1] Lee's images account for about a quarter of all the FSA/OWI images.[2] Lee's work, like that of most of the FSA photographers, includes a number of images focusing on tenant farmers.

Despite this record, Lee was a man of inherited wealth who probably did not need to work for a living. Much of his wealth derived from income from farms worked by Lee's tenants. Although he apparently treated his tenants well and helped keep his farms in good order, Lee derived great benefit from a type of worker, farm tenants, that he—and the FSA in general—documented in order to bring public attention to their sometimes desperate way of life.

Russ Lee was born in Ottawa, Illinois, in 1903. Despite his family's modest wealth, Lee endured tragedy as a child, seeing his mother run down and killed by a car in front of him when he was ten. His father was a troubled personality, and Lee was taken in by his maternal grandmother. She died of kidney disease in 1917, just as Lee was to enter a private boarding high school. Lee then had a number of different guardians, including his great-uncle, Milton Pope. When Pope died in 1920, he left substantial assets to his young ward.

After graduating from his prep school, Culver Military Academy, Lee entered Lehigh University in Pennsylvania, earning a degree in chemical engineering there. He took a job as a chemist after graduation, returning to Illinois. He married a woman from Ottawa, Doris Emrick, in 1927. The Lees seemed poised for a conventional and affluent life.

But they would take a very different tack. Doris was a painter, and Lee took up the art. Not needing to work to live, he resigned from his position—he was now a plant manager—to study painting full time. The Lees lived in the San Francisco area, then moved to Woodstock, New York, wintering in New York City.

Doris Lee gained some recognition as a painter, but Russ Lee did not. In 1935, Lee bought a then state-of-the-art 35 mm camera and began to pursue photography. In this medium, rather than painting, Lee found his muse.

***Facing,* Figure 6.1.** Portrait of Russell Lee, Farm Security Administration (FSA) photographer.

Circa 1942. Library of Congress, Prints & Photographs Division, FSA-OWI Collection, LC-USW3-019997-C.

A friend brought the Resettlement Administration's photography to Lee's attention, and with the help of Ben Shahn, he sought out Roy Stryker. When photographer Carl Mydans left Stryker's group for *Life* magazine in 1936, Stryker hired Russ Lee to replace him.

Lee spent the next six years with the FSA/OWI. After leaving the agency as it wound down during its OWI period, Lee served in World War II as a military photographer.

By that time, Lee and first wife Doris had divorced. She had long had an intimate relationship with her artistic mentor, Arthur Blanch, and she and Lee, who were also still lovers, lived in an open marriage. A chance encounter—like Marion Post meeting Lee Wolcott—was to change all this. In 1938, Lee met reporter Jean Smith while on an assignment in Louisiana. They became lovers, and Lee began taking her with him on FSA assignments. The difference between this arrangement and, for example, Jack and Irene Delano's was that Lee and Smith were not married; in fact, Smith was Lee's mistress. As awareness of the Doris Lee/Arthur Blanch/Russ Lee/Jean Smith scenario spread, Stryker pressured Lee to divorce Doris and marry Jean, who was also married to her estranged husband, reporter George Martin. Lee then divorced Doris, Smith divorced George Martin, and Lee and Smith married. They would remain together for the rest of Russ Lee's life.

Now living in Texas, his second wife's home state, Lee worked as a freelance photographer. A number of his assignments were for Roy Stryker's photography project at Standard Oil of New Jersey. Lee also did assignments for Stryker's projects with the Pittsburgh Photographic Library and Jones and Laughlin Steel. By the 1960s, Lee was retired from doing fieldwork, and he, along with many of his FSA/OWI counterparts, gained recognition as Stryker's photographic project garnered artistic notice such as "The Bitter Years: 1935–1941," an exhibit presented by New York's Museum of Modern Art (MOMA) in 1962.[3] Lee gained his first single-artist book in 1978 with the publication of F. Jack Hurley's *Russell Lee: Photographer.* Lee died of cancer at his home in Austin, Texas, in 1986.

Lee's photos for the FSA/OWI, and from his career following his work with those agencies, resemble Arthur Rothstein's and John Vachon's in terms of both the expanse of his work and his photojournalistic bent. Of the photographers featured in this book, these three perhaps best demonstrate a progression from government photographer to professional photojournalist. Lee is also notable for his early and creative use of flash photography.

This review of Lee's railroad-subject work for the FSA/OWI begins with an image of railroad workers taking a lunch break in Windsor Locks, Connecticut, which was located on the New York, New Haven and Hartford Railroad, plate 53. Plate 54 shows Black railroad workers taking a break at a very different place, Port Barre, Louisiana, on the Missouri Pacific Railroad, while plate 55 shows three Black men sitting on the railroad station platform at New Roads, Louisiana. New Roads was on the Texas and Pacific Railway.

Images of railroad track workers—"section gangs"—are relatively scarce. Plate 56 is Lee's image of a railroad gang in Texas, including a hammer-driver with a spike hammer at the left third of the image. It is notable that we are in the Southern US and the section workers depicted are not Black.[4]

Plates 57 and 58 continue to demonstrate the broad geographic and subject range of Lee's work. Plate 57 shows a train dispatcher at work in an office in San Augustine, Texas, while plate 58 shows a log train passing a lumber camp in Forest County, Wisconsin.[5]

Plates 59–67 are a short photo-essay demonstrating Lee's extensive work on the Colorado narrow-gauge railroads: work that is not extensive enough to form a book but that could easily stand as an article on its own. Plates 59 and 60 show the now-vanished role of US railroads in shipping livestock, scenes taken on the Denver and Rio Grande Western in Cimarron, Colorado. Plate 61 shows a narrow-gauge train with a lead engine and a helper some cars back. The image caption states the photo was taken in Ouray County—the locomotive is Rio Grande Southern 455, acquired from the Denver and Rio Grande Western in 1939.[6] Plate 62 demonstrates another key role of the US railroad: hauling the products of mines and quarries, in this case gold ore concentrate being loaded on the Denver and Rio Grande Western in Ouray, Colorado.

Like plate 61, plates 63–67 take us to the fabled Rio Grande Southern Railroad, which took a circuitous path from Durango north to Ridgway, Colorado. Plates 63, 64, and 65 show an uncommon Rio Grande Southern topic, its branch to Telluride,

Colorado. Plate 66 is an iconic view of the Rio Grande Southern depot at Ophir, Colorado. Plate 67 shows what Lee called a "motor locomotive": this is the homegrown Rio Grande Southern motorcar No. 2, better known as a "Galloping Goose."[7]

Plate 68 takes us to the Pacific Northwest, showing a logging railroad locomotive in Baker, Oregon, a town best known for its narrow-gauge railroad, the Sumpter Valley Railway.

Much of Lee's work for the FSA/OWI focused on disadvantaged Americans. The FSA's involvement with the evacuation of Japanese Americans from the Pacific Coast during World War II led to Lee's documenting this action authorized by an executive order of President Franklin Delano Roosevelt. Most of the resettlement of Japanese Americans to inland "relocation centers" was by train. The final image in this portfolio, plate 69, shows a well-dressed Japanese American mother and child waiting for the train that will take them away from their home in Los Angeles to such a center.

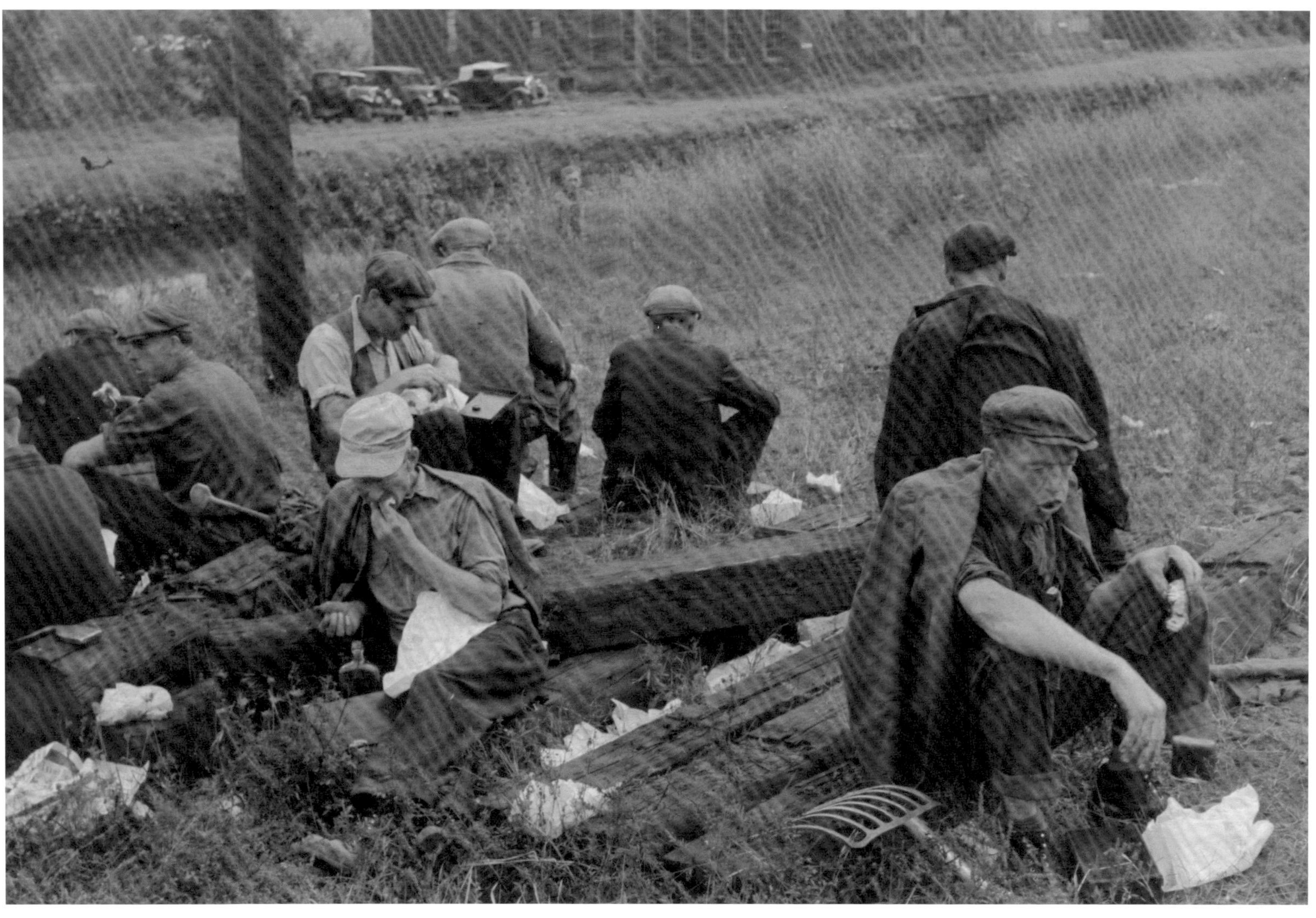

Plate 53. Railroad workers eating lunch along the railroad tracks. Windsor Locks, Connecticut.

Russell Lee. October 1939. Library of Congress, Prints & Photographs Division, FSA-OWI Collection, LC-USF33-012438-M1.

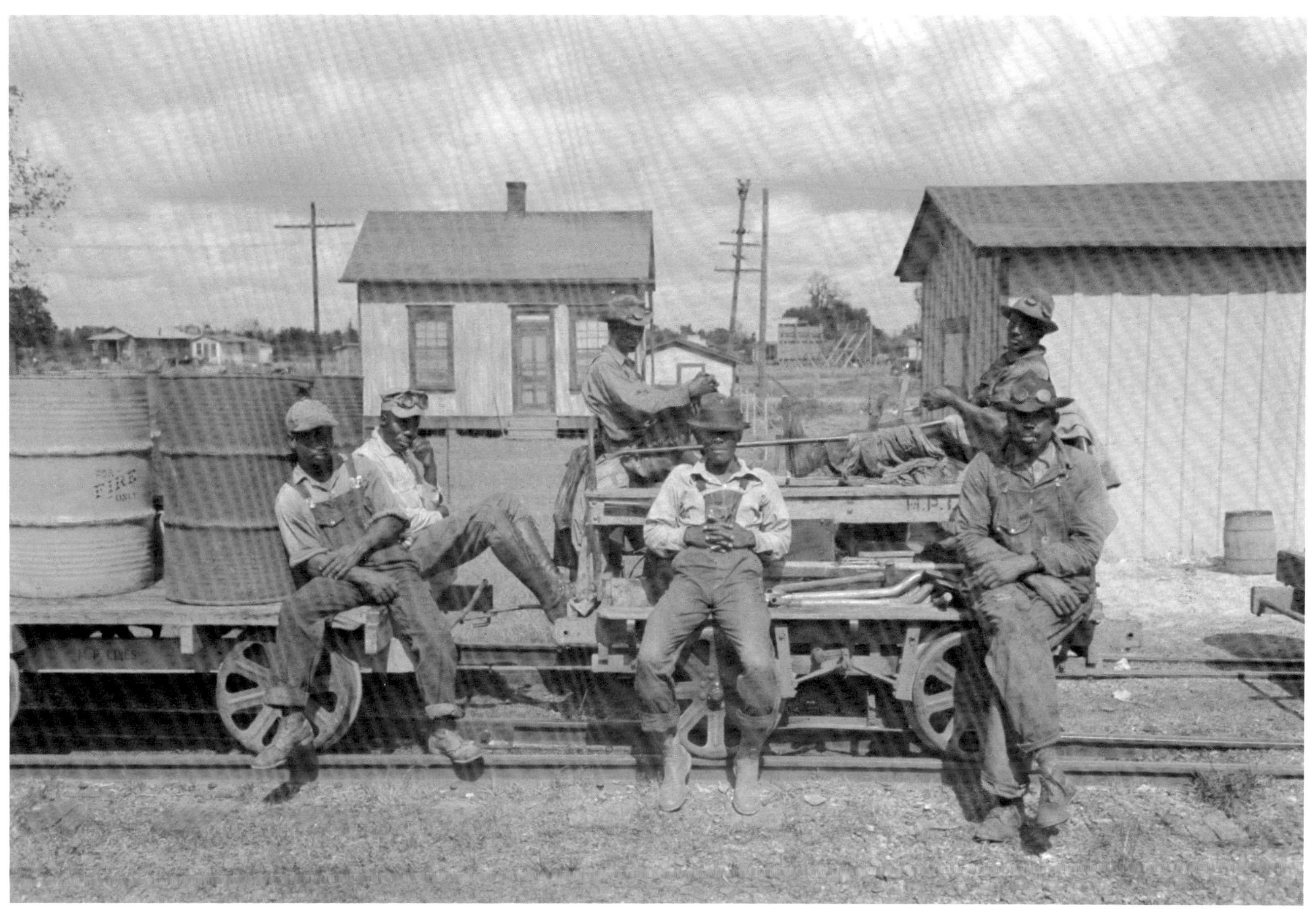

Plate 54. Railroad workers, Port Barre, Louisiana.

Russell Lee. October 1938. Library of Congress, Prints & Photographs Division, FSA-OWI Collection, LC-USF33-011870-M4.

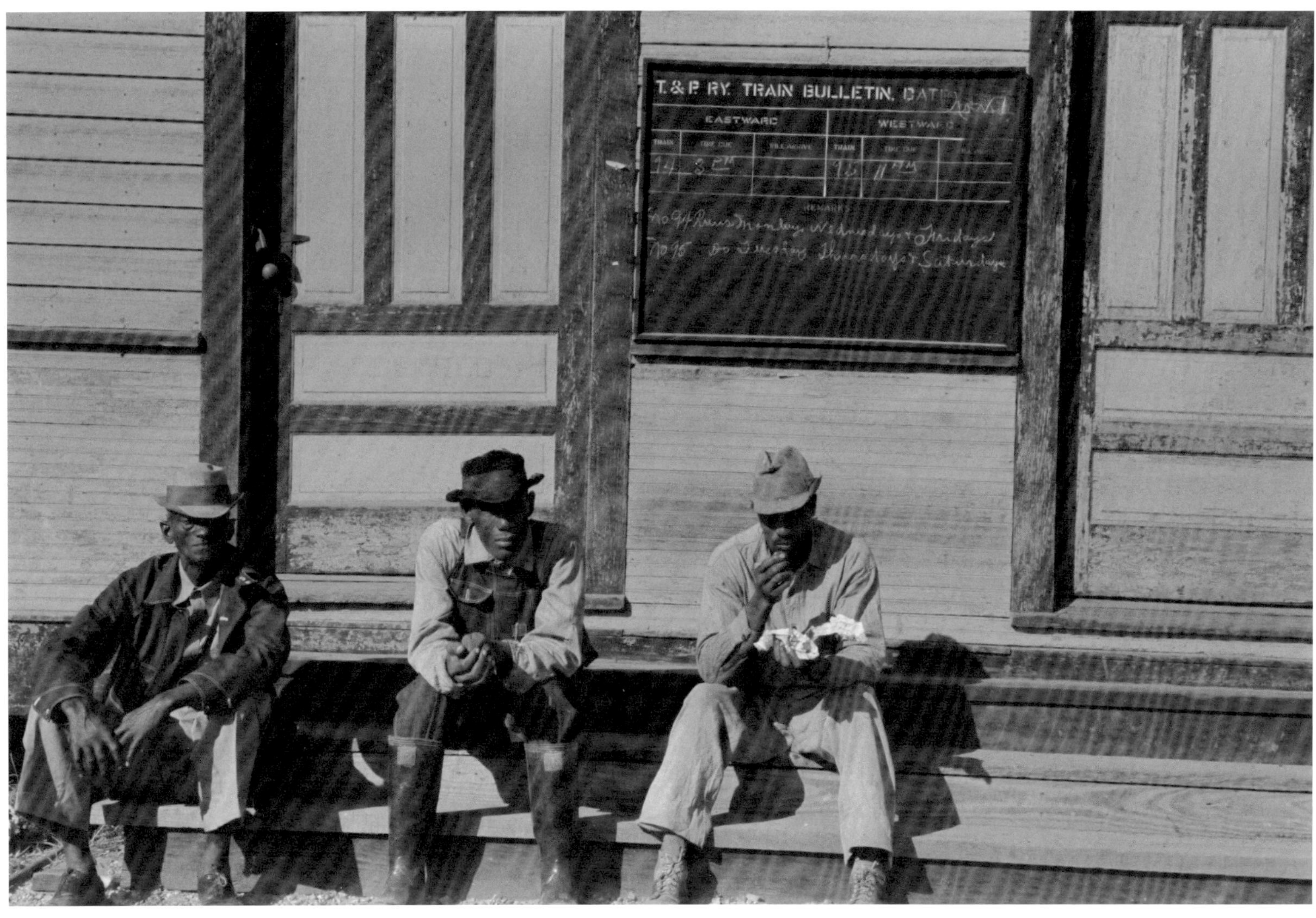

Plate 55. Black men sitting on foot of the T&P (Texas and Pacific) railroad station, New Roads, Louisiana. Note frequency of train operations.

Russell Lee. November 1938. Library of Congress, Prints & Photographs Division, FSA-OWI Collection, LC-USF33-011903-M2.

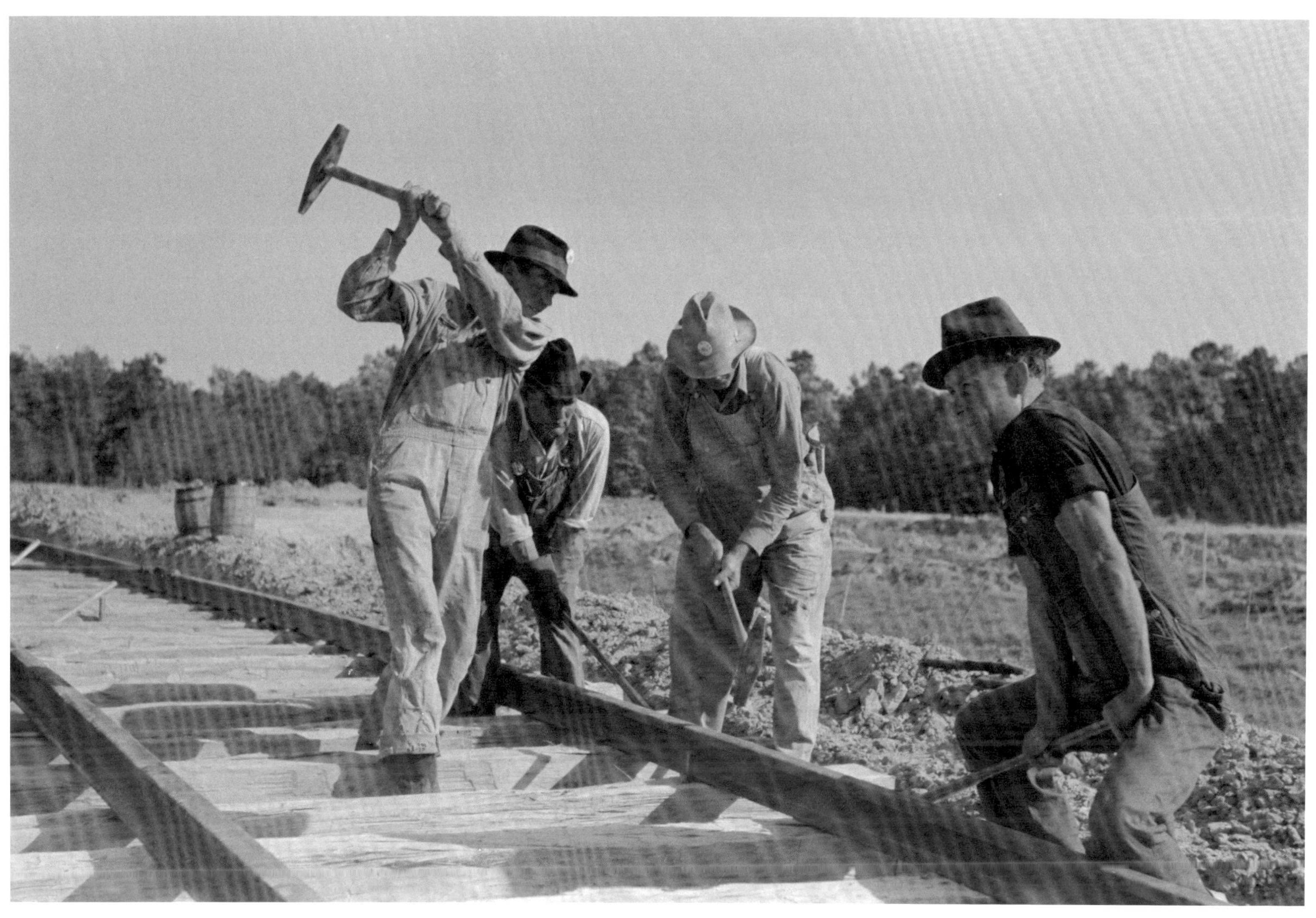

Plate 56. Railroad gang, Southern Paper Mill construction crew. Lufkin, Texas.

Russell Lee. April 1939. Library of Congress, Prints & Photographs Division, FSA-OWI Collection, LC-USF33-012161-M2.

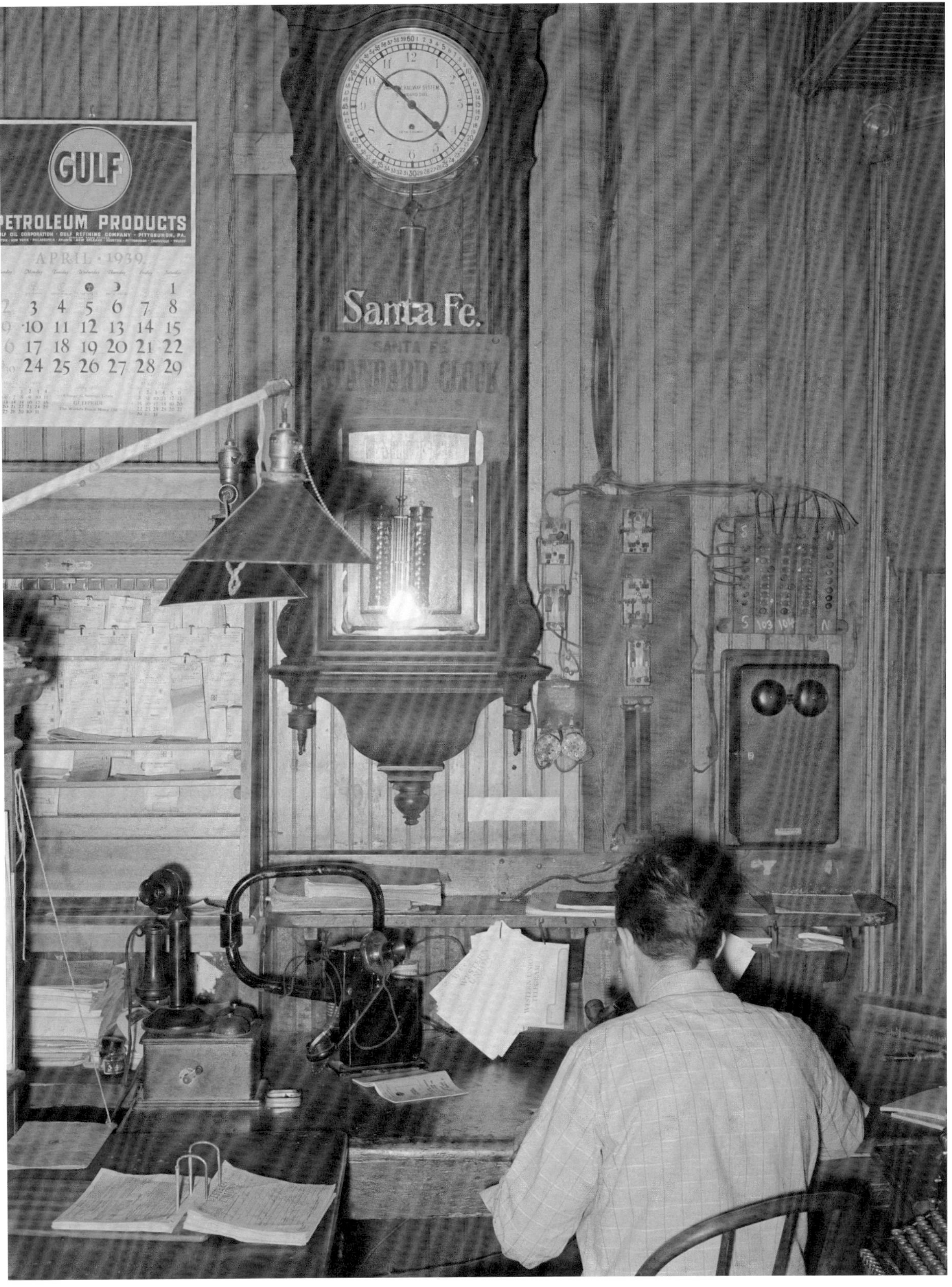

***Left,* Plate 57.** Office of train dispatcher and Western Union. San Augustine, Texas.

Russell Lee. April 1939. Library of Congress, Prints & Photographs Division, FSA-OWI Collection, LC-USF34-032989-D.

***Facing,* Plate 58.** The log train passes through the lumber camp en route to Rhinelander, Wisconsin, where the sawmill of the lumber camp is located. Forest County, Wisconsin.

Russell Lee. April or May 1937. Library of Congress, Prints & Photographs Division, FSA-OWI Collection, LC-USF34-010784-E.

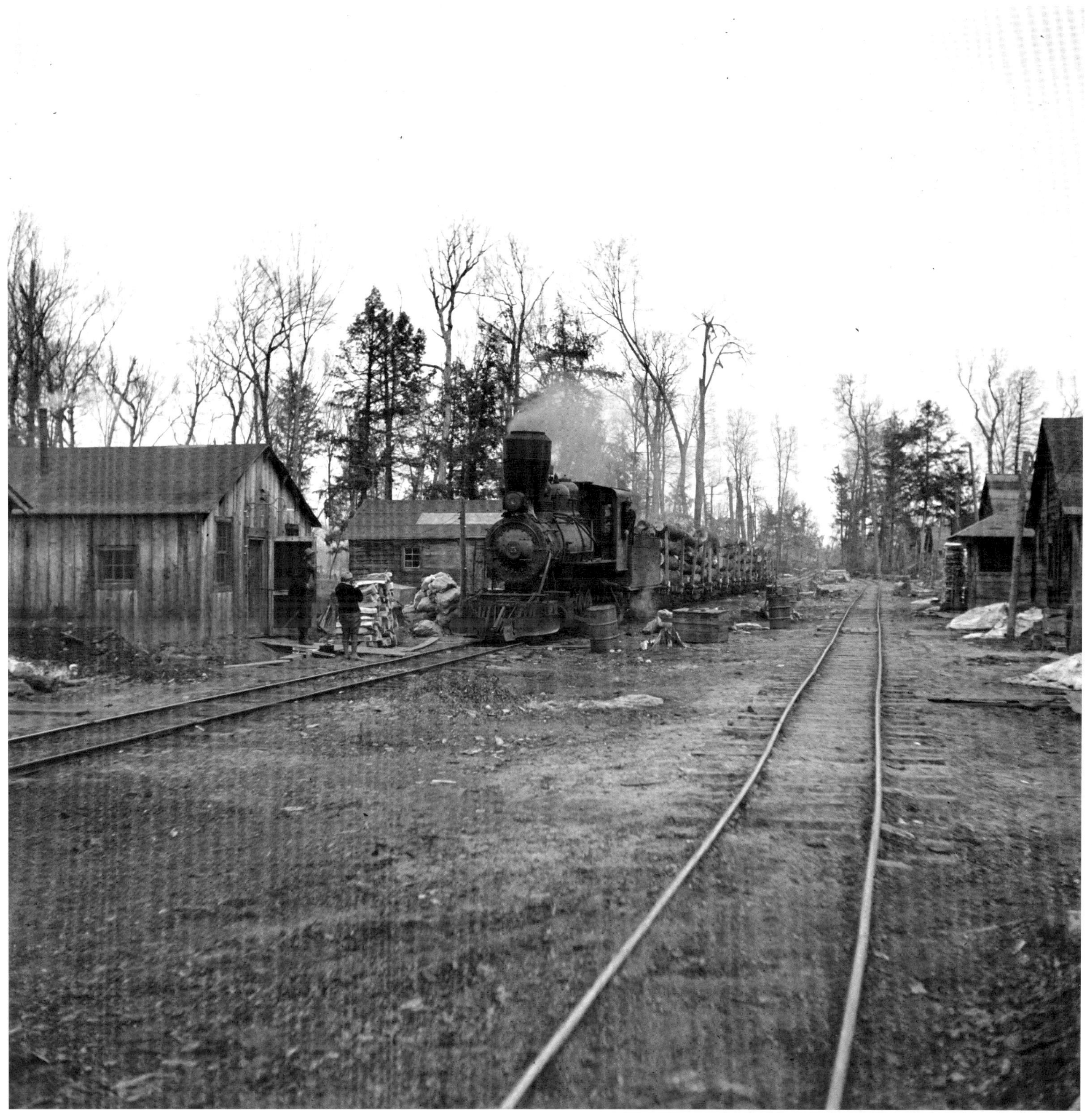

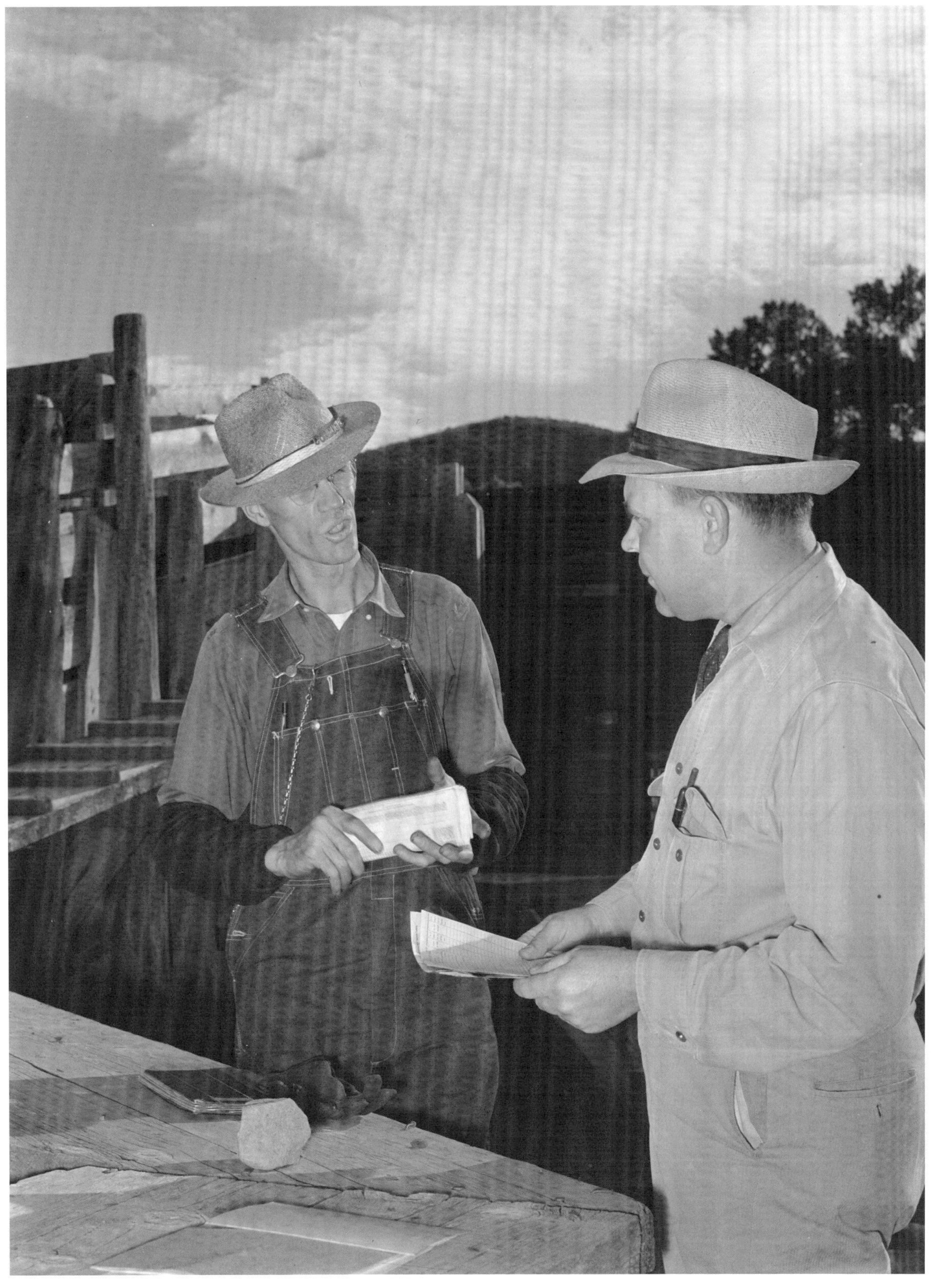

Plate 59. Freight train conductor talking to railroad man who was in charge of shipping livestock. Cimarron, Colorado.

Russell Lee. September 1940. Library of Congress, Prints & Photographs Division, FSA-OWI Collection, LC-USF34-037492-D.

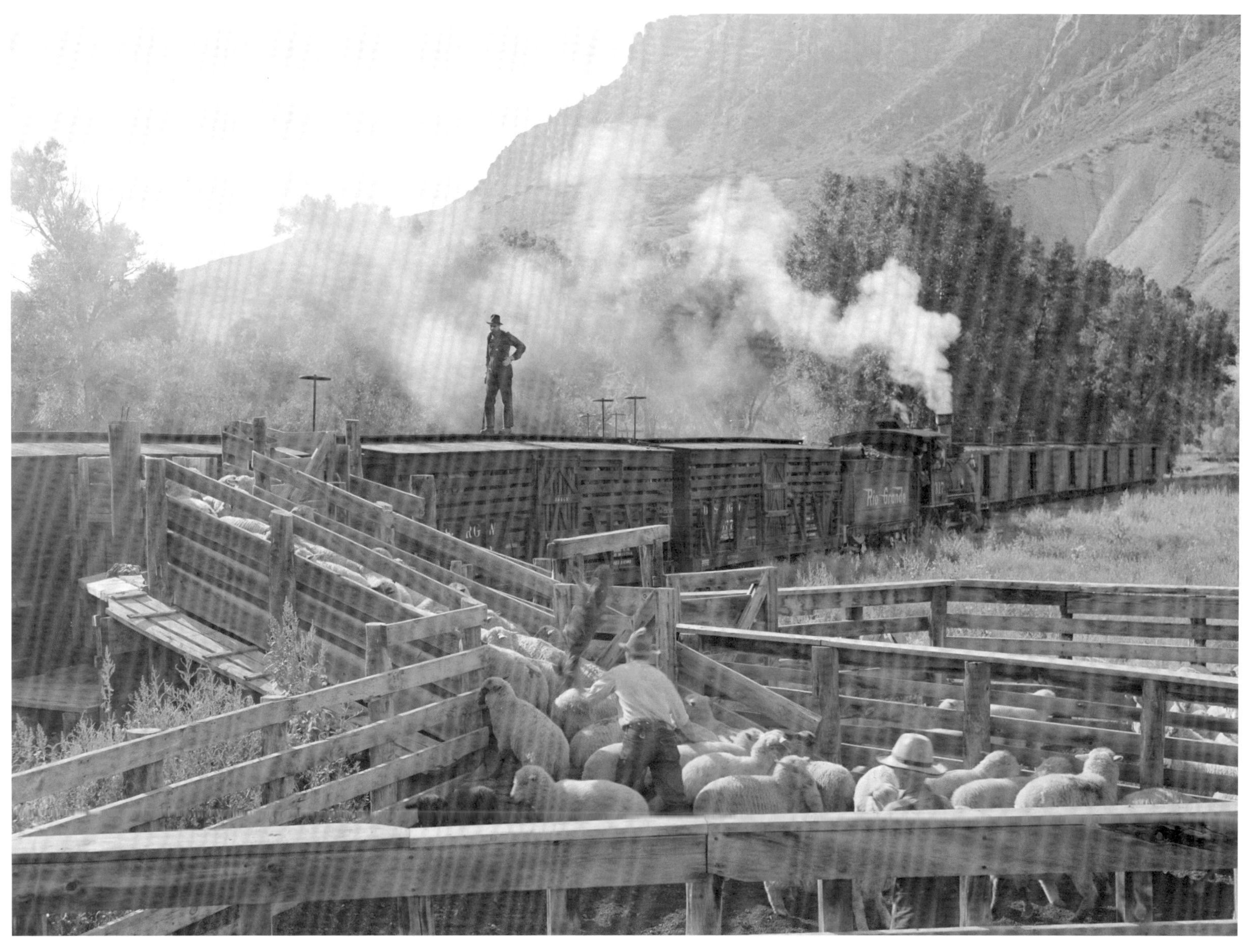

Plate 60. Loading fat lambs on narrow-gauge railway for shipment to Denver market. Cimarron, Colorado.

Russell Lee. September 1940. Library of Congress, Prints & Photographs Division, FSA-OWI Collection, LC-USF347-037468-C.

Plate 61. Train coming up the valley on a narrow gauge track, Ouray County, Colorado. Notice the two engines.

Russell Lee. September 1940. Library of Congress, Prints & Photographs Division, FSA-OWI Collection, LC-USF33-012910-M1.

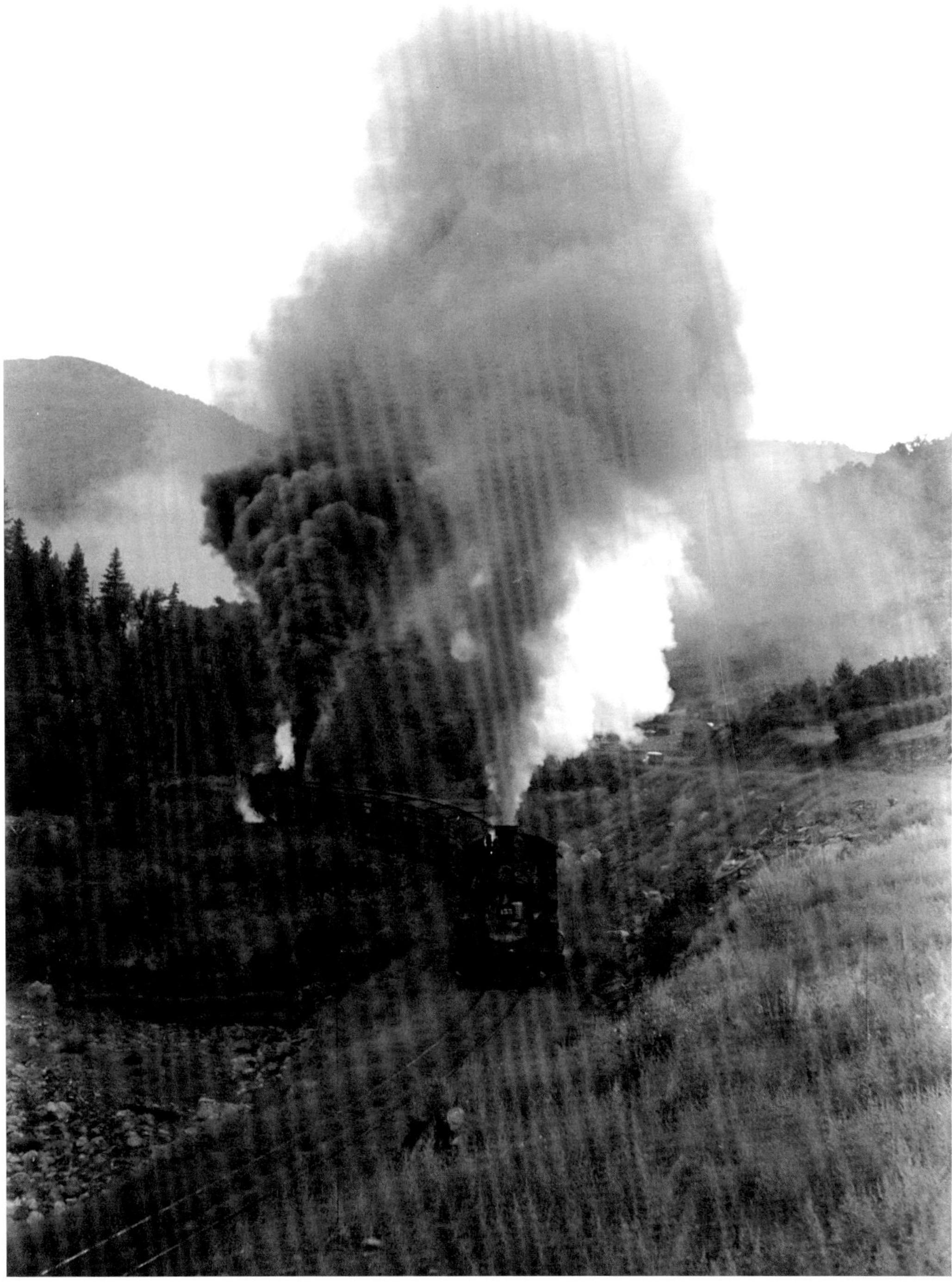

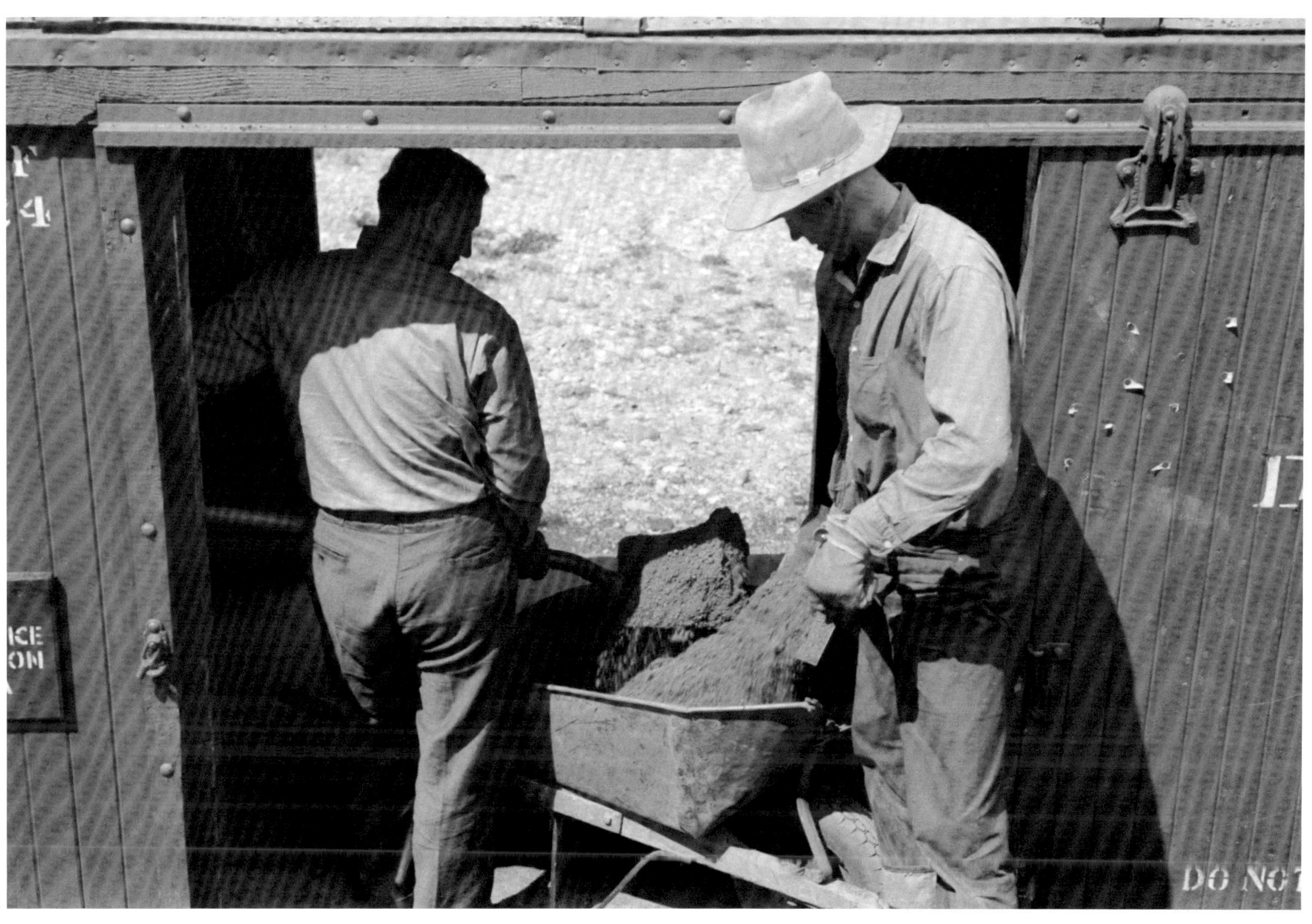

Plate 62. Loading gold ore concentrate into freight cars of narrow-gauge railroad. Ouray, Colorado.

Russell Lee. September 1940. Library of Congress, Prints & Photographs Division, FSA-OWI Collection, LC-USF33-012896-M1.

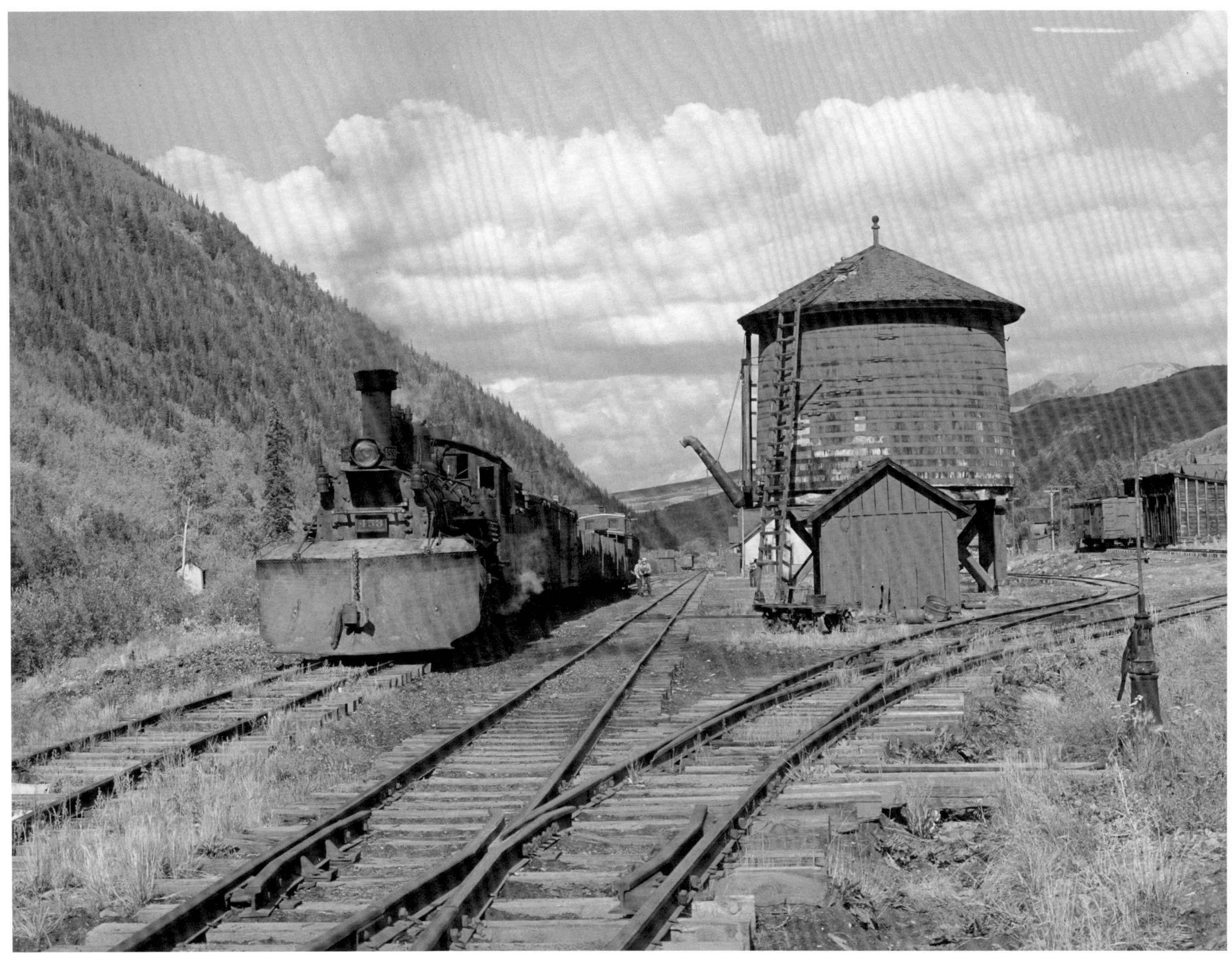

Plate 63. Narrow-gauge railway yards, train, and water tank at Telluride, Colorado.

Russell Lee. September 1940. Library of Congress, Prints & Photographs Division, FSA-OWI Collection, LC-USF34-037454-D.

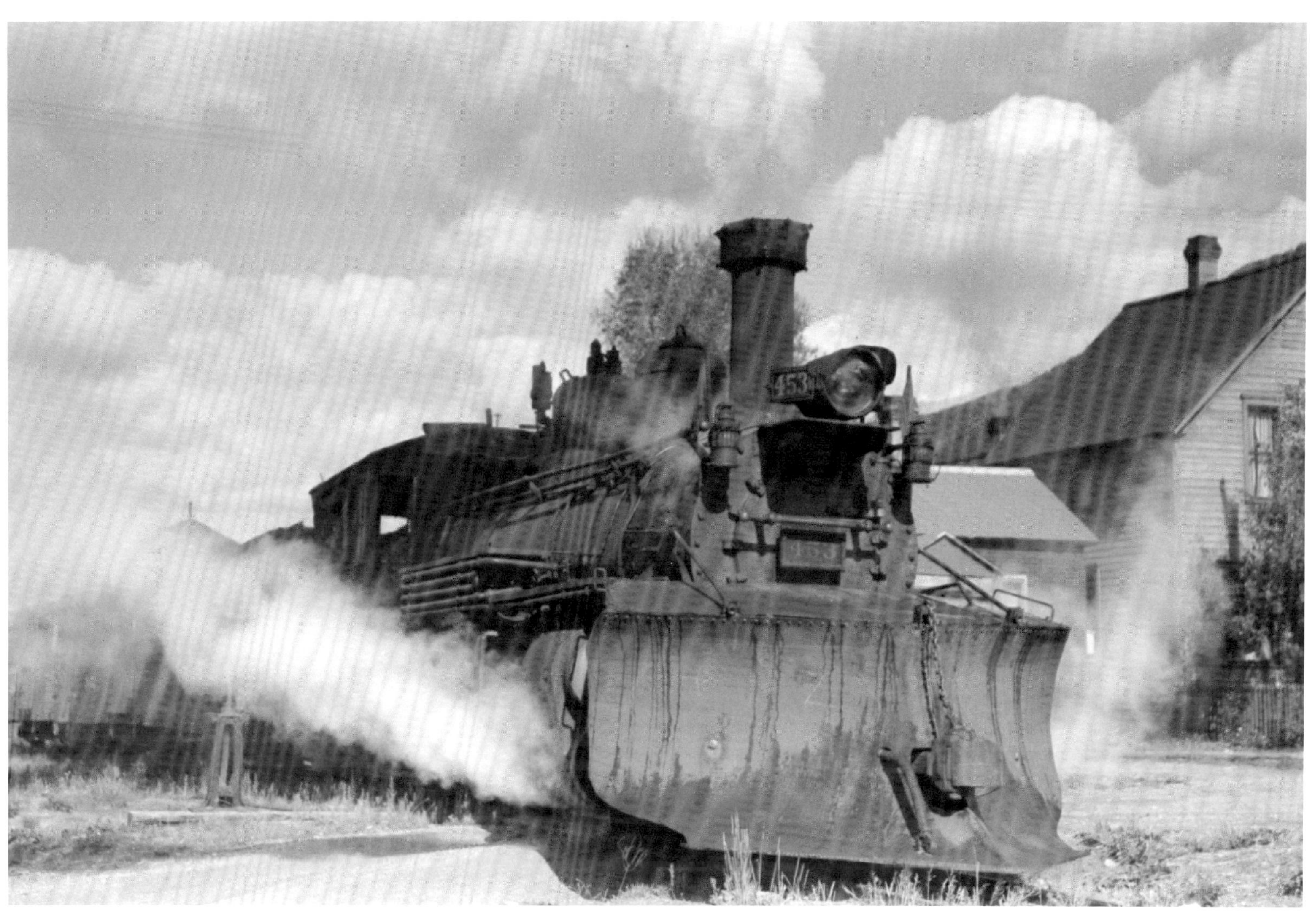

Plate 64. Locomotive with snowplow of narrow-gauge railroad, Telluride, Colorado.

Russell Lee. September 1940. Library of Congress, Prints & Photographs Division, FSA-OWI Collection, LC-USF33-012895-M3.

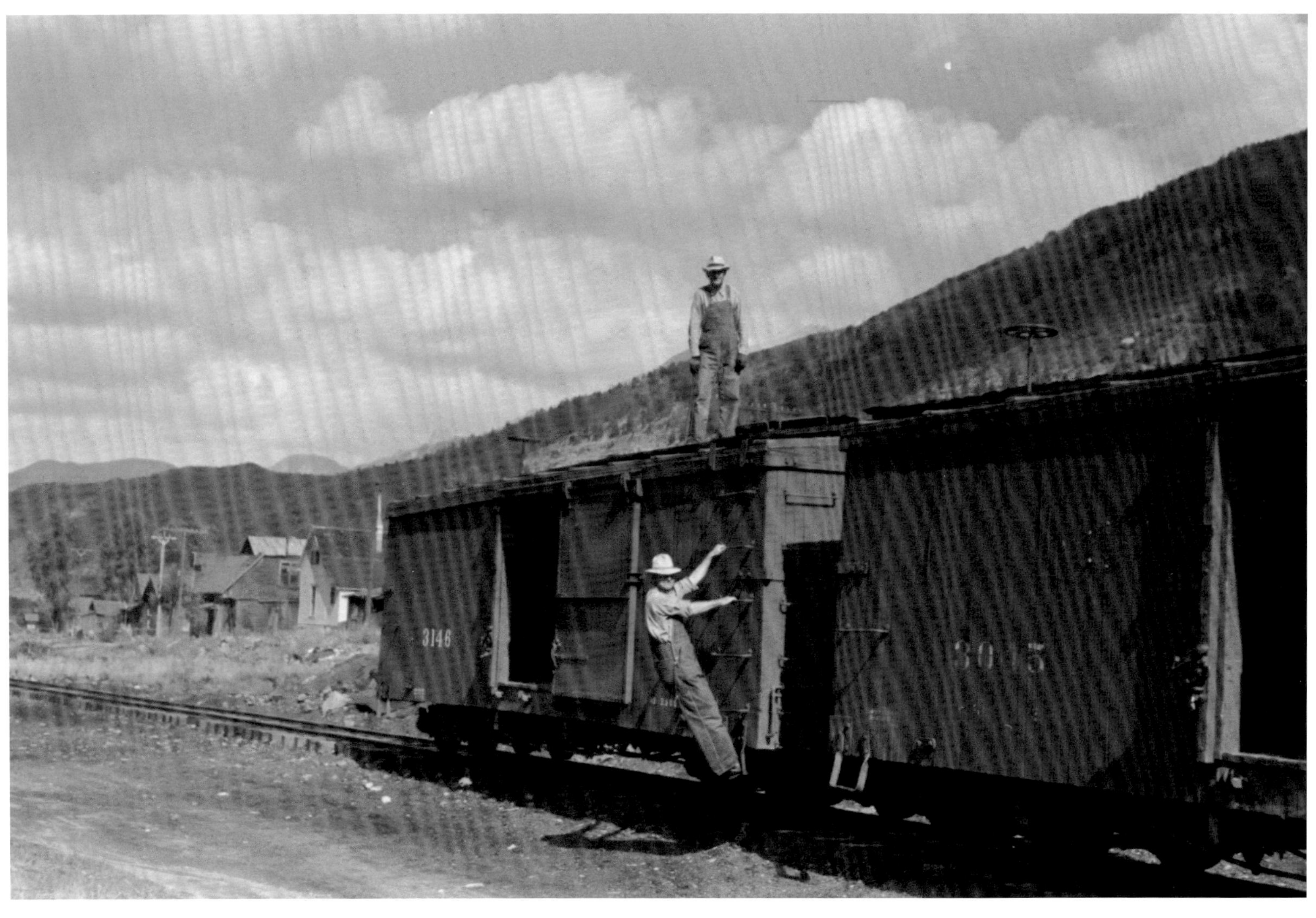

Plate 65. Freight cars of narrow-gauge railway, Telluride, Colorado.

Russell Lee. September 1940. Library of Congress, Prints & Photographs Division, FSA-OWI Collection, LC-USF33-012895-M2.

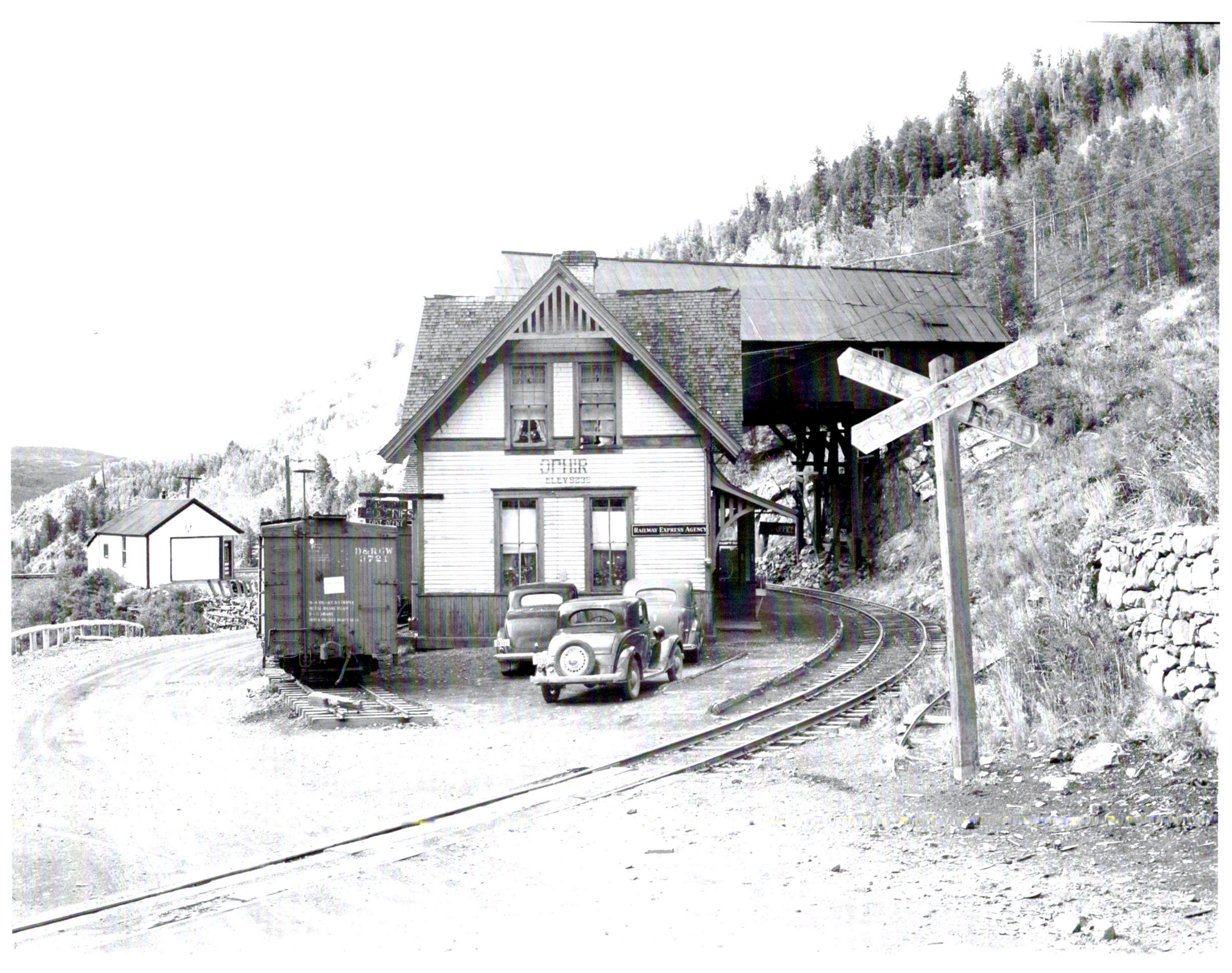

Plate 66. Railway station at Ophir, Colorado.

Russell Lee. September 1940. Library of Congress, Prints & Photographs Division, FSA-OWI Collection, LC-USF34-037642-D.

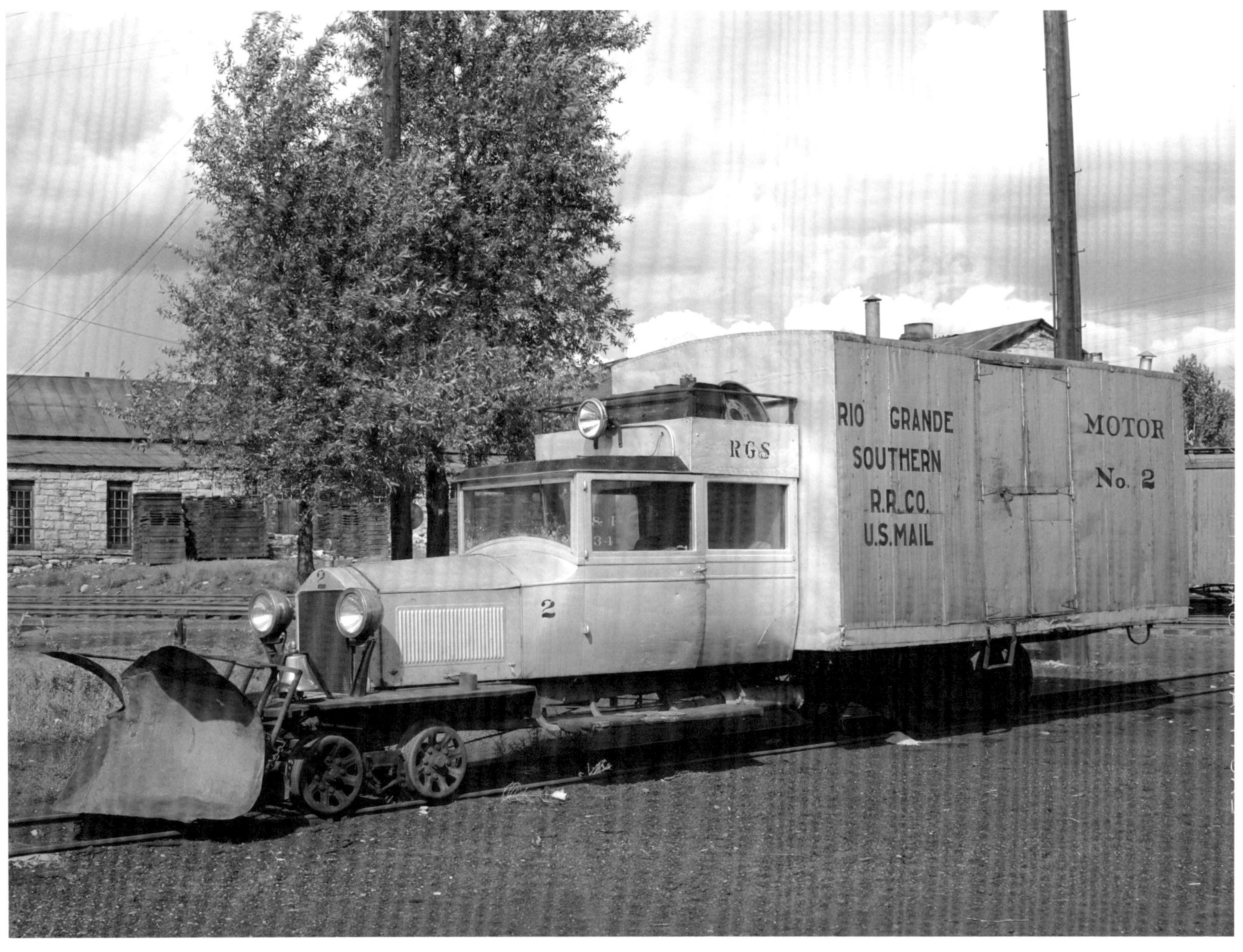

Plate 67. Motor locomotive of railroad equipped with snowplow. Durango, Colorado.

Russell Lee. September 1940. Library of Congress, Prints & Photographs Division, FSA-OWI Collection, LC-USF34-037777-D.

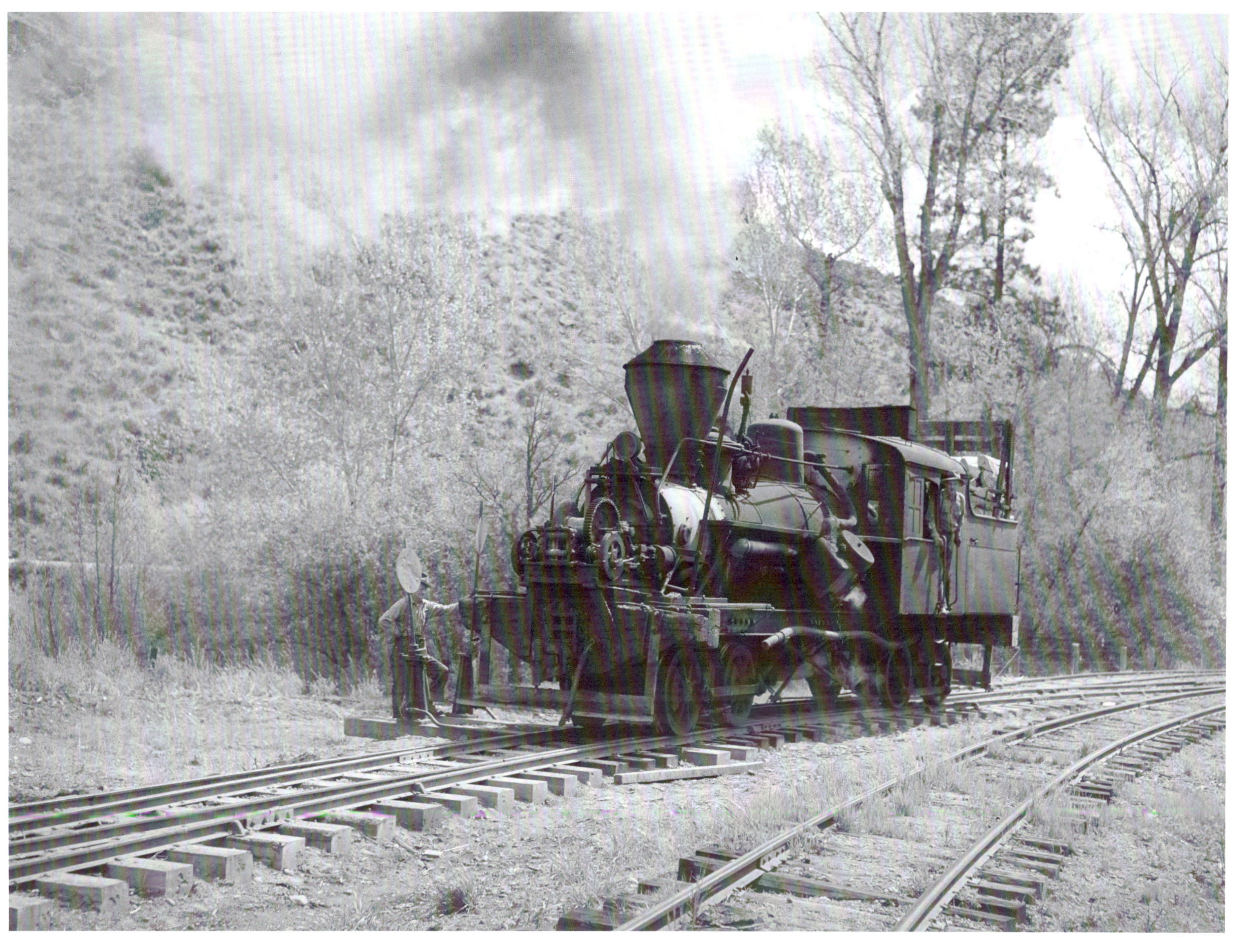

Plate 68. Locomotive of logging train. Baker County, Oregon.

Russell Lee. May 1941. Library of Congress, Prints & Photographs Division, FSA-OWI Collection, LC-USF34-038914-D.

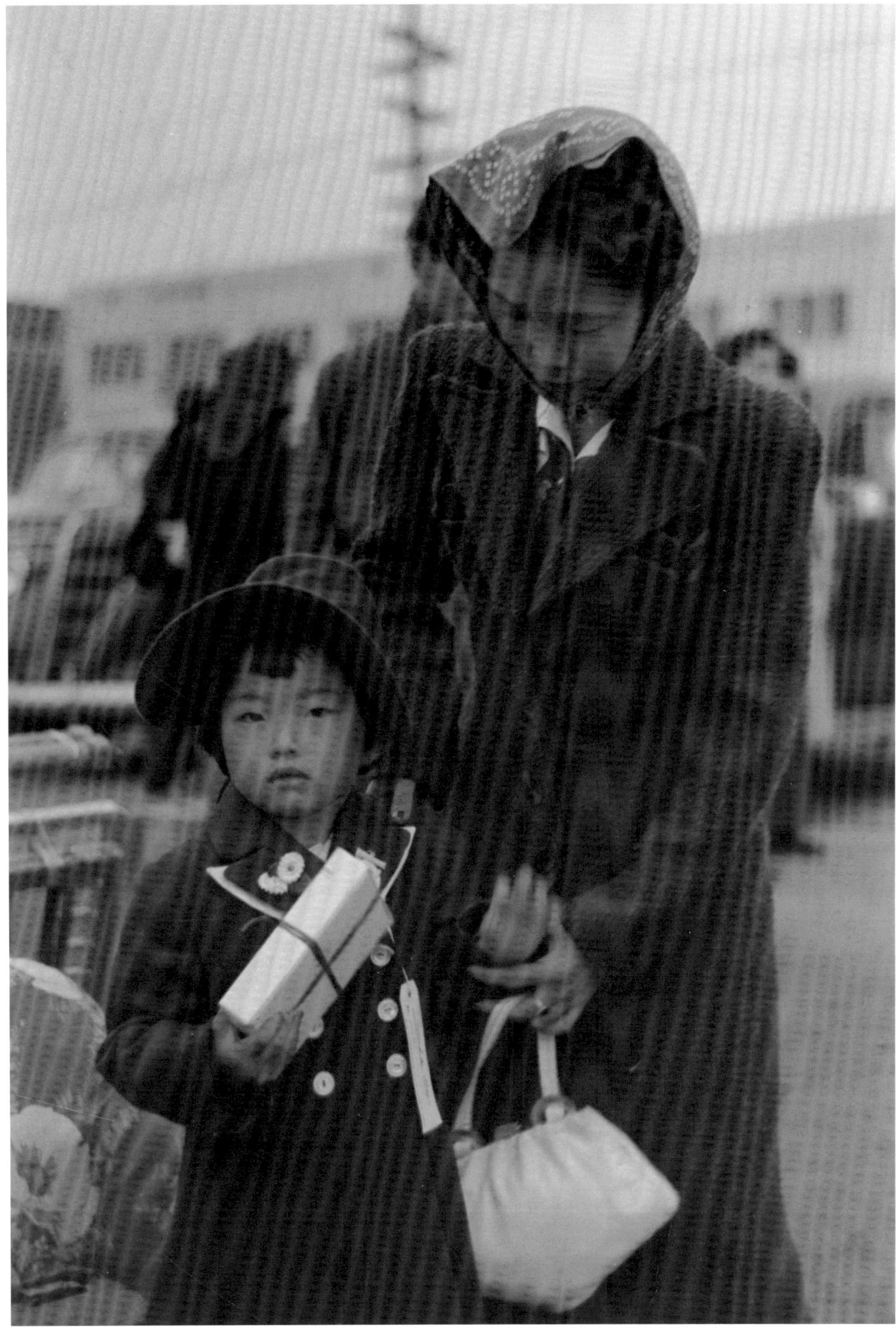

Plate 69. Untitled photo, possibly related to: Los Angeles, California. The evacuation of the Japanese Americans from West Coast areas under US Army war emergency order. Waiting at the old Santa Fe station for the train that will take them to Owens Valley.

Russell Lee. April 1942. Library of Congress, Prints & Photographs Division, FSA-OWI Collection, LC-USF33-013286-M4.

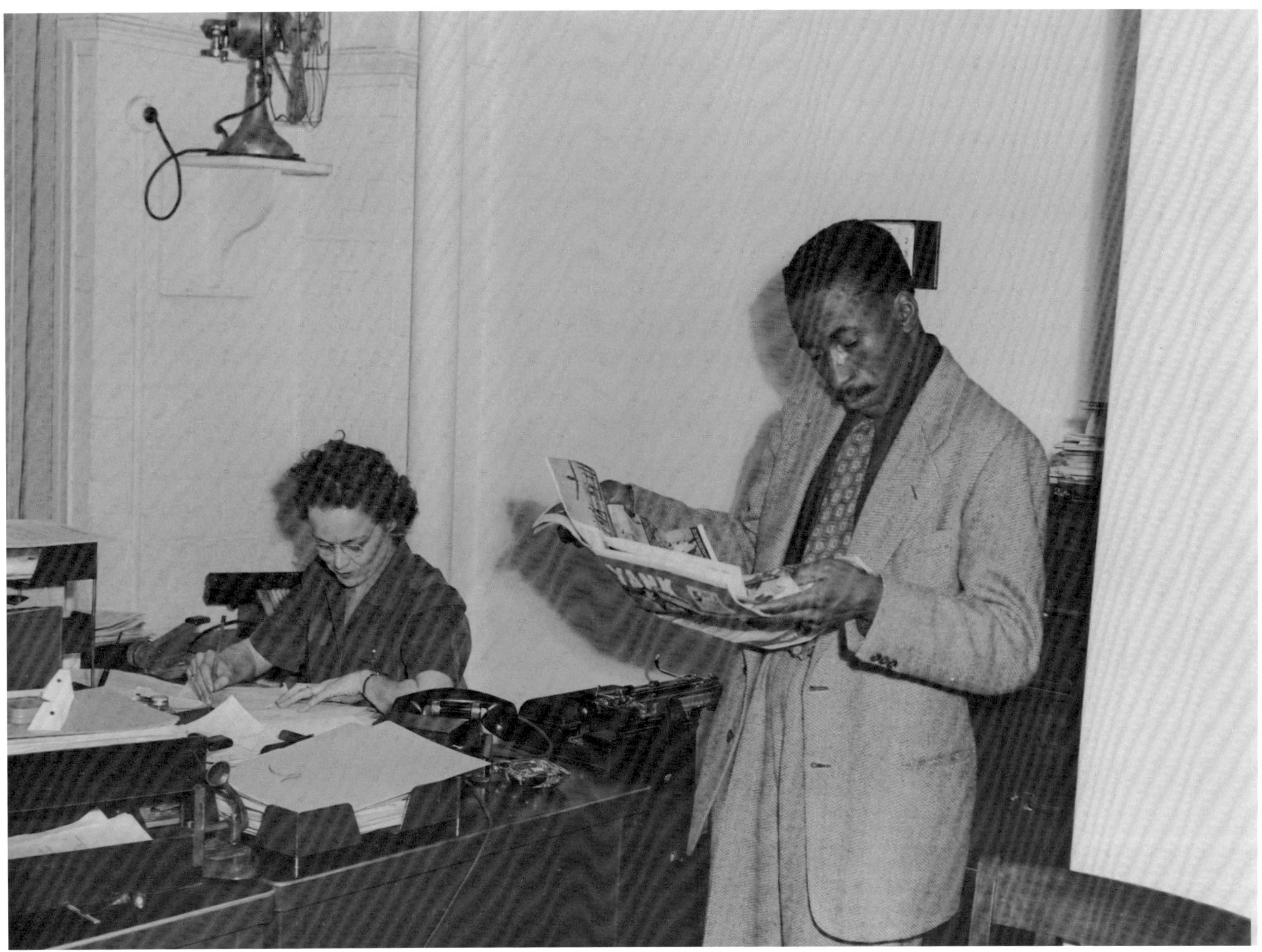

Figure 7.1. Gordon Parks, Farm Security Administration / Office of War Information photographer, standing in office with Helen Wool seated at desk.

Circa 1943. Library of Congress, Prints & Photographs Division, FSA-OWI Collection, LC-USZ62-121074.

PORTFOLIO SEVEN

GORDON PARKS

In 1941, a freelance fashion photographer named Gordon Parks was eking out a living in Chicago, Illinois. His concern for social and racial justice—Parks was an African American originally from Kansas—led him to document the conditions in the city's infamous South Side slums. This work resulted in his being awarded a Julius Rosenwald Fellowship that allowed him to join the FSA and its successor, the OWI.[1]

FSA photographer Jack Delano was instrumental in finding Parks a place at the FSA. Although different in many ways, the men also shared similarities: both faced widespread discrimination (legalized segregation faced Parks in much of the US at the time; Delano, who was a Jewish immigrant, faced discrimination that was real, if perhaps more subtle), both were making their living as photographers, and both shared a focus on depicting the disadvantaged members of American society. Both men were multitalented and found places as musicians, composers, filmmakers, and authors in addition to being photographers.[2]

If Delano is best known for his portraits, Parks is notable for two lines of photographic work. One, which seems natural for an artist of his background, is coverage of people, largely people of color, disadvantaged by their race/ethnicity and by their poverty. The other is fashion/celebrity photography, including images of Gloria Vanderbilt, Ingrid Bergman, Marilyn Monroe, and many noted fashion models of the day. This work by Parks bears comparison with works by contemporaries such as Richard Avedon and Irving Penn.

Parks's variety of accomplishments is also notable. After leaving the OWI, he worked as a photographer for *Vogue*, for Stryker's photographic project at Standard Oil of New Jersey, and for *Life*. He wrote books on photography and moviemaking, autobiographies, books of poetry, and a noted novel, *The Learning Tree*, as well as other works. The film adaptation of *The Learning Tree* led to Parks's career as a Hollywood film director; he also directed *Shaft*, *Shaft's Big Score*, *The Super Cops*, and *Leadbelly*.[3] Parks's musical compositions include a concerto, a symphony, and the music and libretto for a ballet, *Martin*. At the very end of his life, Parks returned to photography, producing abstract images. Parks lived in New York City when he died of cancer in 2006. He is buried in his hometown, Fort Scott, Kansas.

In late 1942, Jack Delano's boss, Roy Stryker, sent him to Chicago to document the role of the railroad industry in the US war effort. One of the key parts of Delano's assignment was to document wartime activity in Chicago's Union Station. At the same time, in November 1942, and a third of a continent away, Gordon Parks shouldered a similar assignment as he documented Washington, DC's Union Station for Stryker and the OWI. But Parks faced a very different situation: he was a Black photographer working in a segregated Southern city, depicting GIs who were white and Black and drawn from other races as well. Unlike his colleague FSA/OWI photographers, Parks also brought personal knowledge to railroad-subject assignments, having served as a porter on the Northern Pacific Railway.[4]

The terrain of a segregated America was nothing new to Parks, and he would continue to work within it: one of his major assignments for the OWI was documenting the 332nd Fighter Group of the US Army Air Forces, the famed Tuskegee Airmen. His OWI oeuvre includes one of the greatest FSA/OWI images, *American Gothic*.[5]

Parks would go on to shoot another railroad-subject portfolio for the OWI (see plates 74–76). These images are much more technically proficient; in fact, almost all of them are publication ready. Parks's technique, under Stryker's masterful direction, had advanced greatly in less than a year. Parks then left the segregated atmosphere of World War II–era Washington, DC, moving to New York City's Harlem neighborhood and finding a position as a fashion photographer for *Glamour* and *Vogue*.

Plates 70–73 exemplify Parks's coverage of Union Station in Washington, DC, during World War II. Like the OWI images taken at great railroad stations in New York and Chicago, the intent seems to be to show American infrastructure strained by war demands but succeeding. There is something more present in these images, however—something perhaps routine today but startling and challenging in then-segregated Washington, DC: Blacks and whites interacting as equals. Look at, for example, plate 71, where a nattily dressed Black serviceman is assisted while a white woman waits just to his left.

Gordon Parks was noted for his appreciation of the female form, and an early view of this factor of his work may be seen in plates 74–76, which provide a sample of Parks's portfolio featuring women working for a railroad express company in New Britain, Connecticut. These were taken on the New York, New Haven and Hartford Railroad during World War II. As is often the case with OWI images intended to show the solidarity of Americans fighting the Axis, the women in the photos are identified by nationality. Parks says in his captions that the women were working for the "American Railway Express Company," but the name of the company at the time was Railway Express Agency.

This portfolio of Gordon Parks's railroad-subject work closes with plate 77, showing a female railroader, a crossing watcher, on the job at the same location, New Britain, Connecticut.

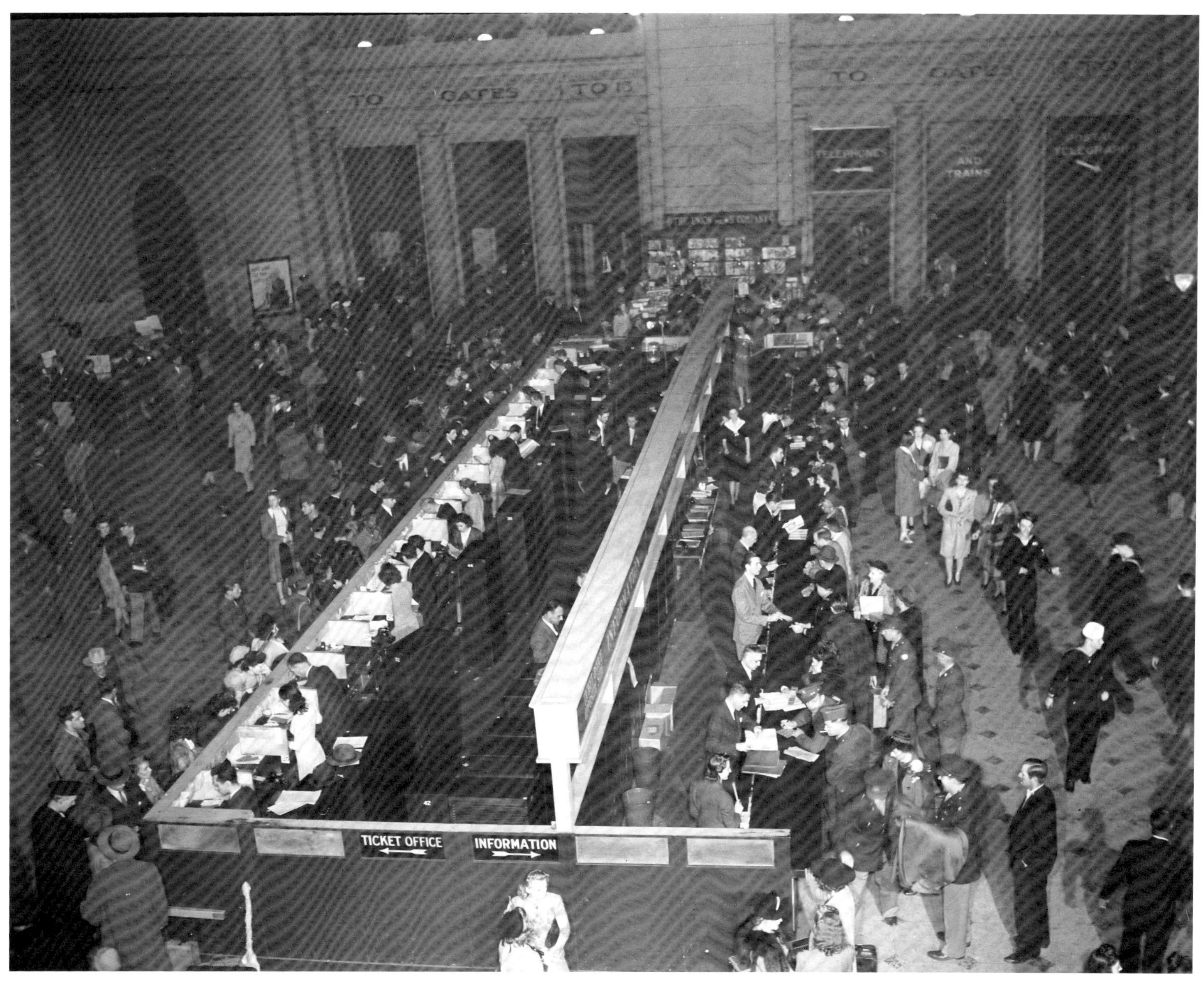

Plate 70 Washington, DC. Ticket office and information desk at the Union Station.

Gordon Parks. November 1942. Library of Congress, Prints & Photographs Division, FSA-OWI Collection, LC-USW3-011393-C.

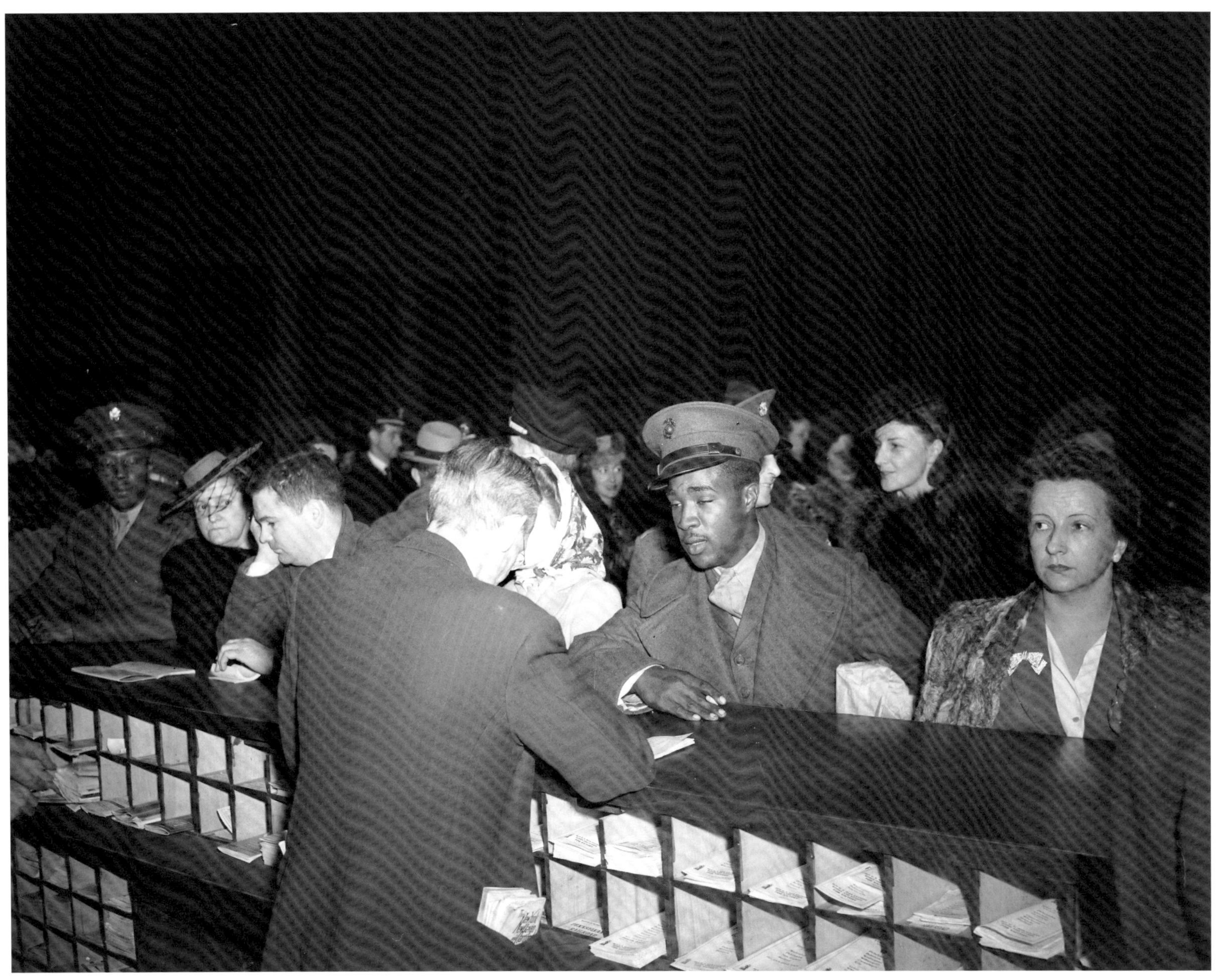

Plate 71. Washington, DC. Soldiers and civilians purchasing tickets at the Union Station.

Gordon Parks. November 1942. Library of Congress, Prints & Photographs Division, FSA-OWI Collection, LC-USW3-012121-C.

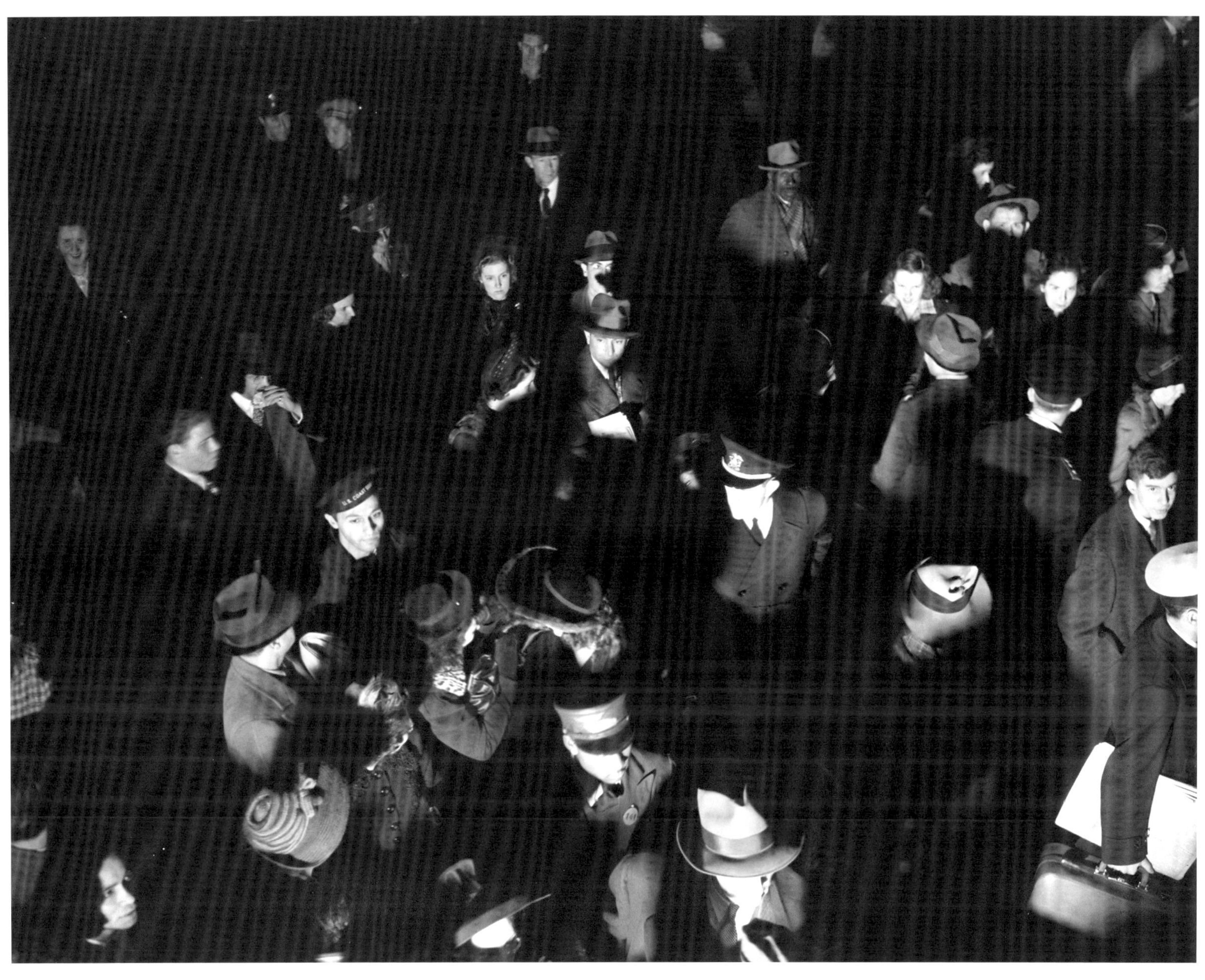

Plate 72. Washington, DC. Crowd waiting for trains at Union Station.

Gordon Parks. November 1942. Library of Congress, Prints & Photographs Division, FSA-OWI Collection, LC-USW3-011382-C.

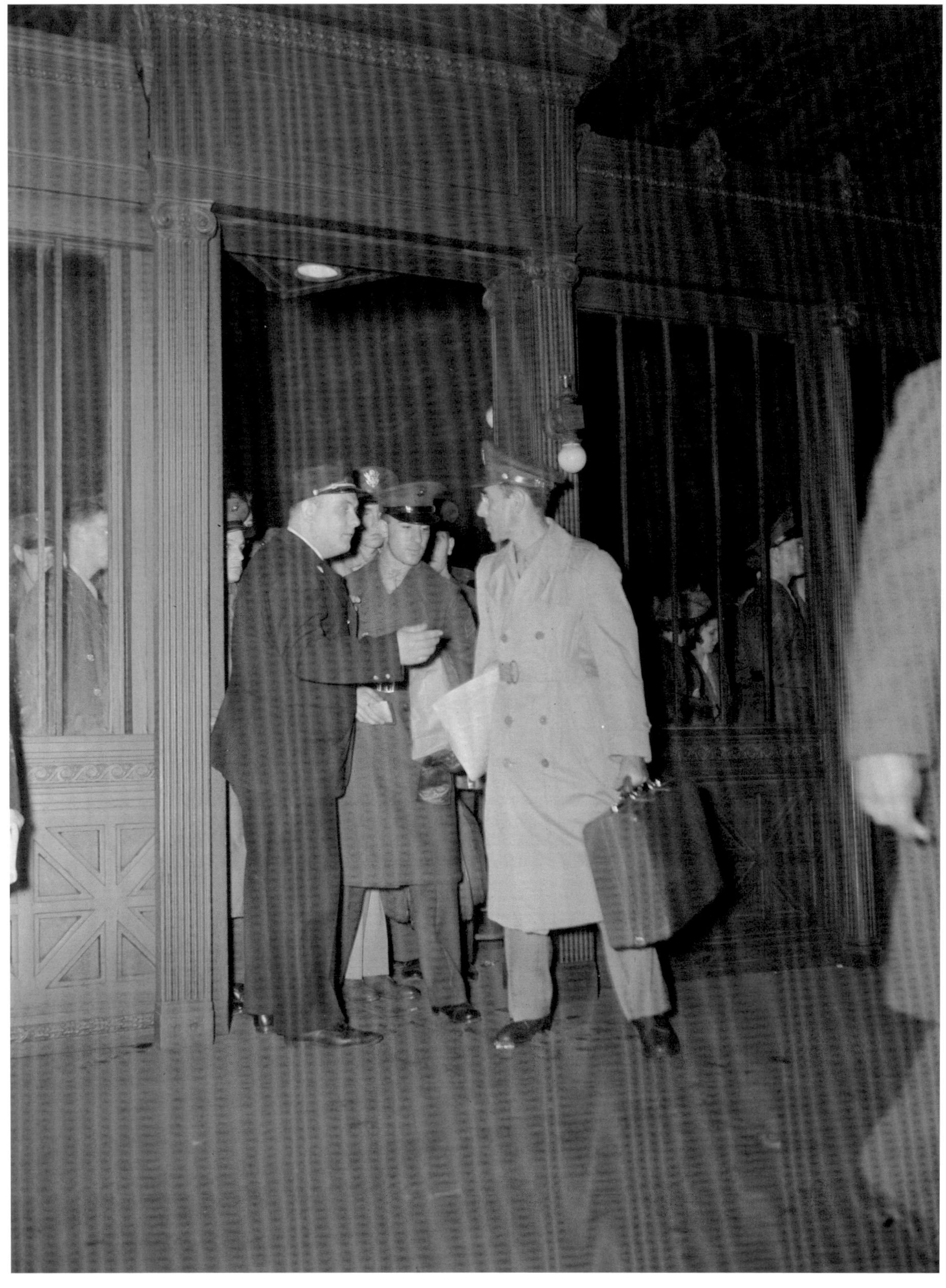

***Left*, Plate 73.** Washington, DC. Soldiers being permitted through the concourse gate at the Union Station.

Gordon Parks. November 1942. Library of Congress, Prints & Photographs Division, FSA-OWI Collection, LC-USW3-011379-C.

***Facing*, Plate 74.** New Britain, Connecticut. Miss Ida Hicks, Lithuanian, twenty-eight years old, employed at the American Railway Express Company, sorting packages, weighting them, etc., earns seventy-nine and one-half cents an hour. She formerly worked in a defense plant.

Gordon Parks. June 1943. Library of Congress, Prints & Photographs Division, FSA-OWI Collection, LC-USW3-034201-E.

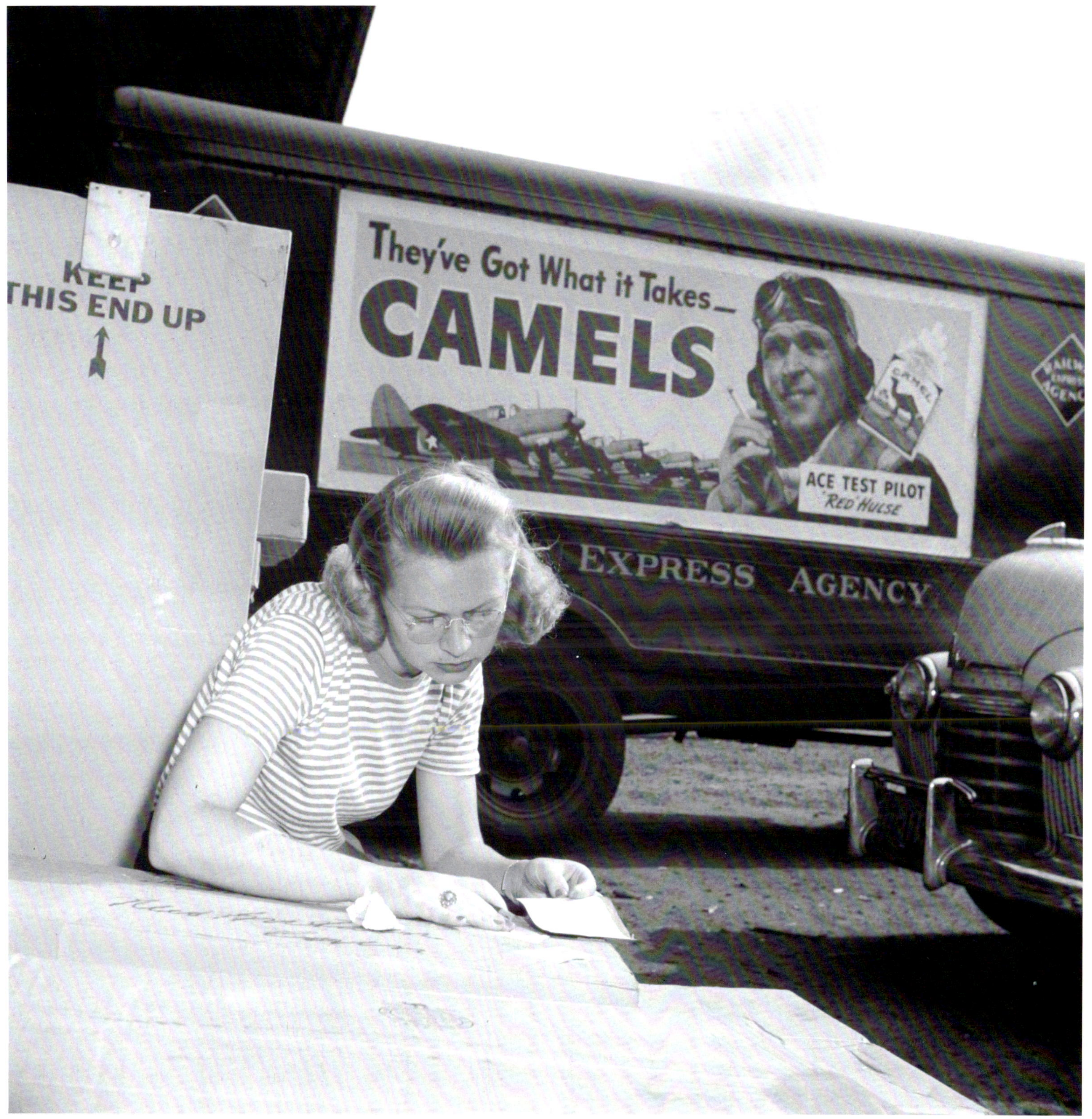
KEEP
THIS END UP
They've Got What it Takes_
CAMELS
ACE TEST PILOT
"RED" HULSE
CAMEL
EXPRESS AGENCY

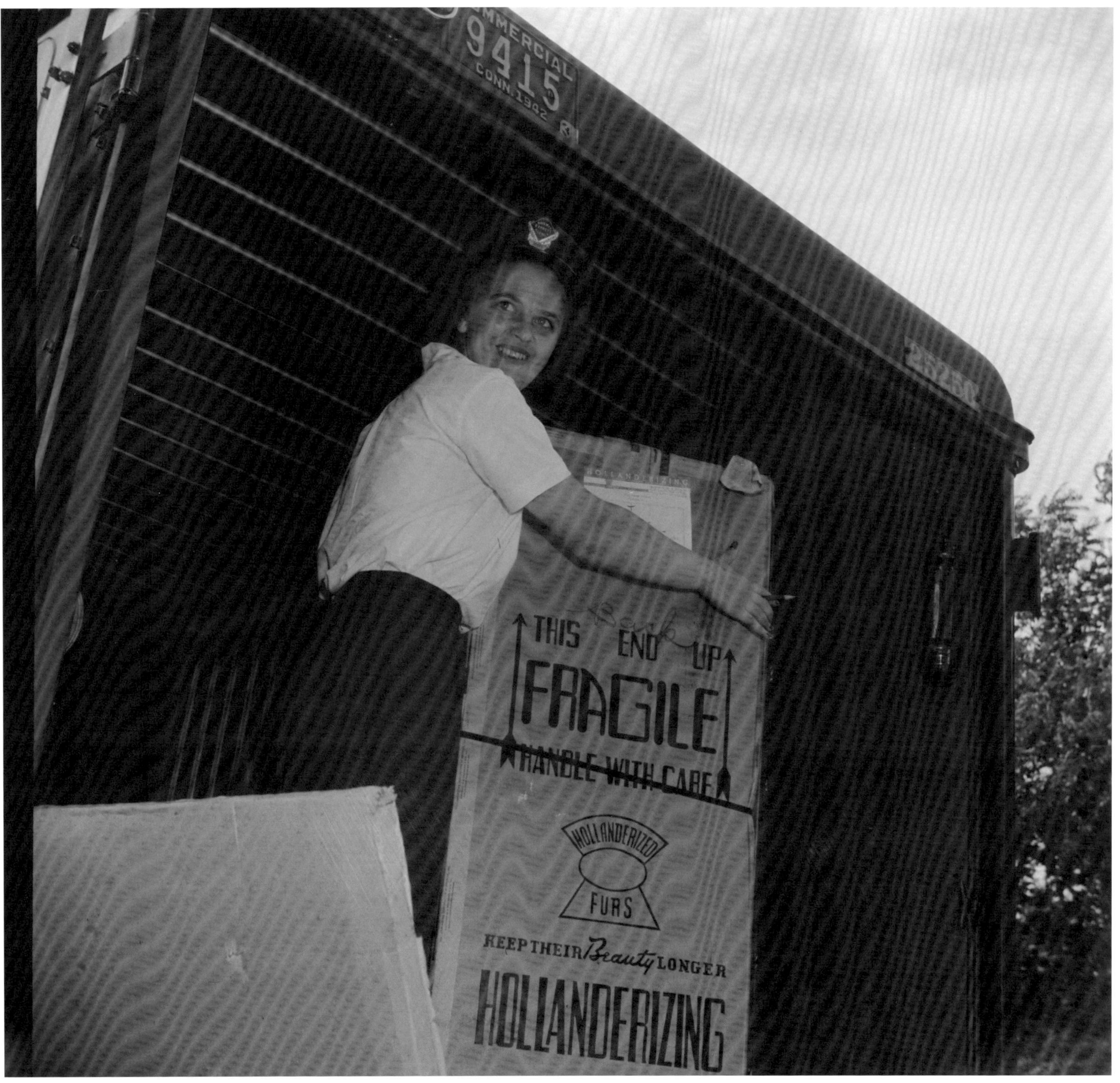
MMERCIAL
9415
CONN. 1942
THIS END UP
FRAGILE
HANDLE WITH CARE
HOLLANDERIZED
FURS
KEEP THEIR Beauty LONGER
HOLLANDERIZING

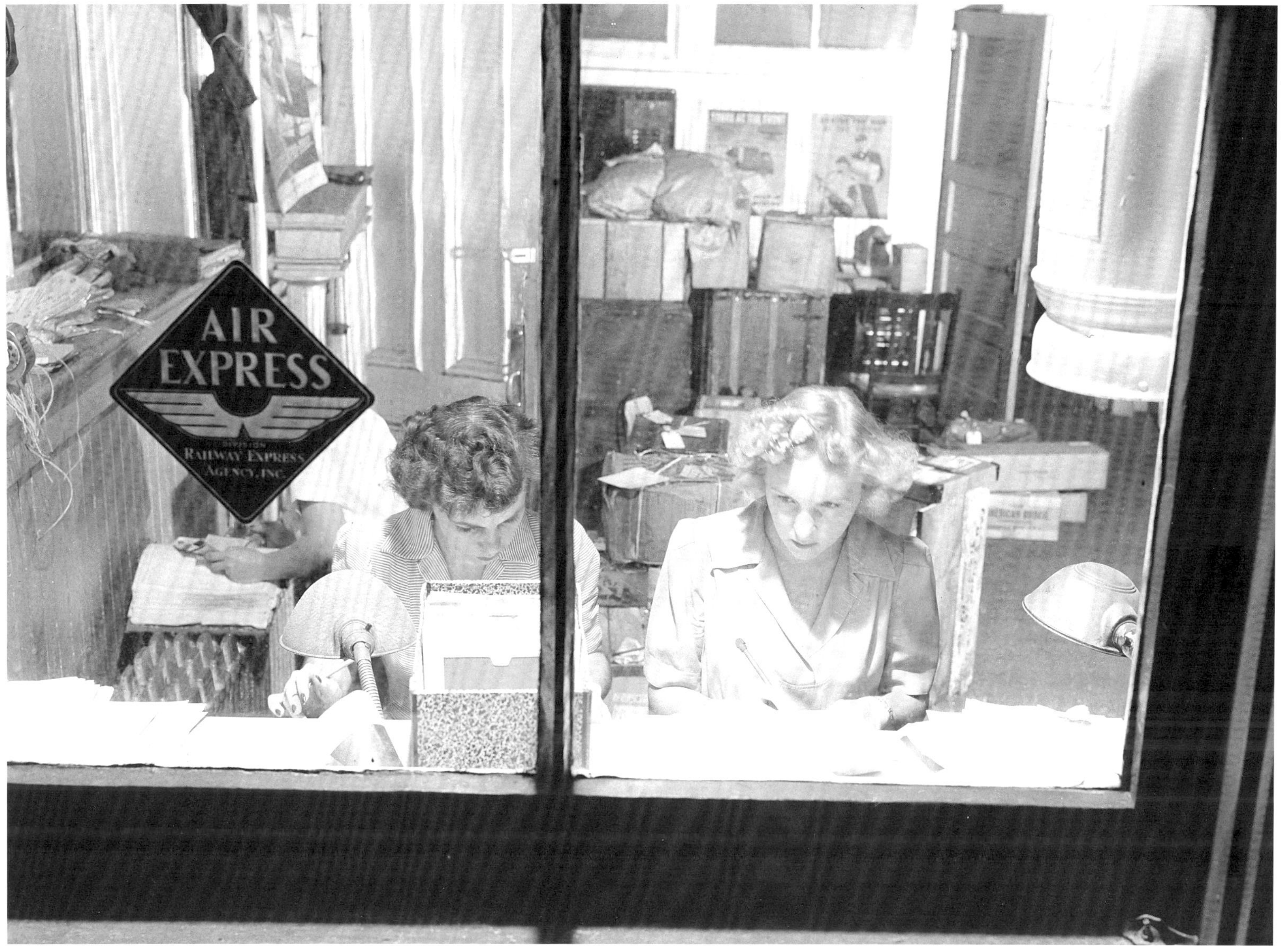

***Facing,* Plate 75.** New Britain, Connecticut. Mrs. Dorothy Bell, Irish German descent, twenty-seven years old, mother of two children, employed at the American Railway Express Company, sorting packages, weighing them, etc., earning seventy-nine and one-half cents an hour.

Gordon Parks. June 1943. Library of Congress, Prints & Photographs Division, FSA-OWI Collection, LC-USW3-034191-E.

***Above,* Plate 76.** New Britain, Connecticut. Miss Florence Janick and Rosalie Starzyk, Polish, employed at the American Railway Express Company, sorting packages, handling accessing charges, etc.

Gordon Parks. June 1943. Library of Congress, Prints & Photographs Division, FSA-OWI Collection, LC-USW3-034223-D.

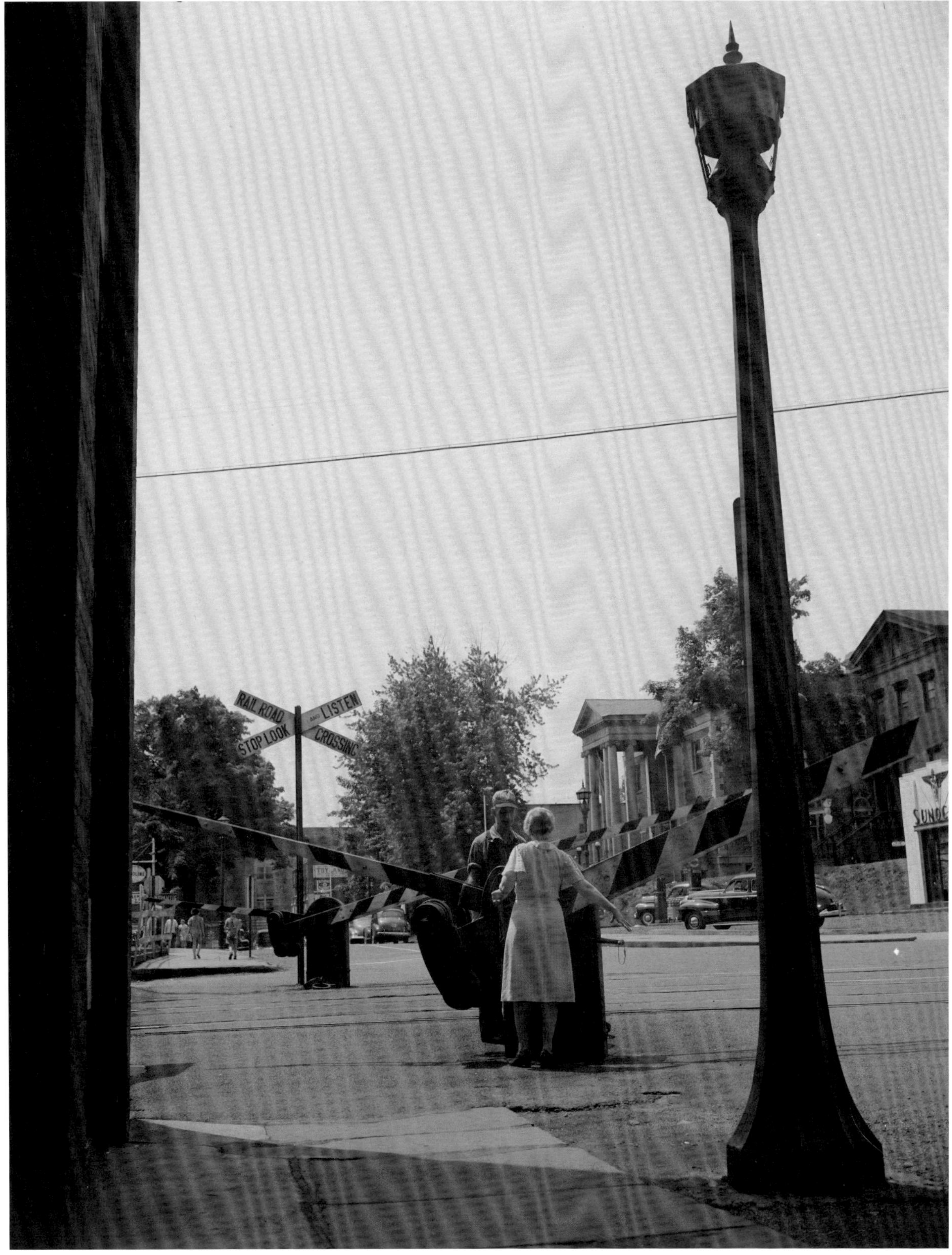

Plate 77. New Britain, Connecticut. A woman railroad crossing watcher letting down the gates until the train passes.

Gordon Parks. June 1943. Library of Congress, Prints & Photographs Division, FSA-OWI Collection, LC-USW3-034277-C.

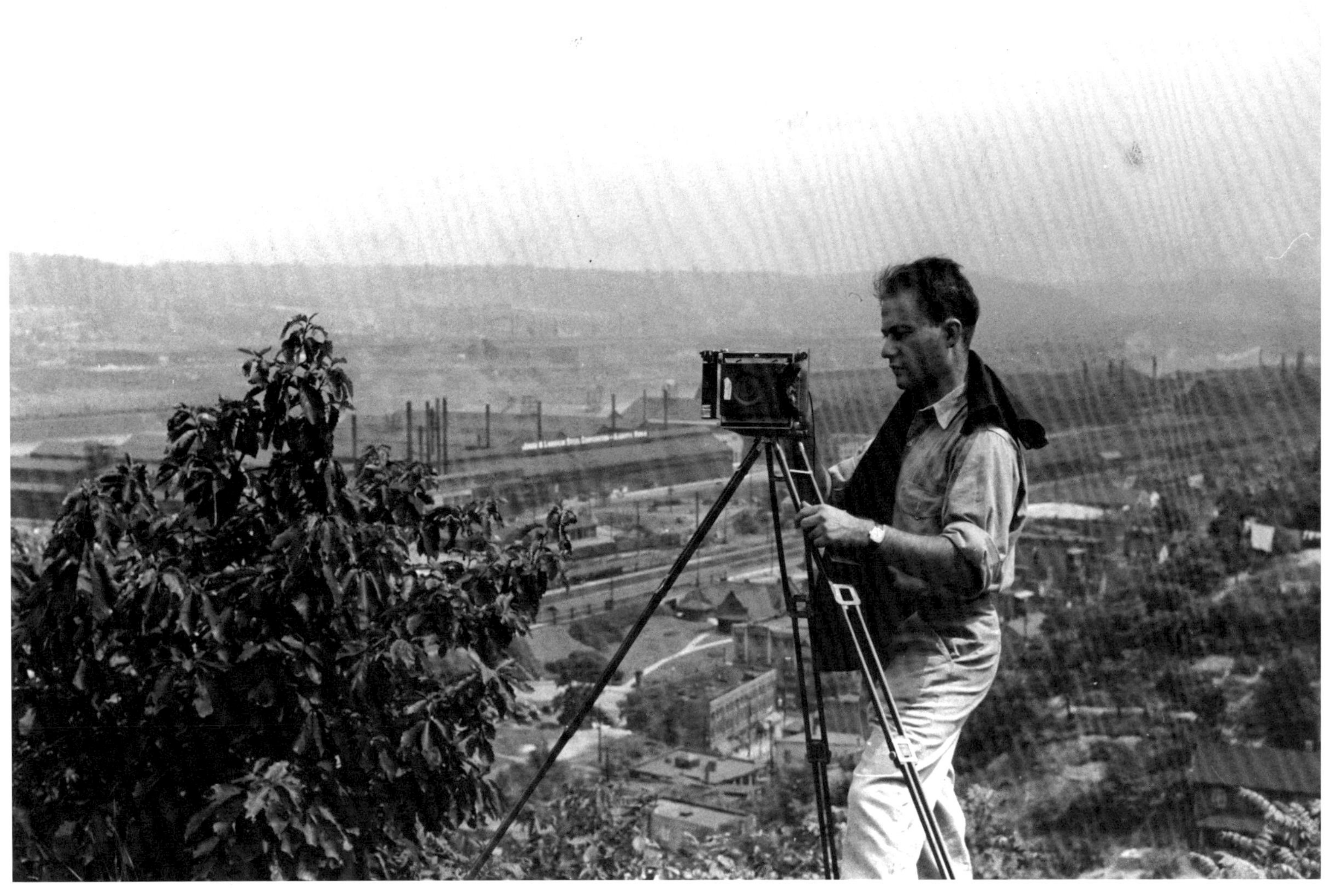

Figure 8.1. Arthur Rothstein, Farm Security Administration (FSA) photographer.

July 1938. Library of Congress, Prints & Photographs Division, FSA-OWI Collection, LC-USF33-002825-M2.

PORTFOLIO EIGHT

ARTHUR ROTHSTEIN

Arthur Rothstein was the youngest of the "first wave" of FSA photographers, a group that included three artistic giants, Walker Evans, Dorothea Lange, and Ben Shahn, as well as Theodor Jung and Carl Mydans. It was the heady first stage of Franklin Delano Roosevelt's (FDR's) New Deal. Rexford "Rex" Guy Tugwell was one of the intellectual leaders of this part of FDR's presidency. He asked Roy Stryker, a protégé from Columbia University, to work on a photography project documenting agriculture in the US, and Stryker in turn called on a student from Columbia, Arthur Rothstein, to assist.

Arthur Rothstein was born in New York to Latvian immigrants in 1915 and attended Columbia University in New York from 1931 to 1935. Toward the end of his undergraduate career, he worked for Roy Stryker at Columbia.

By 1935, Tugwell headed a New Deal agency, the Resettlement Administration, and he asked Stryker to head the administration's Historical Section. Stryker accepted the position, and Arthur Rothstein was his first hire, in 1935.[1] The newly graduated Columbia student was charged with setting up the section's photo lab, but inspired by the work of Evans and Shahn, Rothstein soon convinced Stryker to let him take photos for the Historical Section. Rothstein had long been an amateur photographer, but this transition marked the beginning of the career of one of America's foremost photojournalists.

Rothstein stayed with the Historical Section for five years, including during its transition to becoming part of the Farm Security Administration. He left in 1940 to become a staff photographer at *Look* magazine; he stayed with *Look* for three decades, except for World War II and postwar stints as a photographer for the US Army and the United Nations. He closed his career at *Infinity* and then *Parade* magazines. Rothstein married Grace Goodman in 1947, and they had four children. He taught at a number of institutions, including his alma mater, Columbia, and authored *Photojournalism*, a landmark text in the field. He also authored or illustrated a number of other books, including one that was a collaboration with noted US author William Saroyan. Rothstein's work overall is best characterized by its photojournalistic approach. Arthur Rothstein died of cancer in New Rochelle, New York, in 1985.[2]

Rothstein's best-known work for the FSA includes his photos of Gee's Bend, Alabama, and his images of the Dust Bowl in the US, including his controversial images of a steer's skull taken in

South Dakota. However, his travels for the Resettlement Administration/FSA led him to cover almost the entirety of the continental United States.

Rothstein's railroad-subject images are not as well known as those taken by many of his FSA/OWI peers, and like his overall work, they are wide ranging. Plates 78 and 79 are views of railroading in one of the country's smallest states, Vermont, showing the town of Randolph on what was the Central Vermont Railway.

Plates 80–82 show views of railroads in Maryland—a scene also covered extensively by photographer Phil Hastings about a decade later. Plate 80 pictures a Western Maryland Railway passenger train approaching Hagerstown, Maryland, behind Western Maryland 209, a K-2 4-6-2 Pacific. This train was about to stop at the Western Maryland Railway station in Hagerstown, shown in an interior view in plate 81. This railroad station survives today. Plate 82 depicts a water tank along a little-used rail line in Jennings, Maryland.

Plates 83–87 represent Rothstein's views of the US South and of a border state, Missouri. In plate 83, a steam locomotive pulls an antiquated hopper car on a railroad serving mines in Jefferson County, Alabama. Plate 84 shows a "yardman" in an image taken at about the same time. Since the man in the photo stands in front of a steam engine holding a long-spout oil can, he is more likely an engineer. Bananas were a key product shipped north from southern ports such as New Orleans and Mobile; in plate 85, bananas are loaded into a "reefer"—a refrigerated car—in Mobile, Alabama. Plate 86 shows Terminal Railroad Association of St. Louis locomotive 334, a 0-8-0 switcher, at St. Louis, and plate 87 shows a passenger waiting in a St. Louis station, probably the majestic St. Louis Union Station, which survives today.

Plate 88 takes us to the upper Midwest and shows a groundbreaking technology of the time, the Chicago, Burlington and Quincy Railroad's diesel-powered *Pioneer Zephyr* at La Crosse, Wisconsin.

One of the most noted and popular US railroads is the bonanza short line of Nevada, the Virginia & Truckee Railroad. Lucius Beebe and Charles Clegg's images of the railroad are well known, but Arthur Rothstein was there before them, shooting a portfolio of the noted short line in March 1940, just before he left the FSA. Plates 89–92 represent this work, which justifies a portfolio or article on its own.[3] All were taken at Carson City, Nevada. The locomotive shown in several of the images is Virginia & Truckee 26, a 4-6-0 Ten-Wheeler. Plates 91 and 92 show a type of business that helped keep short lines running—carrying the US mail. Plate 93, likely taken at about the same time, shows, according to the title of the photo, a train crossing the mountains, Eureka County, Nevada. The locomotive is Denver and Rio Grande Western Railroad 3415, a 2-8-8-2. The Rio Grande did not have lines in Nevada; this photograph may have been taken in Utah, or the locomotive may have been operating off its home road.

This portfolio of Arthur Rothstein's FSA railroad-subject work closes with plates 94 and 95, images of the Great Plains states, which must have seemed a world away from New York City and Washington, DC, to this young urbanite in 1939. Plate 94 shows what is unmistakably a Great Northern Railway locomotive at that road's station in Fargo, North Dakota. Great Northern 2578 was an S-2 Northern 4-8-4. The final image in this portfolio, plate 95, shows a grain elevator located next to the Chicago, Milwaukee, St. Paul and Pacific Railroad depot in Fairfield, Montana.

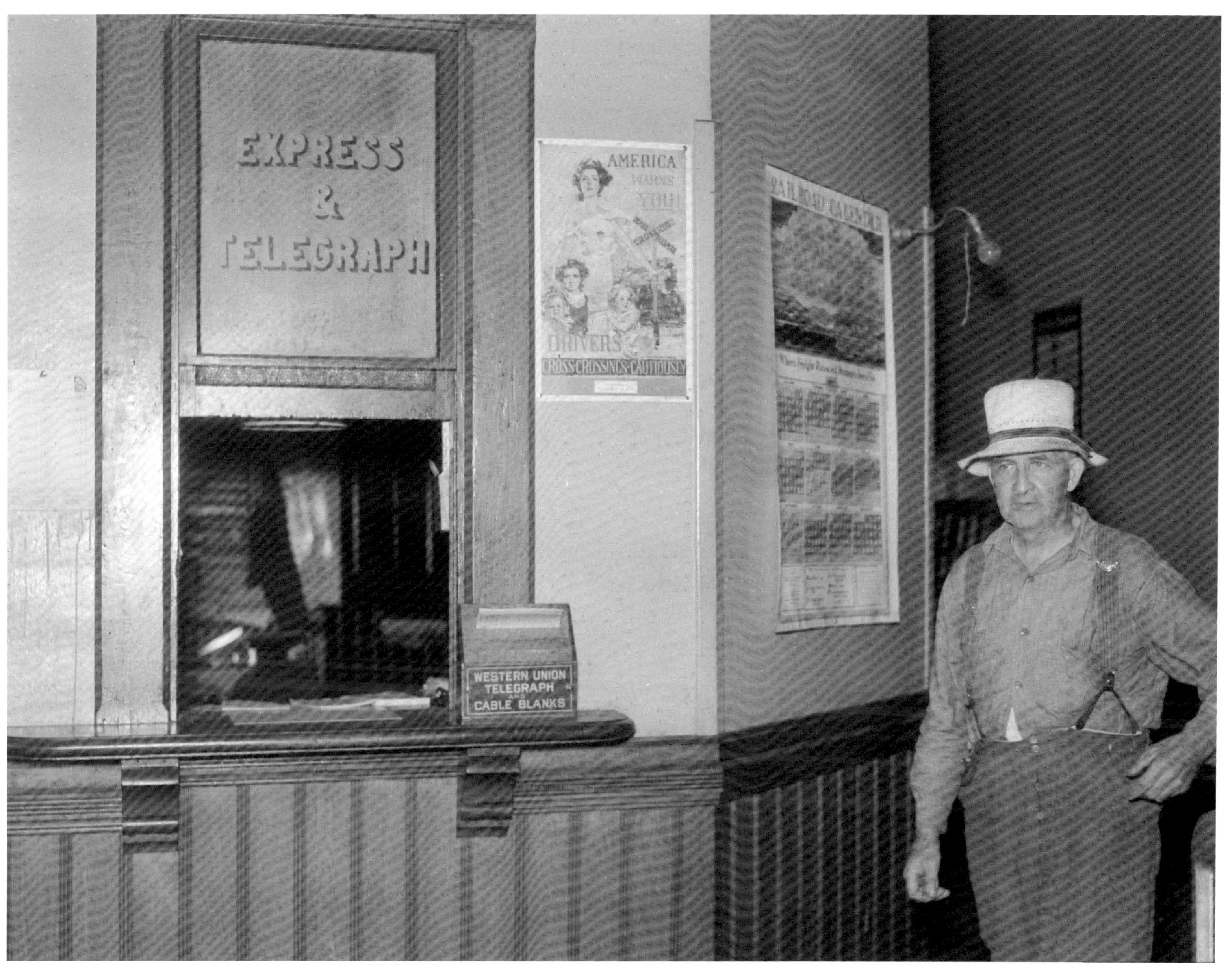

Plate 78. Interior of railroad station. Randolph, Vermont.

Arthur Rothstein. September 1937. Library of Congress, Prints & Photographs Division, FSA-OWI Collection, LC-USF34-025736-D.

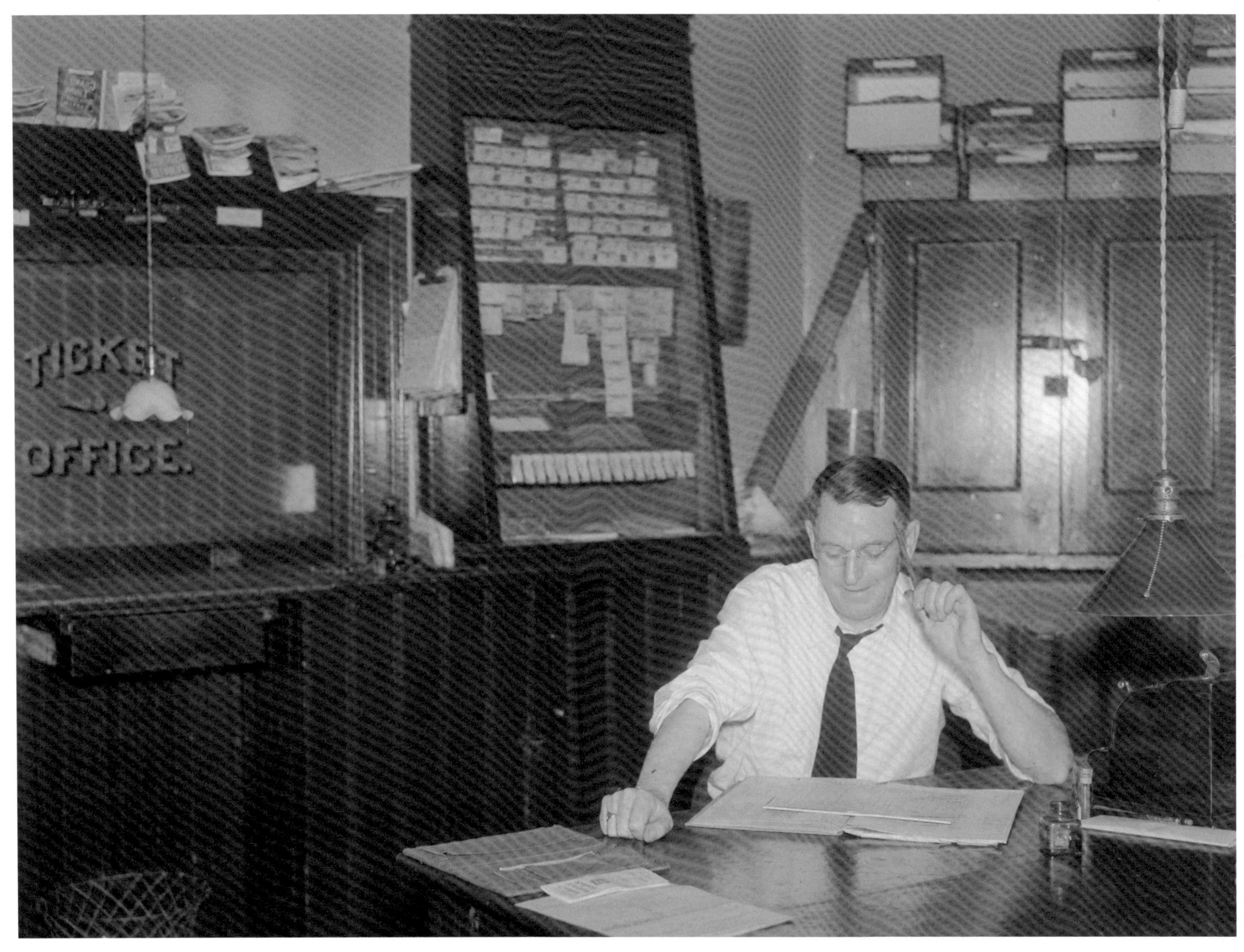

Plate 79. Railroad station agent. Randolph, Vermont.

Arthur Rothstein. September 1937. Library of Congress, Prints & Photographs Division, FSA-OWI Collection, LC-USF34-025744-D.

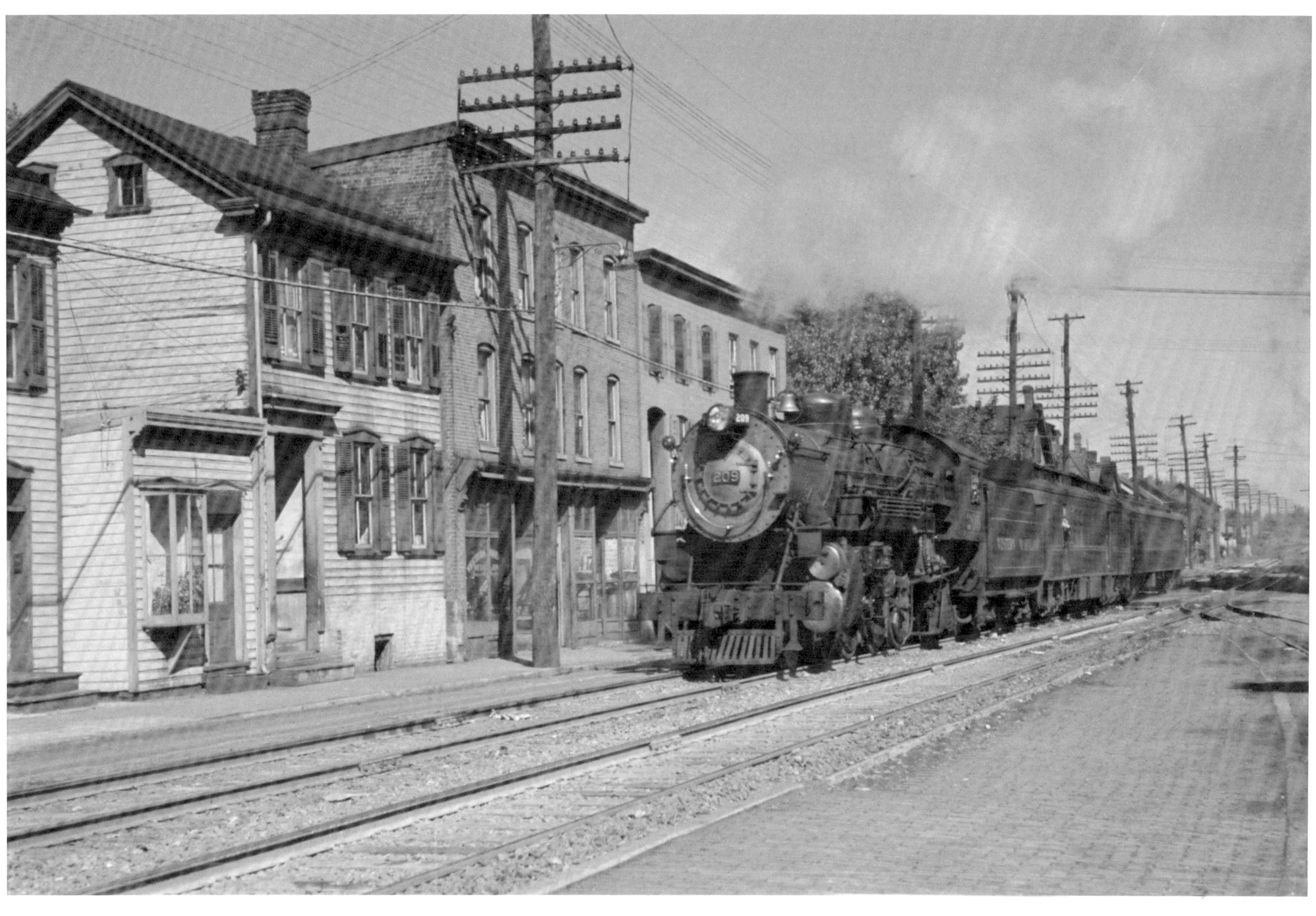

Plate 80. Train arriving from Baltimore. Hagerstown, Maryland.

Arthur Rothstein. October 1937. Library of Congress, Prints & Photographs Division, FSA-OWI Collection, LC-USF33-002655-M1.

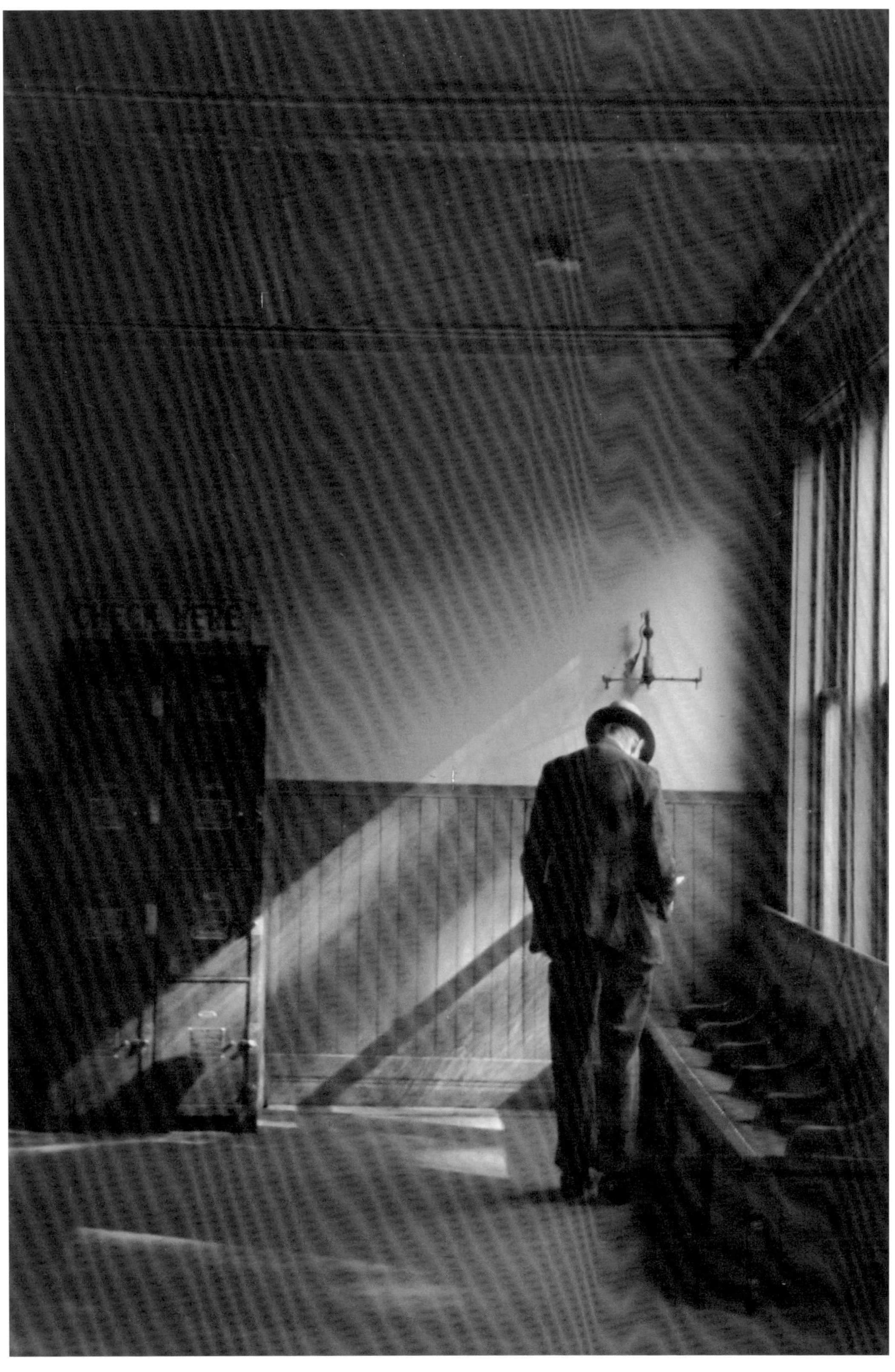

Plate 81. Interior of railroad station, Hagerstown, Maryland.

Arthur Rothstein. October 1937. Library of Congress, Prints & Photographs Division, FSA-OWI Collection, LC-USF33-002649-M5.

***Facing*, Plate 82.** Water tower on railroad through Jennings, Maryland. The train now runs only once a week.

Arthur Rothstein. December 1937. Library of Congress, Prints & Photographs Division, FSA-OWI Collection, LC-USF34-026067-C.

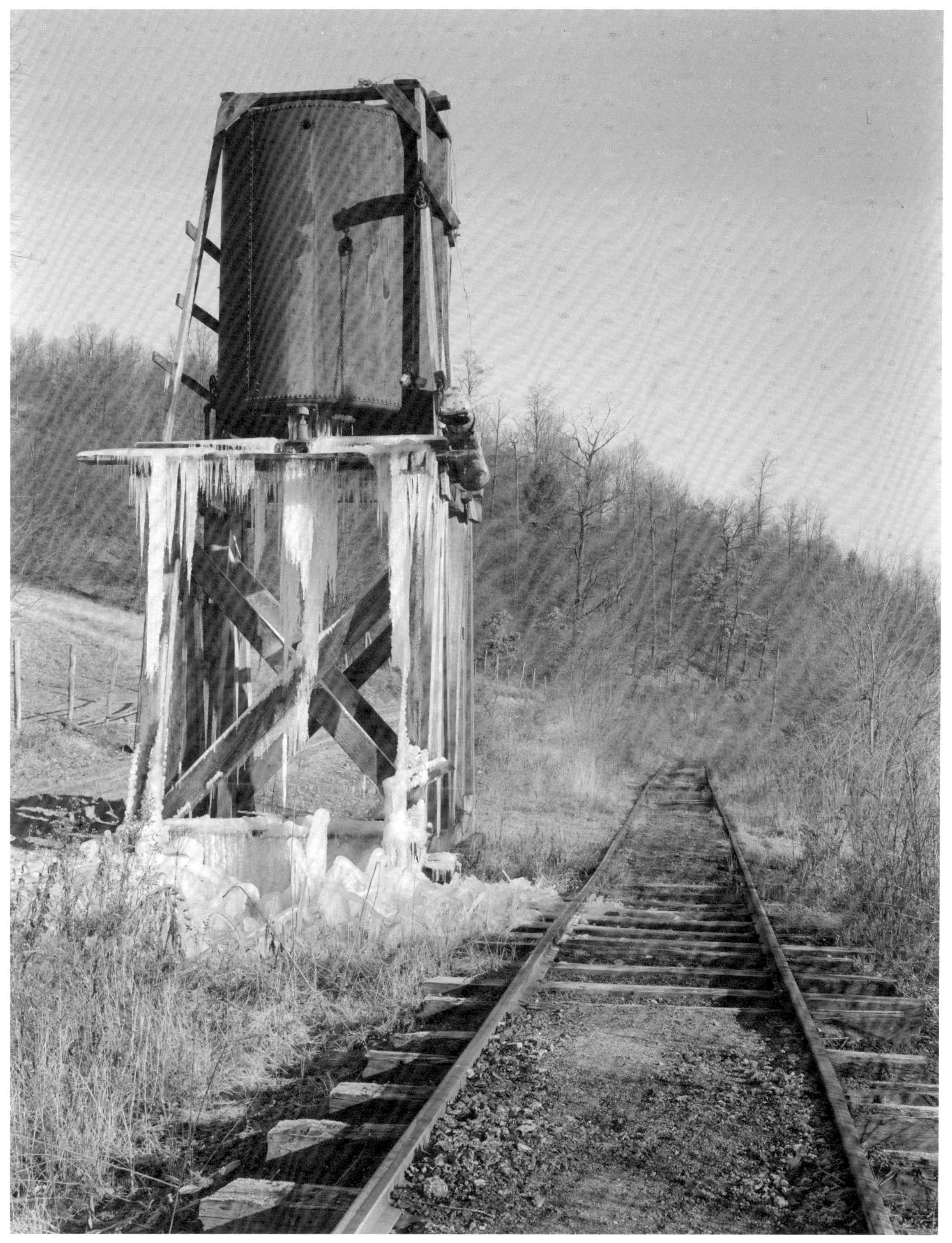

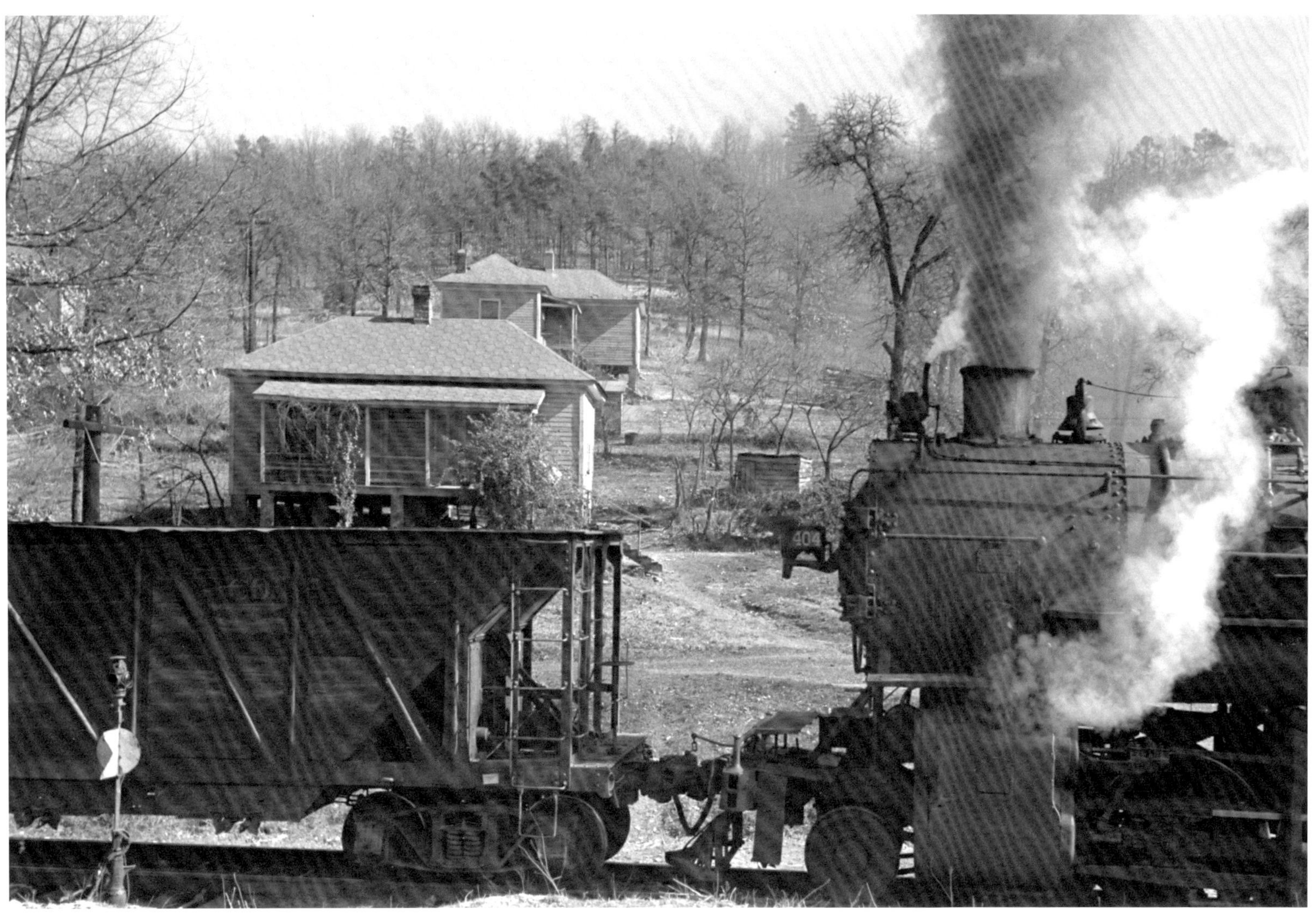

Plate 83. Untitled photo, possibly related to: Yardman on mine railroad, Jefferson County, Alabama.

Arthur Rothstein. February 1937. Library of Congress, Prints & Photographs Division, FSA-OWI Collection, LC-USF33-002393-M5.

Plate 84. Yardman on mine railroad, Jefferson County, Alabama.

Arthur Rothstein. February 1937. Library of Congress, Prints & Photographs Division, FSA-OWI Collection, LC-USF33-002395-M2.

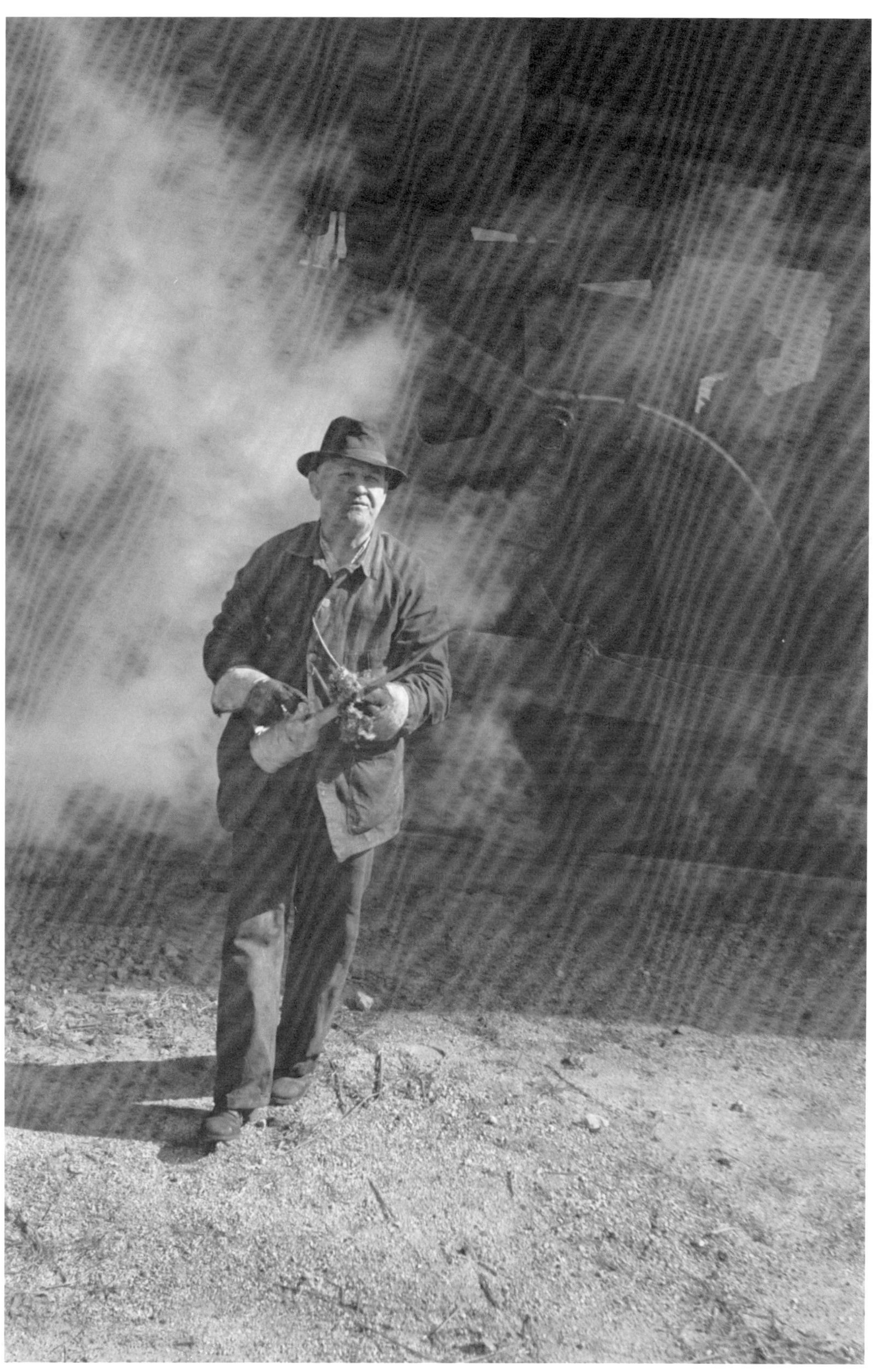

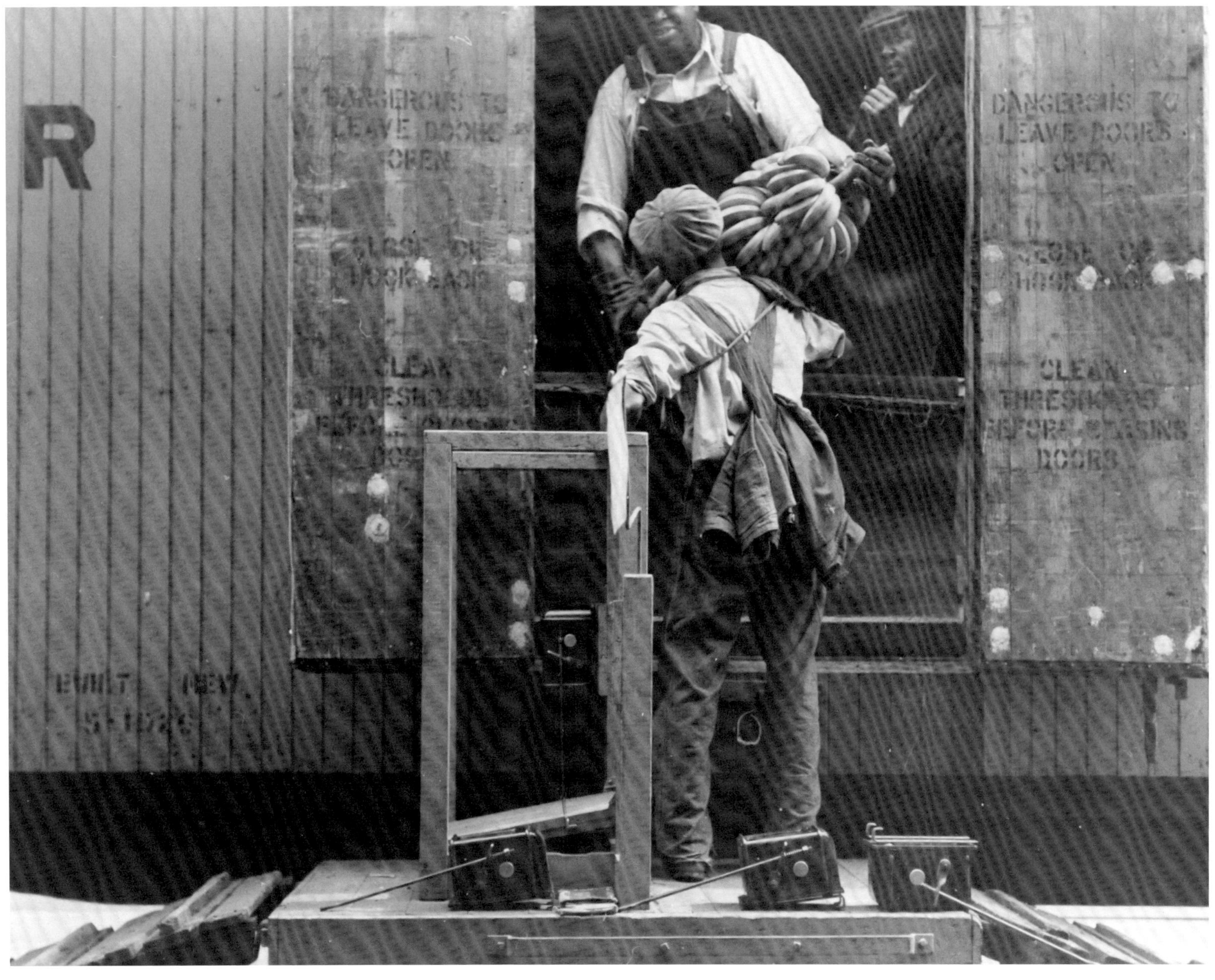

Plate 85. Loading bananas. Mobile, Alabama.

Arthur Rothstein. 1937. Library of Congress, Prints & Photographs Division, FSA-OWI Collection, LC-USF34-025466-D.

Plate 86. Locomotive in railroad yards along river, St. Louis, Missouri.

Arthur Rothstein. January 1939. Library of Congress, Prints & Photographs Division, FSA-OWI Collection, LC-USF33-002988-M5.

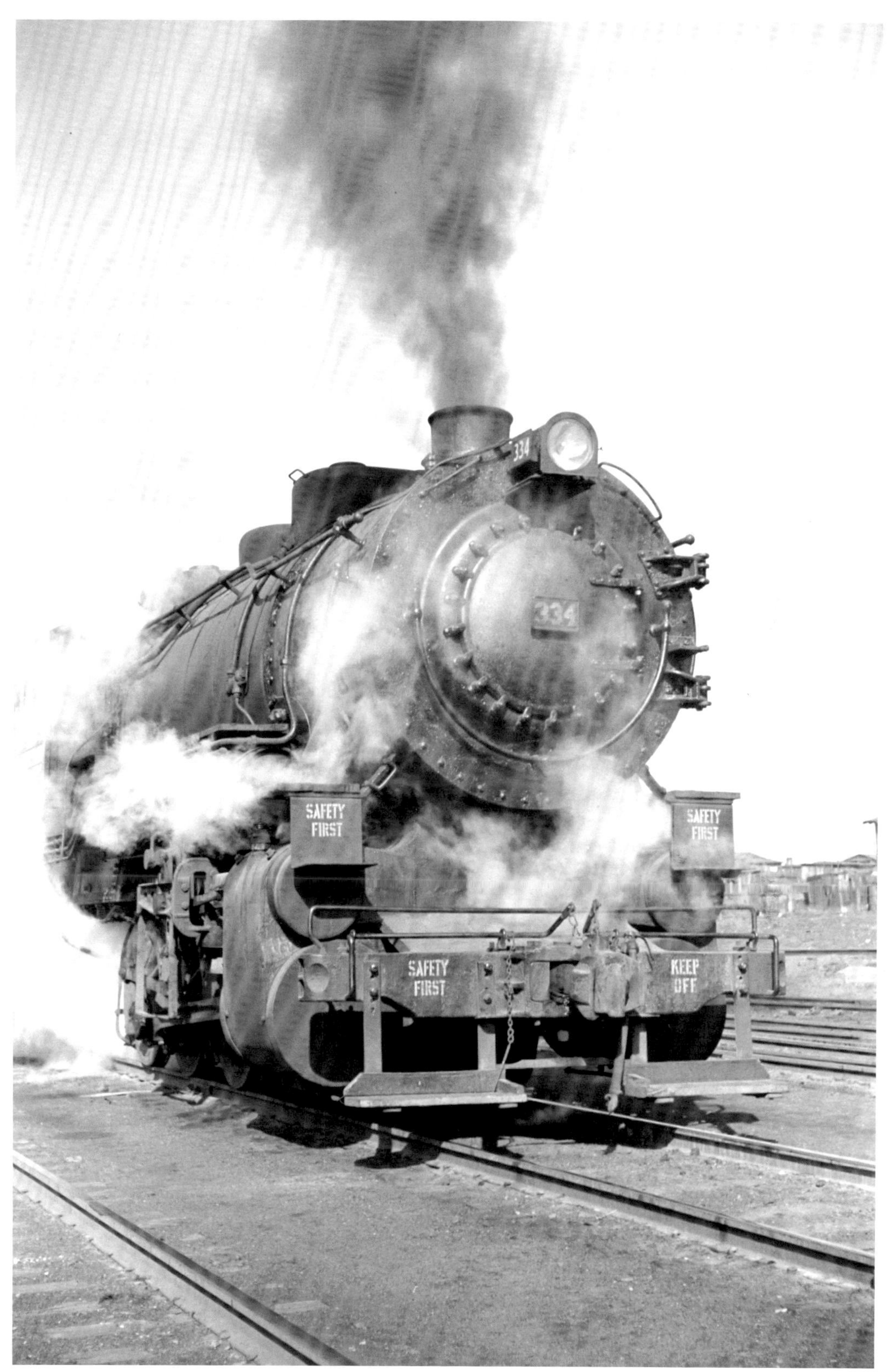

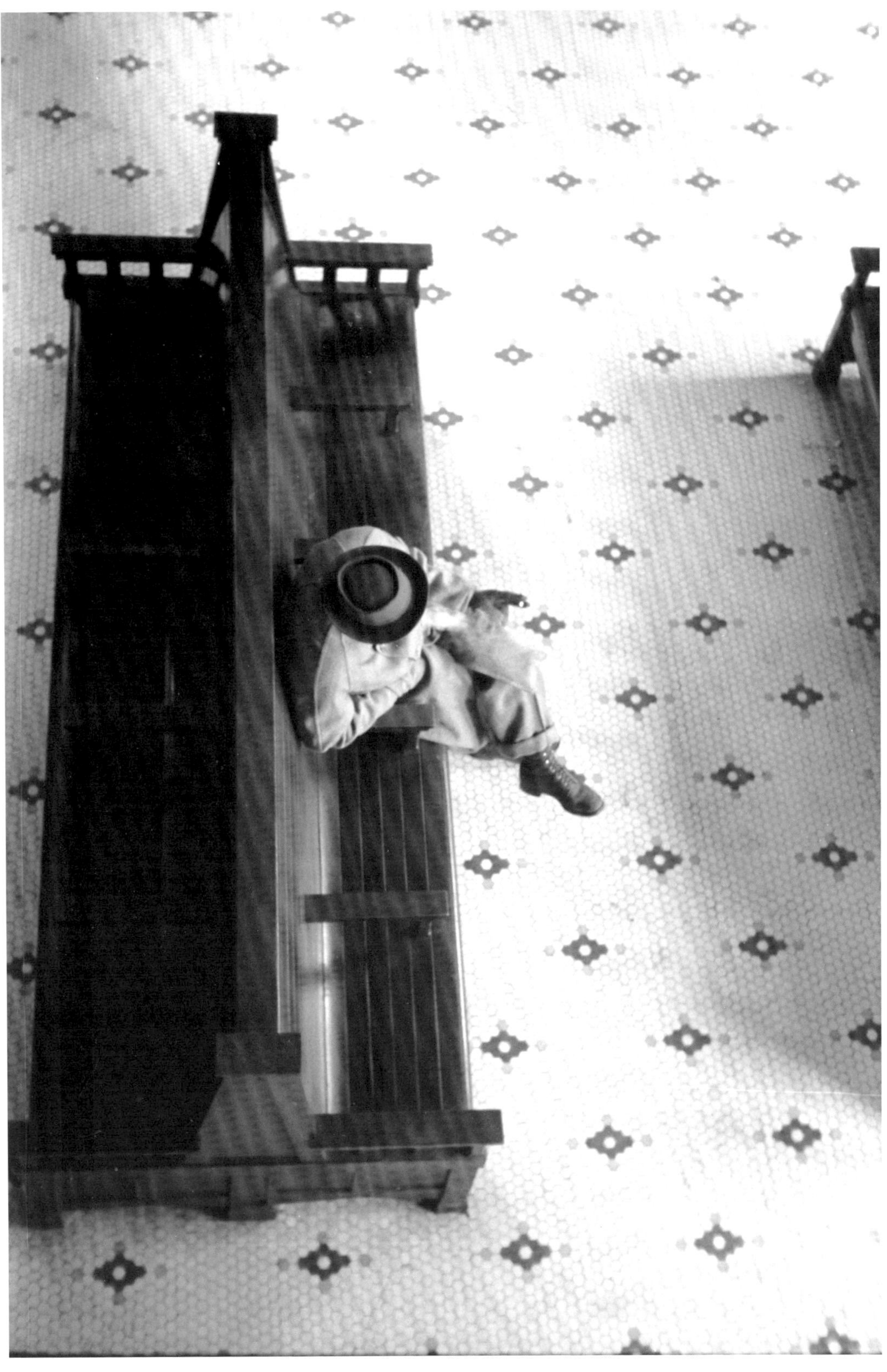

Plate 87. Passenger waiting in railroad station, Saint Louis, Missouri.

Arthur Rothstein. January 1939. Library of Congress, Prints & Photographs Division, FSA-OWI Collection, LC-USF33-003029-M1.

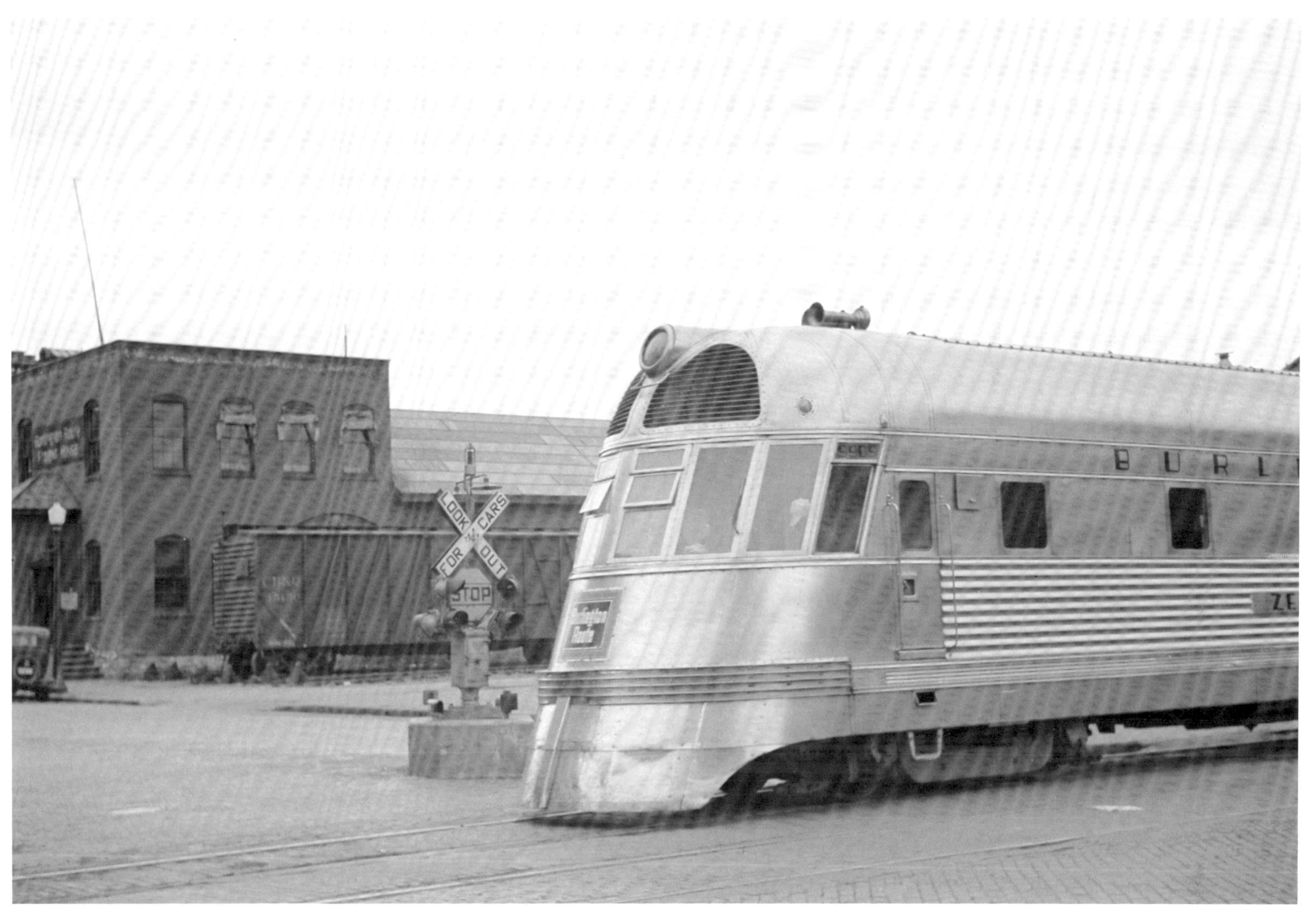

Plate 88. Untitled photo, possibly related to: Streamlined train, La Crosse, Wisconsin.

Arthur Rothstein. 1939. Library of Congress, Prints & Photographs Division, FSA-OWI Collection, LC-USF33-003068-M.

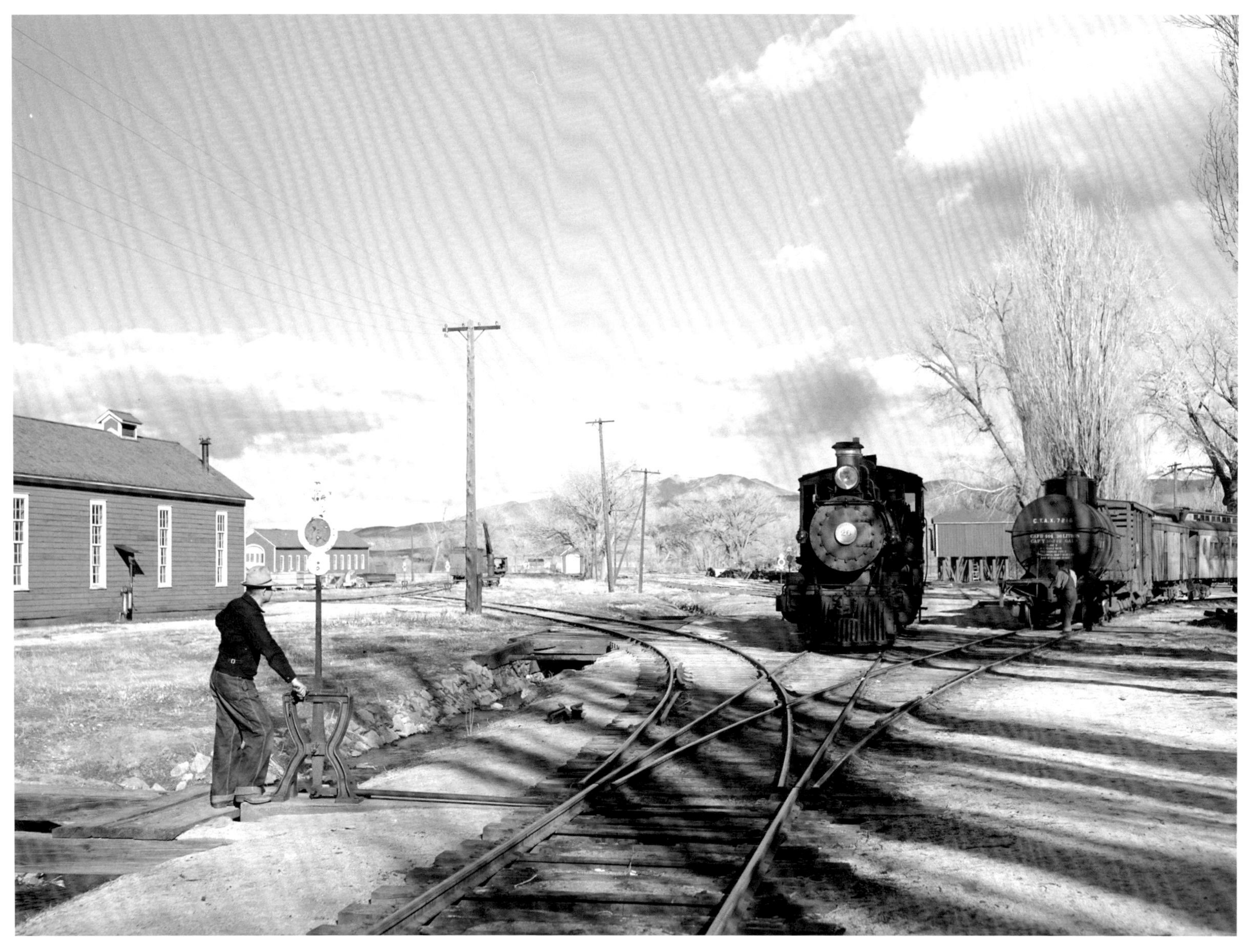

Plate 89. Operating switch at railroad station. Carson City, Nevada.

Arthur Rothstein. March 1940. Library of Congress, Prints & Photographs Division, FSA-OWI Collection, LC-USF34-029973-D.

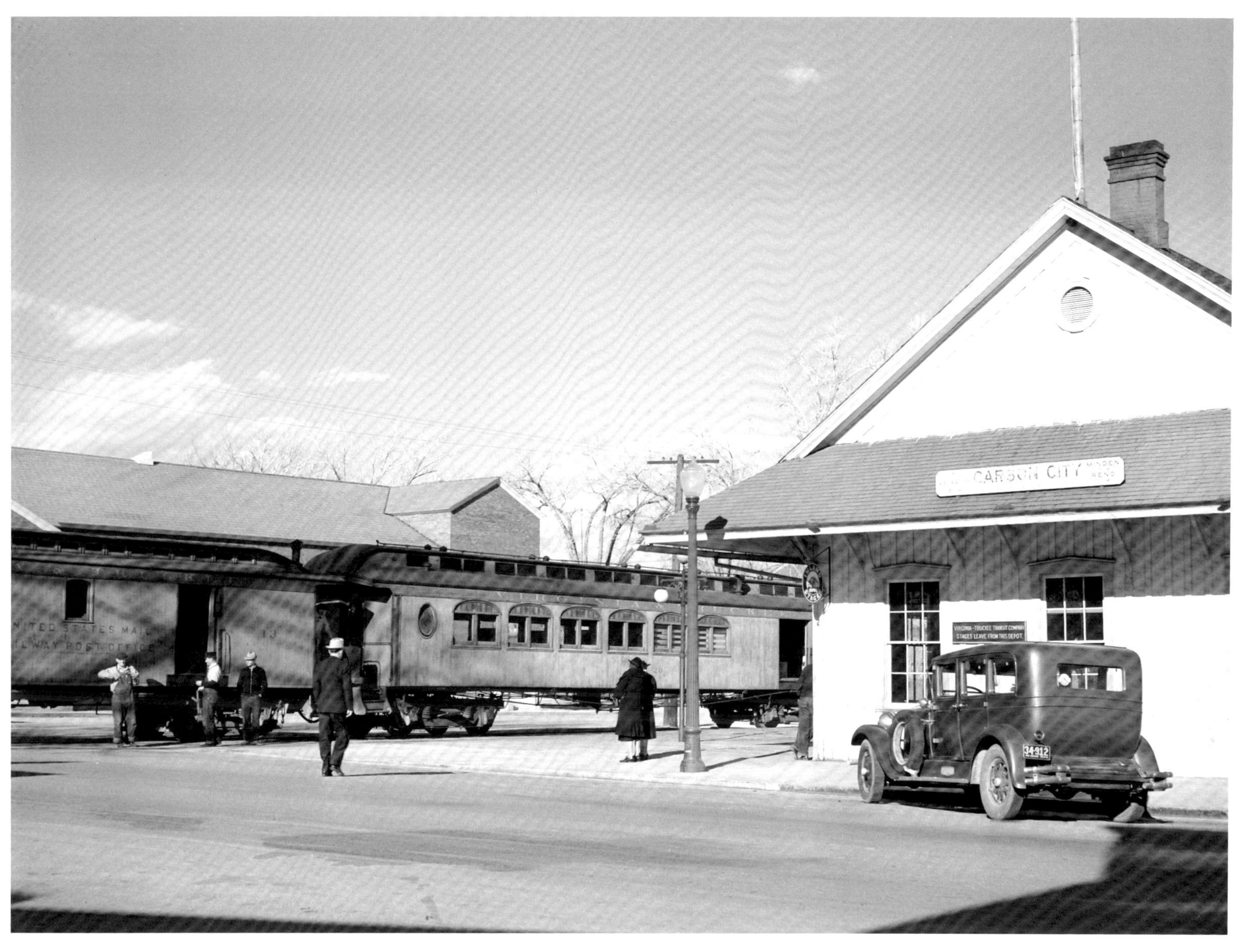

Plate 90. Railroad station. Carson City, Nevada.

Arthur Rothstein. March 1940. Library of Congress, Prints & Photographs Division, FSA-OWI Collection, LC-USF34-029975-D.

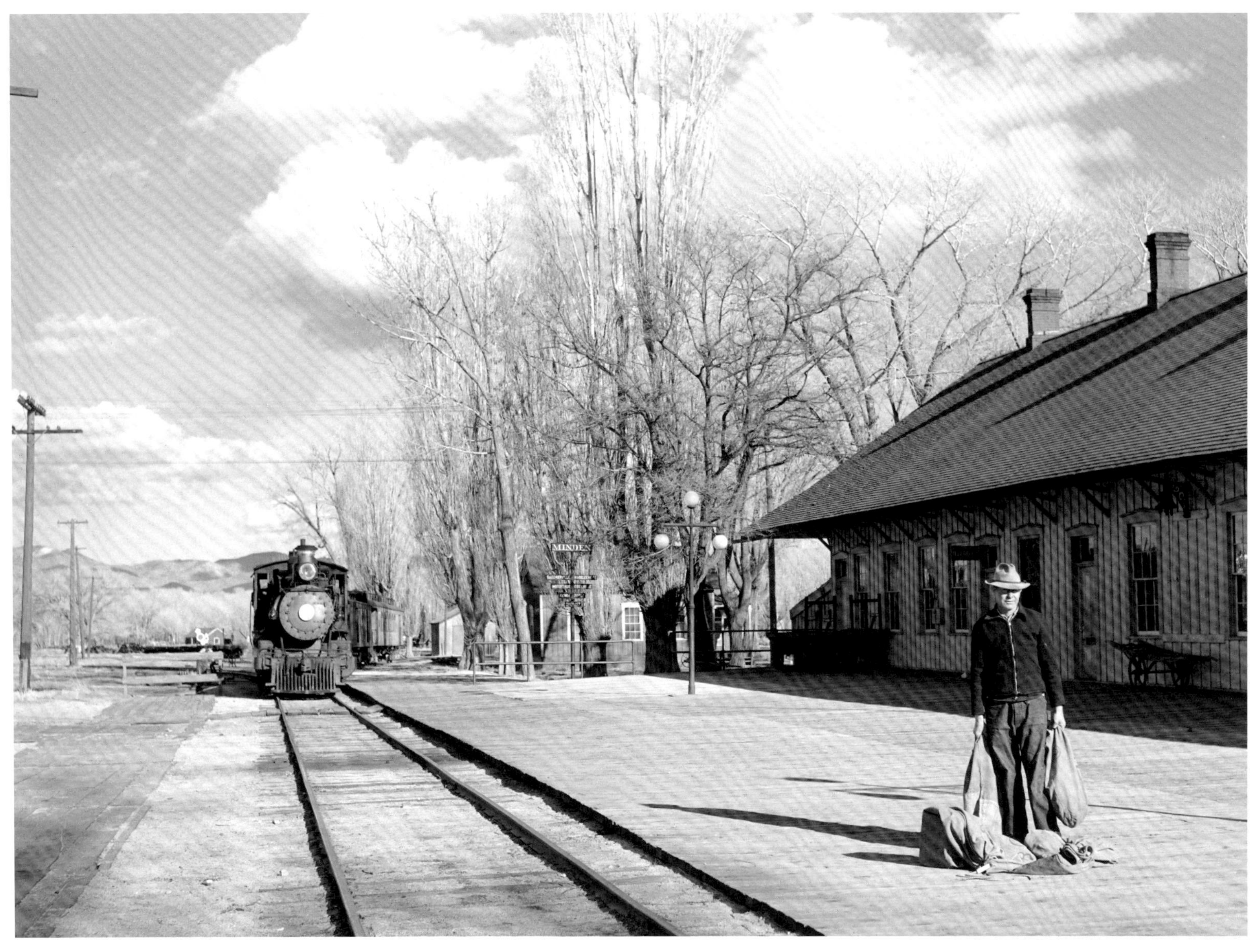

Plate 91. Waiting with mail for train to Reno. Carson City, Nevada.

Arthur Rothstein. March 1940. Library of Congress, Prints & Photographs Division, FSA-OWI Collection, LC-USF34-029935-D.

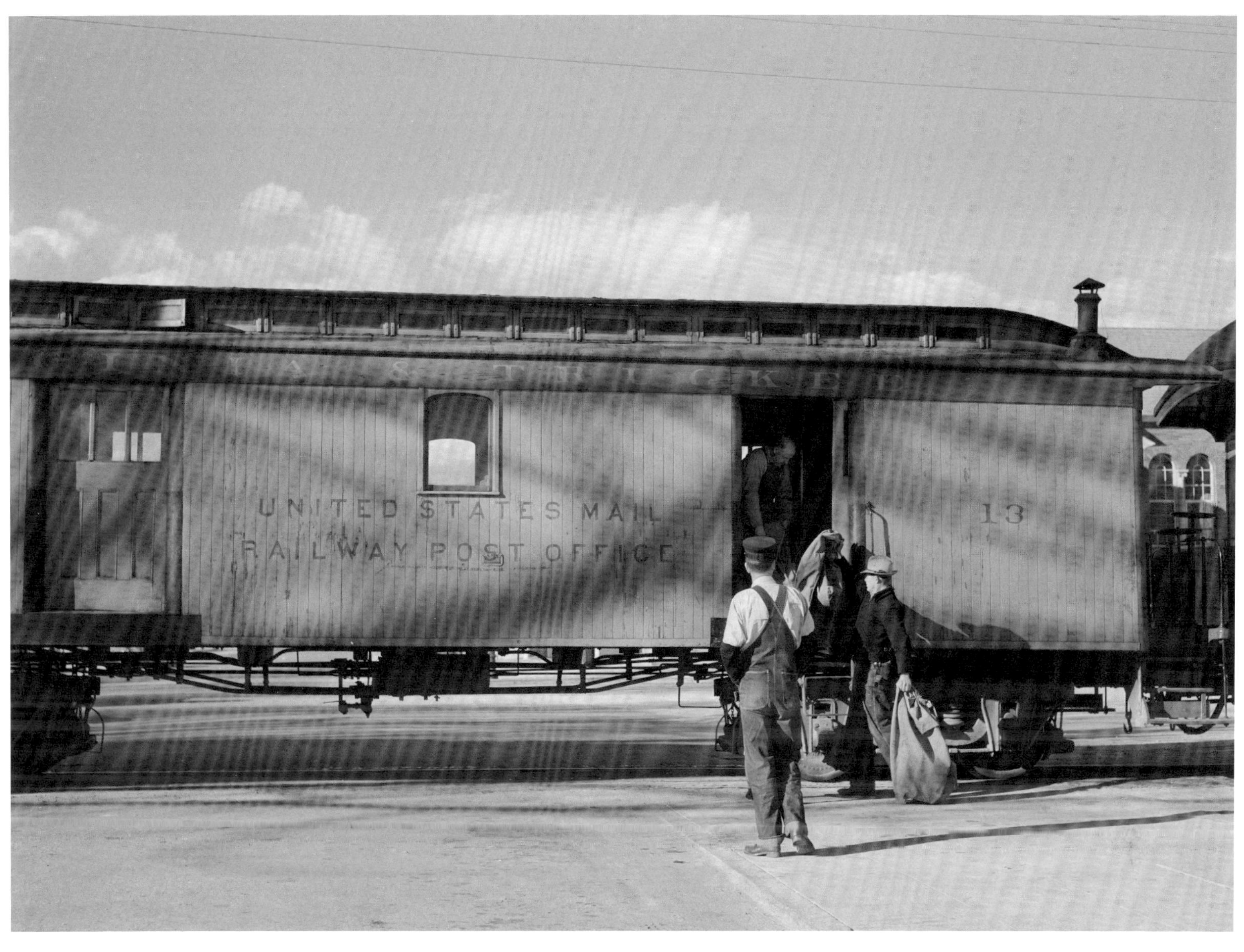

Plate 92. Loading mail into railroad car. Carson City, Nevada.

Arthur Rothstein. March 1940. Library of Congress, Prints & Photographs Division, FSA-OWI Collection, LC-USF34-029936-D.

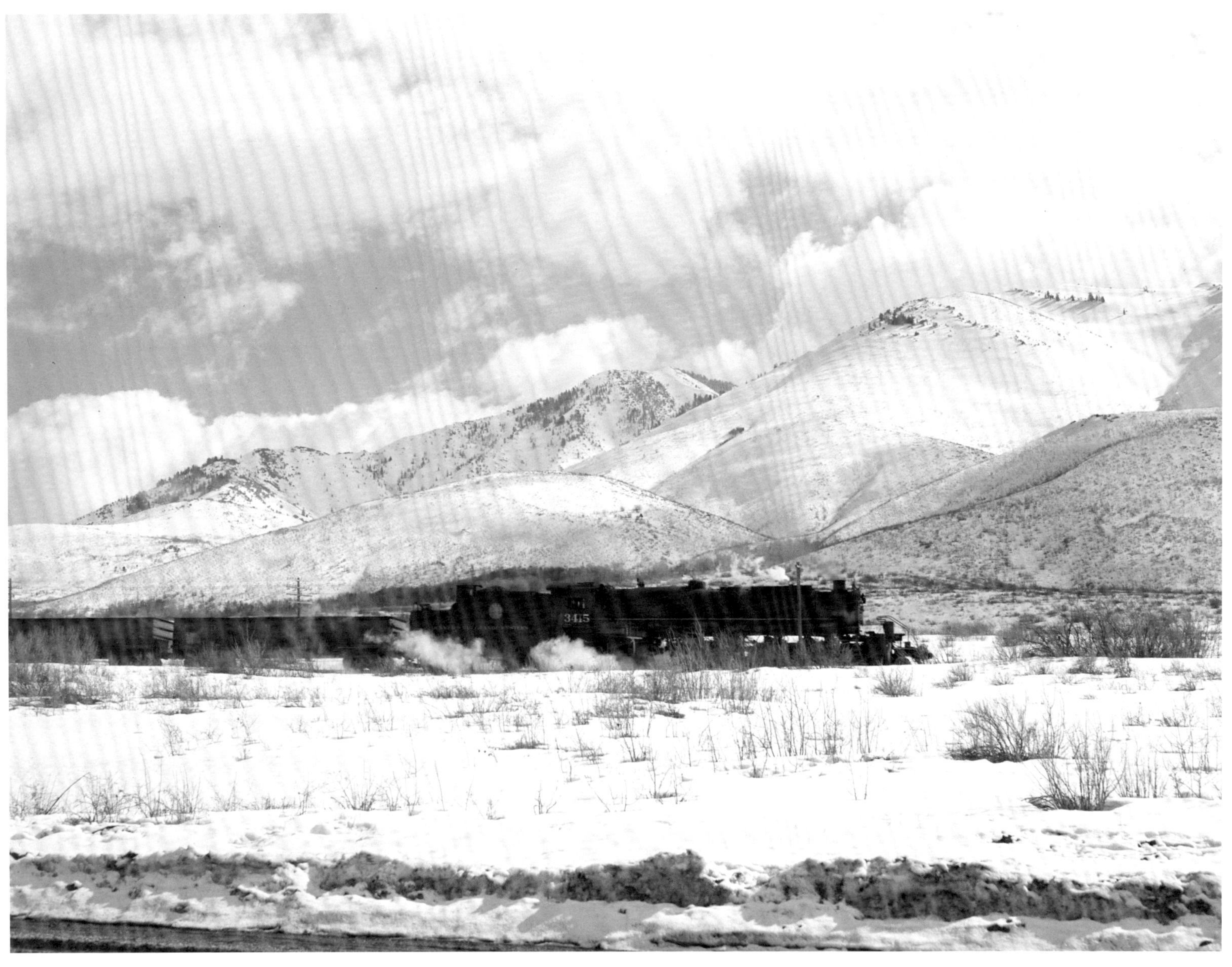

Plate 93. Train crossing the mountains. Eureka County, Nevada.

Arthur Rothstein. March 1940. Library of Congress, Prints & Photographs Division, FSA-OWI Collection, LC-USF34-029588-D.

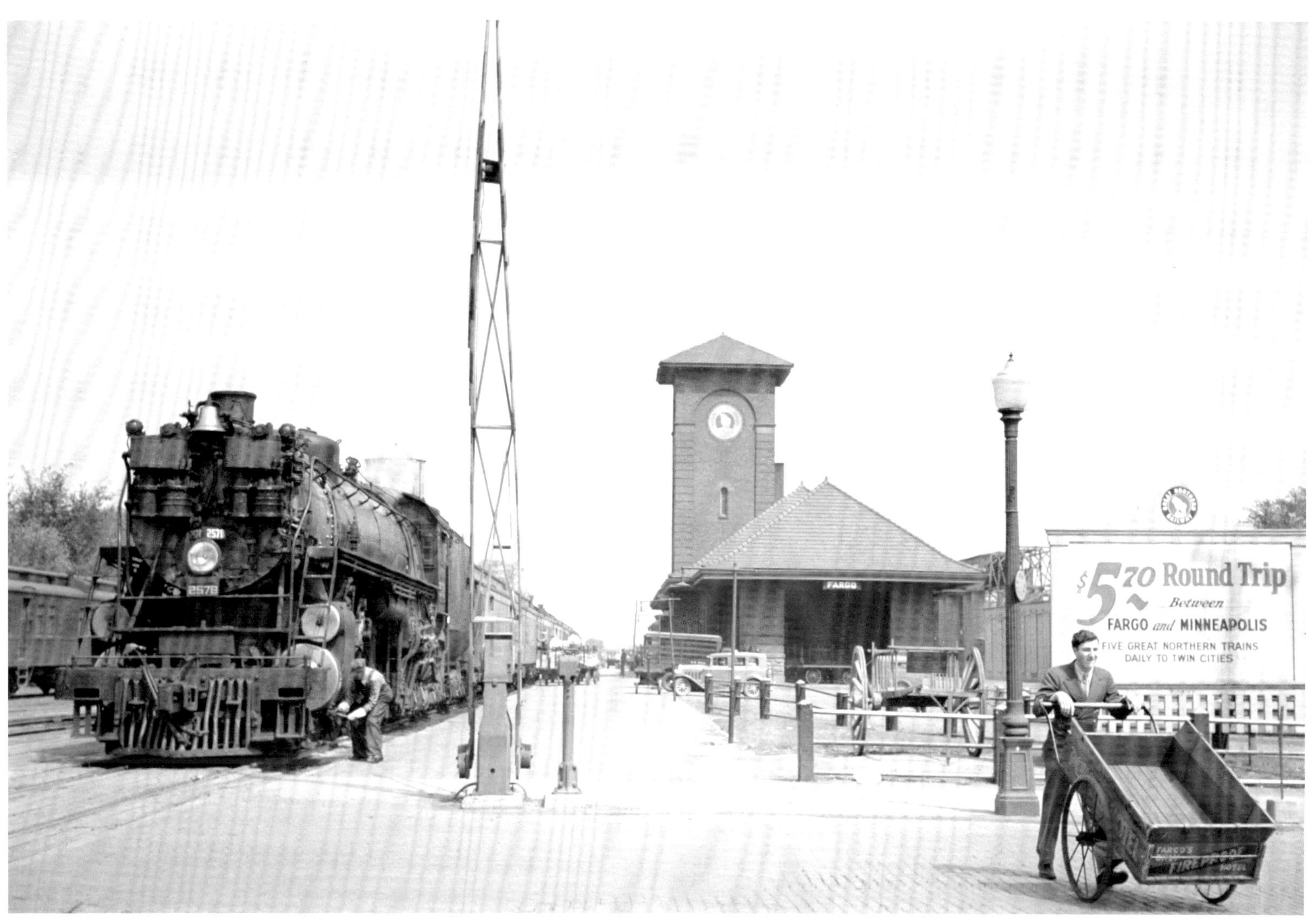

Plate 94. Railroad station, Fargo, North Dakota.

Arthur Rothstein. 1939. Library of Congress, Prints & Photographs Division, FSA-OWI Collection, LC-USF33-003066-M2.

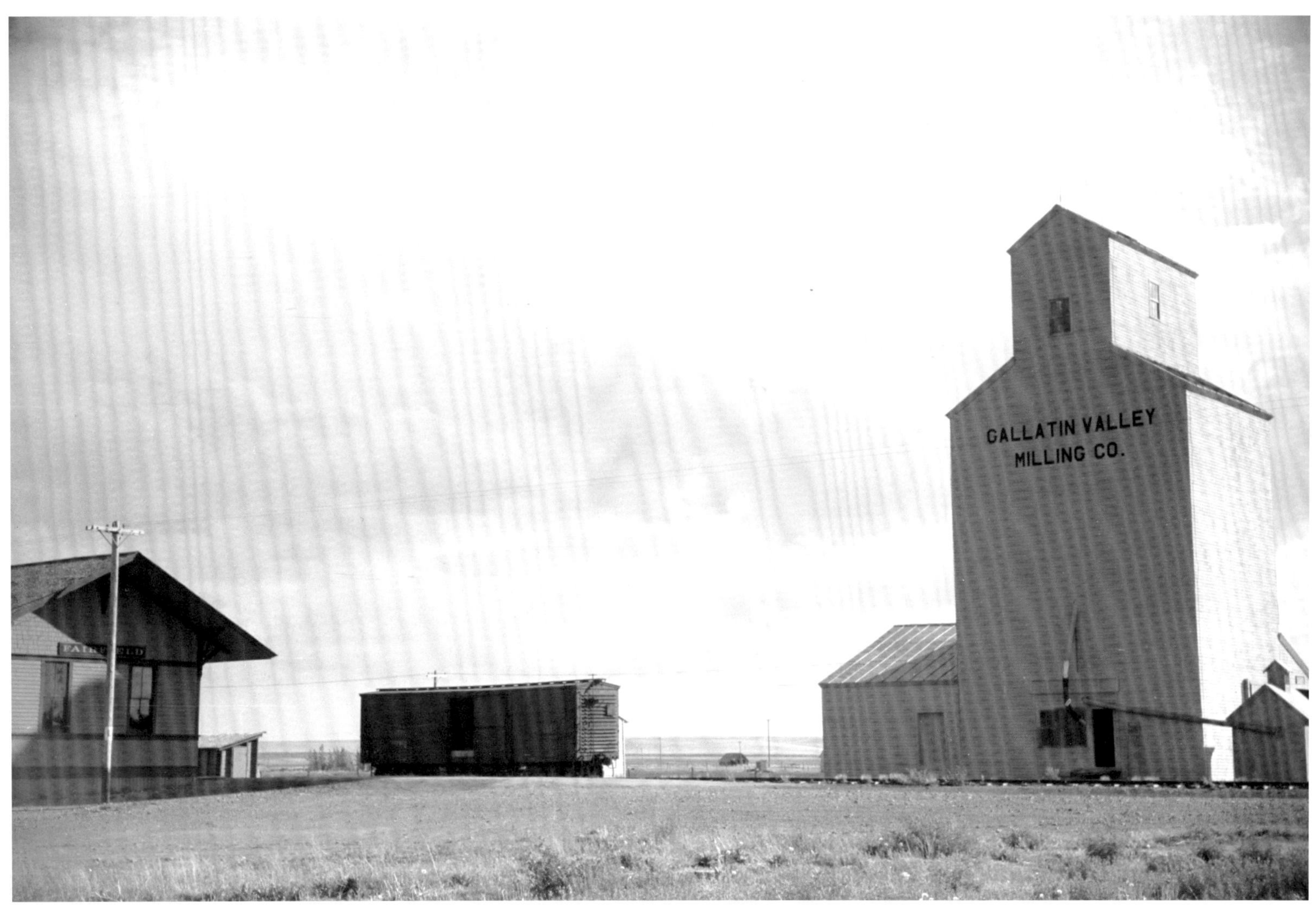

Plate 95. Grain elevator at railroad station, Fairfield, Montana.

Arthur Rothstein. 1939. Library of Congress, Prints & Photographs Division, FSA-OWI Collection, LC-USF33-003107-M2.

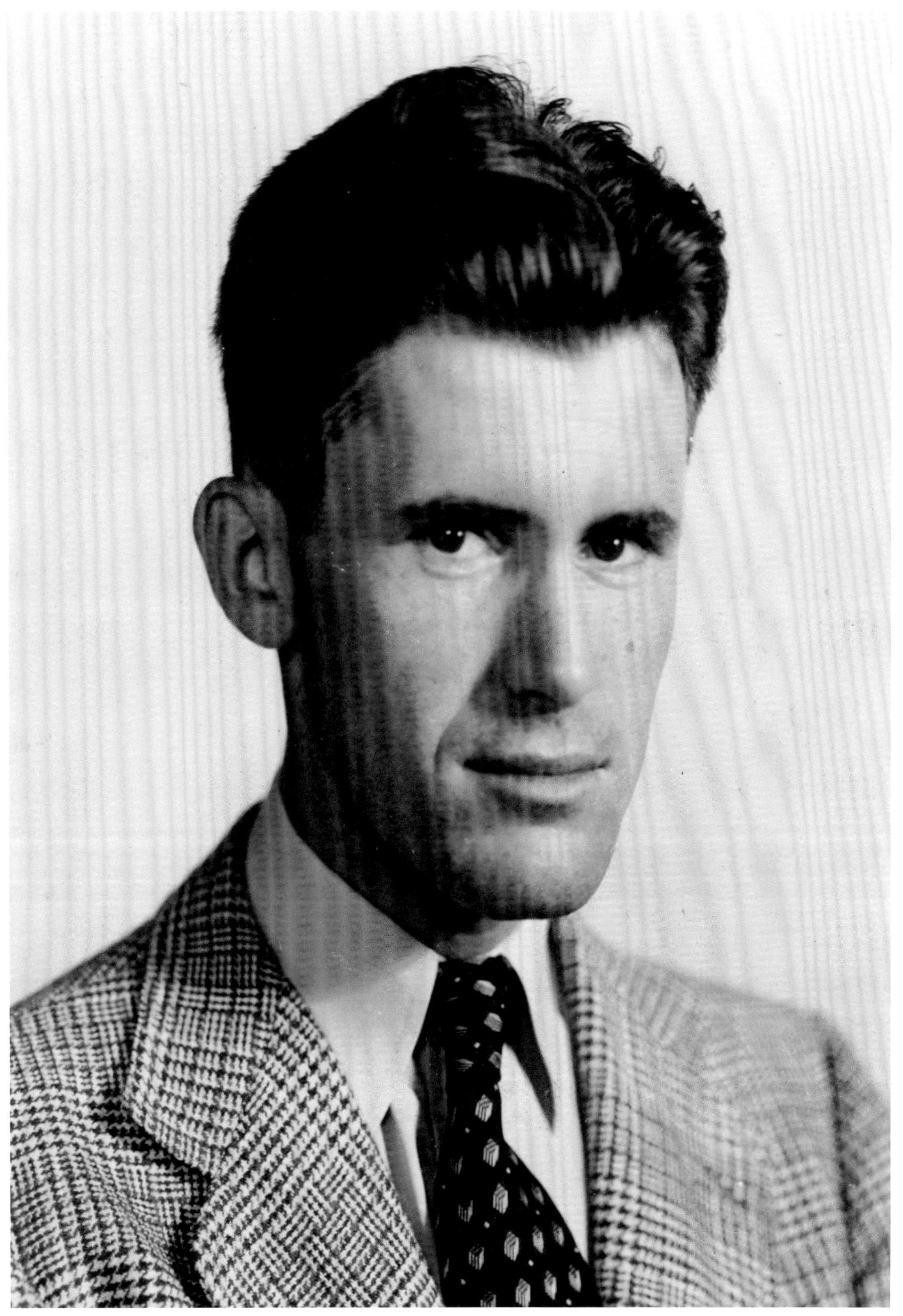

Figure 9.1. John F. Vachon, Farm Security Administration (FSA) photographer.

1942. Library of Congress, Prints & Photographs Division, FSA-OWI Collection, LC-USF341-014695-C.

PORTFOLIO NINE

JOHN VACHON

Like Arthur Rothstein, John Vachon was a FSA photographer who, after he left the agency, spent most of the remainder of his career in photojournalism. And, like Rothstein's work, Vachon's oeuvre is perhaps best characterized as an expansive portfolio of photojournalistic images with a number of portraits that stand out as classic works.[1]

Vachon achieved a successful career despite his substance abuse problems.[2] Born in St. Paul, Minnesota, in 1914, John Vachon earned his undergraduate degree from St. Thomas College. He then moved to Washington, DC, to pursue a graduate degree at Catholic University of America. His substance abuse issue, alcoholism, caught up with him there. Expelled from Catholic University, he found employment at the Farm Security Administration. Quickly discovered and mentored by Roy Stryker, he joined Stryker's team in 1936.[3] He learned to use cameras, including getting instruction from colleague Walker Evans on how to use a large-format camera. Vachon soon also learned how to use the game-changing camera of the era, the compact 35 mm roll film camera.

Vachon did not earn the title of photographer—he was initially an assistant messenger and then a file clerk with the FSA—until 1940 or 1941, but he began taking photos in 1937 and then started going on expansive photographic field trips, initially to Omaha, Nebraska, in 1938. Vachon had one of the longest tenures of any FSA/OWI photographer, staying on with Stryker when the agency moved to the Office of War Information. Vachon followed Stryker from the OWI to Standard Oil in 1943.

Vachon stated that he recognized his own artistic vision as a photographer during his first major solo trip for the FSA, during which he photographed Omaha, Nebraska. Vachon said, "One morning I photographed a grain elevator: pure sun-brushed silo columns of cement rising from behind a C.B. & Q. freight car.[4] The genius of Walker Evans and Charles Sheeler welded into one supreme photographic statement, I thought. Then it occurred to me that it was I who was looking at that grain elevator. . . . I first realized that I had developed my own style of seeing with a camera."[5]

Vachon was drafted soon after joining Standard Oil. After his discharge, he found a job with the United Nations, creating a significant portfolio of images showing Poland in the interregnum between its occupation during World War II and its then becoming a satellite of the Soviet Union.[6] After this 1946 work was over, Vachon worked on the Standard Oil project again for a time and then joined *Look* magazine as a staff photographer in 1948. He remained with *Look* until it stopped publication in 1971. He then worked for *Vermont Life* and, at the very end of his career, taught at the Minnesota Institute of Arts.[7] Vachon died of cancer in 1975.

In addition to his challenges as a "hard-drinking man," Vachon encountered personal tragedy.[8] His first wife, Millicent "Penny" Leeper, was neurodiverse. She committed suicide in 1960, leaving Vachon a single parent with three children.[9] He remarried, to Marie Francoise Fourestier, and they had two children—one of them is noted filmmaker Christine Vachon.

This portfolio of Vachon's FSA/OWI images of American railroading begins with a scene familiar to many railroad enthusiasts—a depot in Connellsville, Pennsylvania, plate 96. This Pennsylvania town is located on today's CSX trackage that includes Sand Patch Grade and is also located on the Great Allegheny Passage rail-trail.[10] Note a now-vanished part of the US railroad scene, the "tell-tales" framing the photo from above. These warned employees working on the roofs of freight cars that a low obstruction was ahead. Catwalks on the roofs of railroad cars, which allowed access to car roofs, were disallowed many years ago.

Plates 97, 98, and 99 were taken nearby. Plate 97 shows a Chesapeake Western locomotive inside a railroad structure. This railroad is a short line with a complex history located in the Shenandoah Valley region of Virginia. Chesapeake Western 109 was a 4-8-0 Twelve Wheeler, also known as a Mastodon. The location appears to be the railroad's shops in Elkton, Virginia. Plates 98 and 99 were taken in remote Elkins, West Virginia. At the time, the town was an operating center for the Western Maryland Railway; today, it is home to the Durbin & Greenbrier Valley Railroad.

Plates 100, 101, and 102 take us to the Deep South, an area emphasized by Vachon's colleague and mentor Walker Evans. Plate 100, showing a railroad station in Manchester, Georgia, on the Atlantic Coast Line Railroad, evidences deep social justice content. As a well-dressed white woman walks by in the background, four Black men stand in the foreground. Two ignore the photographer, while one stares at him, and one glowers. It is a hot day in the pre-air-conditioning US South—the image is dated May 1938—so perhaps the men are cooling off. Or are the Black men avoiding the "Colored Men" waiting room, segregated by race and by sex? Plate 101 is a supremely detailed scene showing the importance of the railroad to US towns like this one, Cordele, Georgia, before the advent of widespread automobile ownership. Cordele was served by a number of railroads at this point in its history. A crowd is gathered at the depot, mail is unloaded from a railway post office car at the front of the train, and a Black worker carries four bags, probably for the well-dressed white woman and child walking a number of paces in front of him. Plate 102 returns us to Manchester, where an elderly, apparently somewhat infirm man stands in front of an antediluvian passenger car. His dress tells us that we are in the US South.

Vachon did a large portfolio of photos focusing on Tulsa, Oklahoma.[11] A number of these are excellent views of the Frisco (St. Louis–San Francisco Railway), which had an important operating center in Tulsa. These show the railroad "at war" during World War II, having been taken in 1942. Plates 103–108 depict views of the Frisco in Tulsa, including an engine dispatching office in plates 103 and 104—an office where engines, engineers, and firemen were assigned to trains.[12]

Plate 105 shows a guard protecting a priority wartime shipment—an oil tank car—in Tulsa during World War II. This photo, like much of Vachon's work, contains layers of content. Oil shipments by rail increased dramatically during early 1942, and although it was not fully understood by the general public at the time, one reason was the debilitating destruction of Allied shipping—many of the ships being tankers—by U-boats off the US Atlantic coast during that year. Also, this scene is taken in wartime, but train inspections such as this were routine closer to the Mexican border, as guards looked for Mexican "illegals" trying to enter the US by train.

Plates 106 and 108 focus on steam locomotives waiting or being serviced in Tulsa, while plate 107 shows a view of shop work, turning a railroad wheel set on a lathe. The identifiable locomotives in plate 108, 4149 and 4103, are 2-8-2 Mikados.

Plates 109–111 are views of US railroading in Texas, including a self-propelled crane at a sulfur plant (plate 109) and the waiting room at a train station in San Augustine on Santa Fe subsidiary Gulf, Colorado and Santa Fe Railway (plate 110). Plate 111 is a rare view—a female railroad employee in a signal tower in

Beaumont, Texas, a town served by a number of railroads. The caboose marks this train as being from the Texas & New Orleans Railroad, a subsidiary of the Southern Pacific. In May 1943, Vachon took a number of views of this female railroad worker, who held a position that—even during wartime—was rarely held by women. The intent was probably to show women assisting the Allied cause during the war.

Vachon grew up in Minnesota, and his feel for the Midwest is evident in his images of that large region. Plates 112–121, the remainder of this portfolio, show the US Midwest, with forays into the Great Plains states. They range from the urban L in Chicago overhanging a trolley car (plate 112) to a railroad station in famously frigid Minot, North Dakota (plate 121), a town then served by the Great Northern and by the Soo, the Minneapolis, St. Paul and Sault Ste. Marie Railroad. This image demonstrates the one-time importance of milk traffic to US railroads.

In plate 113, we see another view of crowded Chicago, while plate 114 takes us to musician Bob Dylan's homeland, the iron-mining region of Minnesota. The iron ore found there stimulated the growth of a number of rail lines. The Danube Mine, shown here, is near Bovey, Minnesota. Bovey was served at the time by the Great Northern and the Duluth, Missabe and Iron Range Railway.

Plates 115 and 116 are images of Vachon's hometown area, Minneapolis, Minnesota, a twin city with Vachon's birthplace, St. Paul. Plate 116 is a notable portrait of a railroad worker, while plate 115 is an innovative view showing the railroad's emerging competitor, a truck, framed in front of a grain elevator through the open doors of a boxcar. Grain is still a key component of railroad freight traffic in the US and Canada today.

Plates 117 and 118 are fascinating Iowa views. In plate 117, a rare FSA/OWI image of an interurban, an interurban car motorman (operator) gets lunch from his wife at Granger Homesteads, Iowa.[13] This interurban is the Des Moines & Central Iowa Railway. In plate 118, one of Vachon's better-known images, he emulates his noted colleague, Dorothea Lange, as he shows a boy undertaking the dangerous move of hopping a freight train, to then be known as a bum or tramp. The location, Dubuque, Iowa, was served by a number of railroads.

Vachon's first major FSA assignment was an extended visit to document the Omaha, Nebraska, area in late 1938. Omaha was and is one of the great rail centers of the United States. It is especially noted in railroad history as the headquarters of one of today's vast US Class One railroads, the Union Pacific. This visit produced some of Vachon's best-known images.[14] Plate 119 is a portrait of an engineer in Omaha. Plate 120 is a view of railroad-served grain elevators in Omaha.[15] The locomotive in the foreground of plate 120 is Rock Island—Chicago, Rock Island and Pacific Railroad—2121, a 2-8-0 Consolidation.

These Midwestern images, closing this Vachon portfolio, reflect his feel for the Midwest and also show the importance of grain farming to this part of the United States.

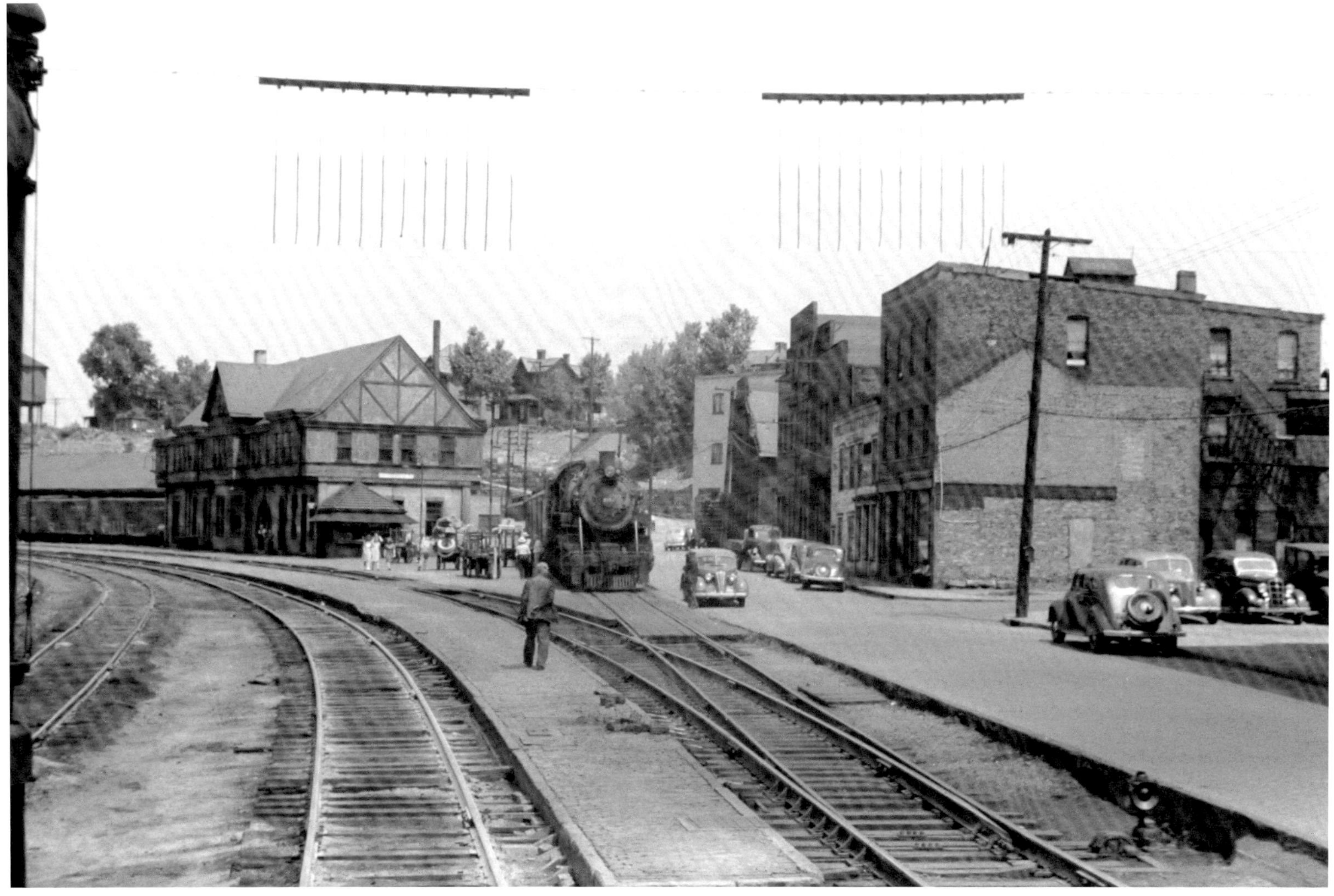

***Above*, Plate 96.** Connellsville, Pennsylvania. A railroad depot.

John Vachon. July 1940. Library of Congress, Prints & Photographs Division, FSA-OWI Collection, LC-USF33-016009-M1.

***Facing*, Plate 97.** Shenandoah Valley. Chesapeake and Western Railway runs through the valley, seventeen miles in length.

John Vachon. May 1941. Library of Congress, Prints & Photographs Division, FSA-OWI Collection, LC-USE6-D-000228.

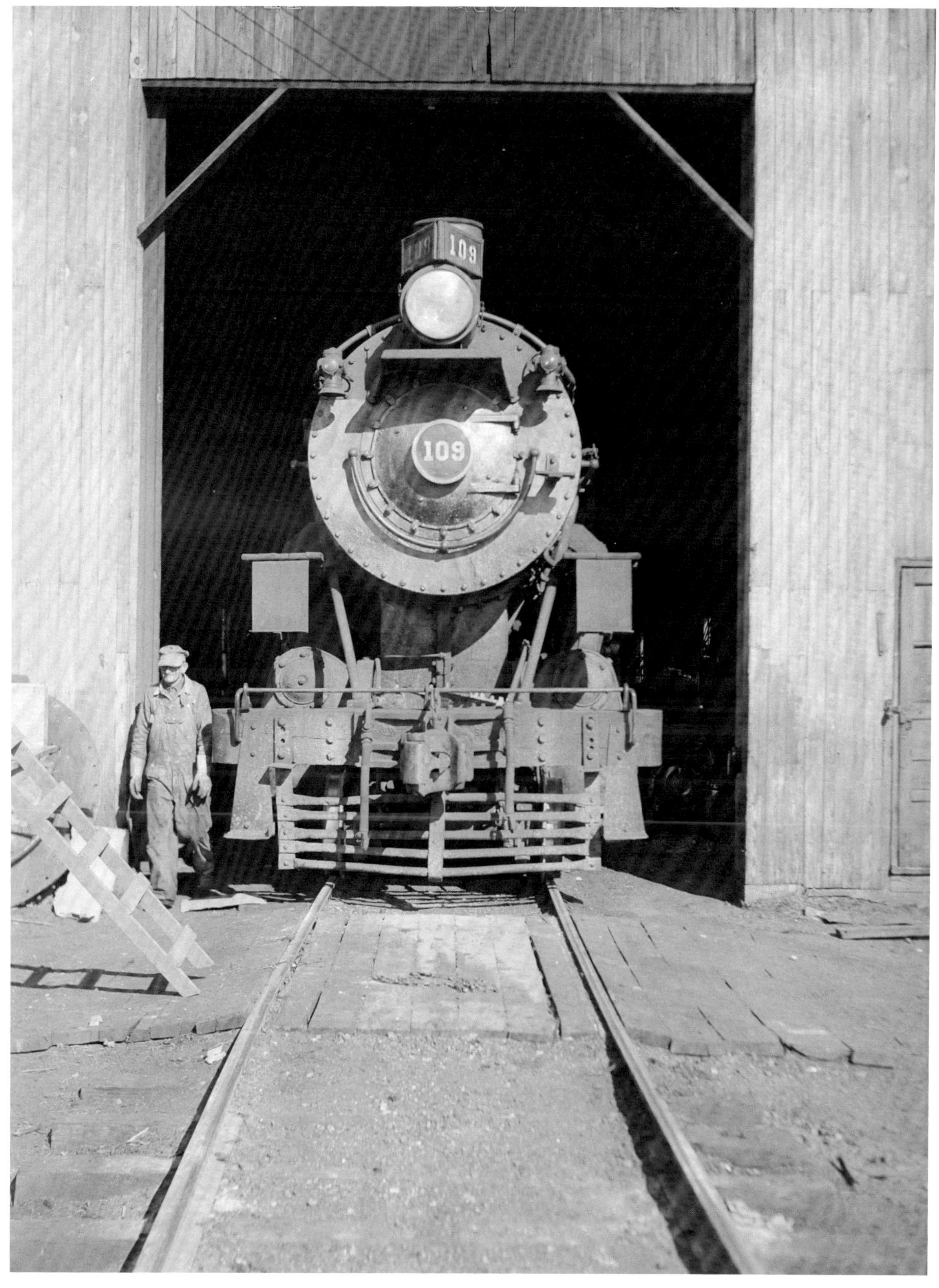
109
109

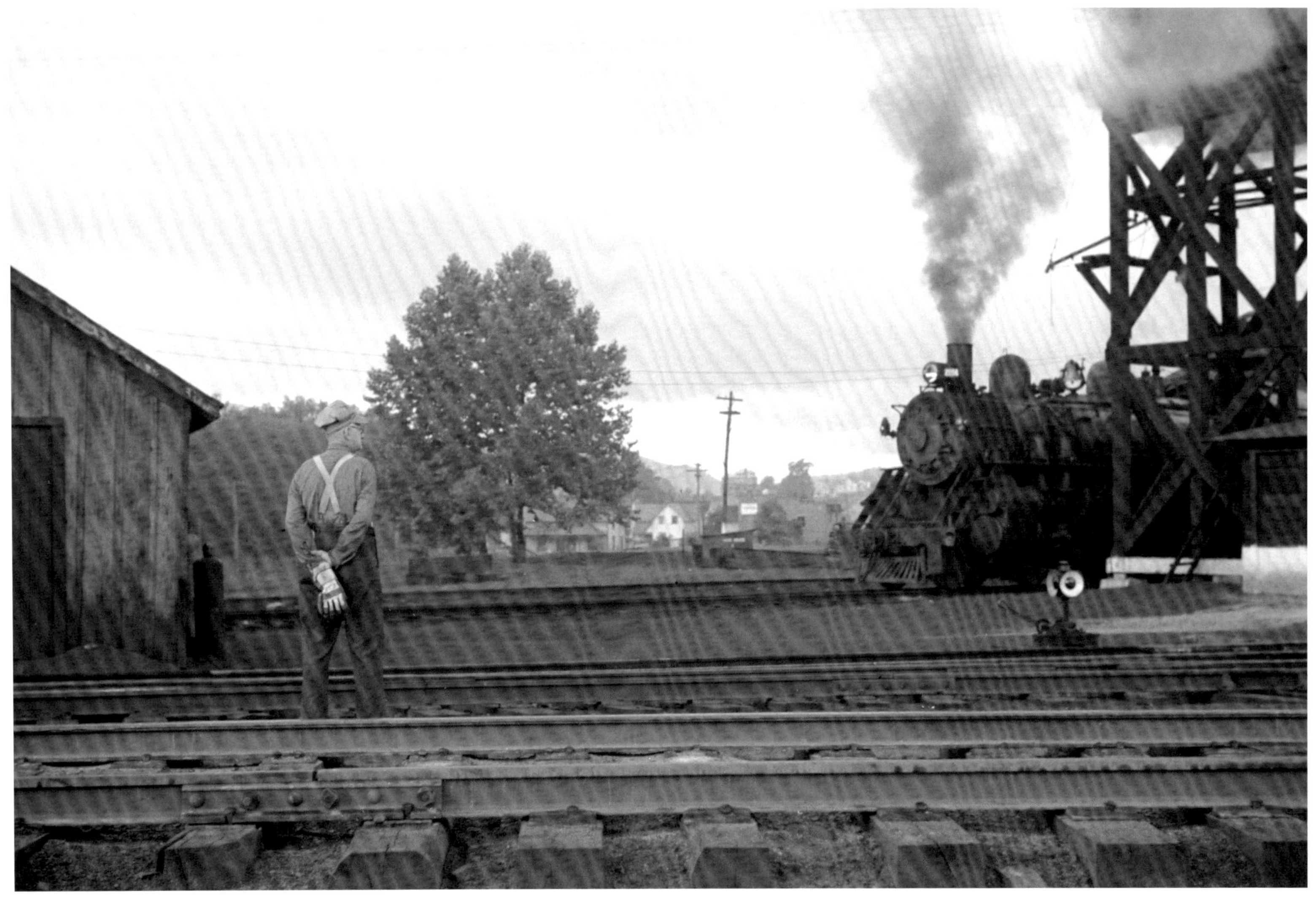

Plate 98. Railroad yards, Elkins, West Virginia.

John Vachon. June 1939. Library of Congress, Prints & Photographs Division, FSA-OWI Collection, LC-USF33-001403-M2.

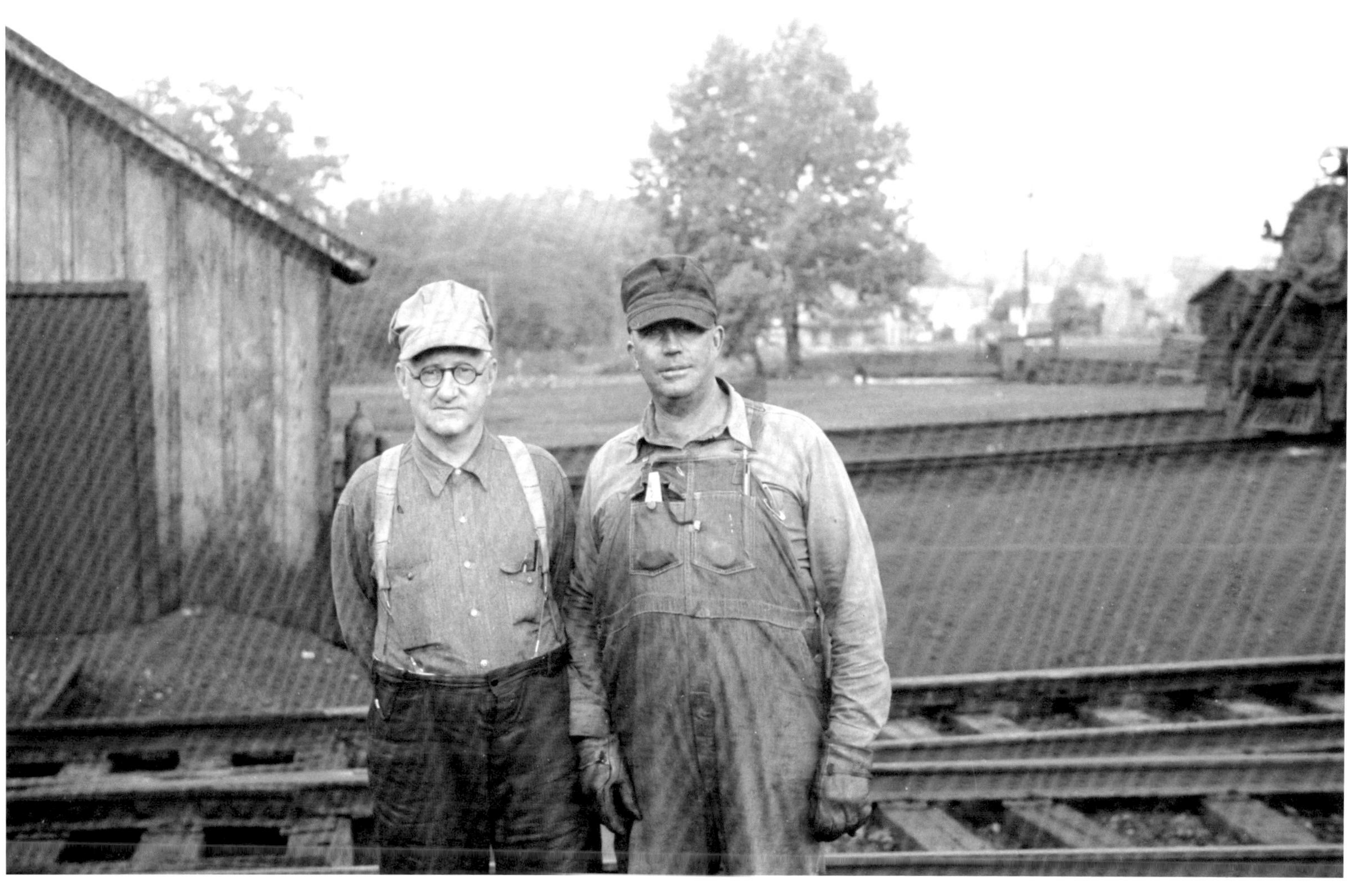

Plate 99. Engineer and brakeman in railroad yards, Elkins, West Virginia.

John Vachon. June 1939. Library of Congress, Prints & Photographs Division, FSA-OWI Collection, LC-USF33-T01-001403-M4.

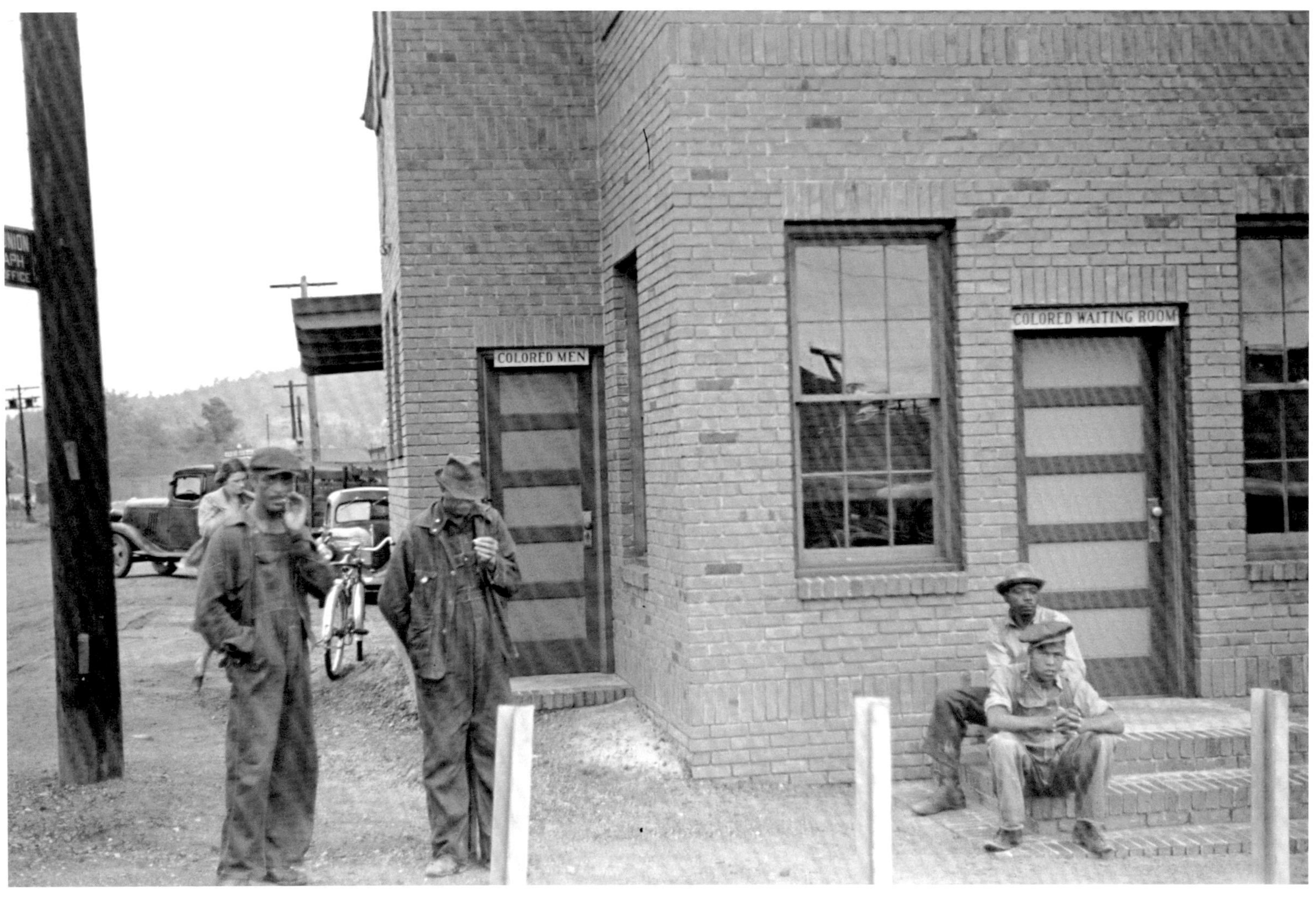

Plate 100. Railroad station, Manchester, Georgia.

John Vachon. May 1938. Library of Congress, Prints & Photographs Division, FSA-OWI Collection, LC-USF33-001172-M4.

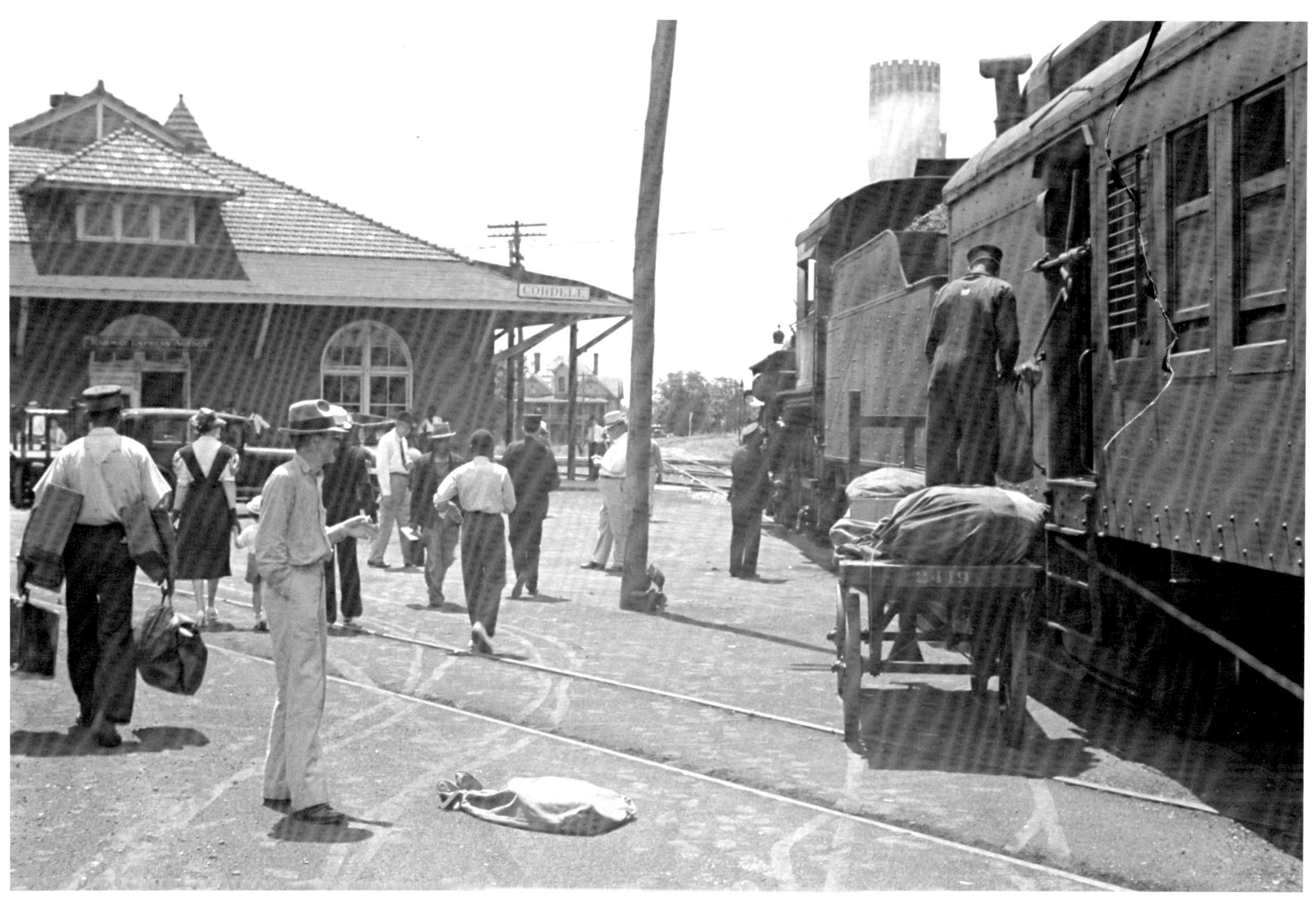

Plate 101. Railroad station, Cordele, Georgia.

John Vachon. May 1938. Library of Congress, Prints & Photographs Division, FSA-OWI Collection, LC-USF33-001148-M1.

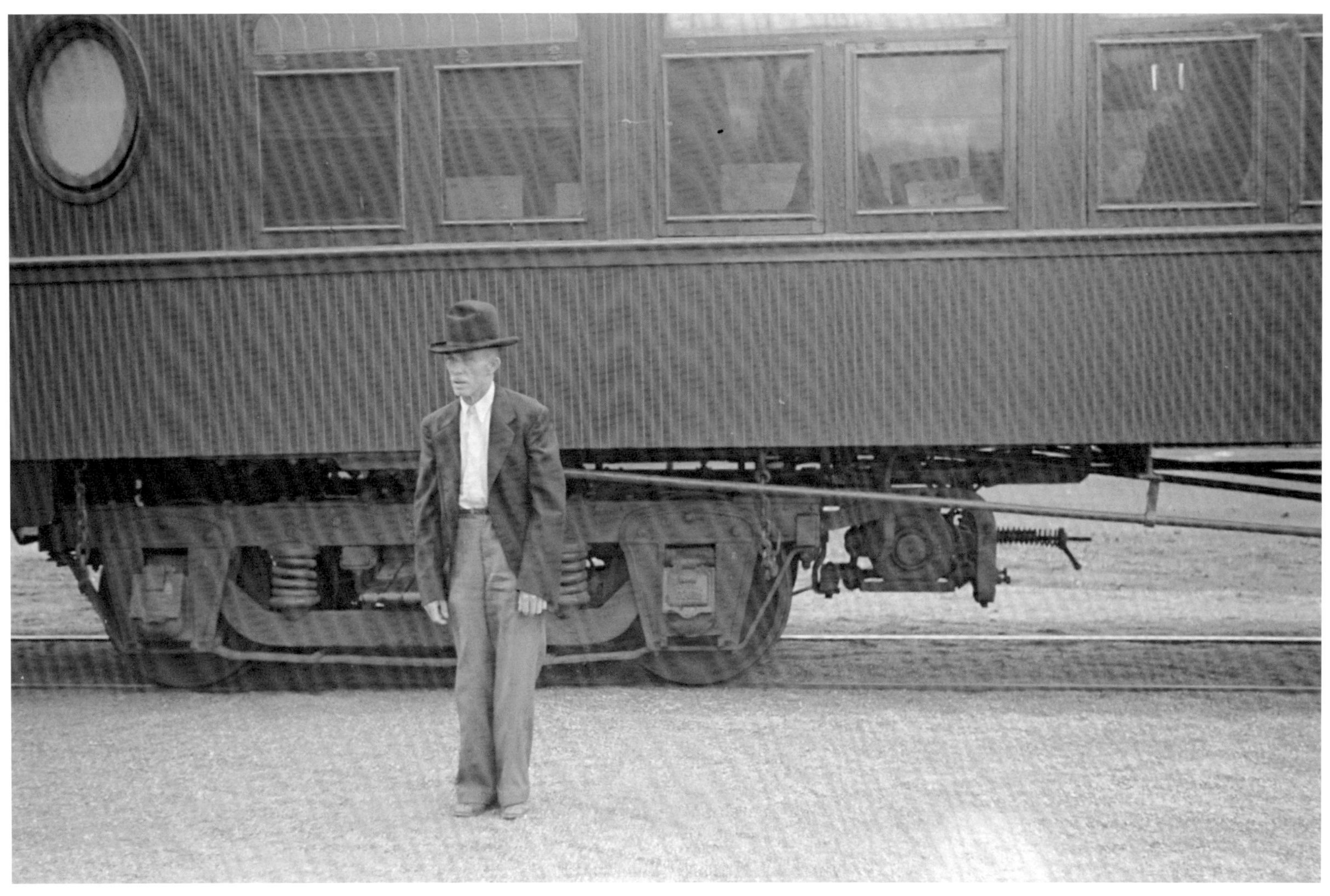

Plate 102. Man in railroad station, Manchester, Georgia.

John Vachon. May 1938. Library of Congress, Prints & Photographs Division, FSA-OWI Collection, LC-USF3301-001172-M3.

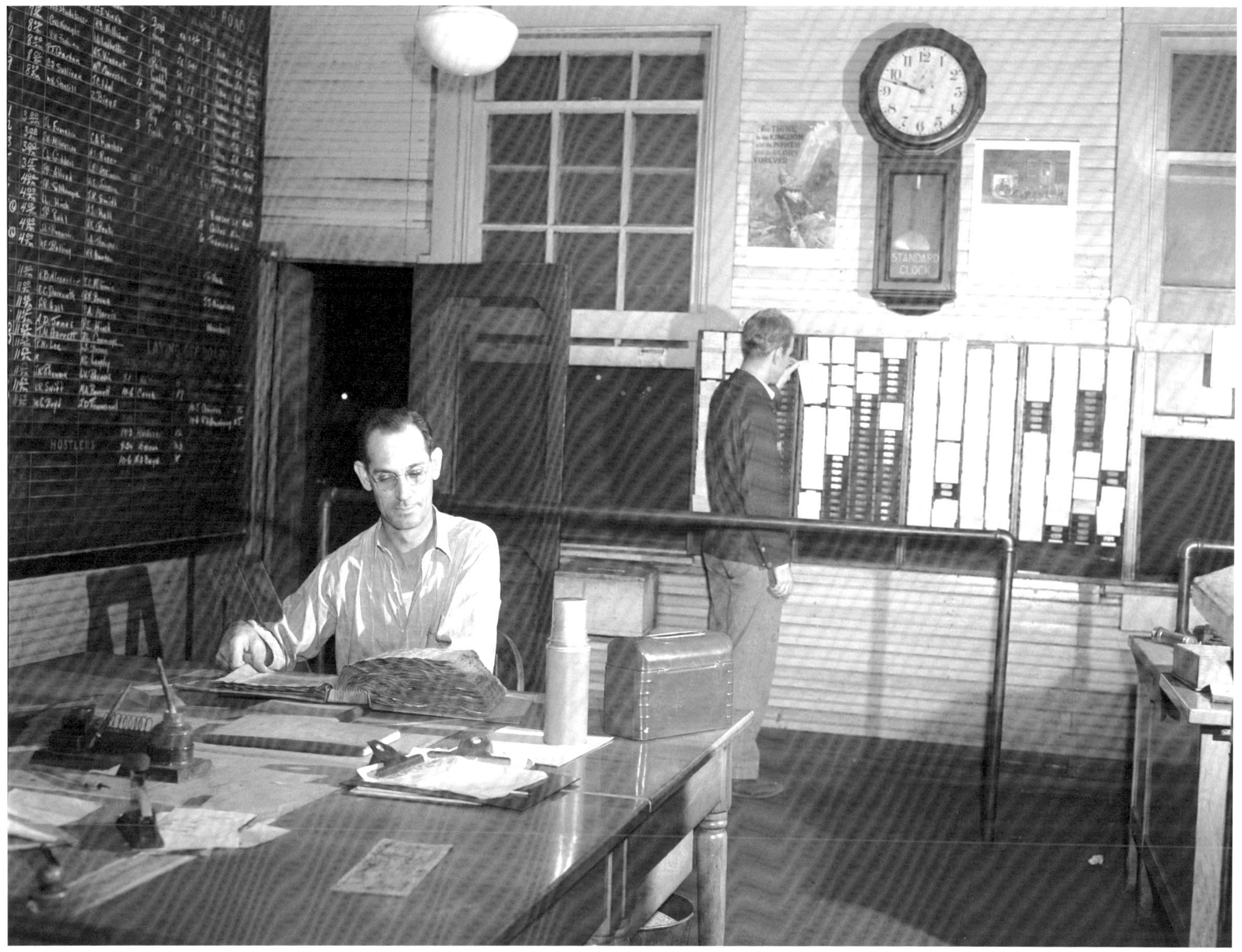

Plate 103. Tulsa, Oklahoma. Engine dispatching office in the Frisco railroad yards.

John Vachon. October 1942. Library of Congress, Prints & Photographs Division, FSA-OWI Collection, LC-USW3-009490-D.

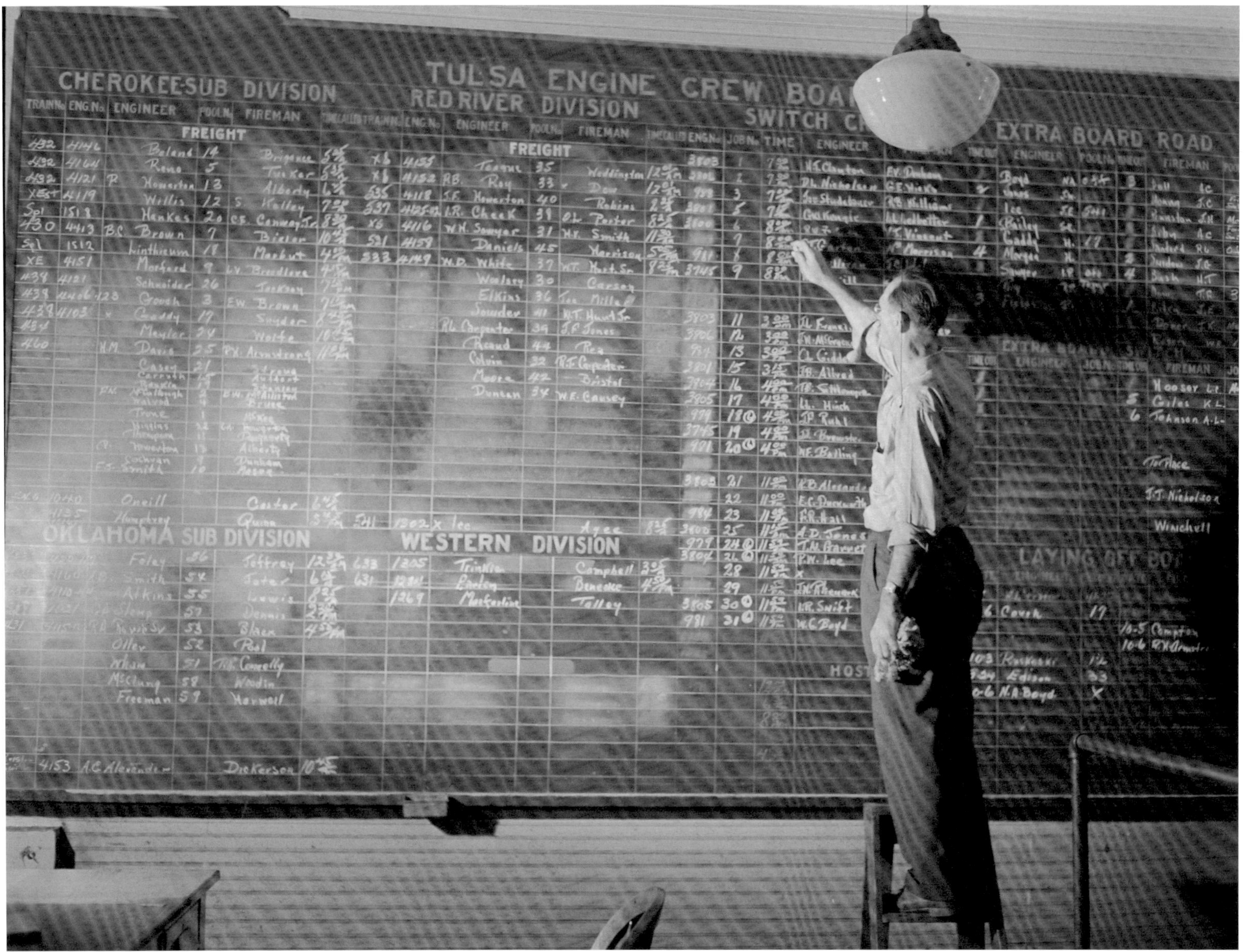

Plate 104. Tulsa, Oklahoma. Engine dispatching office in the Frisco railroad yards.

John Vachon. October 1942. Library of Congress, Prints & Photographs Division, FSA-OWI Collection, LC-USW3-009527-D.

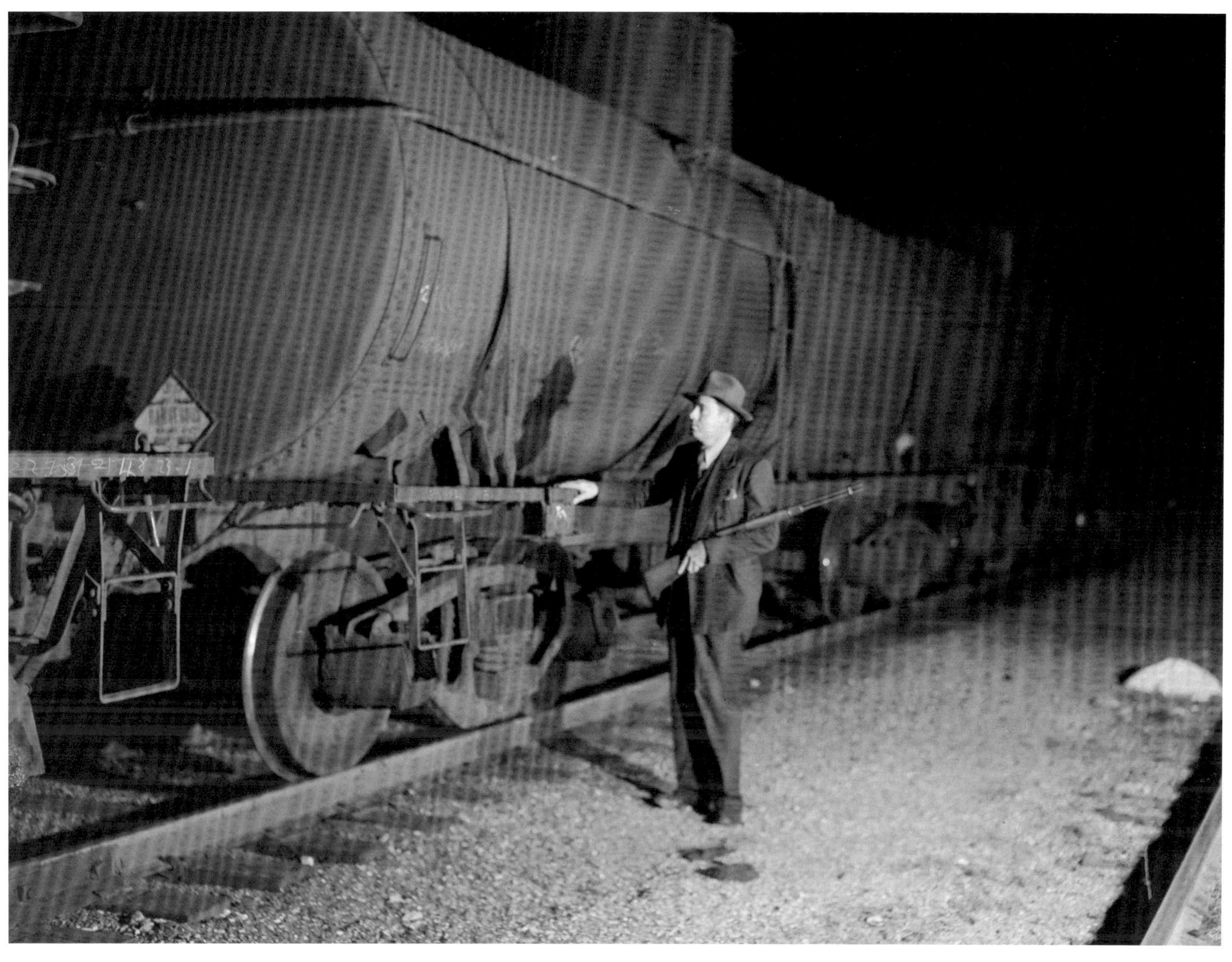

Plate 105. Tulsa, Oklahoma. Armed railroad guard inspecting an oil tank car in the yards.

John Vachon. October 1942. Library of Congress, Prints & Photographs Division, FSA-OWI Collection, LC-USW3-009503-D.

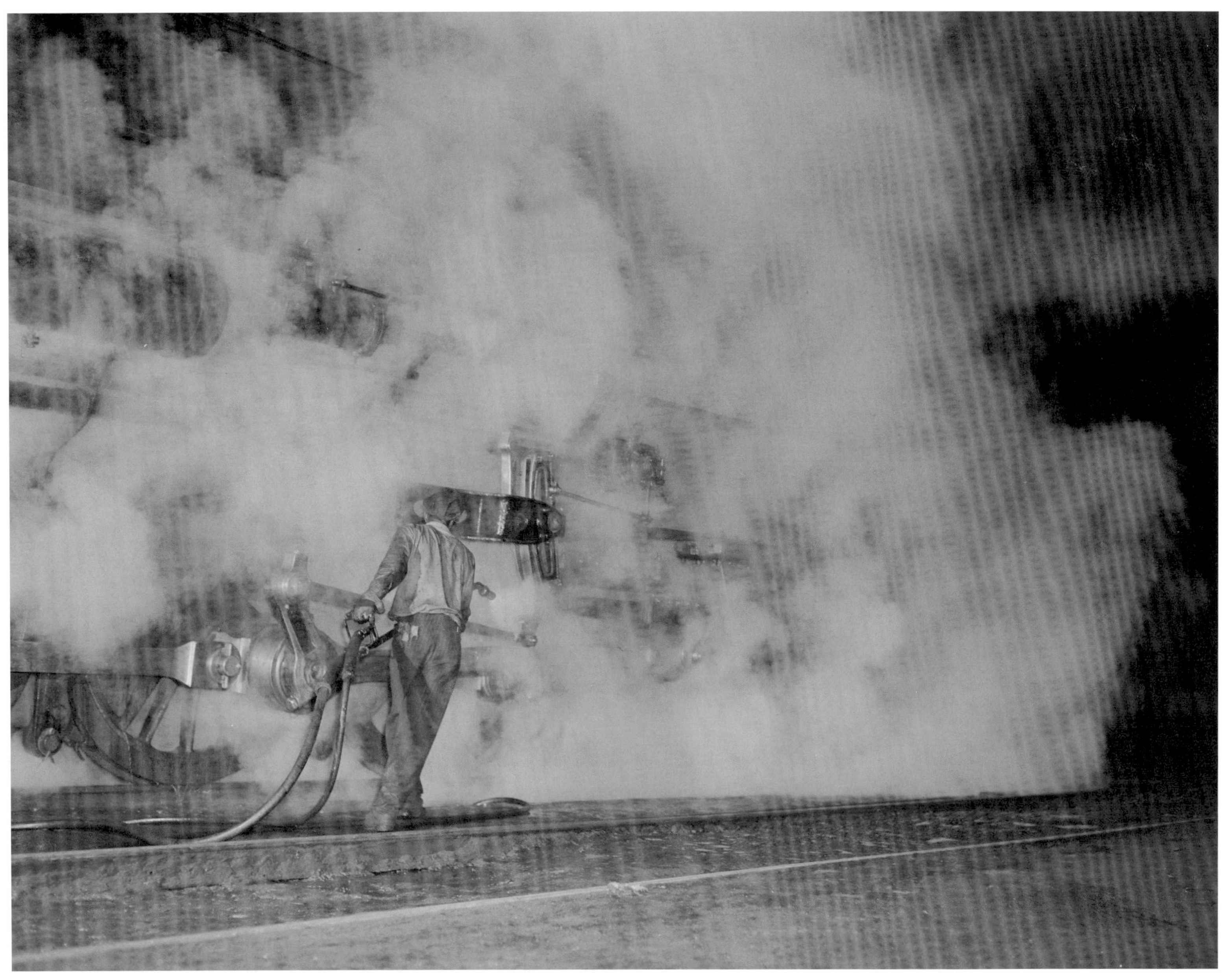

Plate 106. Tulsa, Oklahoma. Cleaning an engine with a steam pressure gun in the Frisco railroad yards at night.

John Vachon. October 1942. Library of Congress, Prints & Photographs Division, FSA-OWI Collection, LC-USW3-009530-D.

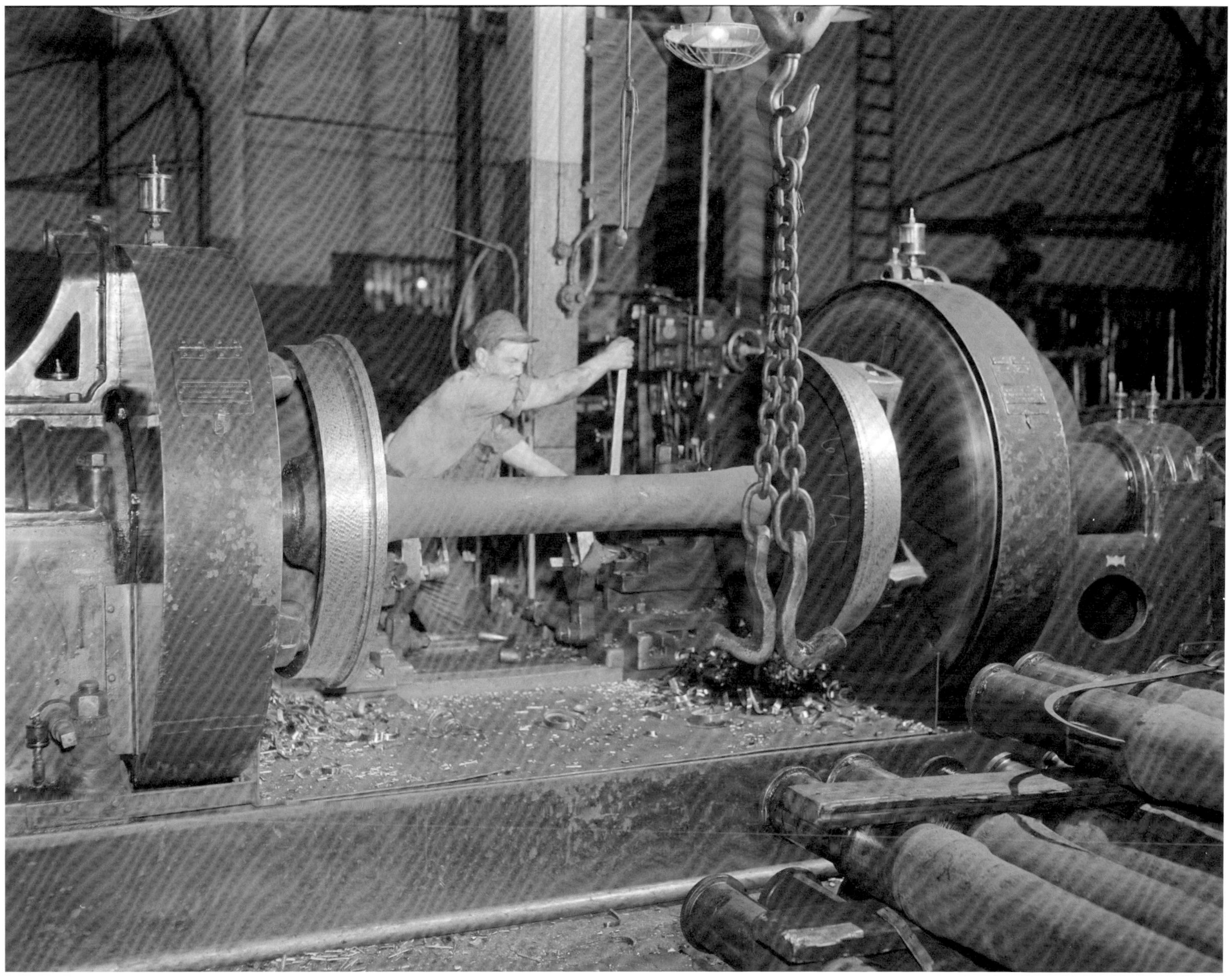

Plate 107. Tulsa, Oklahoma. Repairing railroad wheels in a machine shop of the Frisco railroad yards.

John Vachon. October 1942. Library of Congress, Prints & Photographs Division, FSA-OWI Collection, LC-USW3-009528-D.

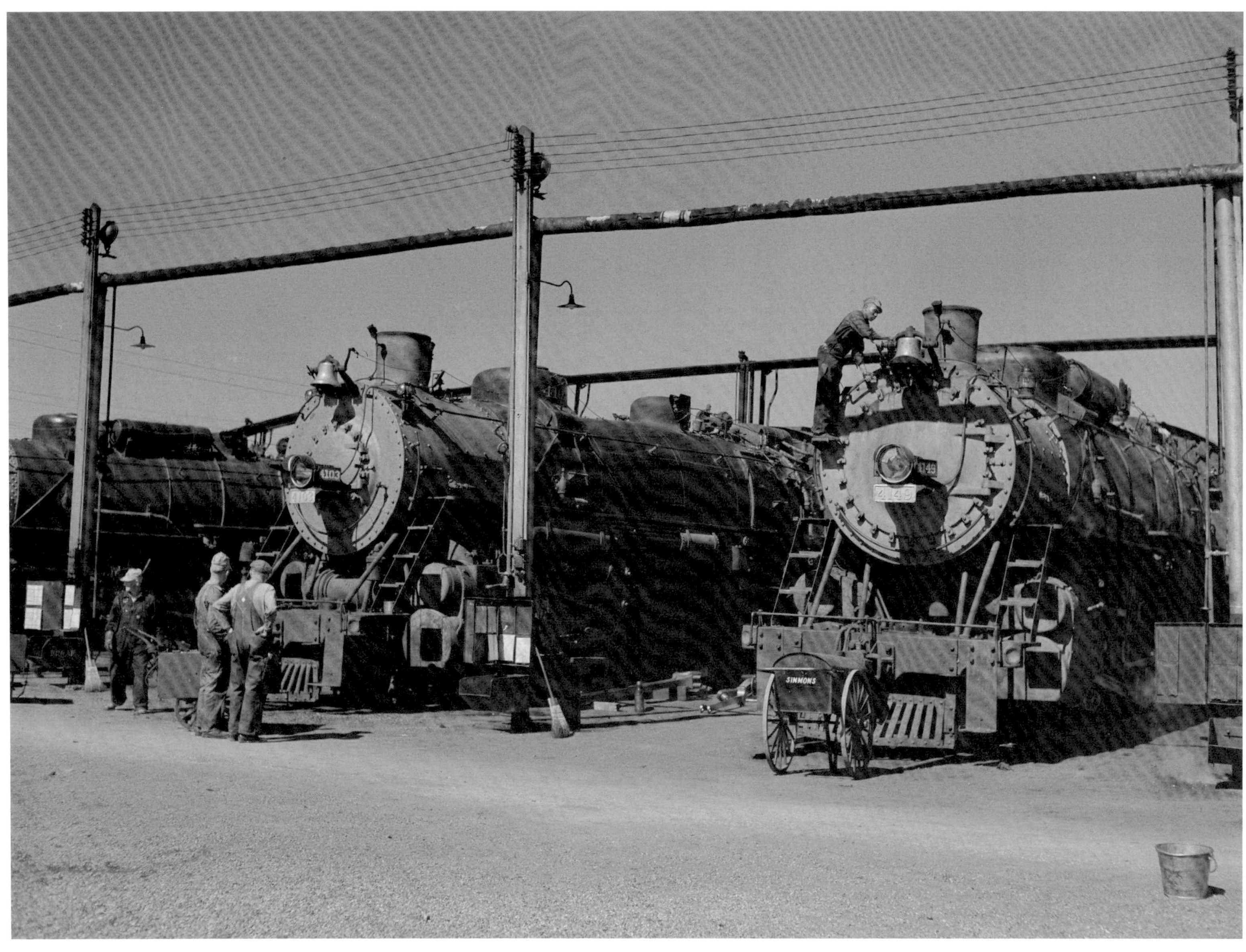

Plate 108. Tulsa, Oklahoma. Engines at the roundhouse at the Frisco railroad.

John Vachon. October 1942. Library of Congress, Prints & Photographs Division, FSA-OWI Collection, LC-USW3-009557-D.

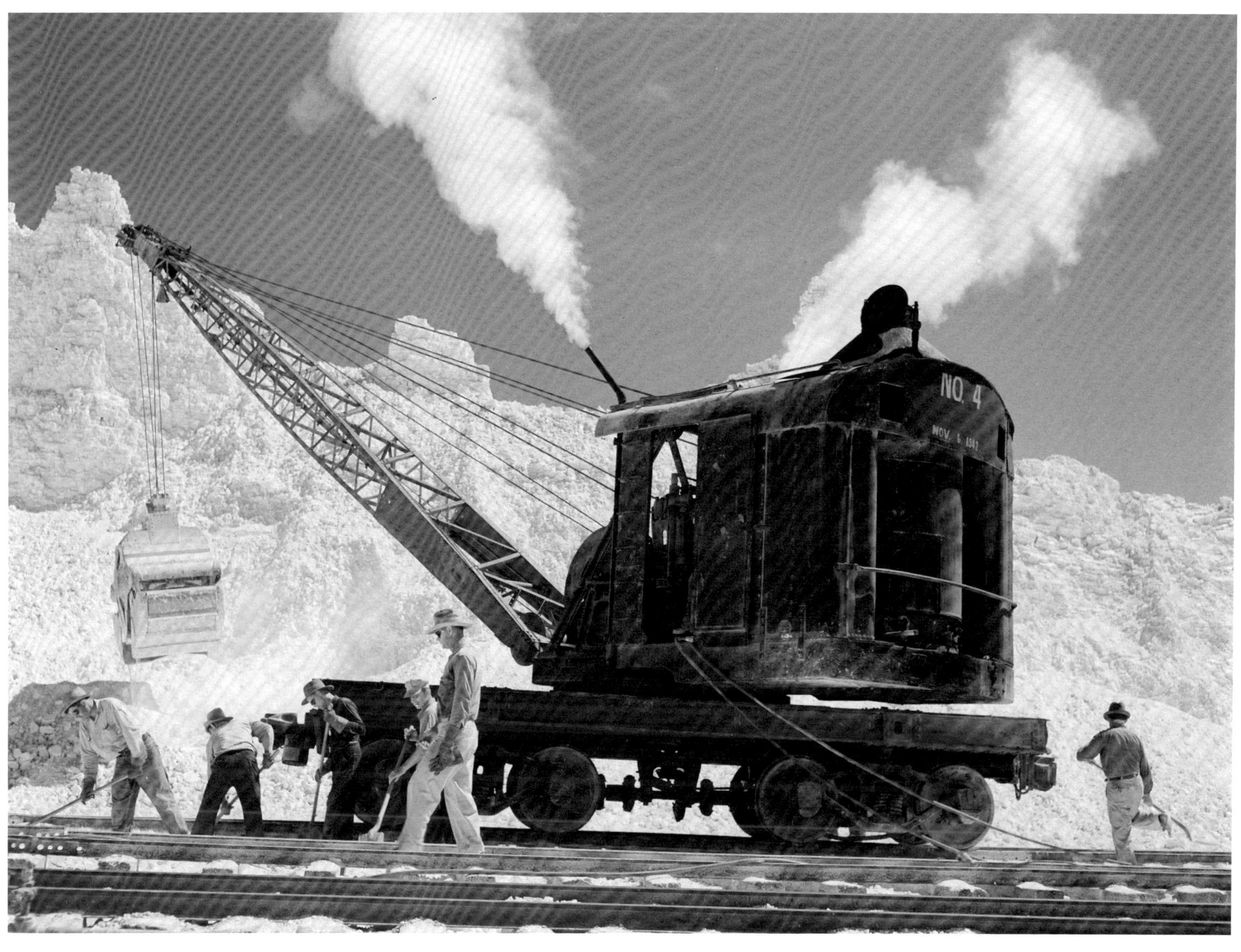

Plate 109. Freeport Sulphur Company, Hoskins Mound, Texas. Cleaning sulfur off railroad tracks after blasting.

John Vachon. May 1943. Library of Congress, Prints & Photographs Division, FSA-OWI Collection, LC-USW3-028839-D.

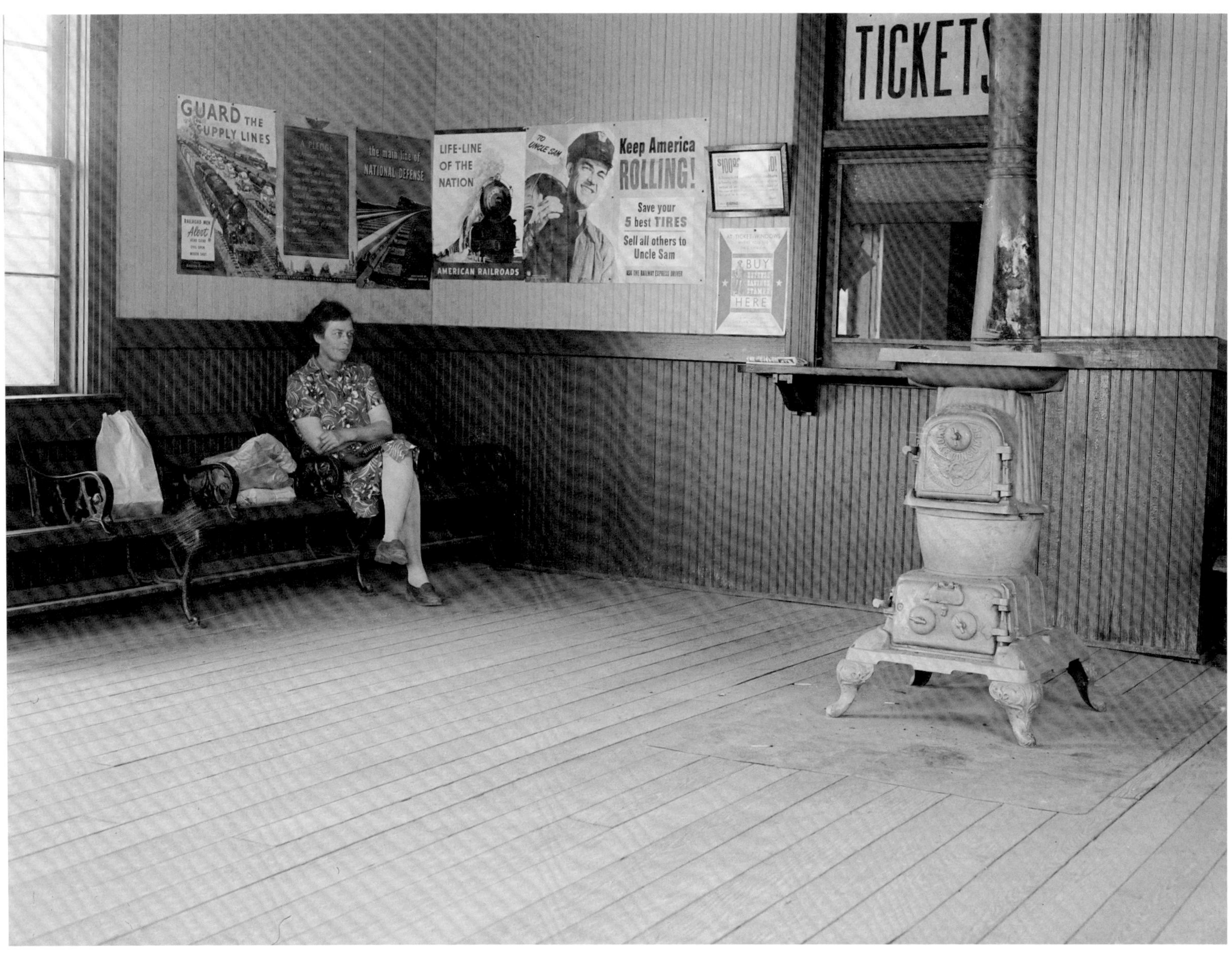

Plate 110. San Augustine, Texas. The waiting room in the railroad station.

John Vachon. April 1943. Library of Congress, Prints & Photographs Division, FSA-OWI Collection, LC-USW3-025220-D.

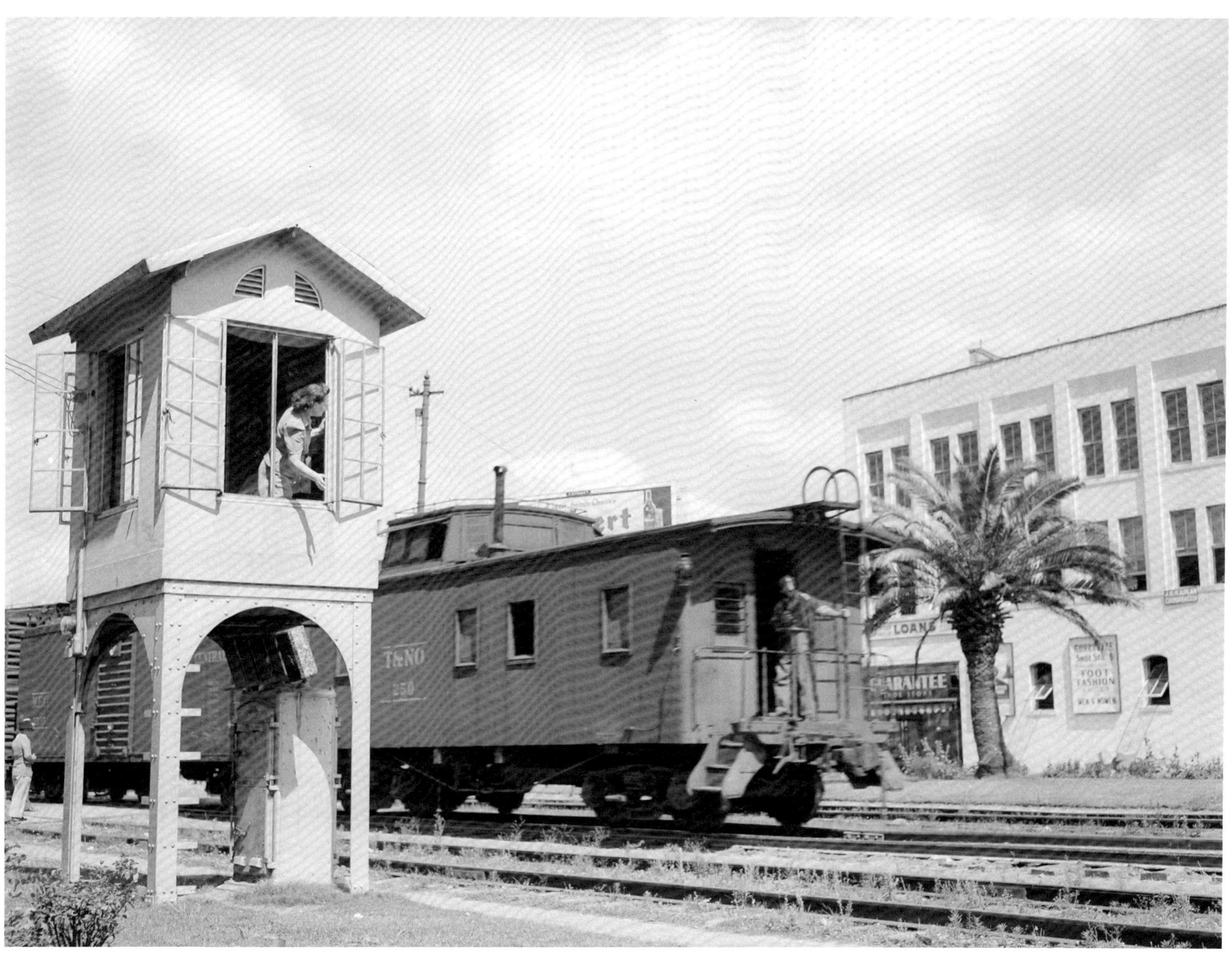

Plate 111. Beaumont, Texas. Lady in a railroad signal tower.

John Vachon. May 1943. Library of Congress, Prints & Photographs Division, FSA-OWI Collection, LC-USW3-030984-D.

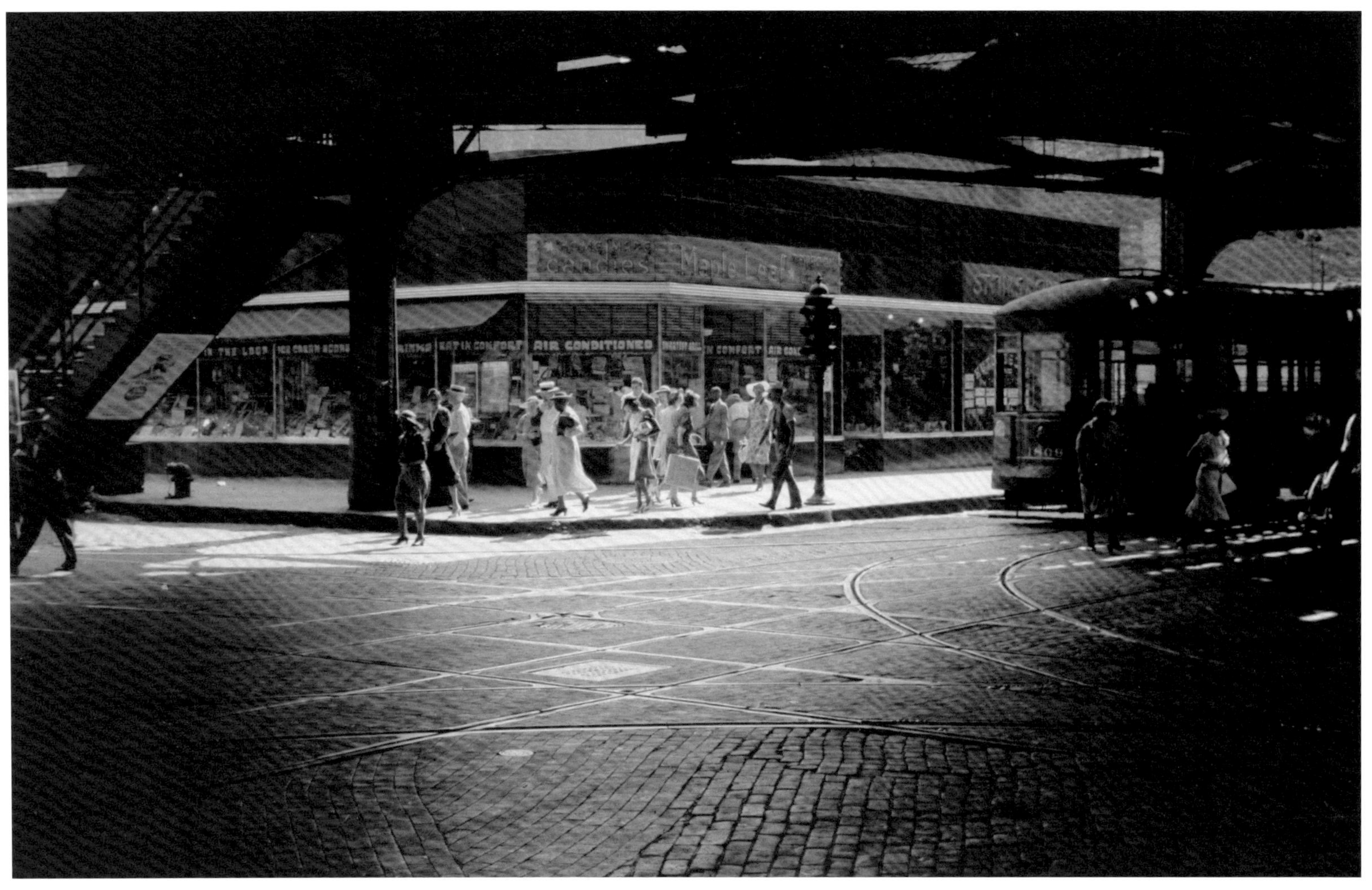

Plate 112. Under the elevated railway, Chicago, Illinois.

John Vachon. July 1940. Library of Congress, Prints & Photographs Division, FSA-OWI Collection, LC-USF33-001962-M3.

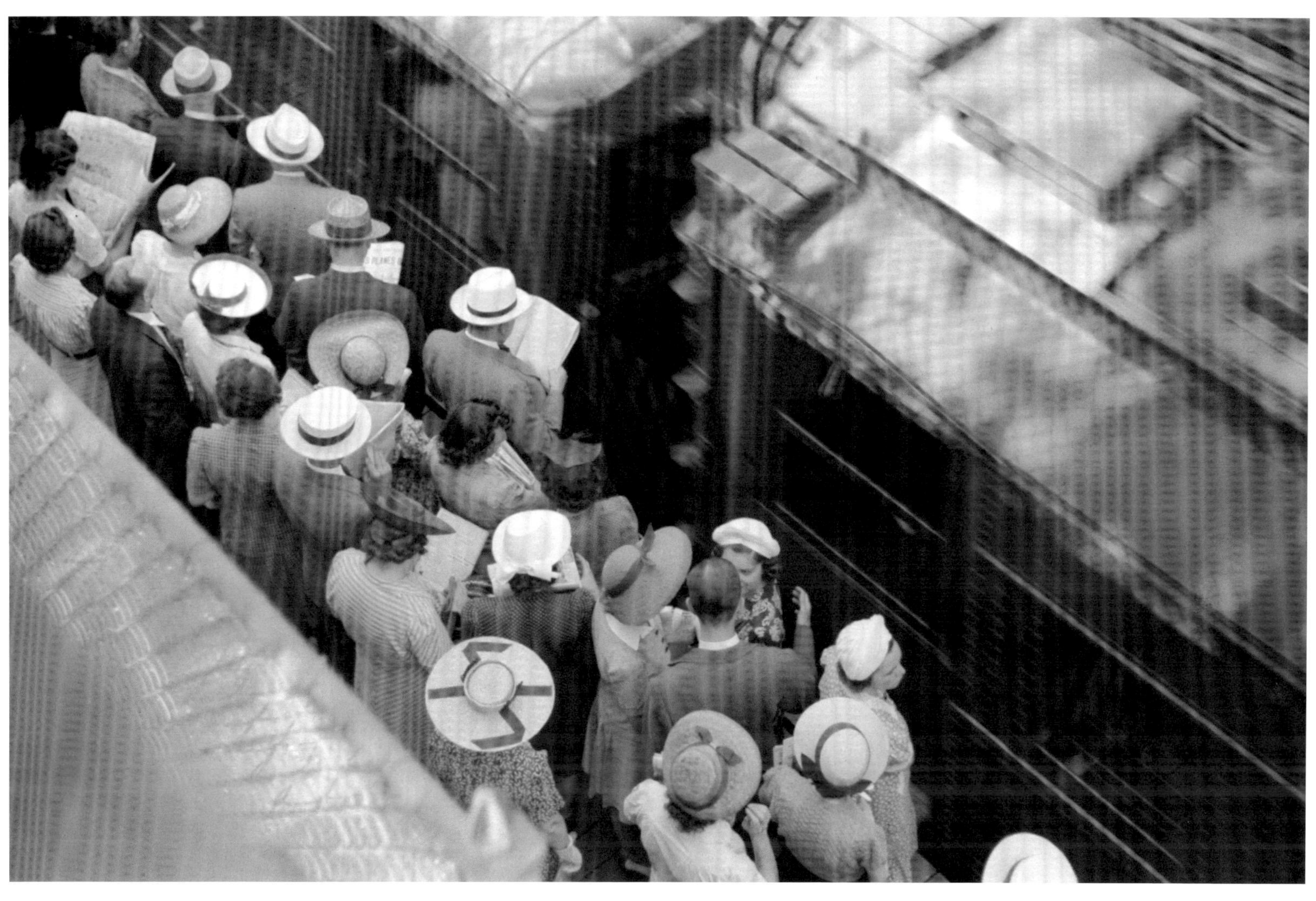

Plate 113. Commuters waiting for southbound trains, Chicago, Illinois.

John Vachon. July 1941. Library of Congress, Prints & Photographs Division, FSA-OWI Collection, LC-USF33-016119-M3.

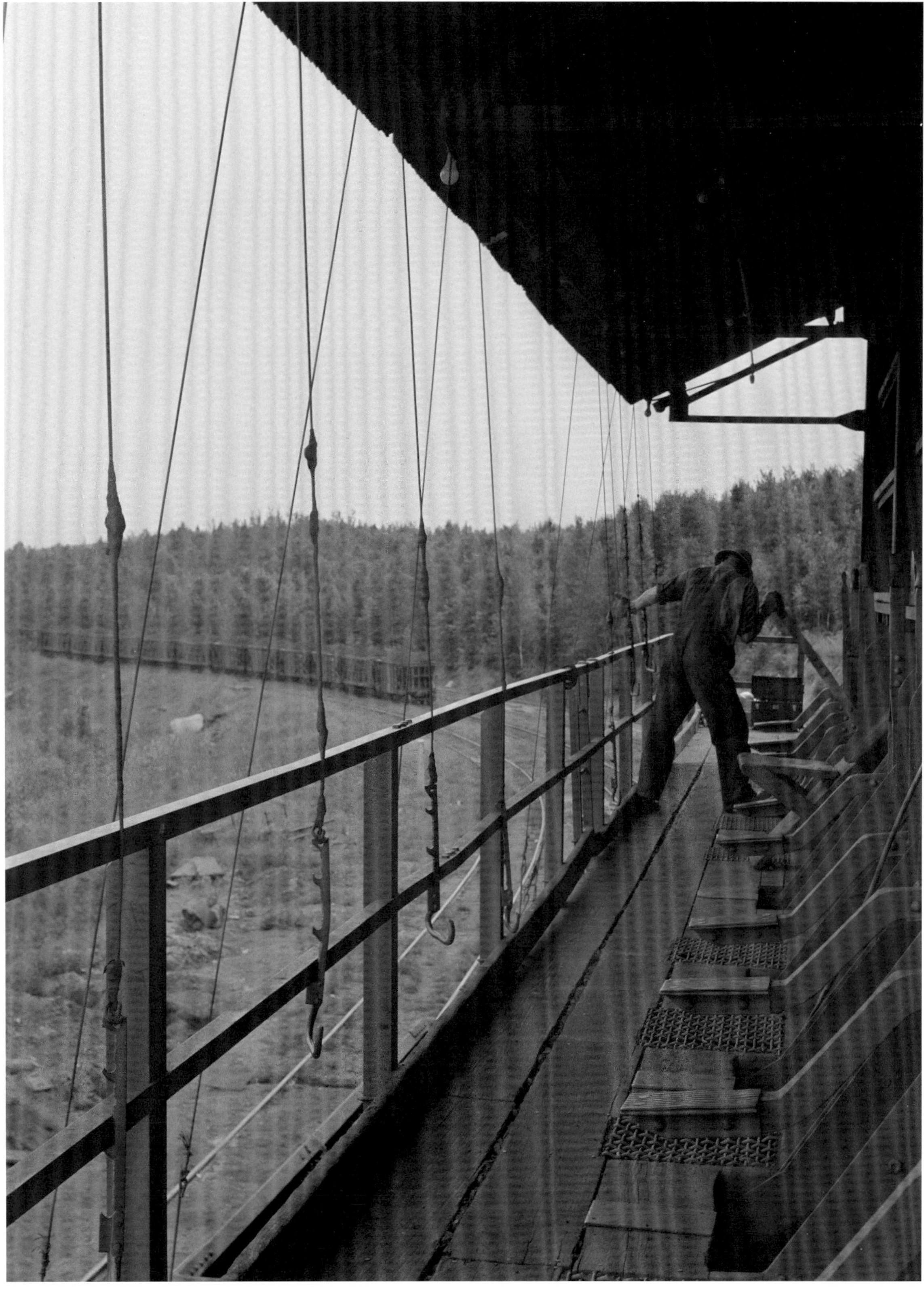

Plate 114. Operating releases that control chutes in loading railroad cars with ore at concentration plant for Danube mine near Bovey, Minnesota.

John Vachon. August 1941. Library of Congress, Prints & Photographs Division, FSA-OWI Collection, LC-USF34-064000-D.

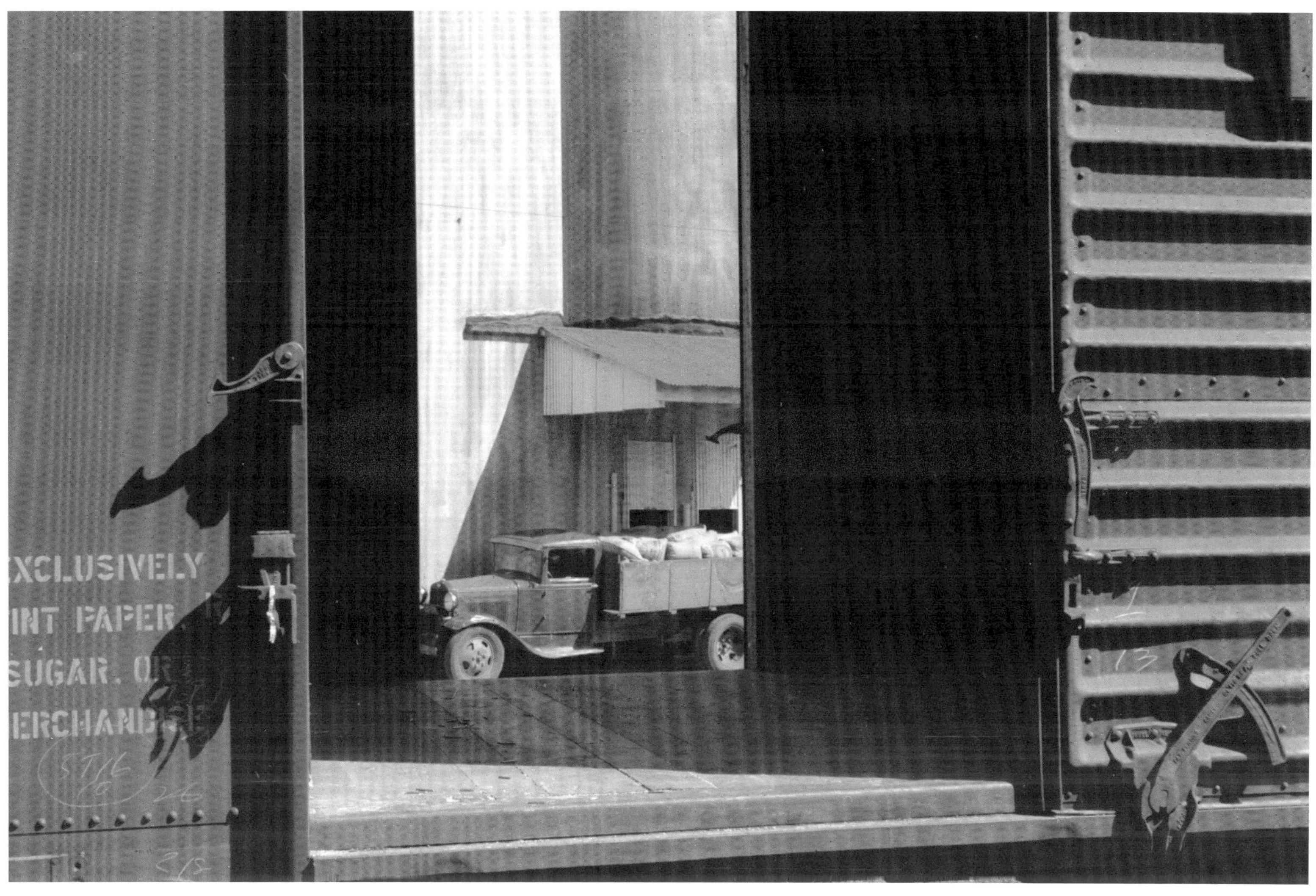

Plate 115. Untitled photo, possibly related to: Truck unloading sacks of wheat at elevator. Most grain is delivered to city elevators by freight train. Minneapolis, Minnesota.

John Vachon. September 1939. Library of Congress, Prints & Photographs Division, FSA-OWI Collection, LC-USF33-001456-M5.

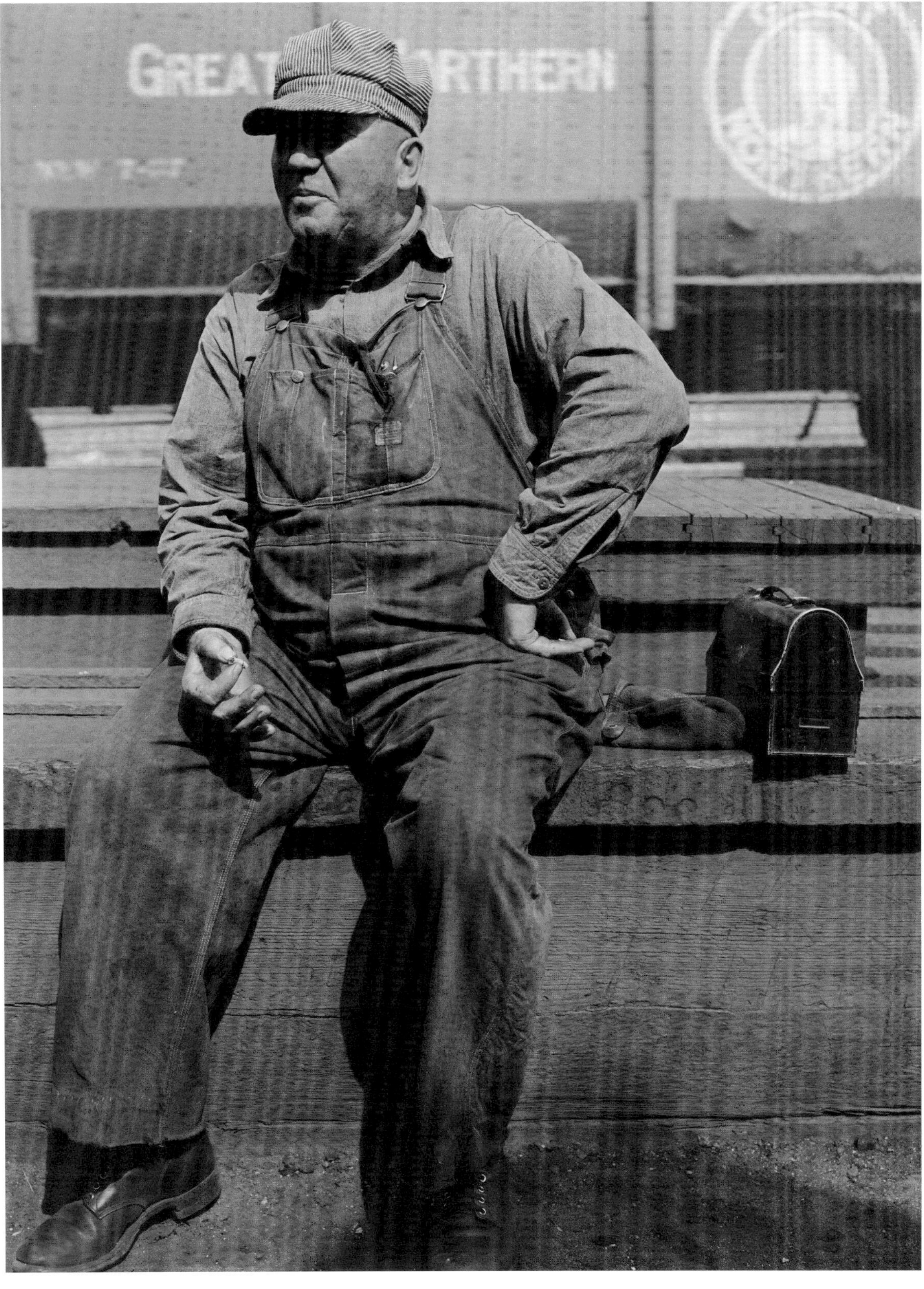

Plate 116. Railroad worker. Minneapolis, Minnesota.

John Vachon. September 1939. Library of Congress, Prints & Photographs Division, FSA-OWI Collection, LC-USF34-060343-D.

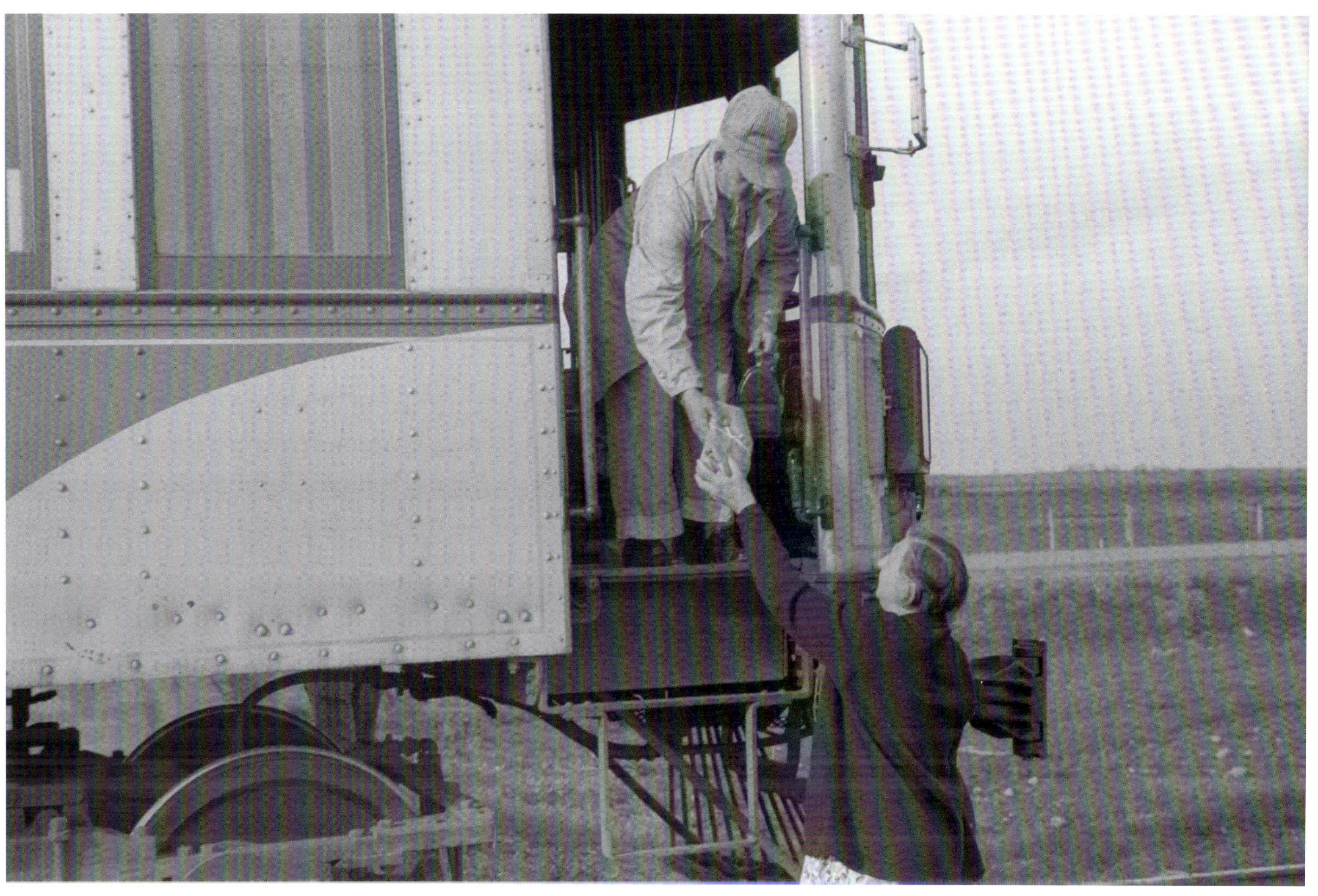

Plate 117. Untitled photo, possibly related to: Motorman of interurban railway receiving lunch from his wife. They are residents of Granger Homesteads, Iowa. The car runs through the project.

John Vachon. April 1940. Library of Congress, Prints & Photographs Division, FSA-OWI Collection, LC-USF33-T01-001829-M3.

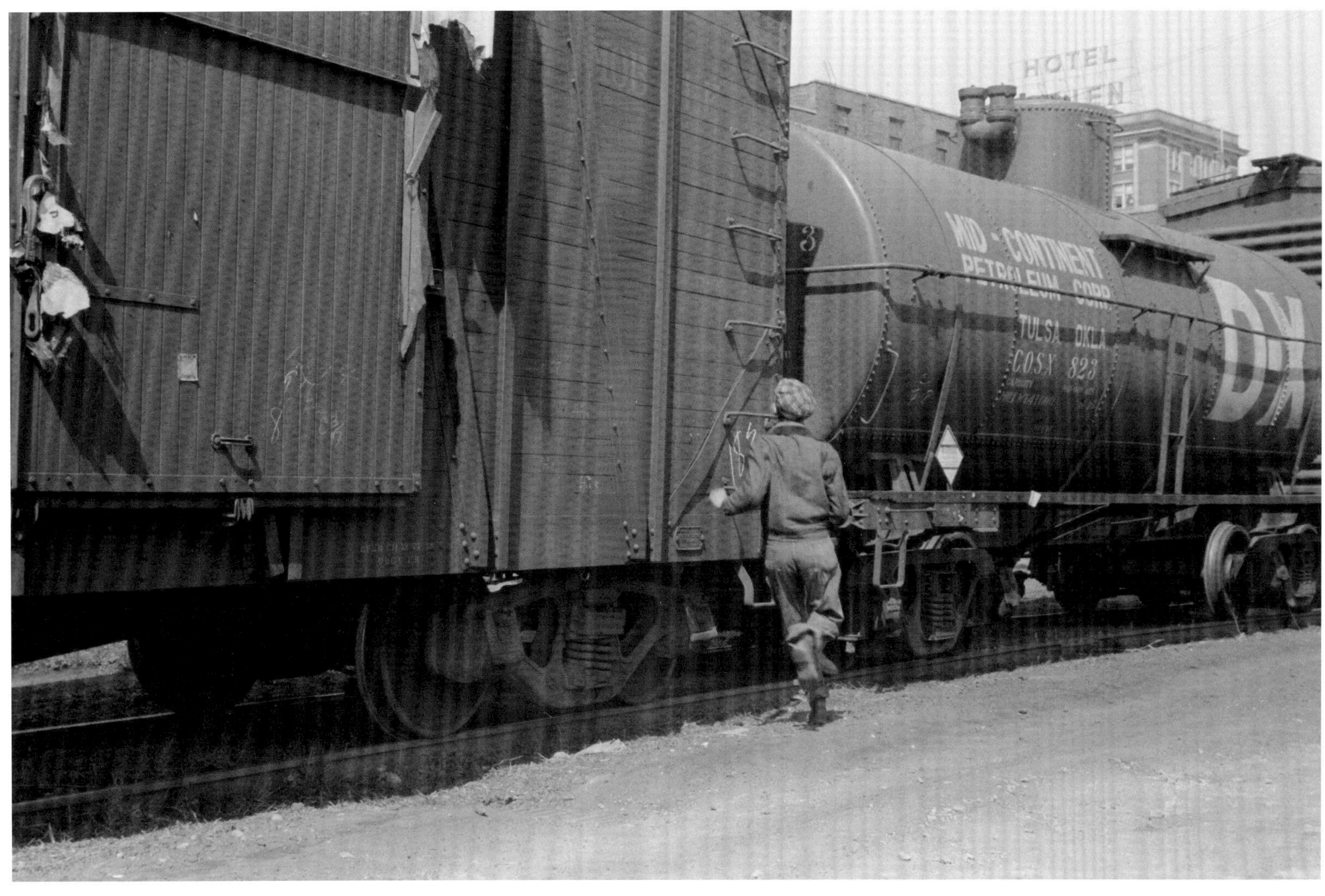

Plate 118. Boy hopping freight train, Dubuque, Iowa.

John Vachon. April 1940. Library of Congress, Prints & Photographs Division, FSA-OWI Collection, LC-USF33-001772-M5.

Plate 119. Railroad engineer. Omaha, Nebraska.

John Vachon. November 1938. Library of Congress, Prints & Photographs Division, FSA-OWI Collection, LC-USF34-008910-D.

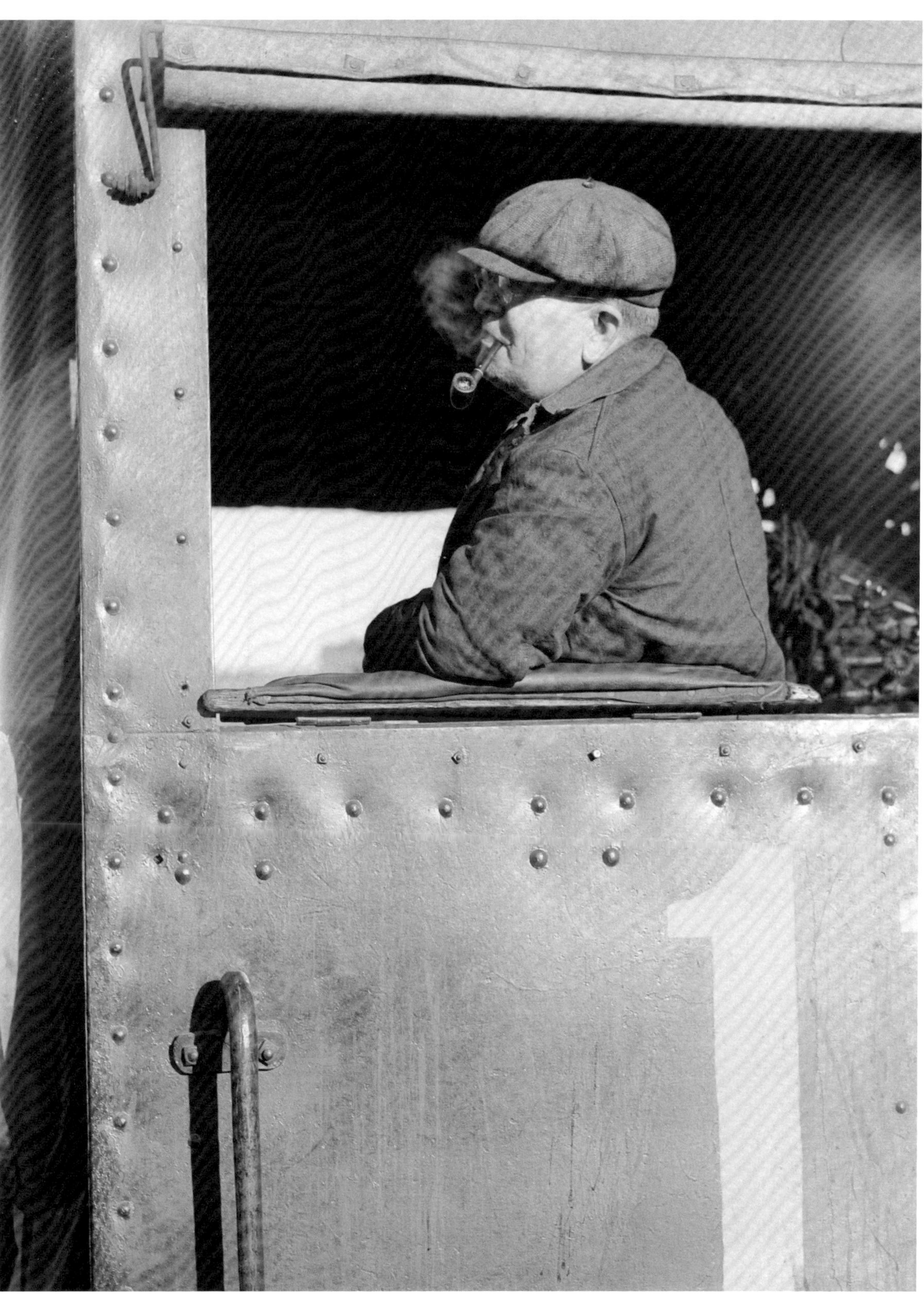

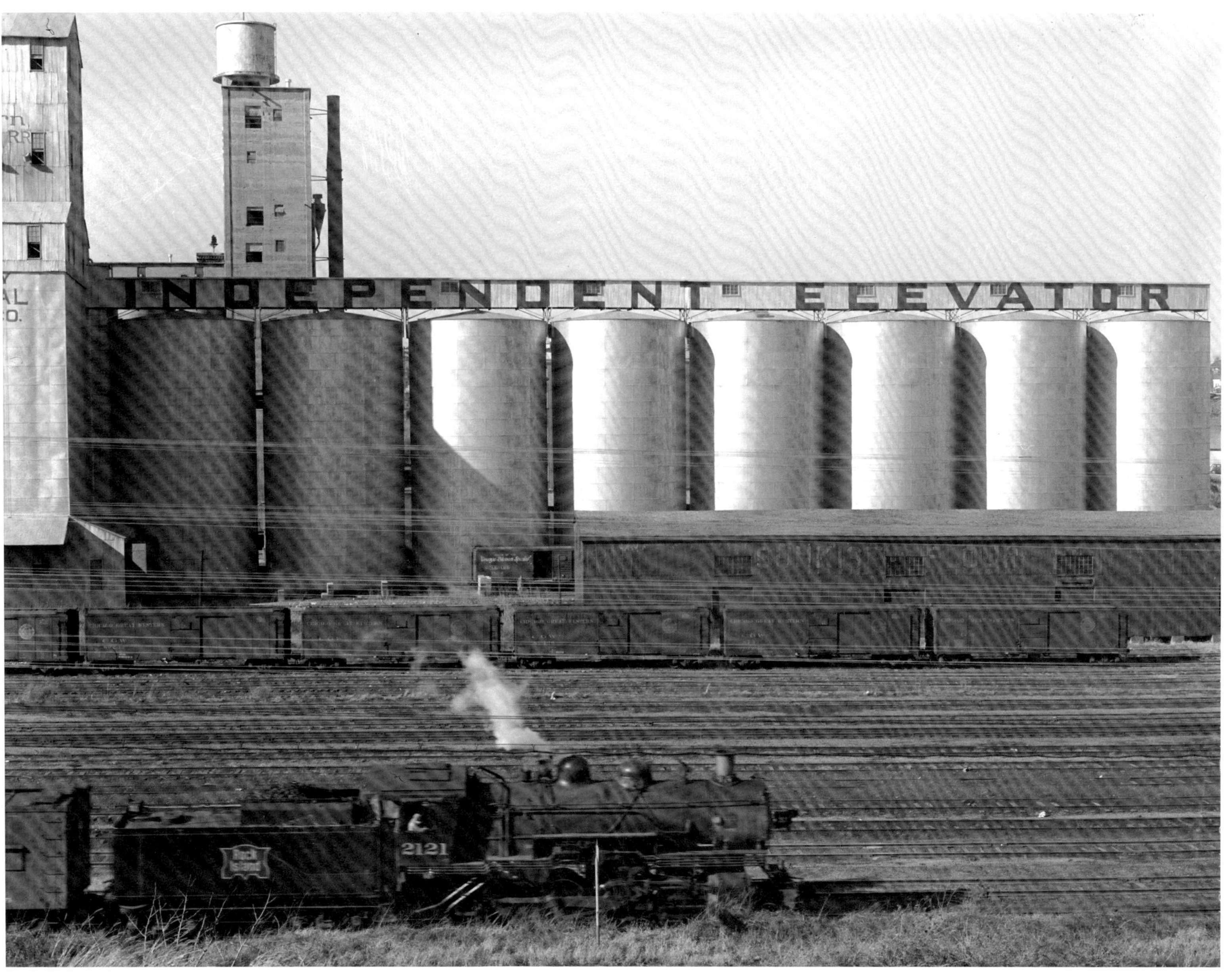

Plate 120. Grain elevators along railroad tracks. Omaha, Nebraska.

John Vachon. November 1938. Library of Congress, Prints & Photographs Division, FSA-OWI Collection, LC-USF34-008825-D.

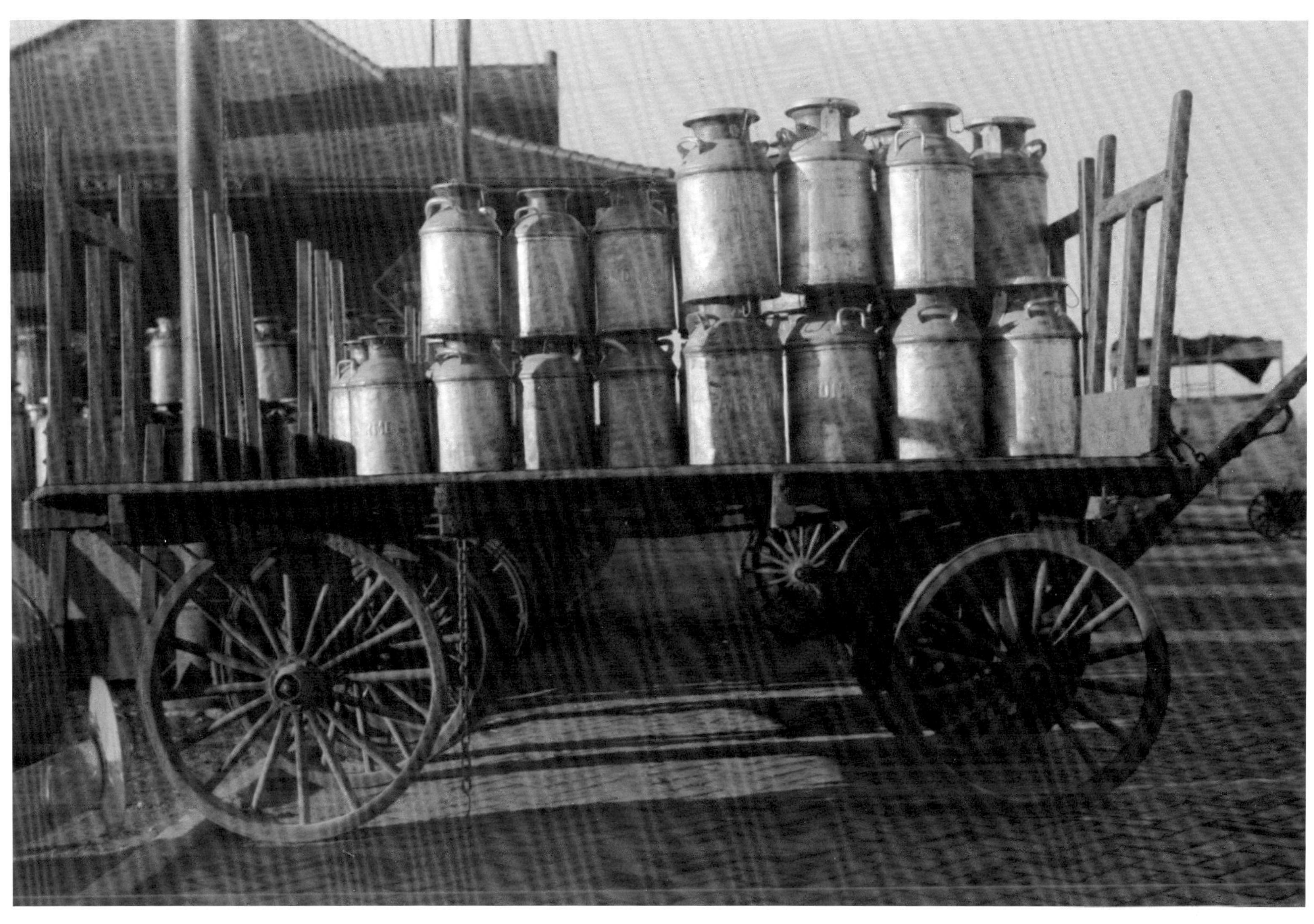

Plate 121. Milk cans at railroad station. Minot, North Dakota.

John Vachon. October 1940. Library of Congress, Prints & Photographs Division, FSA-OWI Collection, LC-USF33-016049-M2.

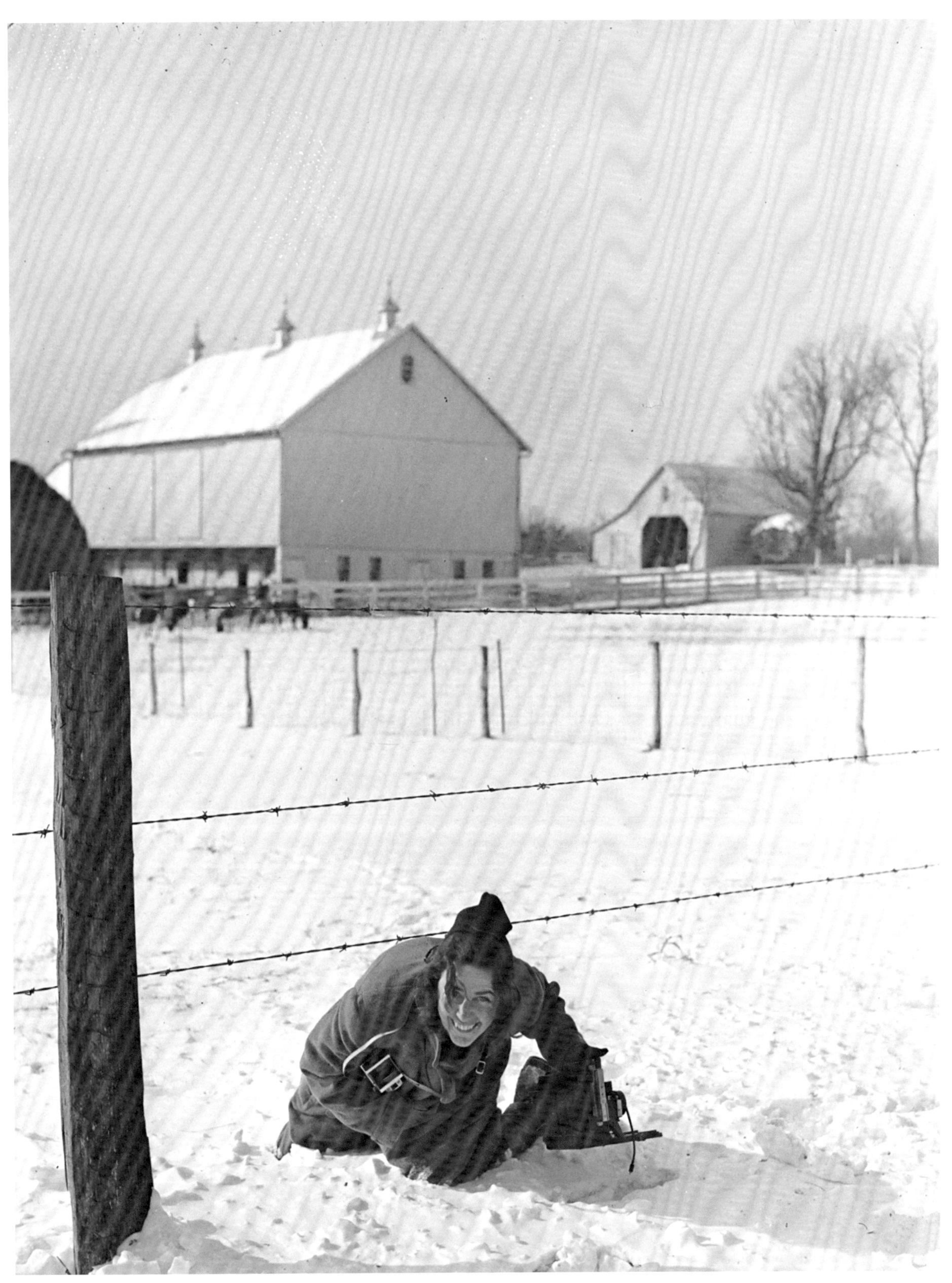

Figure 10.1. Marion Post Wolcott crouched in the snow below a barbed wire fence at a farm in Montgomery County, Maryland.

Arthur Rothstein. January 1940. Library of Congress, Prints & Photographs Division, FSA-OWI Collection, LC-USF34-029245-D.

PORTFOLIO TEN

MARION POST WOLCOTT

In 1964, Marion Post Wolcott heard about Russ Lee's one-person show at the Smithsonian Institution.[1] Post Wolcott drove to the Smithsonian for the opening reception, which was hosted by filmmaker Pare Lorentz. But she had not been invited, and the guard at the door refused her entrance. She gave the guard a note for her old colleague Russ, but after an hour, there was no reply, and so, "as lonely and rejected as she had ever felt in her life," she left.[2] Lee did get the note and go look for Marion, but she was already gone.

This story is shared here for a number of reasons. One is that it characterizes Post Wolcott's complex life as a woman of her time. Raised in affluence and attractive, with a dancer's form, she spent her early career as an avant-garde expatriate. She became a photographer, an art form with outstanding female participants in her day but still dominated at the time by men. When she married, however—and joined herself to a somewhat domineering man, at least by today's standards—she followed the conventional path, giving up her career to become a wife and mother.

The other focal point of this story is how her work was treated with neglect for a very long time—in this observer's view because she was a woman who had given up her career. Being a woman made her suspect to conservative critics of the time, and taking the conventional path made her suspect to progressives. Finally, in the mid-1970s, authors and curators began to feature her work prominently. Today, Marion Post Wolcott is recognized as a great photographer of the twentieth century.

Post Wolcott's early life was complex. She was born in Montclair, New Jersey, where her father was a noted local physician. Her mother was an outspoken progressive, unusual and challenging for the wife of a community leader in that time and place. By the time Post Wolcott was thirteen, her parents had divorced, despite her mother's struggle with uterine cancer. Post Wolcott graduated from a boarding school, Edgewood, and became a teacher. She attended classes at the New School for Social Research in New York City and began to study dance. Despite taking many courses and working as a teacher, she did not earn a college degree.

Her father died in 1932 and left her a trust fund that gave Post Wolcott a stipend as long as she stayed in school. She became an expatriate, living in Paris and then Berlin and traveling in France. Her older sister, Helen, was studying photography in Austria, and Marion joined her there, taking classes at the University of Vienna. While there, she was given a small camera and took her first photographs.

Given the increasingly dangerous politics of pre-Anschluss Austria, Marion and Helen returned to the United States. Post Wolcott continued to work as a teacher but also pursued photography using her sister's darkroom. Ralph Steiner became her mentor and introduced her to Paul Strand. Eventually, her photographic skills led her to a job at Philadelphia's *Evening Bulletin*. A young woman on a team of *boys*, she was assigned work for the ladies' page.[3]

Steiner then did a great service to Post Wolcott, and to observers of American photography, by recommending her to Roy Stryker at the FSA. Stryker had a new position, for a photographer to cover the US South, and hired Post Wolcott.[4] She spent 1938 through 1942 with the FSA.

Her work for the FSA is wide ranging. To this observer, two qualities of Post Wolcott's oeuvre stand out. First, there is a social justice concern for the poor that seems strongly influenced by Dorothea Lange and possibly Margaret Bourke-White. Second, her portraiture—particularly of groups of people—is notable.

Many of the FSA/OWI photographers traveled with a companion who acted as an unpaid assistant. Examples include Dorothea Lange and Paul Taylor, Russell Lee and Jean Smith (later Lee), and Jack and Irene Delano. As an unmarried woman, Post Wolcott traveled alone, often in the US South. She faced many challenges as a result but handled them with dignity and aplomb. She said, "In hotels a single girl, traveling alone, is often annoyed. Men may bribe the bell boys or the clerk to find out her name or room number, or they may watch which room she goes to. . . . It is a liberal education, from anyone's point of view."[5]

In 1941, Marion Post met Lee Wolcott, a widower with two children. They became romantic partners soon after they met and married six weeks later, in June 1941. Lee Wolcott was a government official with the federal Department of Agriculture. By late that year, Marion Post was Marion Post Wolcott—a professional name decided for her by her husband—and by early 1942, she had left the FSA.[6] Lee Wolcott, using his power in the federal government hierarchy, forced Roy Stryker to have the FSA staff go back and recaption the photographer's credit on all of Post Wolcott's photos from *Marion Post* to *Marion Post Wolcott*.

Lee Wolcott would not let his wife spend significant amounts of time on photography.[7] After the end of World War II, Wolcott became a full-time farmer, then, after a serious accident on their farm, a visiting professor at the University of New Mexico. He then joined the Agency for International Development (AID) and was posted to Iran. In association with AID, Lee Wolcott, with Marion beside him, traveled to Pakistan, back to Iran, then returned to Washington, DC. He then traveled to Egypt and, finally, India. After that posting, Wolcott retired, and he and Post Wolcott moved to California. In 1975, a gallery owner, Lee Witkin, sought out Marion Post Wolcott and convinced her to engage with the art-photography community. Her reputation has been rising ever since.[8] Marion Post Wolcott died of lung cancer at her home in Santa Barbara, California, in 1990.[9]

Despite her initial focus on the US South, Marion Post Wolcott took a number of outstanding photographs of New England. Plates 122 and 123 are railroad-subject examples of these, showing the railroad station in Mount Whittier, New Hampshire, on the Boston & Maine.

Plates 124, 125, and 126 are West Virginia views, two of them showing coal trains and one showing a woman walking the railroad tracks in Scotts Run, West Virginia, on the Monongahela Railway. Plate 124 is a portrait of a train passing the station in Davy, West Virginia, on the Norfolk and Western Railway. Plate 125, showing a train practically scraping parked cars on the street in Osage, West Virginia, also on the Monongahela Railway, forcefully demonstrates the ubiquity of coal mining and railroads serving mining areas in the state at the time. The locomotive shown here, Monongahela 140, was a Class H5 2-8-0 Consolidation.

Plates 127–131 take us to the US South. Plate 127, showing cotton bales on a railroad station platform on the Southern Railway in Mebane, North Carolina, at the northern edge of cotton's growing area, demonstrates the importance of that crop to the Southern economy. The locomotive shown here is Southern Railway 4587, a 2-8-2 Mikado. Plate 128, which presages contemporary work by Sebastião Salgado and Edward Burtynsky, demonstrates the environmental degradation that accompanies extractive industries, which are usually linked to the availability of railroad service. The site of this photo and this copper mine, Ducktown, Tennessee, was served by the Louisville & Nashville Railroad. Plates 129 and 130 depict Florida locales. Plate 129 shows a Louisville & Nashville station in northern Florida as a scene of activity. Plate 130 highlights the connection between the sugar industry and the railroad. It depicts a United States Sugar Corporation (USSC) train in Clewiston, Florida, led by USSC 98, a 4-6-2 Pacific. This company still exists and runs excursions behind a restored USSC locomotive, 148, a sister to the engine shown in plate 130.[10] Plate 131 is a classic image of railroading in the Deep South, showing two white "boss men" literally elevated on a platform above two Black men, probably cotton plantation workers, at the Illinois Central Railroad station in Mileston, Mississippi. The white men shown are the station agent and a plantation owner.

Toward the end of her FSA career, Post Wolcott covered the US West. Plates 132–135 are railroad-subject examples of this work, showing the railroad station at aptly named Froid, Montana (plate 132), on the Great Northern Railway; a railroad-served grain elevator at Great Falls, Montana (plate 133); and a freight train, wonderfully silhouetted, leaving Homestead, Montana (plate 134). Great Falls was served by the Great Northern and by the Chicago, Milwaukee, St. Paul and Pacific Railroad, and Homestead by the Great Northern.

This portfolio, and this book, closes with an image showing the destiny of many railroads in the once-overbuilt US railroad network—an abandoned railroad grade used as a road near Leadville, Colorado. This is Carlton Tunnel on the former standard-gauge Colorado Midland Railroad, last used by trains in 1919.[11]

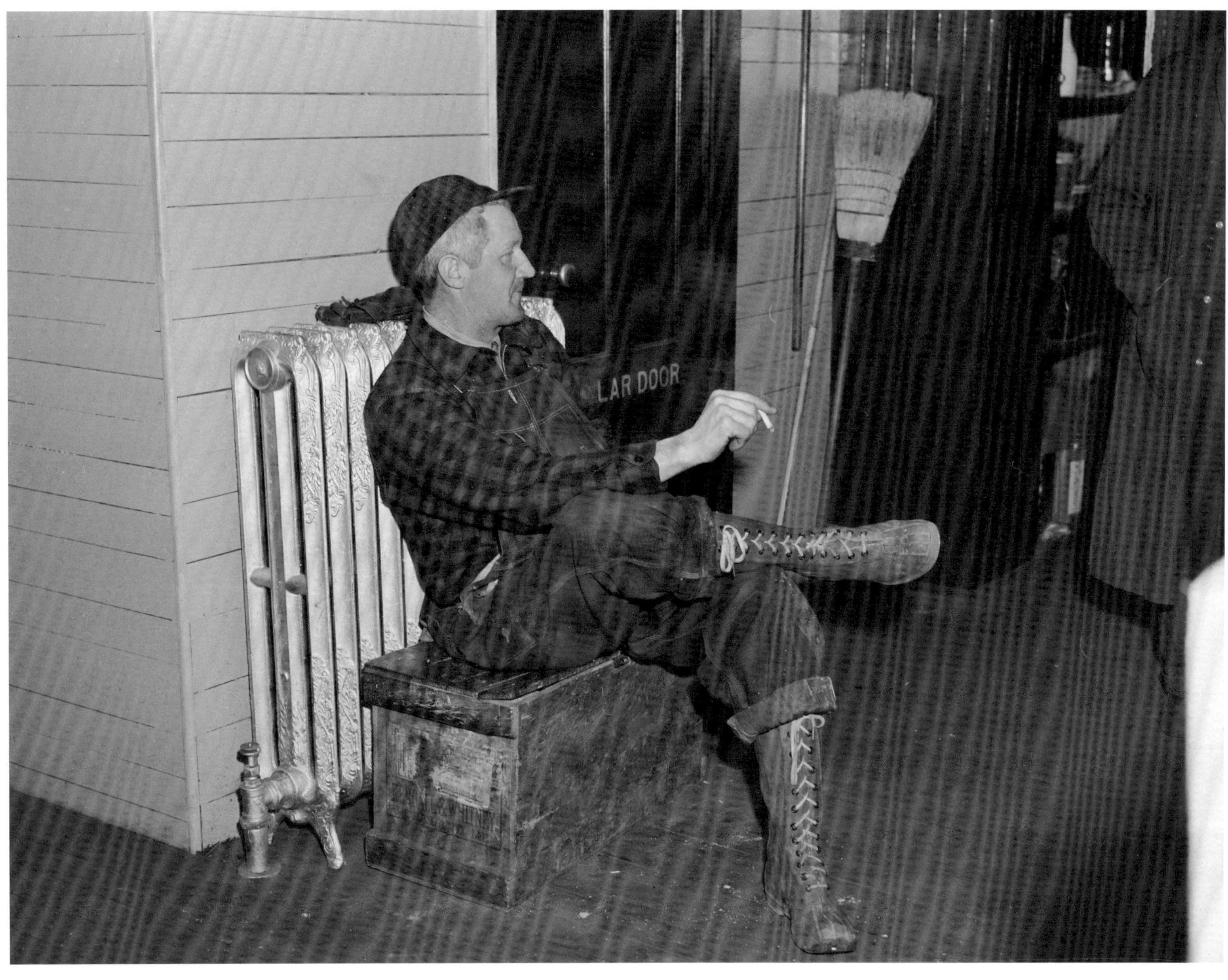

Plate 122. Railroad worker waiting in baggage room for train arrival. Railway station, Mount Whittier, New Hampshire.

Marion Post Wolcott. March 1940. Library of Congress, Prints & Photographs Division, FSA-OWI Collection, LC-USF34-053385-D.

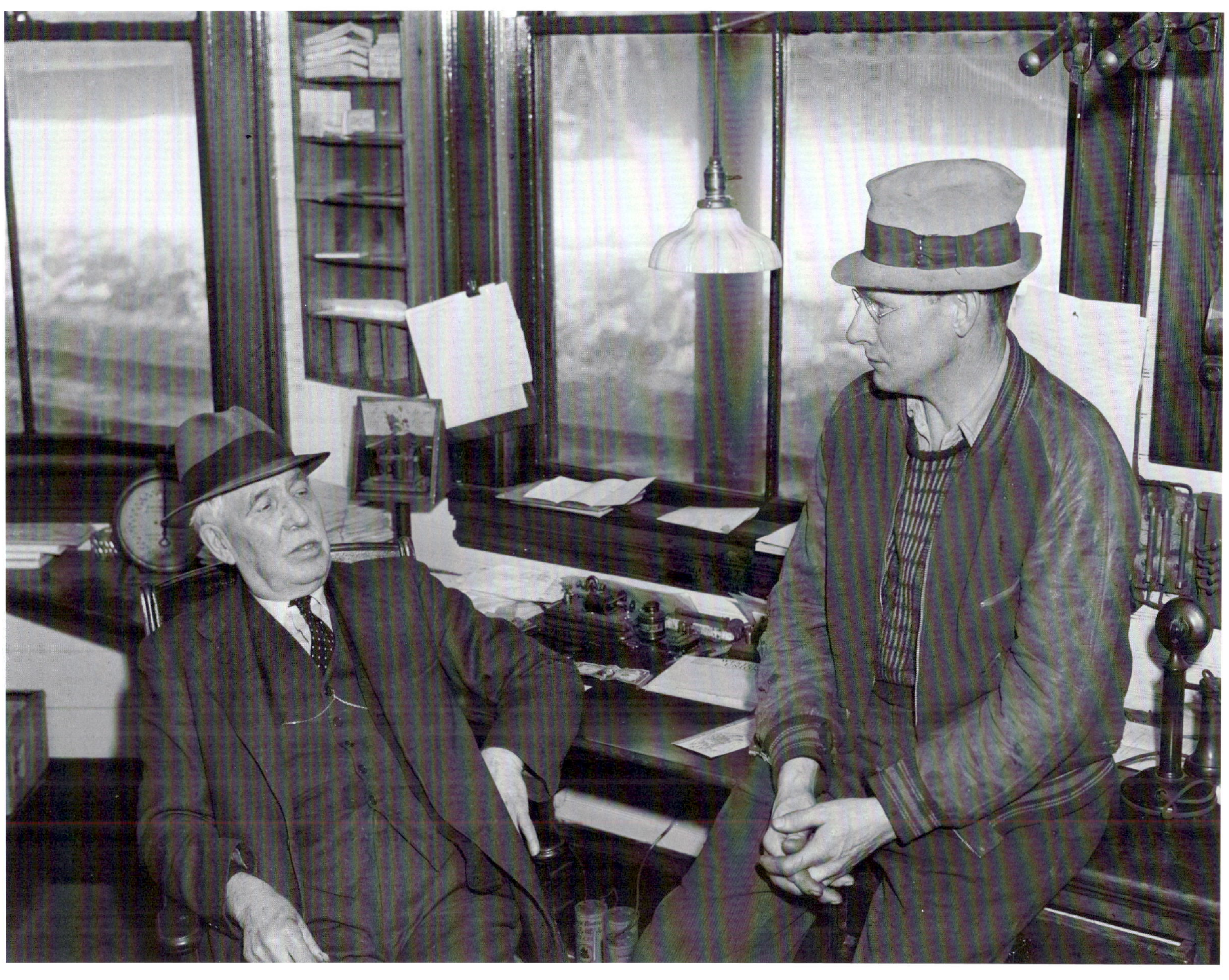

Plate 123. Ticket agent and mail carrier talking in railroad station. Mount Whittier, New Hampshire.

Marion Post Wolcott. March 1940. Library of Congress, Prints & Photographs Division, FSA-OWI Collection, LC-USF34-053404-D.

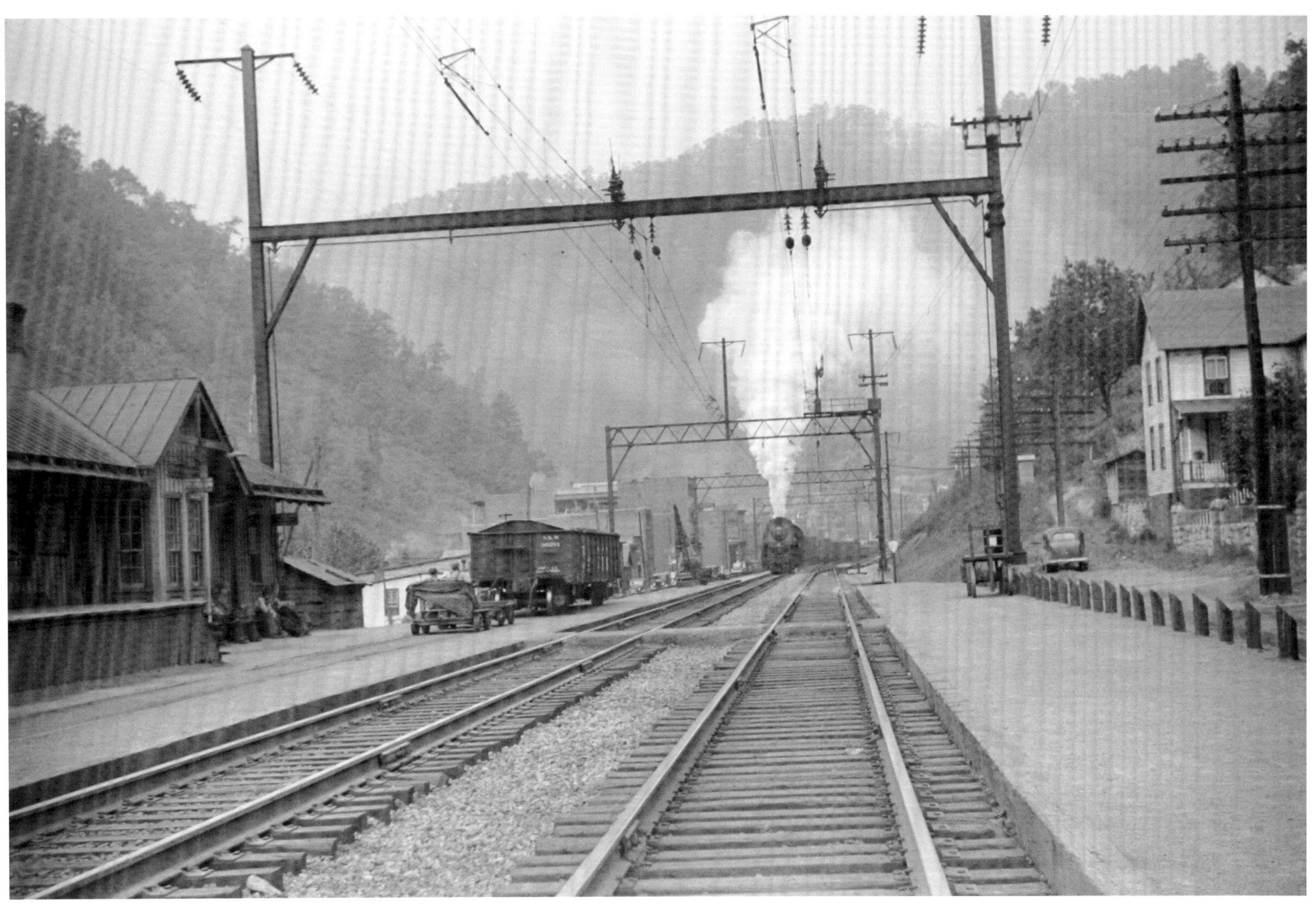

Plate 124. Coal train going through center of mining town. Davey [*sic*], West Virginia.

Marion Post Wolcott. September 1938. Library of Congress, Prints & Photographs Division, FSA-OWI Collection, LC-USF33-030058-M2.

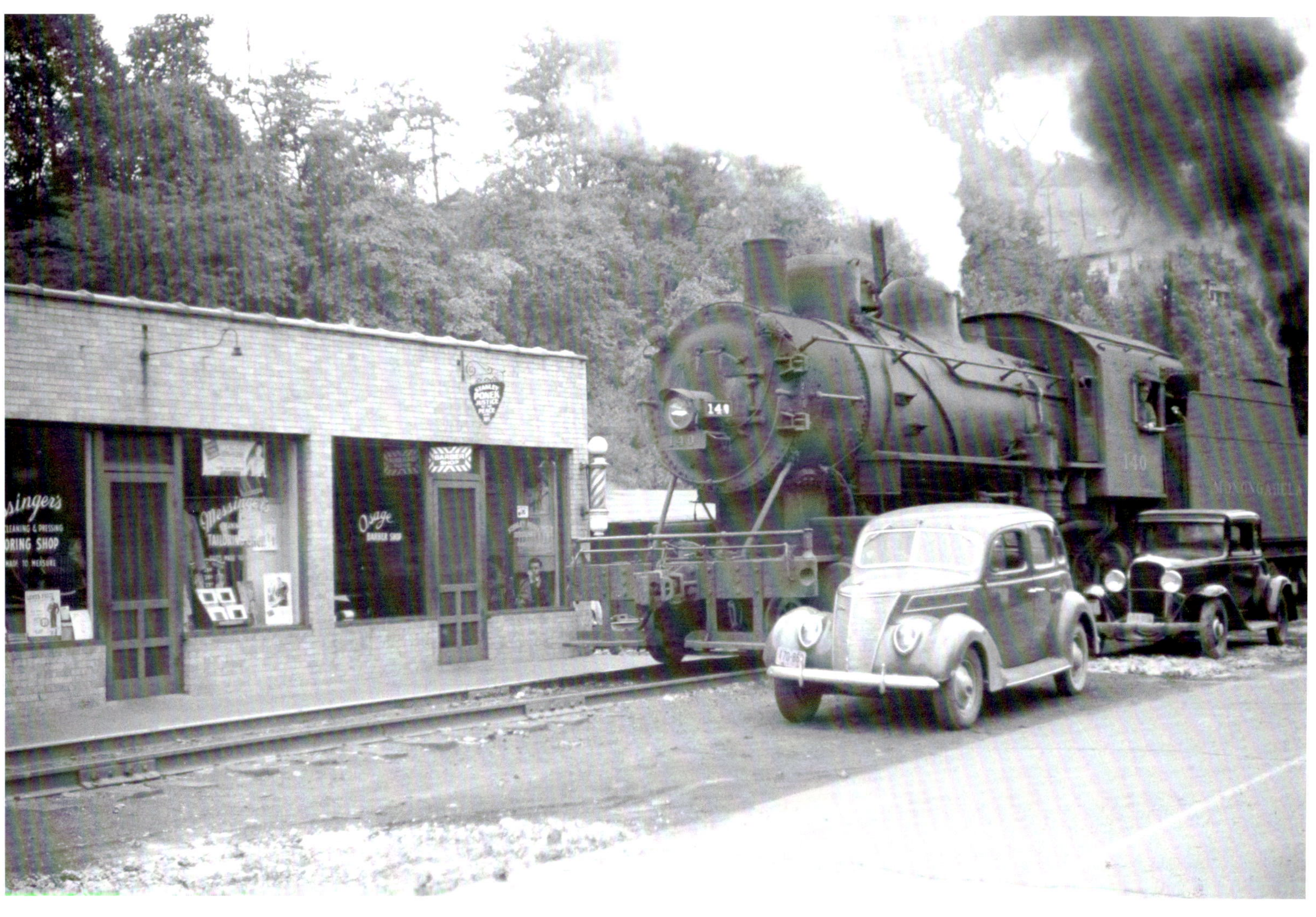

Plate 125. Train pulling coal through the center of town mornings and evenings, Osage, West Virginia.

Marion Post Wolcott. September 1938. Library of Congress, Prints & Photographs Division, FSA-OWI Collection, LC-USF33-030139-M5.

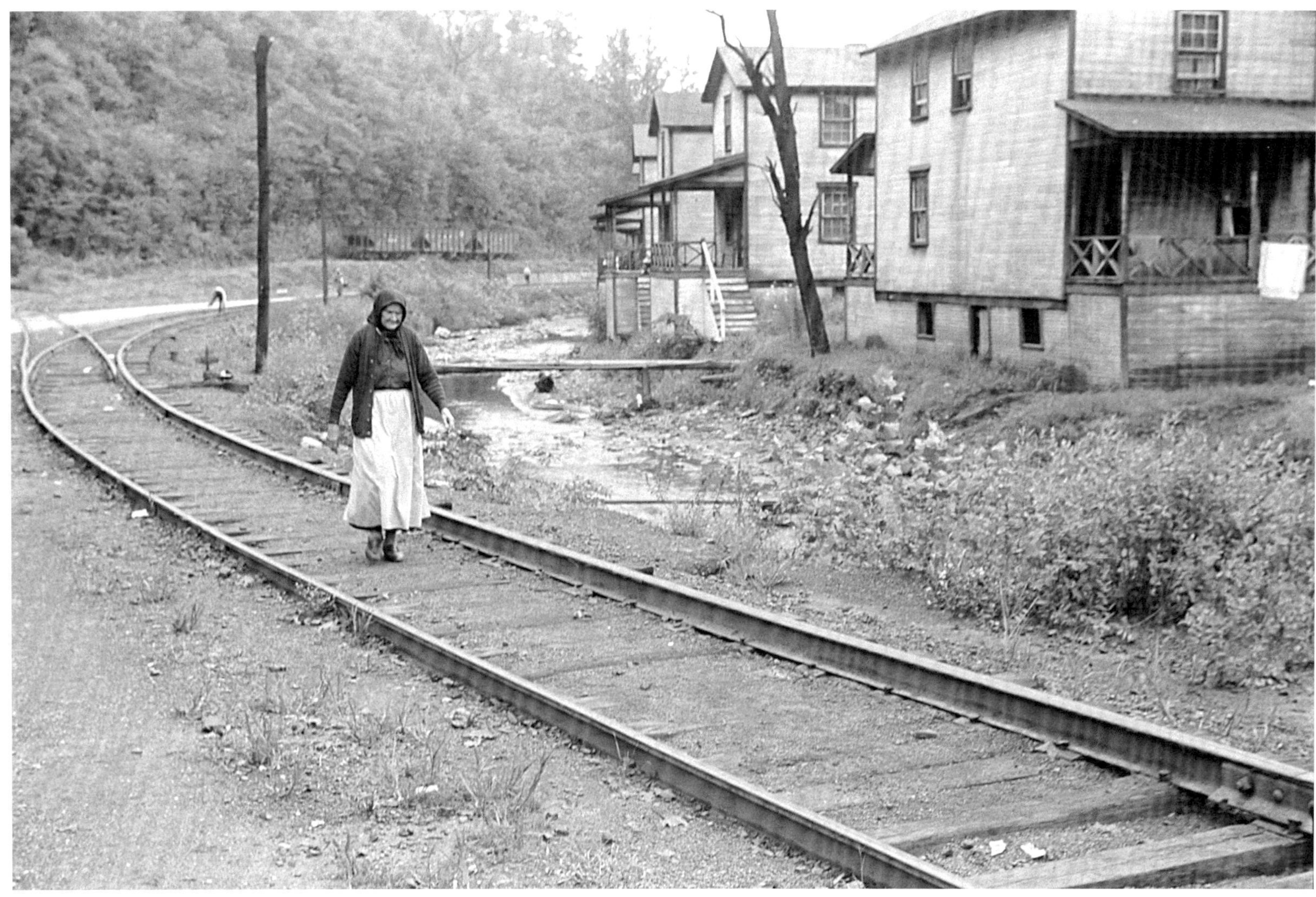

Plate 126. Woman (probably Hungarian) coming home along railroad tracks in coal-mining town, company houses at right, Pursglove, Scotts Run, West Virginia.

Marion Post Wolcott. September 1938. Library of Congress, Prints & Photographs Division, FSA-OWI Collection, LC-USF33-030285-M1.

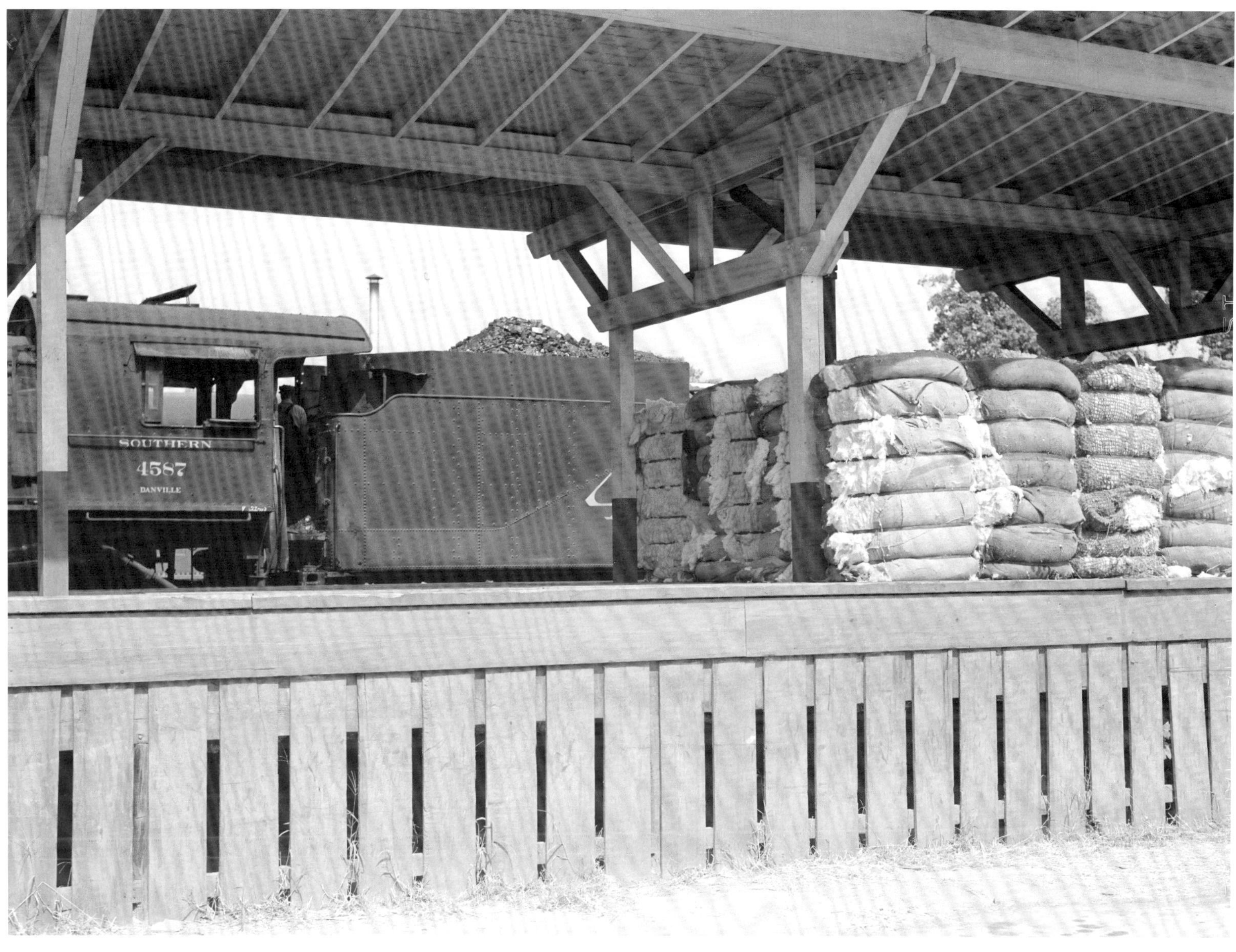

Plate 127. Railway station with bales of cotton on platform. Mebane, North Carolina.

Marion Post Wolcott. October 1940. Library of Congress, Prints & Photographs Division, FSA-OWI Collection. LC-USF34-055995-D.

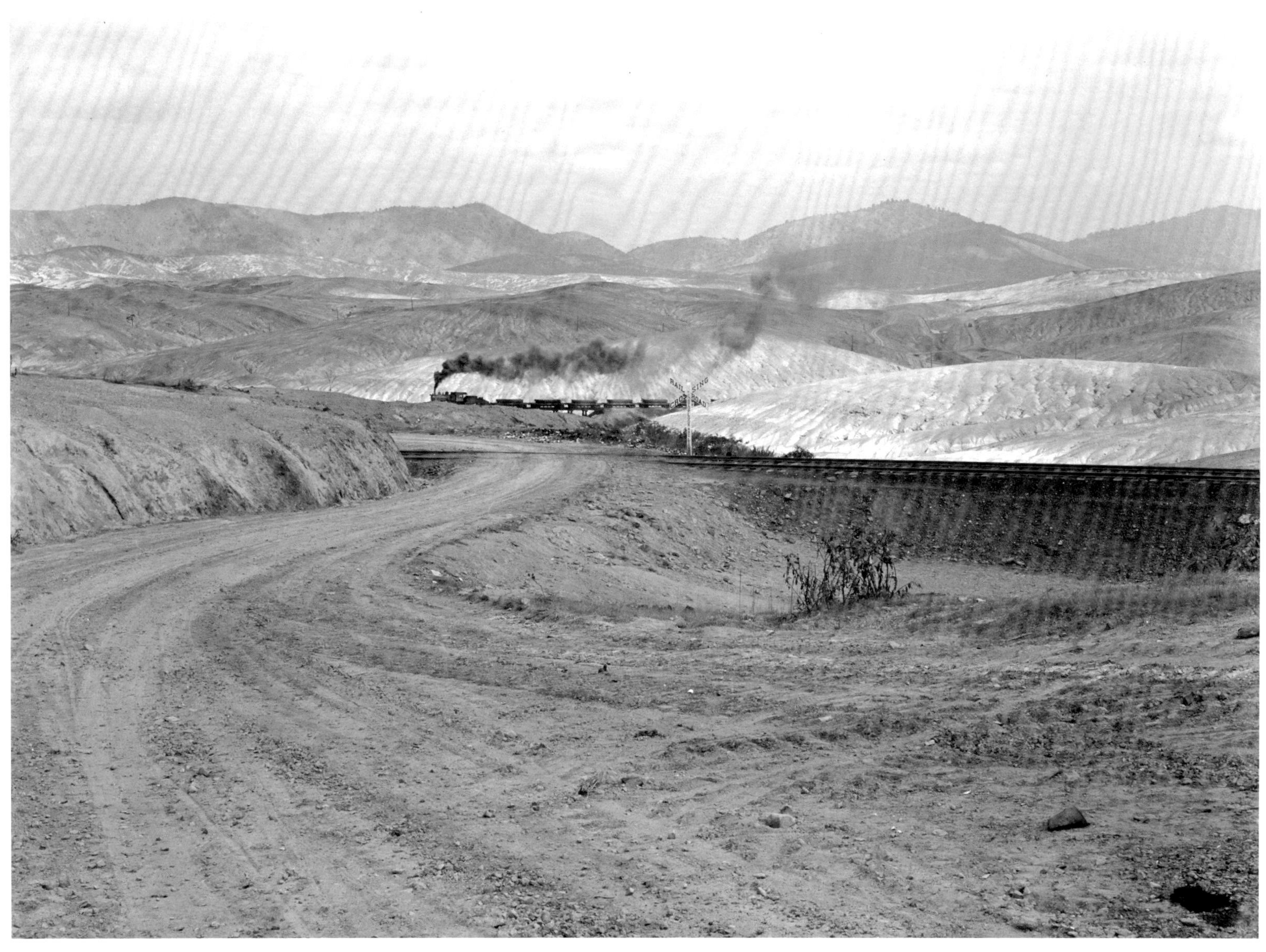

***Above,* Plate 128.** Train bringing copper ore out of mine. Ducktown, Tennessee. Fumes from smelting copper for sulfuric acid have destroyed all vegetation and eroded the land.

Marion Post Wolcott. September 1939. Library of Congress, Prints & Photographs Division, FSA-OWI Collection, LC-USF34-052169-D.

***Facing,* Plate 129.** Loading mail into mail car. L&N railroad station, North Florida.

Marion Post Wolcott. June 1940. Library of Congress, Prints & Photographs Division, FSA-OWI Collection, LC-USF34-054163-E.

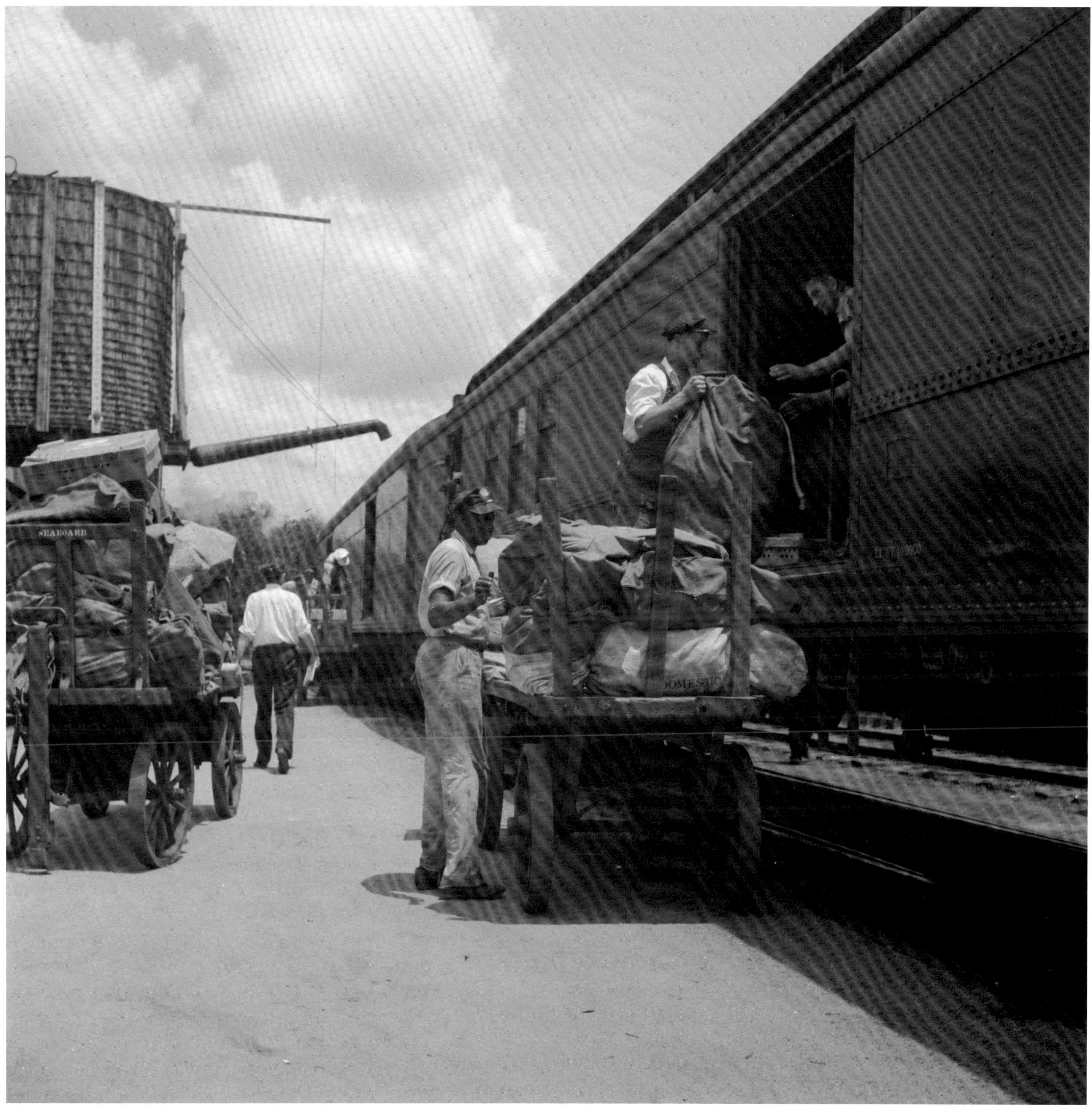
SEABOARD

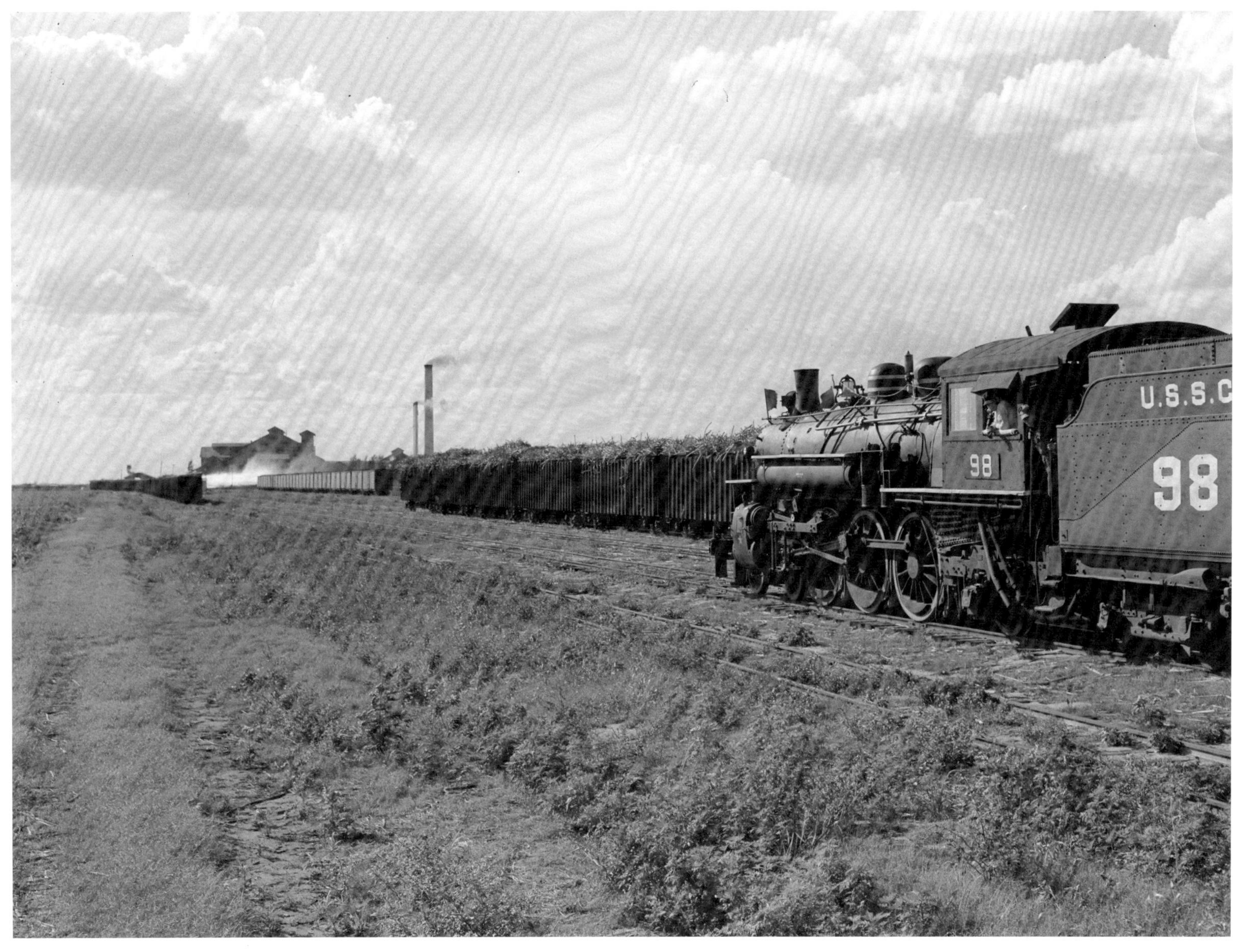

Plate 130. United States Sugar Corporation (USSC) hauls sugarcane from the fields to its mill by its own railroad system. Clewiston, Florida.

Marion Post Wolcott. February 1939. Library of Congress, Prints & Photographs Division, FSA-OWI Collection, LC-USF34-051105-D.

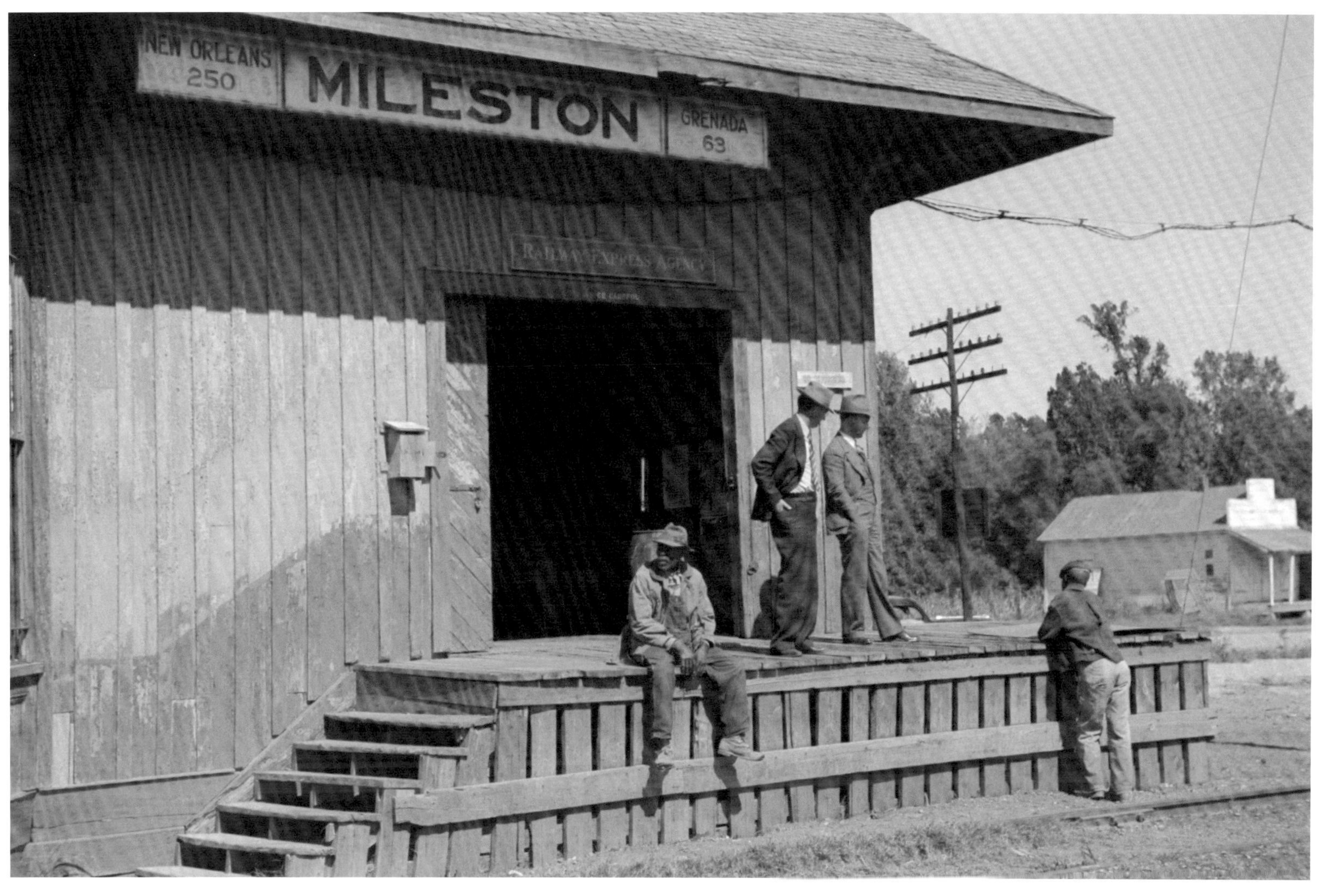

Plate 131. Untitled photo, possibly related to: Railway station on cotton plantation, Mileston Plantation, Mississippi Delta, Mississippi.

Marion Post Wolcott. 1939. Library of Congress, Prints & Photographs Division, FSA-OWI Collection, LC-USF33-030594-M3.

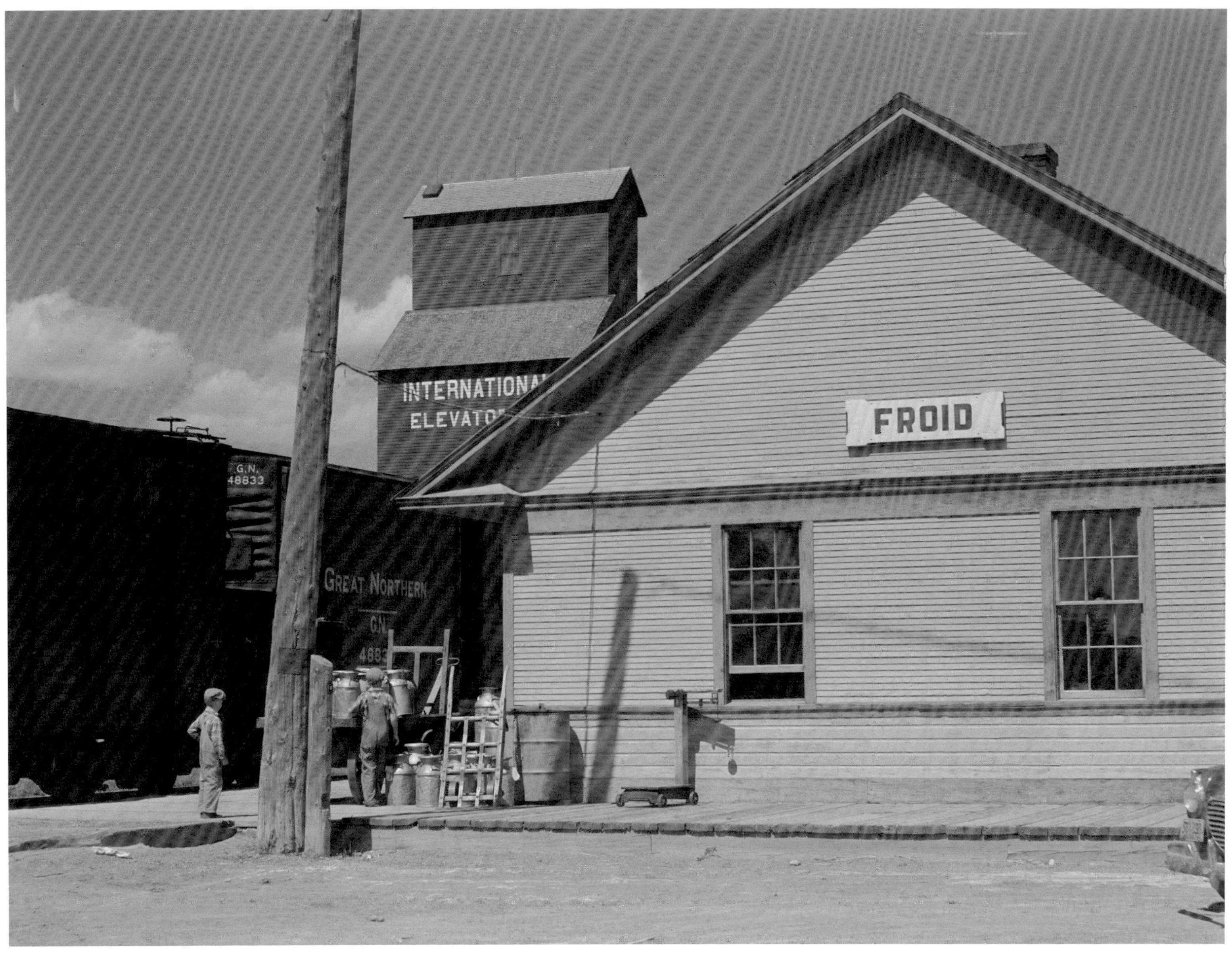

Plate 132. Railroad station. Froid, Montana.

Marion Post Wolcott. August 1941. Library of Congress, Prints & Photographs Division, FSA-OWI Collection, LC-USF34-057967-D.

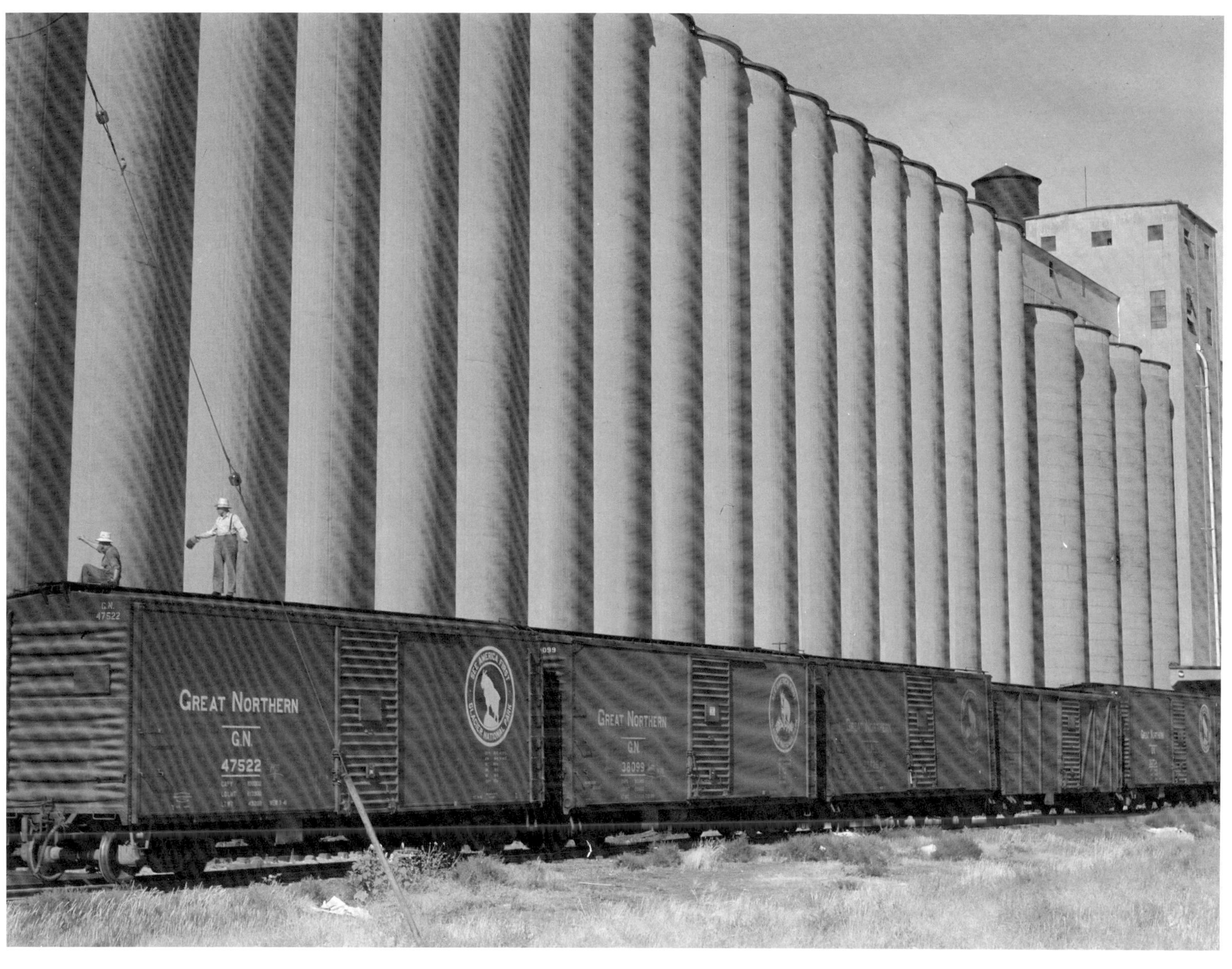

Plate 133. Grain storage, elevators, and freight trains. Great Falls, Montana.

Marion Post Wolcott. August 1941. Library of Congress, Prints & Photographs Division, FSA-OWI Collection, LC-USF34-058157-D.

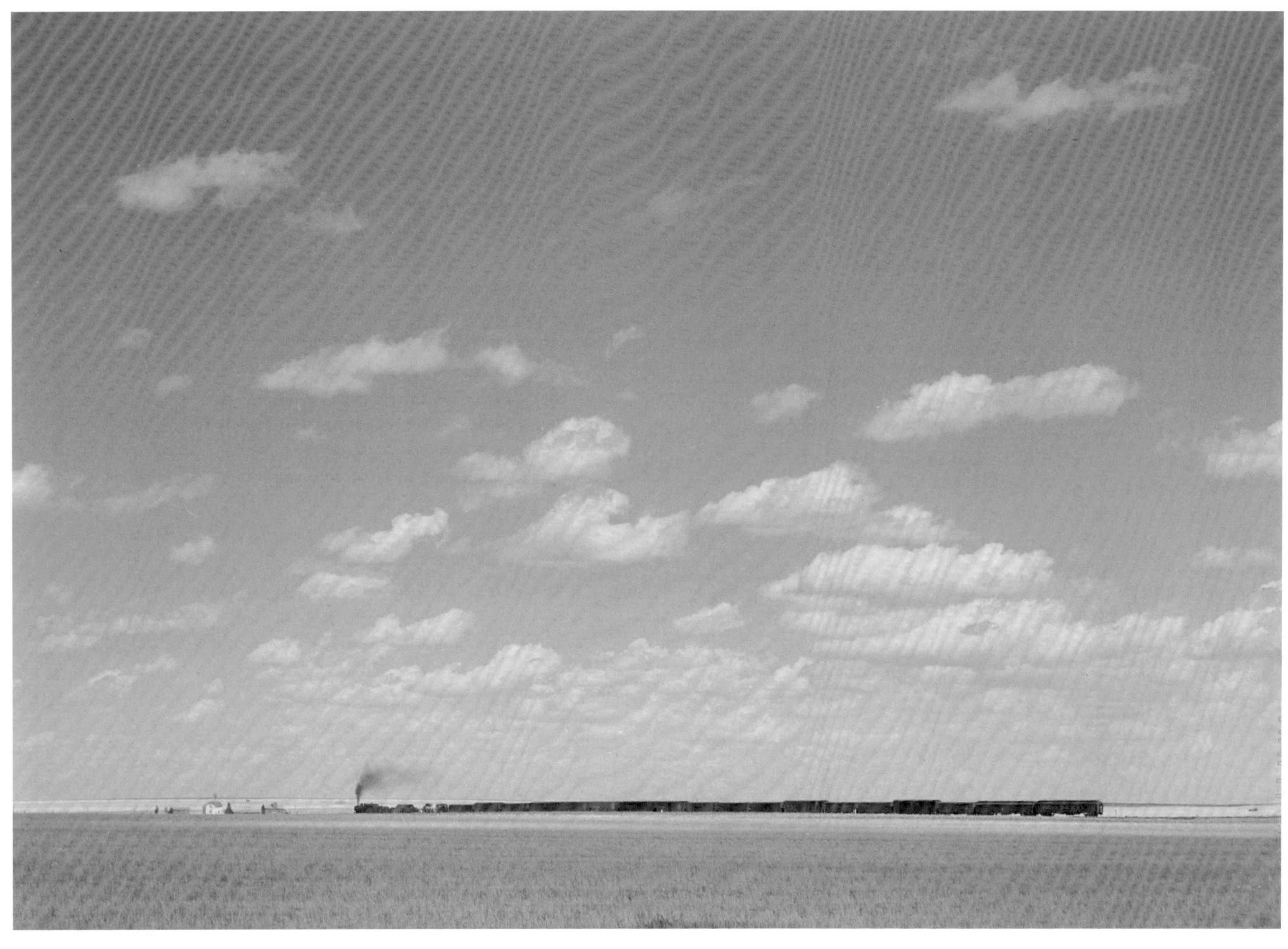

Plate 134. Freight train leaving Homestead, Montana.

Marion Post Wolcott. August 1941. Library of Congress, Prints & Photographs Division, FSA-OWI Collection, LC-USF347-057949-D.

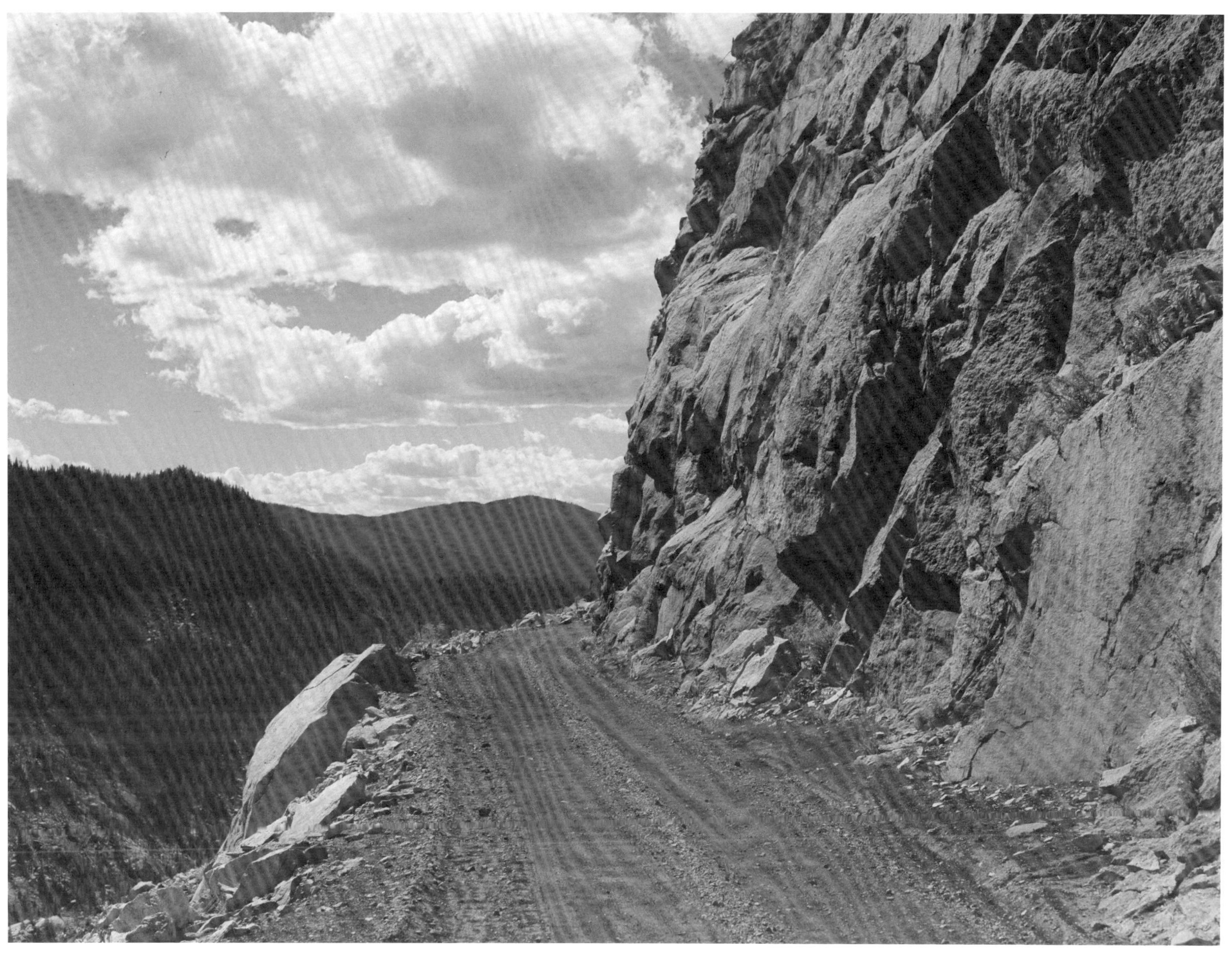

Plate 135. Road leading out of Carlton Tunnel along bed of old narrow-gauge railroad [*sic*] on the west side of the Rocky Mountains from Leadville, Colorado.

Marion Post Wolcott. September 1941. Library of Congress, Prints & Photographs Division, FSA-OWI Collection, LC-USF34-059091-D.

APPENDIX ONE

TECHNICAL NOTE ON THE FSA/OWI PHOTOGRAPHS

It is hard for this observer to believe—my wife and I shot thousands of 35 mm color transparencies and color and black-and-white 35 mm rolls of film over the years—but film photography has transitioned from a societal commonplace to a niche medium. Furthermore, the FSA/OWI photographers lived in a time of transition. Sheet film cameras, the standard for photographers of the time, were being supplemented by roll film cameras such as the Rollei (Rolleiflex) and the 35 mm camera, generally a Leica during this time period. By the 1960s, the 35 mm was the camera of choice for railroad-subject photographers.

For all these reasons, it is useful, even instructive, to consider the equipment the FSA/OWI photographers used. Fortunately, this is easy to do. The original Library of Congress photograph call numbers provide this information. A typical call number is composed as follows:

- LC (Library of Congress)-USF (FSA) or USW (OWI) code number (indicates the type of film used)-xxxxxx (call number)-letter (designates the negative size).

So, each complete call number indicates the type of film used for the photo and the type of negative produced, which tells the researcher what type of camera was used. No color images (generally 4" × 5" sheet film Kodachrome transparencies) are included in this book, so this note will not cover the FSA/OWI color images.

The ending letter in the call number is perhaps the most useful piece of information, as it indicates the size of the original negative. The letters readers will see in the call numbers in this book indicate the following:

- A: 8" × 10"—a large view camera, the equipment preferred by master photographer Walker Evans,
- C: 4" × 5"—a 4 × 5 camera, probably one made by Graflex, the most common size for a Graphic camera;
- D: 3.25" × 4.25"—probably a smaller Graphic, also made by Graflex;
- E: 120 roll film producing about 2.25" square negatives—generally a Rolleiflex; and
- M: 35 mm—generally a Leica.

The prefixes are also useful. As mentioned above, USF indicates FSA provenance, and USW indicates OWI provenance. The two different USF numbers indicate:

- USF33—FSA 35 mm roll film negatives, M ("miniature"); the number refers to the frame on the 35 mm film strip—for example, 1, 2, 3, and so on; and
- USF34—FSA negatives sheet (A, C, D) or roll, E (the E negatives are cut separately and are not filed in film strips like the 35 mm images).

For the purposes of simplification during cataloging, USF, indicating Farm Security Administration provenance, applied to the FSA and also to that agency's previous name, the Resettlement Administration.

For more information, visit https://www.loc.gov/collections/fsa-owi-black-and-white-negatives/about-this-collection/technical-information (accessed May 27, 2024). See also Delano, *Photographic Memories*, 49–51.

APPENDIX TWO

THE US RAILROAD AND THE FSA/OWI PHOTOGRAPHERS NOT PROFILED IN THIS BOOK

One missing piece—surprisingly—in scholarship focusing on the FSA/OWI Historical Section and its staff is research-confirmed lists of all the FSA and OWI photographers. Also missing is confirmation of which OWI photographers worked under Stryker's direction and which did not.[1] As far as is known, all the Resettlement Administration/FSA photographers did.[2] There are lists available of all the photographers who took FSA/OWI black-and-white images at https://www.loc.gov/pictures/collection/fsa/index/names and a list of all the photographers who took FSA/OWI color images at https://www.loc.gov/collections/fsa-owi-color-photographs/index/contributor/?sp=1.

In this appendix, as much as is possible, all FSA photographers are included and all OWI photographers who worked under Stryker's direction.[3] There were OWI photographers who did not work under Stryker's direction, and at least some of their images are included in the FSA/OWI collection at the Library of Congress. Some of the OWI photographers who did not work under Stryker's direction—such as Alfred "Al" Palmer and Arthur Siegel—are significant photographers and deserve further study.[4] The photographers not known to have worked with Roy Stryker will not be covered here. A comprehensive listing of these photographers would be a valuable addition to FSA/OWI photography scholarship.

The roster of FSA/OWI photographers who worked with Roy Stryker in more than freelance roles, then, is Esther Bubley, Paul Carter, John Collier Jr., Marjory Collins, Jack Delano, Walker Evans, Theodor Jung, Dorothea Lange, Russell Lee, Carl Mydans, Gordon Parks, Edwin and Louise Rosskam, Arthur Rothstein, Ben Shahn, John Vachon, and Marion Post Wolcott. Mora and Brannan's *FSA: The American Vision*, arguably the best available source, includes sixteen of these seventeen, leaving out Paul Carter.

THE FSA PHOTOGRAPHERS

Not all the photographers working for Stryker would document the American railroad, often because their tenure with the group did not last long.[5] One of the best of the early FSA photographers, Carl Mydans (1906–2004), stayed with Stryker for only a year during 1935 and 1936 before becoming one of the first photographers for *Life* magazine.[6] Mydans took a handful of railroad-subject images, not enough to form a portfolio.[7] Two other early FSA photographers, Paul Carter and Theodor Jung, who both joined in 1935, did not perform well: Carter stayed only a short time, and Jung about a year.[8] Both of them produced only a small number of images. Carter did not produce any notable railroad-subject photographs, and Jung produced a short series documenting railroad ties.

One of the most noted photographers and artists who worked for Stryker was Ben Shahn (1898–1969).[9] Shahn produced about twenty railroad-subject images set in Louisiana, Ohio, and West Virginia, some of them notable. Along with Mydans, Evans, and Lange—what an exceptional group—Shahn was a mainstay of the early period of Stryker's photographic "file."[10]

Edwin and Louise Rosskam were a husband-and-wife team who joined the FSA after working on an assignment in Puerto Rico for *Life*. Edwin Rosskam took a few photos for the FSA but mostly worked as an editor and packager of the Stryker team's work. After joining the FSA, Louise Rosskam took up photography. The Rosskams' work for the FSA produced a few railroad-subject images of Puerto Rico. They would continue to work with Stryker at Standard Oil of New Jersey and then were hired by Rexford Tugwell when he was governor of Puerto Rico to establish an FSA-style project there with Edwin Rosskam as director. Rosskam then hired Jack Delano to join the project.[11] The Rosskams' work with Standard Oil of New Jersey did result in a notable book in the transportation field, *Towboat River.*

In addition to these photographers, there is a Historical Section staffer, Edwin Locke, who took the portrait of Walker Evans featured in this book. He occasionally did take photographs for the FSA—there are about seven hundred in the "file"—but he did not take any significant railroad-subject images.

Beyond these photographers, who might be considered members of the Historical Section staff,[12] the "file" includes images by photographers who seem to have worked for the FSA on an assignment/contractual/freelance basis. There are many such contributors, but at least three are mentioned in notable works about the Historical Section. FSA photographer Sheldon Dick is mentioned in Carl Fleischhauer and Beverly W. Brannan's *Documenting America 1935–1943*.[13] The Library of Congress website shows about 450 photos taken by Dick but no significant railroad-subject images.[14] Photographer Royden Dixon is mentioned in the Library of Congress's listing of photographers who took color images as an FSA photographer. He took a limited number of images, none of them of railroad-subject interest.[15] The Library of Congress online resource, Photographers of the FSA, includes an image of Howard Liberman. Liberman may have worked for both the FSA and the OWI and took a handful of images of Black workers building a railroad line for the federal government in August 1942—these are USW images taken for the OWI.

THE OWI PHOTOGRAPHERS WHO WORKED WITH ROY STRYKER

A number of FSA photographers followed Roy Stryker to the OWI, and so all these are covered here. The roster of FSA photographers who followed Stryker to the OWI includes John Collier Jr., Jack Delano, Russell Lee, Gordon Parks, Edwin and Louise Rosskam, and John Vachon. All these took significant railroad-subject images except for the Rosskams, as mentioned above.

There is also a pair of photographers who worked for Roy Stryker in the brief period between the Historical Section's transfer to the OWI and its disbandment. These artists are Esther Bubley and Marjory Collins. Collins is profiled in Portfolio Two in this book.

Esther Bubley (1921–1998) joined the OWI as a darkroom technician. She counted Edward Steichen as a mentor. Stryker soon moved Bubley into a photography position. Her best-known OWI work focuses on a US passenger transportation mode, the Greyhound bus.[16] Bubley also worked for Stryker at Standard Oil of New Jersey and produced another bus portfolio while working there, "Bus Story." Her work later influenced Robert Frank.[17] Bubley took a handful of railroad-subject images for the OWI, but later in her career, she took a number of such images for the Standard Oil project.[18]

NOTES

INTRODUCTION

1. Despite the complexity of the first two years of the Historical Section's history and governance, scholars generally call the section's photographers the FSA or the FSA/OWI photographers. This convention is followed throughout this book for clarity's sake.

2. For additional information about the founding of the Historical Section, see Mora and Brannan, *FSA*, 9–10.

3. Tugwell became a political liability and left the Roosevelt administration in late 1936. See Mora and Brannan, *FSA*, 15. After a period working in the private sector, he reemerged as Roosevelt's appointed governor of Puerto Rico. As such, he brought three of Stryker's mentees, Edwin and Louise Rosskam and Jack Delano, to the territory to document Puerto Rico as Stryker had documented the United States as a whole. For a brief review of Tugwell's career, see *Britannica*, "Rexford Guy Tugwell," accessed June 8, 2024, https://www.britannica.com/biography/Rexford-Guy-Tugwell.

4. Another key book in the history of the FSA/OWI photographers is J. Russell Smith's *North America*. Stryker asked all of his photographers to read it as background for their work.

5. From Gabriel Bauret, "Testimony or Instrument of Propaganda: What Is the Role of Photography?," in Poos, *Bitter Years*, 22.

6. See Mora and Brannan, *FSA*, 124–125, and Rothstein, *Photographs of Arthur Rothstein*. Rothstein is the author of the influential book *Photojournalism*.

7. Also known as Marion Post, the name by which she joined the FSA. Marion Post Wolcott is the name she used after she married in 1941.

8. Many of Stryker's employees were Jewish, and of course, they faced daunting discrimination in this period of US history.

9. Parks was the only FSA/OWI photographer who had been a railroad employee.

10. For a discussion of the end of the Historical Section, see Hurley, *Portrait of a Decade*, 162–173.

11. For a complete set of all known railroad-related FSA/OWI shooting scripts, see Appendix Two in Reevy, *Railroad Photography*, 167–175.

12. See Reevy, *Railroad Photography*, 167. See also a discussion of this work in Fleischhauer and Brannan, *Documenting America*, 59–60.

13. Reevy, *Railroad Photography*, 170.

14. Valle, *Iron Horse at War*, 253.

15. Montrose, Colorado, on the railroad historically known as the Denver and Rio Grande or Denver and Rio Grande Western, today's Union Pacific. The Montrose railroad station is now a museum.

16. Because of its inclusion in some editions of *Let Us Now Praise Famous Men* and in many works about Evans, this is

arguably one of the most influential railroad-subject photographs of all time.

17. Stryker and Wood, *In This Proud Land*, 15.

18. This book intentionally focuses on the FSA/OWI black-and-white images. The FSA/OWI photographers, especially Delano, also took color images. Generally, these are 4" × 5" sheet film Kodachrome transparencies or the small images from 35 mm film that today we would call color slides. Color transparencies that are 3" × 4" and 2½" × 2½" also exist in the file. The large Kodachrome images generate outstanding reproductions. See Reevy, *Railroad Photography*, for more about Delano's color images of US railroading. For information about this color work in general, see Jeremy Adamson, "Kodachrome: The New Age of Color," in Hendrickson, *Bound for Glory*, 190–191.

19. Appendix Two briefly reviews the railroad-subject work of the FSA/OWI photographers not profiled in this book.

20. Also known in this period as the Puerto Rico Railroad & Transport Company.

21. John Collier Jr., Gordon Parks, the Rosskams, and John Vachon also worked with the Standard Oil project. See "Chronologies," in Mora and Brannan, *FSA*, 348–353.

22. See "Standard Oil (New Jersey) Collection [SONJ]," University Libraries, University of Louisville, accessed June 9, 2024, https://archivescatalog.library.louisville.edu/resources/standard-oil-new-jersey. This collection deserves further study.

23. "Documentary Photography Collections," University Libraries, University of Louisville, accessed June 9, 2024, https://library.louisville.edu/archives/photo/documentary.

24. The Standard Oil of New Jersey project also produced *Towboat River* by Edwin and Louise Rosskam, a notable book about a neglected aspect of American transportation: water transport of freight. The overall project was profiled by Steven W. Plattner in *Roy Stryker: U.S.A., 1943–1950*. Roy Stryker's Pittsburgh project did not produce much published documentation except for a few photos in *A Pittsburgh Album 1758–1958*, by Roy Stryker and Mel Seidenberg, and a survey, *Witness to the Fifties: The Pittsburgh Photographic Library, 1950–1953*, by Constance B. Schulz and Steven W. Plattner. The records of this project, the Pittsburgh Photographic Library, are held by the Carnegie Library of Pittsburgh. The Jones and Laughlin Steel Corporation project is not well documented. The images it produced are held by the University of Louisville. Recent research by this author at the University of Louisville identified railroad subject images taken for the SONJ project by John Collier Jr., Gordon Parks, and John Vachon.

25. To review the black-and-white FSA/OWI images, see "Farm Security Administration/Office of War Information Black-and-White Negatives," accessed June 9, 2024, https://www.loc.gov/pictures/collection/fsa.

26. Carl Mydans also had a long career at *Life* magazine.

27. Ben Shahn also taught at North Carolina's Black Mountain College and Harvard University.

28. Their tradition is also carried on by descendants such as Malcolm Collier, Pablo Delano, and Christine Vachon. Also, there are at least seventeen FSA/OWI photographers, but two of them, Theodor Jung and Paul Carter, are not included as significant here.

29. See Mora and Brannan, *FSA*, 349, and Ken Johnson, "Soul Searching across America," *New York Times*, July 18, 2013, https://www.nytimes.com/2013/07/19/arts/design/walker-evanss-american-photographs-at-moma.html.

30. The late Rogers E. M. Whitaker is popularly known as E. M. Frimbo.

31. If you include rapid transit systems in US railroading, the images in Evans's book, *Many Are Called*, which features portraits of people riding the subways of New York City, also stand as excellent railroad-subject work by this photographic artist.

32. See Moedinger, "Silver San Juan Scenic Line," which features three of these Russell Lee images.

33. In some cases, captions may have been assigned by FSA/OWI staff.

JOHN COLLIER JR.

1. Collier and Collier, *Visual Anthropology*, xiii–xiv.

2. "Collier, John," Encyclopedia.com, accessed July 27, 2024, https://www.encyclopedia.com/people/social-sciences-and-law/sociology-biographies/john-collier.

3. Many of these facts come from one of the few biographic sketches of Collier available: "The American Image: The Photographs of John Collier Jr.," accessed March 9, 2024, https://americanimage.ideum.com/biography.html.

4. Charles Hagen, "John Collier Jr., 78, a Teacher, Writer and Photographer," *New York Times*, March 5, 1992, https://www.nytimes.com/1992/03/05/arts/john-collier-jr-78-a-teacher-writer-and-photographer.html.

5. See "John Collier, Jr.: Pennsylvania Coal Mines," in Mora and Brannan, *FSA*, 290–310.

6. "Made in Maryland: The Phillips Packing and Seafood Company," *Preservation Maryland*, accessed July 21, 2024, https://preservationmaryland.org/maryland-history-the-phillips-packing-and-seafood-company/.

7. See "Falco Is a Real Ghost Town," *Brewton Standard*, March 1, 2017, https://www.brewtonstandard.com/2017/03/01/falco-is-a-real-ghost-town; and "Remember When: Covington County's Only Ghost Town," *Andalusia Star News*, May 19, 2023, https://www.andalusiastarnews.com/2023/05/19/remember-when-covington-countys-only-ghost-town.

MARJORY COLLINS

1. Beverly Brannan, "Marjory Collins (1912–1985), Biographical Essay," accessed January 27, 2024, https://webarchive.loc.gov/all/20210903001252/https:/loc.gov/rr/print/coll/womphotoj/collinsessay.html.

2. Collins married twice more and, like fellow photographer O. Winston Link, faced disaster when her third husband destroyed most of her photographic prints and negatives. This occurred sometime between 1948 and 1950.

3. Brannan, "Marjory Collins (1912–1985), Biographical Essay." As far as can be determined, Palmer did not work in Stryker's Historical Section but in a different OWI group.

4. See Fleischhauer and Brannan, *Documenting America*, 252.

5. In a notable omission in the FSA/OWI file, New York City's Grand Central Terminal did not receive this extensive coverage.

6. For an excellent review of this movement, see Burman's *Sisters of the Iron Road*. For a corresponding view of the Black experience as railroaders in the US, see Kornweibel's *Railroads in the African American Experience*.

JACK DELANO

1. According to Delano, this was the second such grant for a photography project; the first was awarded to famed photographer Edward Weston. Delano, *Photographic Memories*, 109–110.

2. Most of this narrative comes from Reevy, *Railroad Photography of Jack Delano*. See also the timeline in Mora and Brannan, *FSA*, 348–349; and Delano, *Photographic Memories*.

3. For an overview of these images, see Delano, *From San Juan to Ponce*.

4. See also "Union Station," in Fleischhauer and Brannan, *Documenting America*, 276–293. For many more Delano images, including a selection of his color railroad-subject images, see Reevy, *Railroad Photography of Jack Delano*.

WALKER EVANS

1. Much of the information here is from this author's article in *Railroad Heritage*, "Walker Evans, American Communities, and the Railroad."

2. This date is according to the timeline for Walker Evans in Mora and Brannan, *FSA*, 349.

3. The book has a very complex history, including a connection with *Fortune* magazine. It was finally published by Houghton Mifflin in 1941.

4. A New York City to Washington, DC, passenger train officially known as *The Morning Congressional* or *The Afternoon Congressional*. Frank's influential 1959 book, *The Americans*, includes several outstanding railroad-subject photos.

5. These photos were taken earlier, in the 1930s and 1940s, and some had appeared in journal articles before the book was published.

6. At about this time, David Plowden, who has produced a great deal of superb railroad-subject photography, became a protégé of Evans.

DOROTHEA LANGE

1. Lange was her mother's maiden name; Dorothea began calling herself Dorothea Lange in about 1920. See Gordon, *Dorothea Lange*, 42.

2. Cox, *Dorothea Lange*, 6.

3. Dixon was John Collier Jr.'s artistic mentor.

4. Gordon, *Dorothea Lange*, 155.

5. Gordon, *Dorothea Lange*, 158.

6. Most of the FSA/OWI photographers died of cancer. One wonders if the darkroom chemicals and film products they used contributed to this unfortunate tendency.

7. The terminal is still used by ferries today. It is now part of Liberty State Park, and ferries for Ellis Island and the Statue of Liberty depart from here.

8. "La Bestia."

9. A bindle is a carrying device associated with US railroad hobos, formed of cloth—often the owner's blanket—rolled or bundled to hold articles inside it.

RUSSELL LEE

1. Some sources say Lee joined the army in 1943.
2. Appel, *Russell Lee*, x. The factual information here comes mostly from Appel's book and from the Russell Lee timeline in Mora and Brannan, *FSA*, 350.
3. After he stepped back from fieldwork, Lee established a photography program at the University of Texas at Austin and retired from this work in the late 1970s.
4. This is probably the Southland Paper Mills, Inc. See "Southland Paper Mills, Inc.," Historical Marker Database, accessed July 27, 2024, https://www.hmdb.org/m.asp?m=28963.
5. San Augustine was located on the Gulf, Colorado and Santa Fe Railway, a subsidiary of the Atchison, Topeka and Santa Fe Railway.
6. Ferrell, *Silver San Juan*, 589. Locomotive "rosters," found both in print and online, were used to identify locomotives such as Rio Grande Southern 455, a 2-8-2 Mikado. The Rio Grande Southern roster in Ferrell's book is a good example of these rosters.
7. Galloping Goose No. 2 survives at the Colorado Railroad Museum in Golden, Colorado.

GORDON PARKS

1. According to Parks, Roy Stryker was originally reluctant to hire him, worrying about the reactions of others in the federal government as well as people in the city of Washington, DC, to the presence of a Black photographer on his staff. Parks recalled that former FSA head Will Alexander, then with the Rosenwald Fund, convinced Stryker to hire Parks. See Fleischhauer and Brannan, *Documenting America*, 226–227.
2. Much of the material in this portfolio introduction comes from this author's *Railroad History* article "Off to War: Gordon Parks' Photographs of Washington Union Station During World War II." See also the timeline in Mora and Brannan, *FSA*, 350. The Mora and Brannan timeline gives an incorrect release year for Parks's film *The Learning Tree*.
3. Parks had previously directed public television documentaries.
4. Roth, "Introduction," , n.p.
5. LC-USF34-T01-013407-C.

ARTHUR ROTHSTEIN

1. Rothstein, *Photographs of Arthur Rothstein*, ix.
2. See the timeline in Mora and Brannan, *FSA*, 352.
3. Plate 90, showing the Virginia & Truckee station, with a train, in Carson City, achieved what might be the first publication of an FSA/OWI photo in a railroad-subject book—it is featured in Archie Robertson's *Slow Train to Yesterday*. The photo is credited in the book to "Farm Security Administration." The book includes three other FSA images.

JOHN VACHON

1. Like most, but not all, of the photographers profiled in this book, a Library of Congress Fields of Vision book focusing on Vachon, *The Photographs of John Vachon* (introduction by Kurt Andersen), provides a succinct introduction to his work.
2. Vachon has not gained a biographer. Biographic information here comes from *The Photographs of John Vachon* and from the online *MNopedia* entry about Vachon by R. L. Cartright: MNopedia, "Vachon, John (1914–1975)," accessed March 16, 2024, https://www.mnopedia.org/person/vachon-john-1914-1975. See also the timeline in Mora and Brannan, *FSA*, 353.
3. See Vachon's Getty record: ULAN Full Record Display (Getty Research), "Vachon, John," accessed March 16, 2024, https://www.getty.edu/vow/ULANFullDisplay?find=&role=&nation=&prev_page=1&subjectid=500036523.
4. The "C.B. & Q." is the Chicago, Burlington and Quincy Railroad. The freight car in Vachon's best-known Omaha shot of this type is from the Chicago Great Western.
5. Fleischhauer and Brannan, *Documenting America*, 91. For a similar photo, see plate 120 in this book. See also O'Neal, *A Vision Shared*, 267–268.
6. See Vachon, *Poland, 1946*.
7. See John Vachon's Prabook entry: Prabook, "John Vachon, Photographer, Journalist," accessed March 16, 2024, https://prabook.com/web/john.vachon/2225843.
8. Vachon, *The Photographs of John Vachon*, x.
9. Some sources say she died in 1959.
10. *Grade* is a transportation engineering term for a significant change in elevation. These changes are generally given in percentages (2% is a two-foot rise in one hundred feet). Railroads can tolerate only moderate grades.

11. Was Vachon aware of the Tulsa race massacre of 1921? The author has found no documentation of this. Knowledge of events such as this was suppressed until recently.

12. This is not to be confused with a train dispatcher, who in this period used telegraph and possibly telephone communications, usually combined with train orders, to control train traffic on a certain portion of a railroad system.

13. An interurban is a heavy-duty electrified version of the urban trolley/streetcar. The only legacy interurban surviving today is in the Chicago area, although Philadelphia has a surviving electrified line many would consider an interurban.

14. Such as *Mildred Irwin, Entertainer in a Saloon in North Platte, Nebraska, October 1938*. LC-USF34-008760-D.

15. This view is published as an alternate to the much-published *Freight Car and Grain Elevators, Omaha, Nebraska, November 1938*, LC-USF34-T01-008906-D. The image shown in plate 120 is perhaps less artistic but has the advantage of showing more railroad-subject content.

MARION POST WOLCOTT

1. Marion's last name was Post until she married, and she then began to use the name Marion Post Wolcott. For simplicity's sake, in this book she will be referred to as Marion Post Wolcott or Post Wolcott.

2. Hurley, *Marion Post Wolcott*, 137.

3. Hurley, *Marion Post Wolcott*, 20–21.

4. In her years with the FSA, she also covered other sections of the US.

5. Hurley, *Marion Post Wolcott*, 81.

6. Hurley, *Marion Post Wolcott*, 118.

7. Hurley, *Marion Post Wolcott*, 123.

8. This phenomenon of rediscovery and reengagement also applies to the 1983 exhibitions that focused attention on O. Winston Link and the railroad-subject books, beginning in the late 1970s, that focused attention on Jack Delano.

9. Beverly W. Brannan, "Marion Post Wolcott (1910–1990): A Biographical Essay," accessed March 29, 2024, https://www.loc.gov/rr/print/coll/womphotoj/wolcottessay.html.

10. See "Sugar Express—Historic Train Rides in South Central Florida," accessed July 27, 2024, https://sugarexpress.com.

11. "Carlton Tunnel—Leadville, CO," accessed July 27, 2024, https://www.waymarking.com/waymarks/WM72FB_Carlton_Tunnel_Leadville_CO.

APPENDIX TWO: THE US RAILROAD AND THE FSA/OWI PHOTOGRAPHERS NOT PROFILED IN THIS BOOK

1. One clue is the "Selected Bibliography and Related Resources" online listing in the Library of Congress in the Library's Farm Security Administration/Office of War Information Black-and-White Negatives site, accessed August 11, 2024, https://www.loc.gov/pictures/collection/fsa/bibliography.html. It has a section of works about these photographers.

2. For one listing of FSA photographers, presumably only the ones for whom the Library of Congress has portrait images, see Library of Congress, *Photographers of the FSA: Selected Portraits*, accessed August 11, 2024, https://www.loc.gov/pictures/collection/fsa/sampler.html.

3. Mora and Brannan, in *FSA*, identify John Collier Jr., Jack Delano, Gordon Parks, the Rosskams, and John Vachon as joining Stryker in the move from the FSA to the OWI. The new biography of Russell Lee by Mary Jane Appel, *Russell Lee: A Photographer's Life and Legacy*, confirms Lee's brief work with the OWI, as does a search of the Farm Security Administration/Office of War Information Black-and-White Negatives site, accessed August 31, 2024, https://www.loc.gov/pictures/search/?q=jung%20railroad&co=fsa.

4. Al Palmer is mentioned in this book due to his criticism of fellow OWI photographer Marjory Collins's work. He was prolific, but he did not work under Stryker's direction. During his time with the OWI, Palmer captured about thirty railroad-subject images.

5. For a list of FSA/OWI photographers, see Fleischhauer and Brannan, *Documenting America*, 337, although Theodor Jung is missing from the list. Poos also offers a list, composed originally by Edward Steichen, of twelve FSA photographers. It does not include any who joined Stryker's group after it became part of the OWI. See Poos, *Bitter Years*, 48. O'Neal, *A Vision Shared*, profiles eleven FSA/OWI photographers.

6. "Carl Mydans," International Center of Photography, accessed June 1, 2024, https://www.icp.org/browse/archive/constituents/carl-mydans.

7. FSA/OWI black-and-white images were searched from the Farm Security Administration/Office of War Information Black-and-White Negatives site, accessed June 1, 2024, https://www.loc.gov/pictures/collection/fsa.

8. Available information about Paul Carter is limited. For a discussion of Carter and Jung, see Hurley, *Portrait of a Decade*, 76–78. For additional information on Jung, see Mora and Brannan, *FSA*, 110–123.

9. "Ben Shahn," International Center of Photography, accessed June 1, 2024, https://www.icp.org/browse/archive/constituents/ben-shahn.

10. For insight about how Stryker felt about his "file" of photographs, see Hurley, *Portrait of a Decade*, 168–170.

11. Mora and Brannan, *FSA*, 148–149.

12. The actual employment of Ben Shahn and Dorothea Lange by the FSA is complex, but authorities always include them in lists of significant FSA photographers.

13. On page 62, a letter from Stryker to Dick, about Dick's assignment to photograph a Pennsylvania coal town, is quoted. The letter is dated October 17, 1938.

14. Farm Security Administration/Office of War Information Black-and-White Negatives site, accessed July 6, 2024, https://www.loc.gov/pictures/collection/fsa.

15. See Library of Congress, "Contributors in Farm Security Administration/Office of War Information Color Photographs," accessed August 11, 2024, https://www.loc.gov/collections/fsa-owi-color-photographs/index/contributor/?sp=1.

16. See "Cross-Country Bus Trip," in Fleischhauer and Brannan, *Documenting America*, 312–329.

17. "Esther Bubley," International Center of Photography, accessed June 1, 2024, https://www.icp.org/browse/archive/constituents/esther-bubley; and Mora and Brannan, *FSA*, 334–335.

18. James E. Valle's *The Iron Horse at War*, which focuses on Jack Delano's railroad-subject photographs, has an opening section featuring other FSA/OWI photographers and their images. Alfred "Al" Palmer, Howard Hollem, Ann Rosener, and Andreas Feininger are all featured here; they were OWI photographers but apparently did not work closely with Stryker. Palmer captured thirty or so railroad images; Hollem took a handful. About half of Rosener's small set of railroad-subject photos are images of the Baltimore & Ohio Railroad station in Silver Spring, Maryland. Feininger shot a few images of railroading at the Utah Copper Company mines. Howard Hollem is identified as Jack Hollem in Valle's book; this may be a nickname. Andreas Feininger is identified as Andreus Finenger. Paul Hendrickson's *Bound for Glory: America in Color 1939–43* features a number of color images by OWI photographers who did not work with Roy Stryker.

BIBLIOGRAPHY

Agee, James, and Walker Evans. *Let Us Now Praise Famous Men*. With an introduction to the new edition by John Hersey. Boston: Houghton Mifflin, 1988.

Anderson, Sherwood. *Home Town*. New York: Alliance, 1940.

Appel, Mary Jane. *Russell Lee: A Photographer's Life and Legacy*. New York: Liveright, 2021.

Ball, Don, Jr., and Rogers E. M. Whitaker. *Decade of the Trains: The 1940s*. Boston: New York Graphic Society, 1977.

Burman, Shirley. *Sisters of the Iron Road*. Sacramento, CA: SRS, 2022.

Caldwell, Erskine, and Margaret Bourke-White. *You Have Seen Their Faces*. New York: Arno, 1975.

Chéroux, Clément. *Walker Evans*. Paris: Éditions du Centre Pompidou, 2017.

Collier, John, Jr., and Malcolm Collier. *Visual Anthropology: Photography as a Research Method*. Albuquerque: University of New Mexico Press, 1986.

Colson, J. B., Malcolm Collier, Jay Rabinowitz, and Steve Yates. *Far from Main Street*. Albuquerque: University of New Mexico Press, 1994.

Cox, Christopher. *Dorothea Lange*. New York: Aperture, 1987.

Crane, Hart. *The Bridge*. Paris: Black Sun, 1930.

Delano, Jack. *From San Juan to Ponce on the Train*. Río Piedras, Puerto Rico: Editorial de la Universidad de Puerto Rico, 1990.

———. *Photographic Memories*. Washington, DC: Smithsonian Institution Press, 1997.

———. *The Photographs of Jack Delano*. Introduction by Esmeralda Santiago. Washington, DC: Library of Congress, 2010.

———. *Puerto Rico Mio: Four Decades of Change*. Washington, DC: Smithsonian Institution Press, 1990.

Doty, C. Stewart, Dale Sperry Mudge, and Herbert John Benally. *Photographing Navahos: John Collier, Jr. on the Reservation, 1948–1953*. Albuquerque: University of New Mexico Press, 2002.

Evans, Walker. "Along the Right-of-Way." *Fortune*, September 1950, 106–113.

———. "America's Heritage of Great Architecture Is Doomed . . . It Must Be Saved." *Life*, July 1963, 52–60.

———. "Before They Disappear." *Fortune*, March 1957, 141–145.

———. "The Last of Railroad Steam." *Fortune*, September 1958, 137–141.

———. *Many Are Called*. With an Introduction by James Agee. Boston: Houghton Mifflin, 1966.

———. "The U.S. Depot." *Fortune*, February 1953, 138–143.

———. *Walker Evans: American Photographs*. With an Essay by Lincoln Kirstein. New York: Museum of Modern Art, 1938.

Ferrell, Mallory Hope. *Silver San Juan: The Rio Grande Southern*. Boulder, CO: Pruett, 1973.

Fleischhauer, Carl, and Beverly W. Brannan. *Documenting America, 1935–1943*. Berkeley: University of California Press, 1989.

Frank, Robert. *The Americans*. New York: Grove, 1959.
———. "The Congressional." *Fortune*, November 1955, 118–122.
Garver, Thomas H. *Just before the War; Urban America from 1935 to 1941 as Seen by the Photographers of the Farm Security Administration*. Balboa, CA: Newport Harbor Art Museum, 1968.
Gordon, Linda. *Dorothea Lange: A Life beyond Limits*. London: W. W. Norton, 2009.
Greenough, Sarah. *Walker Evans: Subways and Streets*. Washington, DC: National Gallery of Art, 1991.
Gruber, John, ed. *Railroaders: Jack Delano's Homefront Photography*. Madison, WI: Center for Railroad Photography and Art, 2014.
Hendrickson, Paul. *Bound for Glory: America in Color, 1939–43*. New York: Harry N. Abrams, 2004.
Hine, Lewis. *Men at Work: Photographic Studies of Modern Men and Machines*. New York: Macmillan, 1932.
Horvath, David G., ed. *Roy Stryker Papers 1912–1972: A Guide to the Microfilm Edition*. Sanford, NC: Microfilming Corporation of America, 1982.
Hurley, F. Jack. *Marion Post Wolcott: A Photographic Journey*. Albuquerque: University of New Mexico Press, 1989.
———. *Portrait of a Decade: Roy Stryker and the Development of Documentary Photography in the Thirties*. Baton Rouge: Louisiana State University Press, 1972.
———. *Russell Lee, Photographer*. Dobbs Ferry, NY: Morgan and Morgan, 1978.
Kornweibel, Theodore. *Railroads in the African-American Experience: A Photographic Journey*. Baltimore, MD: Johns Hopkins University Press, 2010.
Lange, Dorothea, and Paul Taylor. *An American Exodus: A Record of Human Erosion*. New York: Reynal & Hitchcock, 1939.
Lewis, Lloyd, and Stanley Pargellis. *Granger Country*. Boston: Little, Brown, 1949.
MacLeish, Archibald. *Land of the Free*. New York: Harcourt Brace, 1938.
Melville, Annette. *Farm Security Administration Historical Section: A Guide to Textual Records in the Library of Congress*. Washington, DC: Library of Congress, 1985.
Moedinger, William T. "Silver San Juan Scenic Line." *Trains*, February 1942, 8–25.
Mora, Gilles, and Beverly W. Brannan. *FSA: The American Vision*. New York: Harry N. Abrams, 2006.
Mora, Gilles, and John T. Hill. *Walker Evans: The Hungry Eye*. New York: Harry N. Abrams, 1993.
Niemann, Linda. *Boomer: Railroad Memories*. Berkeley: University of California, 1990.
Niemann, Linda, and Joel Jensen. *Railroad Noir: The American West at the End of the Twentieth Century*. Bloomington: Indiana University Press, 2010.
Nixon, Herman Clarence. *Forty Acres and Steel Mules*. Chapel Hill: University of North Carolina Press, 1938.
O'Neal, Hank. *A Vision Shared: A Classic Portrait of America and Its People, 1935–1943*. New York: St. Martin's Press, 1976.
Parks, Gordon. *Gordon Parks*. Introduction by Paul Roth. London: Thames & Hudson, 2013.
Plattner, Steven W. *Roy Stryker: U.S.A., 1943–1950: The Standard Oil (New Jersey) Photography Project*. With a Foreword by Cornell Capa. Austin: University of Texas Press, 1983.
Plowden, David. *Requiem for Steam: The Railroad Photographs of David Plowden*. New York: W. W. Norton, 2010.
———. *A Time of Trains*. New York: W. W. Norton, 1987.
Poos, Françoise, ed. *The Bitter Years: Edward Steichen and the Farm Security Administration Photographs*. New York: Distributed Arts, 2012.
Prince, Richard E. *Southern Railway System Steam Locomotives and Boats*. Millard, NE: R. E. Prince, 1983.
Raper, Arthur Franklin. *Tenants of the Almighty*. With FSA Photographs by Jack Delano. New York: Macmillan, 1943.
Raper, Arthur Franklin, and Ira De A. Reid. *Sharecroppers All*. Chapel Hill: University of North Carolina Press, 1941.
Reevy, Tony. "Artist of the Rail: Jack Delano." *Railroad History* 201 (Fall–Winter 2009): 30–41.
———. "Men at Work: Lewis Hine's Photographs of Railroad Workers." *Railroad History* 204 (Spring–Summer 2011): 42–51.
———. "Off to War: Gordon Parks' Photographs of Washington Union Station during World War II." *Railroad History* 212 (Spring–Summer 2015): 38–47.
———. *O. Winston Link: Life along the Line*. New York: Harry N. Abrams, 2012.
———. *The Railroad Photography of Jack Delano*. Bloomington: Indiana University Press, 2015.
———. "Walker Evans, American Communities, and the Railroad." *Railroad Heritage* 20 (2009): 12–19.
Reid, Robert L., and Larry A. Viskochil, eds. *Chicago and Downstate: Illinois as Seen by the Farm Security Administration*

Photographers, 1936–1943. Urbana: Chicago Historical Society and University of Illinois Press, 1989.

Riis, Jacob. *How the Other Half Lives: Studies among the Tenements of New York*. New York: C. Scribner's Sons, 1890.

Robertson, Archie. *Slow Train to Yesterday*. Boston: Houghton Mifflin, 1945.

Rosskam, Edwin and Louise. *Towboat River*. New York: Duell, Sloan and Pearce, 1948.

Rothstein, Arthur. *The Photographs of Arthur Rothstein*. Introduction by George Packer. Washington, DC: Library of Congress, 2011.

———. *Photojournalism*. Garden City, NY: American Photographic Book, 1979.

Saroyan, William. *Look at Us*. With photographs by Arthur Rothstein. New York: Cowles Education, 1967.

Schulz, Constance B., and Steven W. Plattner, eds. *Witness to the Fifties: The Pittsburgh Photographic Library, 1950–1953*. With text by Clarke Thomas. Pittsburgh, PA: University of Pittsburgh Press, 1999.

Smith, J. Russell. *North America: Its People and the Resources, Development, and Prospects of the Continent as the Home of Man*. New York: Harcourt, Brace, 1940.

Steichen, Edward, ed. *The Bitter Years, 1935–1941: Rural America As Seen by the Photographers of the Farm Security Administration*. New York: Museum of Modern Art, 1962.

Stilgoe, John. *Metropolitan Corridor*. New Haven, CT: Yale University Press, 1983.

Strand, Paul. *Paul Strand*. New York: Aperture Foundation, 1987.

———. "Photography." *Seven Arts* 2 (August 1917): 524–526.

Stryker, Roy Emerson, and Mel Seidenberg. *A Pittsburgh Album 1768–1958*. Pittsburgh, PA: *Pittsburgh Post-Gazette*, 1959.

Stryker, Roy Emerson, and Nancy Wood. *In This Proud Land: America 1935–1943 as Seen in the FSA Photographs*. Greenwich, CT: New York Graphic Society, 1973.

Tugwell, Rexford G. *The Democratic Roosevelt*. Garden City, NY: Doubleday, 1957.

Tugwell, Rexford G., Thomas Munro, and Roy E. Stryker. *American Economic Life*. New York: Harcourt, Brace, 1925.

Vachon, John. *John Vachon's America*. Berkeley: University of California Press, 2003.

———. *Poland, 1946: The Photographs and Letters of John Vachon*. Washington, DC: Smithsonian Institution Press, 1995.

———. *The Photographs of John Vachon*. Introduction by Kurt Anderson. Washington, DC: Library of Congress, 2010.

Valle, James E. *The Iron Horse at War*. Berkeley, CA: Howell-North, 1977.

Walther, Peter. *Lewis Hine: America at Work*. Cologne, Germany: Taschen, 2018.

Wright, Richard. *12 Million Black Voices*. Photo direction by Edwin Rosskam. New York: Viking, 1941.

INDEX

Page numbers appearing in italics refer to illustrations.

TONY REEVY is Assistant Vice Provost for University Interdisciplinary Initiatives Development at North Carolina State University. He is a graduate of North Carolina State University, UNC-Chapel Hill, and Miami University. His previous publications include *Ghost Train!*, *O. Winston Link: Life Along the Line*, *Old North*, *Passage*, *The Railroad Photography of Jack Delano*, *Socorro*, *The Railroad Photography of Lucius Beebe and Charles Clegg*, *Turbulence*, and *The Railroad Photography of Phil Hastings*. He resides in Durham, North Carolina.

JEFF BROUWS is a fine-art photographer whose works can be found in numerous institutions across the country, including the Whitney Museum of American Art. Alongside his photographic practice, over the past thirty years Brouws has researched and written about the historic and aesthetic development of railroad photography in America as seen in such books as *The Call of Trains: Railroad Photographs by Jim Shaughnessy* and *A Passion for Trains: The Railroad Photography of Richard Steinheimer*. He is a board member of the Center for Railroad Photography & Art and lives with his wife, Wendy, in Stanfordville, New York.

FOR INDIANA UNIVERSITY PRESS

Sabrina Black *Editorial Assistant*

Tony Brewer *Artist and Book Designer*

Anna Francis *Assistant Acquisitions Editor*

Anna Garnai *Production Coordinator*

Samantha Heffner *Marketing Production Manager*

Katie Huggins *Production Manager*

Alyssa Nicole Lucas *Marketing and Publicity Manager*

Annie L. Martin *Editorial Director*

David Miller *Lead Project Manager/Editor*

Dan Pyle *Online Publishing Manager*

Jennifer Wilder *Senior Artist and Book Designer*